ROME IN THE DARK AGES

ROME IN
THE DARK AGES

PETER LLEWELLYN

PRAEGER PUBLISHERS

New York · Washington

BOOKS THAT MATTER

Published in the United States of America in 1971
by Praeger Publishers, Inc., 111 Fourth Avenue,
New York, N.Y. 10003

© 1970 in London, England, by Peter Llewellyn

Library of Congress Catalog Card Number: 78-109479

Printed in Great Britain

To Lucinda

ACKNOWLEDGEMENTS

I wish to express my thanks to Mr. Peter Brown of All Souls College, Oxford, and to Professor Donald Bullough of Nottingham University for their advice and criticism in the preparation of this book; the shortcomings are mine alone.

My aim has been to provide a general account of Rome's history through this period at the expense, perhaps, of detailed discussion of many points of controversy; the bibliography, which is by no means exhaustive, is intended to allow the gaps in my treatment to be filled and the emphasis therefore has been on the secondary literature rather than the source material.

My thanks are also due to those who have helped in completing this book; to my mother, Mrs. Elizabeth Llewellyn, and to Mrs. M. Cullimore, Miss Suzanne Forbes, Miss Sally Purcell and Mrs. M. Reade, for their generous aid in typing; and to Miss Lucinda Rodd and Miss Frances Lynch for the preparation of the maps.

9

CONTENTS

ILLUSTRATIONS

Plates

Maps

ABBREVIATIONS

Sources, collections of sources and periodicals

AASS   *Acta Sanctorum* (ed. Bollandists)
AB   *Analecta Bollandiana.*
ALMA   *Archivum Latinitatis Medii Aevi et Bulletin Ducange.*
ASR   *Archivio della Reale Deputazione Romana di Storia Patria.*
BHL   *Bibliotheca Hagiographica Latina.*
BISI   *Bollettino per l'Istituto Storico Italiano per il Medio Evo e Archivio Muratoriano.*
CIL   *Corpus Inscriptionum Latinorum.*
CSEL   *Corpus Scriptorum Ecclesiasticorum Latinorum.*
CSHB   *Corpus Scriptorum Historiae Byzantinae.*
EL   *Ephemerides Liturgicae.*
FHG   *Fragmenta Historica Graeca.*
LC   *Liber Censuum Ecclesiae Romanae.*
LD   *Liber Diurnus Ecclesiae Romanae.*
LP   *Liber Pontificalis Ecclesiae Romanae.*
MAH   *Mélanges d'archeologie et d'histoire de l'Ecole française de Rome.*
Mansi   J. D. Mansi, *Sacrorum Conciliorum Nova et Amplissima Collectio.*
MGH   *Monumenta Germaniae Historica:*
     AA   Auctores Antiquissimi
     Epp   Epistolae
     LL   Leges, Concilia.
     SS   Scriptores
     SS   Rer. Long. et Ital: Scriptores Rerum Longobardicarum et Italicarum.
     SS   Rer. Mer. Scriptores Rerum Merovingicarum.
OR   *Ordines Romani.*
PG   Migne, *Patrologia Graeca.*
PL   Migne, *Patrologia Latina.*
RAC   *Rivista di archeologia cristiana.*
RSR   *Recherches de Science Religieuse.*

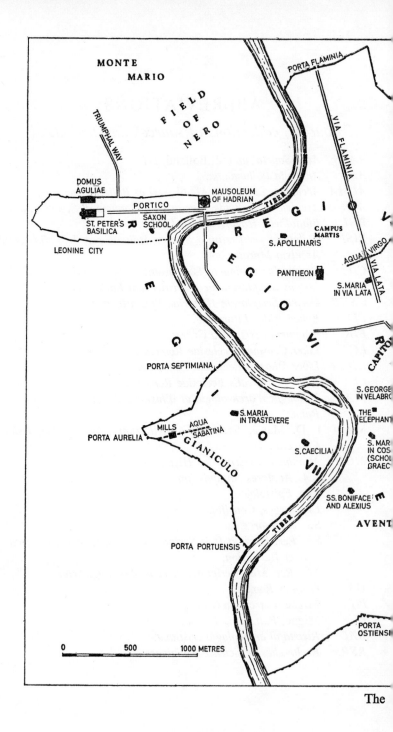

MONTE MARIO

FIELD OF NERO

PORTA FLAMINIA

VIA FLAMINIA

TRIUMPHAL WAY

DOMUS AGULIAE

PORTICO

MAUSOLEUM OF HADRIAN

TIBER

REGIO

ST. PETER'S BASILICA

SAXON SCHOOL

CAMPUS MARTIS

S. APOLLINARIS

LEONINE CITY

REGIO

AQUA VIRGO

PANTHEON

S. MARIA IN VIA LATA

VIA LATA

REGIO

VI

PORTA SEPTIMIANA

CAPITO

S. GEORGE IN VELABRO

THE ELEPHANT

S. MARIA IN TRASTEVERE

MILLS

AQUA SABATINA

S. MAR IN COS (SCHOL GRAEC

PORTA AURELIA

GIANICULO

O

S. CAECILIA

SS. BONIFACE AND ALEXIUS

VII

AVENT

TIBER

PORTA PORTUENSIS

PORTA OSTIENS

0   500   1000 METRES

The

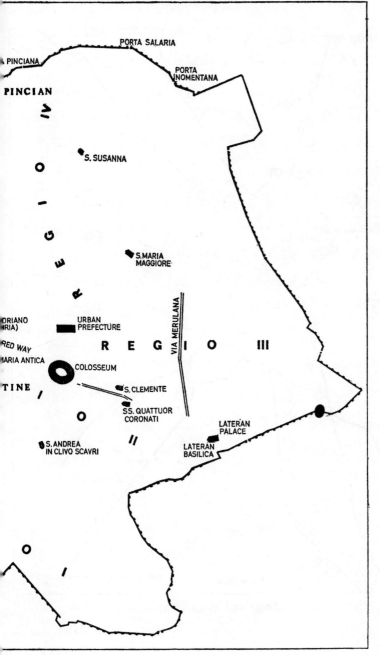

PORTA PINCIANA

PINCIAN

REGIO IV

S. SUSANNA

S. MARIA MAGGIORE

PORTA SALARIA

PORTA NOMENTANA

VIA MERULANA

ADRIANO (RIA)

RED WAY

MARIA ANTICA

TINE

URBAN PREFECTURE

R E G I O   III

COLOSSEUM

S. CLEMENTE

SS. QUATTUOR CORONATI

S. ANDREA IN CLIVO SCAVRI

LATERAN PALACE

LATERAN BASILICA

O

I

O

II

O

I

Rome

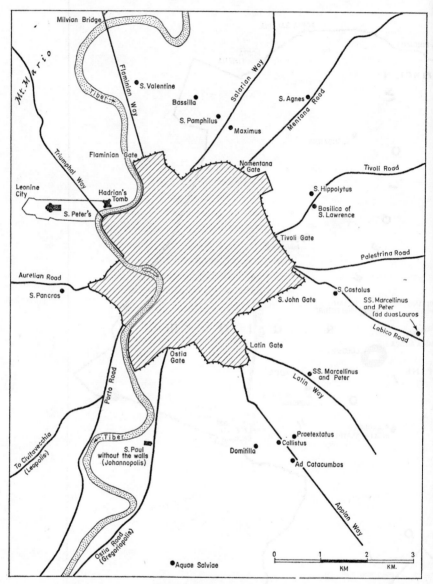

Rome and its environs

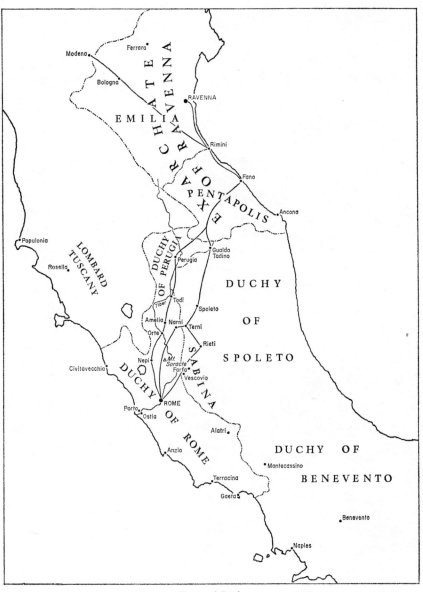

Central Italy

1

ROME AND THE OSTROGOTHS

On a day in the year 500 the African monk Fulgentius, later bishop of the small town of Ruspe, fulfilled a life's ambition in visiting Rome. The circumstances were unhappy; he had been driven into exile by the persecutions of the Vandal king of North Africa and had wandered, homeless and dependent on charity, through Sicily and southern Italy; but Rome, centre alike of law and the tradition of human authority and of Christian orthodoxy and primacy, had beckoned to him. He had read in the pagan poets their eulogies of this city, elevated to the status of a goddess, to be revered and justly revered throughout the world, but what he saw amazed him. 'How wonderful,' he exclaimed, 'must be the heavenly Jerusalem, if this earthly city can shine so greatly.'[1] For Rome was the centre, *the* city, the lawgiver, the fact that had dominated and made the world men knew. From Iraq to Wales, from the Baltic to the Sudan, she had fashioned and left all in her image. On the countryside her language had left the place-names men used; in the towns men lived by her organization, her law, her peace. 'What was once a world, you have left one city', a poet of the previous century had declared.[2] The good monk, from the small white towns on the edge of the desert, with their memories of things unRoman, of Carthage and Rome's greatest enmities, could yet know that he was at home.

All this was the work of time. Rome was now in the thirteenth century of her foundation, and in the eleventh of her domination, a matter to move men's minds in awe. From the establishment of the

[1] Ferrandus, *Vie de Saint Fulgence de Ruspe*, (ed. and French trans. by G-C Lapeyre, 1929). See also H. J. Diesner, *Fulgentius von Ruspe als Theologe und Kirchenpolitiker*, 1966.
[2] Rutilius Namatianus, *Carmen de Reditu suo*, I, 66. For the place acquired by Rome in Western thought in the last century of Antiquity see F. Paschoud, 'Roma Aeterna, études sur le patriotisme romain dans l'occident latin a l'epoque des grandes invasions', (*Bibliotheca Helvetica Romana*, 7, 1967).

21

peace of Augustus she had seemed unshakeable, eternal. The thirty legions of the empire had guarded her, the luxuries of the world had sustained her. Rebellion and civil war had appeared to leave her untouched; her official acts were dated as they had been since the expulsion of the kings, by the years of her consuls; her senate still met as it had met to direct the war against Hannibal, as it had assembled when the Gauls broke into the city. The crowd, the great, idle, roaring Roman crowd, demanding distraction and entertainment, was still there to riot or cheer, as in the time of the Gracchi. The palace of the Caesars' sprawled on the Palatine, carrying proof in brick and mortar and marble of the succession of emperors. But Rome was weary beyond the days of her strength. The expense of maintaining a luxurious court and an idle population sapped the provinces; the legions, permanently encamped on the frontiers, put down their roots and lost mobility and flexibility. A great tide of peoples was building up, clamouring for admission to the sweets of empire; and the emperors, strangers to their city, remained permanently on guard, moving to threatened points, shoring up the overloaded structure. Drastic measures were taken; control of all aspects of their subjects' lives was rigorously enforced; prices, jobs and homes were all frozen to support stability. The emperors lost sight of the republican origins of their office and with lavish oriental ceremony surrounded their persons with the mystique of divine kingship. Furthermore, the Empire itself was divided by Diocletian, since it had grown beyond the powers of government by any one man, even by a man who arrogated something of godhead to his office, and Constantine founded his city, the new Rome, at Byzantium to serve the East. Here still the model of the city on the Tiber was retained; the new Rome had its senate and its city magistrates, and some inconspicuous rises were promoted to the status of Seven Hills. Taxation and the bureaucracy increased; the margin of survival narrowed. The successors of Constantine engaged whole tribes to fight their battles; these came and settled. Their chieftains, dignified with imperial titles, remained too, to gain power and vie with ministers for influence. In the West, Rome was an anachronism; as the pressures increased its emperors held court in the safety of the marshes of Ravenna.

Fulgentius was fortunate in the moment of his arrival, for the city was *en fête* to greet its ruler. The senate and the magistrates were there, with speeches whose periods rolled back to Cicero; the city clergy, headed by Pope Symmachus, came to join the ruler in prayers of thanksgiving at the tomb of St. Peter; above all, the Roman people were there for the traditional distribution of rations and for the circus games that were an immemorial and essential feature of any Roman occasion. The rejoicing was nonetheless sincere among all sections of the population; they and their city now enjoyed a peace and prosperity that had long been lacking. But the ruler they welcomed was no Roman emperor; he was a king–but a king of a barbarian nation, the Ostrogoths–and an illiterate and a murderer. His name, like that of his younger contemporary Arthur, was to live in legend as Dietrich of Bern; it was Theodoric.[3]

For the final blow had fallen on the West: the ministers and the army commanders had eclipsed and extinguished their overlords the emperors. In 410 the Visigoths under Alaric had sacked Rome itself, eliciting from St. Augustine a great search for the meaning of human and divine government and from the Emperor Honorius, misled by the early reports, acute anxiety for his pet hen, who shared the city's name. The Vandals followed; less amenable than the Visigoths, they broke through Spain into Africa which they had held ever since. Then, briefly and terribly, the Huns followed under Attila until, checked and turned, they dissolved into the East. The provinces of Gaul passed out of direct imperial administration and were settled and ruled by Franks and Burgundians. Ephemeral emperors, sponsored by the generals and ministers, rose and fell until the last, a boy, was placed on a meaningless throne by his father Orestes who– such were the revolutions of the times–had once served as Attila's secretary. This was Romulus, fittingly nicknamed Augustulus, the Little Emperor. He did not last long; an army commander, Odoacer, chieftain of the Rugian tribe in imperial pay, held an emperor to be superfluous for the diminished West and in 476 deposed him, settling him with a pension in a comfortable villa near Naples. The imperial insignia were returned to the East, and Odoacer himself ruled Italy in an undefined lieutenancy for the sole Emperor in New Rome.[4]

[3] Anonymus Valesianus, (ed. and English trans. by J. C. Rolfe in Loeb Library, Ammianus Marcellinus, vol. III, 1939), *pars posterior*, 12, 65.
[4] A. H. M. Jones, 'The Constitutional position of Odoacer and Theodoric', (*Journal of Roman Studies*, 52, 1962). C. Cipolla, 'Considerazioni

For Italy the experiment was successful. Odoacer was a wise and moderate man who won the support of Romans of all kinds, and especially that of the senatorial class which represented the traditions and continuity of power.[5] But the East was also dogged by the problem of large and hungry bodies of German troops, and it merely tolerated Odoacer's assumption of power. In 489 the Emperor Zeno commissioned the King of the Ostrogoths, Theodoric, to reunite Italy to the Empire; unexpressed but more cogent was the desire to remove an embarrassing unemployed force from his own dominions where its interference in politics threatened his own throne. So Theodoric marched, defeated Odoacer and pinned him behind the walls of Ravenna. There he was held for three years until a compromise solution, the sharing of the rule of Italy, was agreed upon. At a celebratory banquet, Theodoric ended an unworkable partnership by murdering his new colleague. Henceforth he too ruled alone, although with the qualified support of persons of great influence.[6]

When Fulgentius saw him in Rome he had been sole ruler for seven years. The odds had been against him achieving a peaceful government. As an illiterate barbarian he might have met opposition from the custodians of culture, the senate; as an Arian heretic, distrust from the Church. Furthermore his troops needed land, the cultivated, fertile land that had set all the barbarian tribes marching, and this land could only be obtained by confiscation. These problems Fulgentius himself knew well. His grandfather, the senator Gordianus, had lost all his lands by the Vandal settlement of 442; his sons had recovered part but Fulgentius as a young man had served as a procurator, a tax-collector for the Vandal government until he resigned in disgust at the brutal methods he had been ordered to employ. Nor had his experience as a churchman been any happier; the Vandal kings were also Arian and were continuously hostile to

sul concetto di Stato nella monarchia di Odoacre', (*Rendiconti della Reale Accademia dei Lincei, Ser.* 5, 20, 1911). G-B. Picotti, 'Il patricius', (*Archivio Storico Italiano*, 1, 1928).

[5] G-B. Picotti, 'Sulle relazioni fra re Odoacre e il Senato e la Chiesa di Roma', (*Rivista Storica Italiana, Ser.* 5, 4, 1939).

[6] Anon. Vales., *loc. cit.*: Procopius, *Bellum Gothicum*, 1, (Loeb ed. and trans. by H. B. Dewing, 1914–40). On Theodoric's departure from the Eastern empire, E. W. Brooks, 'The Emperor Zenon and the Isaurians', (*English Historical Review*, 8, 1893).

their Catholic subjects. In 496 King Thransamund initiated a persecution; all Catholic churches in Africa were closed, the consecration
of bishops was forbidden and the existing bishops exiled to Sardinia,
a backward, uncivilized and pagan island, notoriously unhealthy and
for long used as a penal settlement. But the Ostrogoths were not
Vandals, and the dominating personality of Theodoric overrode the
occasions of friction, for he had acquired a respect for the government of civilization.

The son of a chief who had joined the Huns, Theodoric was born
in the Danube provinces of the Eastern Empire during the turmoil
following the collapse of Attila's power. As a boy he had been sent as
hostage for his nation to Constantinople and been brought up at the
imperial court. He joined the imperial service, bringing his tribe
within the confines of the Empire, rose higher in rank but remained a
restless, ambitious danger in the manoeuvres of the warlords. The
Italian solution satisfied his ambition since he had acquired a respect
for learning and the ways of settled government–by partnership with
the Italian senate he was able to achieve a unity and co-operation
within the peninsula unknown to the other successor-states. The
division of land, whereby one-third passed to the Gothic warriors in
return for their support was effected without incident, guided by the
senator Liberius. There had in recent years been a considerable drift
from the countryside and much land lay unoccupied; nevertheless,
affecting as it did the great landowners of the senate, its accomplishment was a revolution, easily and smoothly executed. Instead of
protest there was universal praise from both aristocracy and churchmen, who looking across to North Africa may have expected something far worse. The Bishop of Pavia, the educator Ennodius,
flattered Liberius in saying 'You have enriched the countless hordes
of the Goths with generous grants of land and yet the Romans have
hardly felt it.'[7] Theodoric's Roman secretary Cassiodorus, in a

[7] Ennodius, *Epistolae*, IX, 23 (*Opera*, ed. G. Harkel; *CSEL*. 6, 1882;
p. 245) S. Leglise, *Les lettres d'Ennode*, 1903. For Liberius' career in Italy
and Provence in the Gothic and in Egypt in the imperial service, see
Pauly–Wissowa, RE. 13, 1, coll. 94–8. On Theodoric, his government
and political relations, see W. Ensslin, *Theoderich der Grosse*, 1947;
E. Caspar, 'Theoderich der Grosse und der Papsttum', (*Kleine Texte für
Vorlesungen*, 162, 1931); B. Rubin, 'Theoderich und Iustinian', (*Jahrbücher
für Geschichte Osteuropas*, 1, 1953); M. Dumoulin, 'Le Gouvernment de

speech that he wrote for his master to deliver to the senate, also praised the settlement and its results; this sharing of estates was producing a new harmony between the races, a new friendship securing the tenure of the land.[8] A more adulatory chronicler summed up the reign in fulsome but not over-exaggerated terms. 'So great was the happiness that even wayfarers were at peace. He did no wrong. He governed the two nations, Goths and Romans, and though he himself belonged to the Arian sect yet he attempted nothing against the Catholic faith. . . . Merchants from the various provinces flocked to him for so good was the order he maintained that if anyone wished to leave gold or silver on his country estate it was considered as safe as if in a walled town. Throughout the whole of Italy Theodoric made no gates for any city, and what gates there were to the cities were never closed. Anyone with business to transact could do it at any time of night as safely as by day.'[9]

'He maintained the civil service for the Romans as it had been under the emperors', the same chronicler noted, and therein lay the key to the harmony he achieved. It was the senate that held the traditions of culture and of service to the state, as well as the gaudier rewards and the vast wealth. Its numbers had fallen in the previous century and under Odoacer and Theodoric it had only between sixty and eighty effective members, reflecting a similar decline in the city population as a whole.[10] But like the city the senate received flattering attention from the barbarian kings. Their meeting-place, the curia in the Forum, was rebuilt under Theodoric and after centuries the right was restored to them of striking their own copper coinage.[11]

Theodoric d'après les oeuvres de Ennodius', (*Revue Historique*, 79, 1902); W. G. Sinnigen, 'Comites Consistoriani in Ostrogothic Italy', (*Classica et Mediaevalia*, 24, 1963); Sinnigen, 'Administrative Shifts of Competence under Theodoric', (*Traditio*, 21, 1965).

[8] Cassiodorus, *Variae*, 11, 16 (in *MGH. AA*, XII). Abridged translation by T. Hodgkin, *The Letters of Cassiodorus*, 1886.

[9] Anon. Vales, 12, 60, 172–3.

[10] See A. Chastagnol, 'Le Sénat Romain sous le règne d'Odoacre: Recherches sur l'épigraphie du Colisée au Ve siècle', (*Antiquitas*, Ser. 3, fasc. 3, 1966) and, 'Le revitaillement de Rome en viande au Ve siècle', (*Revue Historique*, 210, 1953).

[11] See P. de Francisci, 'Per la Storia del Senato Romano e della Curia nei secoli V e VI', (*Rendiconti della Pontificia Accademia romana di Archeologia* 22, 1946); A. Bartoli, 'Lavori nella sede del Senato Romano al tempo di

Although compelled to give admission to some of the new men from the administrative capital at Ravenna, including even Goths,[12] the senate was corporately more concerned with the city administration than with the wider aspects of government; with the maintenance of the water-supply system and the aqueducts, the care of the river banks and of the many statues, both bronze and marble, that commemorated gods, heroes and emperors. The Romans, as Procopius noted later, were distinguished by a passionate antiquarianism, especially in anything that concerned their own city, an antiquarianism that expressed itself in their literature and their adherence to the forms of their ancestors. The closely-knit families that composed it were proud and ancient; they held the consulships and the greater magistracies, sources of pride and prestige if now actually meaningless.[13] A description inserted into the *Church History* of Bishop Zachary of Mytilene conveys something of the awe of Rome dominated by these princely families; a description at second-hand, cobbled from handbooks of statistics, but reflecting the work of generations in administration, in public service and in patronage. Like Fulgentius the author can only compare the effect to the heavenly Jerusalem:

'Now the description of the decorations of the city, briefly given, is as follows, with regard to the wealth of its inhabitants, their great and pre-eminent prosperity and their grand and glorious objects of luxury and pleasure, as in the great city of wondrous beauty. Now its surpassing adornments are as follows, without mentioning the splendours within the houses, the beautiful formation of the columns within their halls, their colonnades, their staircases, their towering heights, as in the city of wondrous beauty.

'It contains 24 churches of the blessed apostles, Catholic churches. It contains 2 great basilicas, where the king sits and the senators are assembled before him every day. It contains 324 great and spacious streets, 2 great Capitols, 80 golden gods, 64 ivory gods. It contains

Teodorico, (*Bollettino della Commissione archeologica Comunale di Roma*, 73, 1949–50): G. Della Valle, 'Teodorico e Roma', (*Rendiconti della Accademia di Archeologia, Lettere e Belli Arti di Napoli*, 34, 1959).

[12] See V. Gianlorenzo, 'I barbari nel Senato al VI secolo', (*Studi e Documenti di storia e diritto*, 20, 1899).

[13] For the praetorate see Boethius, *de Consolatione Philosophiae*, III, 4.

46,603 dwelling houses and 1,797 houses of the magnates.' The description continues with lists of the city's amenities; the bakeries, the reservoirs and aqueducts of the water-supply, and the depots of the food-supply; the theatres, the circuses, the parks and the brothels; the machinery for maintenance, the police-barracks, the ward-masters, the great circle of the Aurelian Walls with their gates.[14]

This was the glory of Rome, the inheritance and plunder of centuries; standing above all else were the height and splendour of the palaces of the Roman nobility. Among the greatest families the influence of the Anicii and the related Symmachi was empire-wide; their relations and cadet branches held estates in Gaul and the East as well as in Italy and Africa. From them had come many of the emperors of the previous century and their traditions went back to republican days. More than a century earlier they had provided the last stronghold for the pagan religion, cults and associations. Macrobius had written of the *conversazioni* in the house of the senator Symmachus; and Symmachus himself has left in his letters the abiding monument of a great aristocrat, secure, snobbish and dilettante. He hopelessly led against St. Ambrose the fight for the preservation of the traditional cults of the senate's meeting, the reverence to the statue of Victory.[15] But the families in their turn became Christian and made Christianity fashionable, taking its management and patronage into their care, as they maintained at great cost the civic amenities, the games in the circus, the city services and the senate. They stood out beyond the confines of Theodoric's Italian dominions and interests; they represented still, after its effective disappearance as a political unit, the old international order; their ties of family and connection matched their wide culture, their patronage of learning and education.[16]

[14] R. Valentini and G. Zucchetti, *Codici Topografici della Città di Roma*, (4 vols, Fonti per la Storia d'Italia, 1940), vol. I.

[15] See J. McGeachy, *Quintus Aurelius Symmachus and the Senatorial Aristocracy of the West*, (Chicago, Diss., 1942).

[16] See also M. A. Wes, 'Das Ende des Kaisertums im Westen des Römischen Reichs' (*Archeologische Studien van het Nederlands Historisch Institut te Rome, D. II*, 1967), for opinion in Rome following the fall of the Western Empire. A. Momigliano, 'Gli Anicii e la storiografia latina del VI secolo', (*Rendiconti dell' Accademia dei Lincei, Ser. 8, vol. II, fasc.* 11–12,

Bishop Ennodius of Pavia was of a Gallic branch of the Anicii, born near Arles in 474. He studied in Pavia where he became a priest, having acted as secretary to his uncle the Bishop of Milan at the Roman synod of 500. In Milan he had opened a school at which he had educated many of the younger generation of Roman nobles, such as Parthenius, a grandson of the Western Emperor Avitus, who afterwards returned to his native Gaul and became a senior minister to the Merovingian Franks; and also Arator, the poet and civil servant, who later took orders. Ennodius was a man of some diplomatic ability and reputation. He was sent by the shadowy claimant to the Western throne as envoy to the Visigothic King Euric whose regard he won: 'In my view the person of the ambassador holds more weight than the power of him who sent him.' From Odoacer he obtained a considerable lightening of the taxes due on Church property; while Theodoric used him to heal dissent in the Church and on missions to Constantinople. He represented a northern wing of the nexus of Anician contact and patronage, receiving aid for his educational venture from Rome.[17] Anician connections with North Africa were equally strong. The lady Proba, a cousin of the senator Boethius, had a great admiration for the works of St. Augustine, a complete set of which she kept in her Roman house. It was with her that Fulgentius, himself a theologian in the African tradition of Augustine, lodged on his visit to the city; to her that Eugippius, abbot of the Lucullanum monastery converted from Romulus's villa, dedicated his anthology of Augustine's works.

Strongly orthodox and traditionally opposed alike to Arianism and the unorthodoxies of the East, the Anicii, like others of their class, had nevertheless a legacy of co-operation with the new rulers in the West as well as an instinctive and sentimental accord with the imperial hegemony in the East. An Anicia, Faltonia Proba, had been suspected of opening the gates of Rome to the Visigoths in 410 in furtherance of better relations between Romans and barbarians. The senator Flavius Maximus, consul in 523, married into the Gothic royal family which in 537 caused him to be held disloyal to the imperial cause. Flavius Rufus Petronius Nichomachus Cethegus,

1956). See also P. Riché, *Education et culture dans l'Occident barbare*, 1962, ch. 3.

[17] Ennodius, *Opera*, (*ed. cit.*).

consul in 504, who succeeded to the leadership of the aristocracy after the deaths of Symmachus and Boethius, was a Gothic sympathizer who represented the Roman senate in Constantinople from 546 to 554 and was spokesman for Italy in the negotiations leading to the Pragmatic Sanction in the latter year.

The Anicii also had cousins in the Eastern capital. Flavius Anicius Olybrius, consul in 472, lived until the early years of the sixth century; he was married to Placidia, a daughter of the Western Emperor Valentinian III, who brought her husband considerable wealth; from her came to the Roman Church the *domus Placidiae*, the residence of the papal legates in Constantinople. The daughter of Placidia and Olybrius, Anicia Juliana, who died in 528, had been offered in marriage by the Emperor Zeno to Theodoric himself, but she married Flavius Areobindus Dagalaifus, consul in 506 and previously an unsuccessful general against the Persians in the campaigns of 504. Anicia Juliana was a woman of culture and influence, a correspondent of Pope Hormisdas and owner of a magnificent manuscript, copied specially for her about the year 514, of the works of the first century physician Dioscorides, which occupies an important place in the history of scientific illustration. Her Western imperial connections were not forgotten in Constantinople; when in 512 the great riots broke out and threatened to depose Anastasius it was outside the *domus Placidiae* that the crowd assembled to beg Juliana to choose a husband as emperor. Members of the Western senate passed frequently to the East on embassies concerned with religious or political matters and renewed contact with their confrères and relations in the capital.[18]

In the East there was a corresponding interest and pride in the West, nostalgic but real. The Emperor Justinian was himself proud to be sprung from a Latin-speaking province and was Latin-speaking by birth. The chronicler Marcellinus Comes, writing in Constantinople, shows more than a trace of regret at the loss of the West. Above all the bureaucrat John of Lydia, writing his treatise *On Magistracy* in the middle of the century, regarded the decision taken after the publication of Justinian's Code to promulgate all future laws in Greek, and the abandonment of Latin as the official language effected early in the fifth century, as disastrous to the imperial idea.

[18] Marcellinus Comes. *Chronicon* (*MGH. AA.* XI, a, 512).

John had a personal interest in that he had been to some trouble to learn Latin himself, but his great pride in the historical continuity of the administration, which he traces back to republican and even regal days, is the mainspring of his regret. This sympathy with the West received powerful support through contact with the senate and men of letters; refugees from Vandal North Africa, such as the grammarian Priscian, aroused new concern for the old imperial tongue and centre.[19]

The horizons of Roman society therefore outstripped, in contact and in sentiment, the dominions of Theodoric. But that implied no necessary conflict; it was from these men that Theodoric received his greatest support and in return they gained security and respect shown by too few emperors. Not since the Principate had the senate been taken into such close partnership in government. The Gothic occupation did not interrupt their traditional enjoyment of the prestigious republican offices but rather reinforced it. 'Happy man', wrote the king's secretary Cassiodorus to a nominee to the consulship, 'who has all the honour of supreme power and yet leaves to others the drudgery of affairs.' Their pursuit of letters, a real service to civilization in Europe, was permitted to go forward unhindered; it was the age not merely of the philosopher Boethius and of Dionysius Exiguus but also of lesser, yet still important activity. Boethius's father-in-law, Symmachus, wrote a history of Rome while under sentence of death in Ravenna–Cassiodorus with a fine republican touch calls him a Cato for his calmness–and he also produced an edition of Macrobius. Flavius Mavortius, the consul of 527, edited Horace's poems. The Lucullanum monastery near Naples, under the abbacy of Eugippius and the patronage of Rome, became a centre for the dissemination of Augustinian theology and literature. Indeed it was familiarity with letters and the classical education in philosophy and rhetoric which for Cassiodorus distinguished the Roman from the barbarian: 'Let others bear arms, but the Romans be armed forever only with eloquence.'

But the military achievements of Theodoric, purely Gothic though they were, assumed also some part in reconciling the Romans to Germanic rule. There was security; there was perhaps more direct profit. Theodoric may have exaggerated when he stated that

[19] *Ibid.* Johannes Lydus, *De Magistratibus*, (ed. I. Bekker, *CSHB.*, 1837).

Cassiodorus's father could mount the entire Gothic army from his own Calabrian estates, but by the end of the century Gregory I had discontinued horsebreeding on the papacy's Sicilian properties, since the lack of any such assured market made it unprofitable. Occasional crises of harvest or maladministration apart, Ostrogothic Italy was prosperous and peaceful.[20] Furthermore, under Theodoric Italy had again assumed the leadership of the western Mediterranean; a network of marriage alliances, of one sister to the Vandal king, another to the heir of Burgundy, and his daughter to the heir to the Visigothic throne, assured him a patriarchal status in Europe. His rule was firm over southern France and extended into modern Austria and Yugoslavia. Rome could, vicariously, again regard itself as ruler of the West after the humiliations of the previous century. To the city itself Theodoric showed favour, through the agency of the senate, by maintaining its monuments and its amenities, by keeping in constant repair its drainage system, its water-supply and the river embankment, and by providing circus games and ensuring the corn-supply. 120,000 bushels of wheat were annually given by the government to the people of Rome at a cost of 2,000 gold *solidi*, for 'the love of the people is strong and reliable only when they are preserved from hunger'. Life as yet was uninterrupted. Thomas, the leading charioteer of the hippodrome of Constantinople, found it worthwhile to move to Rome and perform there; he was granted a public salary for, as Cassiodorus remarked, he was 'the first in his art'.[21]

Cassiodorus himself, Theodoric's Roman secretary, most fully represented this co-operation between king and senate. His family was not ancient, but had for four generations served the state in the lesser ranks, belonging to the palatine service rather than the senate. His great-grandfather had helped to defend the south of Italy, where the family estates lay, from Vandal raids; his grandfather had been sent as envoy to obtain peace from Attila. A cousin, Heliodorus, was for eighteen years prefect in the Eastern Empire, where the family

[20] See M. Lecce, 'La vita economica d'Italia durante la dominazione dei Goti nelle "Variae" di Cassiodoro', (*Economia e Storia*, 3, 1956); G. A. Punzi, *L'Italia del VI Secolo nelle 'Variae' di Cassiodoro*, 1927; On the Italian economy in general in Late Antiquity, L. Ruggini, 'Economia e Società nell' Italia Annonaria, rapporti fra agricoltura e commercio dal IV al VI secolo d.C'. (*Coll. Fond. Guglielmo Castelli*, 30, 1961).
[21] *Variae*, III, 51.

originated. Cassiodorus's father had governed the south well for both Odoacer and Theodoric and launched his son early on a career in the palace at Ravenna. Of modest family and modest wealth, as the senate estimated it, circumstances had soon put the young Cassiodorus in the role of adviser-general to the German king. It was a role that suited his talents for, although erudite and well-read, he was not an original or critical thinker; his tastes turned towards the elegant framing of correspondence and the preservation of what he felt was in danger of being lost–the whole learning of the ancient world. His writing was encyclopaedic and forced: 'Speech, 'he declared, 'is the common gift of all mankind; it is embellishment alone that distinguishes the learned from the unlearned.' His official writings, extensively preserved, bear out this criterion; full of pedantic, irrelevant, uncritical digressions into mythology, literature and a natural history compiled from the writings of the ancients, a gentle admonition to some official to take some action being added as an afterthought. He dramatized his work: his collection of official memoranda was undertaken since friends 'wanted me to do this that future generations might recognize the painful labours I have undergone for the public good and the hardships of my unbribed conscience'. But in partnership with his king he worked sincerely and well for the peace and prosperity of Italy.[22]

He did have a wider vision of the need to preserve and foster learning. In 536 he urged upon Pope Agapetus the need to found a university at Rome, equipped with libraries, to continue both ancient and Christian traditions. 'Seeing that the schools were swarming with students with a great longing for secular letters ... I was, I confess, extremely sad that the Divine Scriptures had no public teachers; for there was beyond doubt rich and most distinguished instruction in the worldly authors. I urged upon the most holy Agapetus ... to collect subscriptions and to have Christian rather than secular schools in the city of Rome, with professors, just as there had been for so long in Alexandria.' In the Lateran there may have been a collection

<hr>

[22] A. Van der Vyver, 'Cassiodore et son Oeuvre', (*Speculum*, 6, 1931); J. Fridh, 'Terminologie et Formules, dans les Variae de Cassiodore', (*Studia Graeca et Latina Gottoburgensia*, 2, 1956); O. Zimmermann, *The Vocabulary of the Variae of Cassiodorus*, (Catholic University of America, 1944).

of books started in the previous century by Pope Hilary, while the greater churches, such as St. Peter's, acted as natural focuses for collections. The Lateran held the records of the Roman Church, while St. Peter's from the beginning of the century, and perhaps through Pope Symmachus's residence there during the Laurentian schism, had had a bureau for book-production and archives of its own. But there was no unified centre for teaching and edition. When Fulgentius, in exile in Sardinia, required books for the school he was organizing, it was to his friend Eugippius at the Lucullanum, where Dionysius Exiguus had carried out most of his work, that he wrote.

Agapetus fell in readily with Cassiodorus's urgings. A start was made by providing a library and reading-room at the church of SS. John and Paul where Agapetus's father Gordianus had been priest. An inscription in the reading-room proclaimed it as the pope's foundation: 'He made this splendid place for books', but the enterprise was cut short by the Gothic Wars and never afterwards resumed. Theodoric himself frowned on the attempt to make Goths into Romans by education, a prejudice shared by most of his people. Cassiodorus, following the collapse of all his hopes for the Romano–Gothic state, retired to his home in Squillace in Calabria where he founded the 'Vivarium', a monastic community devoted to effecting his projects for the correct edition and production of literary, historical and educational works.[23]

The other figure of Ostrogothic Rome who towered above his surroundings and whose influence was to sustain Europe in the succeeding centuries was an Anicius, the philosopher Manlius Severinus Anicius Boethius. His inclinations were primarily academic and philosophical; he had entered public life only, he states in the *Consolations of Philosophy*, in accordance with the dictate of Plato

[23] E. K. Rand, 'The New Cassiodorus', (*Speculum*, 13, 1938); A. Momigliano, 'Cassiodorus and the Italian Culture of his time', (*Proceedings of the British Academy*, 41, 1955); H-I. Marrou, Autour de la bibliothèque d'Agapet', (*MAH.*, 48, 1931); P. Courcelle, 'Le site du monastère de Cassiodore', (*MAH.*, 55, 1938); L. Teutsch, 'Cassiodorus Senator: Grunder der Klosterbibliothek von Vivarium', (*Libri*, 9, 1959); L. Szymanski, *The Translation Procedure of Epiphanius-Cassiodorus*, (Catholic University of America, 1963); W. Weinberger, 'Handschriften von Vivarium', (*Miscellanea Francesco Ehrle*, 4, *Studi e Testi*, 40, 1924); G. Ludwig, *Cassiodor: über den Ursprung der Abendländischen Schule*, 1967.

that 'States would be happy if either philosophers ruled them or their rulers turned philosopher.' He held the consulship in 510 and devoted himself to the well-being of Italy; his reputation stood high as a leader of moderate opinion and his popularity was great when he intervened with the government to reduce the effects of a severe economic depression in southern Italy and Campania. Theodoric called upon his mathematical and mechanical skills to devise diplomatic gifts for neighbouring rulers. He too, like Cassiodorus, was concerned for Western education, but his concern lay in constructing an adequate bridge to keep the West in contact with the founts of philosophy in the East. His death—the result of a welter of theological, political and personal interest at Rome and Ravenna—gave him the status in Western Europe of a martyr and a father of the church.[24]

Boethius, Symmachus, Liberius, even Cassiodorus, stood out among the senatorial group by their learning, moderation or vision. They were not typical, for the senate contained many men who accepted the light rule of Theodoric and the privileges he granted them as an encouragement to emphasize their patrician status and imperial connections. Rome, a city with no industrial or commercial but only social and traditional justification, retained one prerogative of civilization, the formation of factions to occupy the inhabitants. The Blues and the Greens, though quieter than in Constantinople where there was the meat of power to seize, still flourished. In 509 a riot erupted: a meeting had been held to plan the mimes to be presented by the Green faction and two candidates were competing for favour. One was Helladius, a Greek of Emesa who in Constantinople under Zeno had been employed by the Red faction. Helladius's partisans, led by the consul Importunus and his brother the patrician Theodore of the proud Decian family, were not members of the Greens but of the aristocratic Blues. Some misappropriation of public funds may have been involved, for the Greens, who represented a large proportion of the poorer citizens, were in receipt of an annual public subsidy. Fighting broke out between citizens and the household servants of the senators, and a man was killed; the mob, more law-abiding than that in Constantinople, which in 501 had caused riots which killed 3,000 and set most of the city on fire,

[24] See H. M. Barrett, *Boethius—some aspects of his life and work*, 1940; H. R. Patch, *The Tradition of Boethius*, 1935.

appealed to Theodoric. He acted with his usual good sense: arrogance was out of place in the circus since the mob did not possess the virtues of Cato and indeed, the king declared, he only permitted the games, which he considered a foolish and expensive waste of time, because it was impossible to abolish them. They were a part of the tradition of Rome.[25]

Arrogance, favouritism to an Oriental and sympathy for the East may have determined the two senators' conduct. But there was still one further consideration which prevented senatorial nostalgia from being effectively realized. These men were Christians, Catholic Christians, obedient to the pope. In the phrase now gaining currency, Rome was the *urbs ecclesiae*, the Church's city, as distinct from the *urbs regiae*, the imperial seat in the East. The Bishop of Rome, wielder of the authority of the princes of the apostles, and now being acknowledged as the prime pope or father of the Western Christian communities, with a vast moral authority in the East, was also head of a powerful and rich corporation, based on the endowments of emperors and the achievements of his predecessors.[26] The senatorial class had, as it had attempted with paganism, assumed some right of patronage over the established religion. The churches of Rome had been founded by the first Christians among the senate in their private houses and named after their founders; their maintenance and that of the small domestic monasteries of the city was largely in their hands. They had also tried to place themselves squarely within the history and tradition of the dominant religion by utilizing the new legends of the saints that were now acquiring a wide popularity. So the account of the martyrdom of SS. Rufina and Secunda, and of St. Marius and his companions whose cults centred around Boccea, a few miles north of Rome, evidently appear to have been inspired by the pretensions of the family of Asterius Turcius, consul in 504; an ancestor figures as the magistrate presiding at the saints' trials. Similarly the Anicii appear to have adopted into their family St. Melania, wife of

[25] E. Condurachi, 'Factions et jeux du Cirque au début du VIe siècle', (*Revue Historique du Sud-Est Européen*, 18, 1941); A. Maricq, 'Factions du Cirque et partis populaires', (*Bulletin de la classe des lettres et des sciences morales et politiques de l'Academie royale de Belgique*, 36, 1950); C. Pietri, 'Le Senat, le peuple chrétien et les partis du Cirque sous le pape Symmaque', (*MAH.*, 78, 1963).

[26] See P. de Labriolle, 'Papa', (*ALMA*. 4, 1928).

Pinianus, a wealthy and charitable matron of the *gens Valeria* early in the fifth century; by the mid-sixth century her actions and attributes, including her husband, and the prestige arising from them had passed to Lucina, an Anicia of about the same date. St. Marius and his companions were reputedly Persian and their popularity marks the beginnings of Roman interest in things of the East, an interest which was to grow in the course of the sixth century. Also early in the sixth century the cult of St. Anastasia from the East achieved prominence in Rome and, the first of non-Roman saints, she was given the dedication of a *titulus* and commemorated by a special Mass on Christmas Day. The doctor-brothers of Arabia, SS. Cosmas and Damian, were also introduced into the Roman calendar. This fascination persisted; the stories of the saints of the East and the magicians they encountered, the wonders, such as the phoenix and the king of Persia's tomb carved from a single, huge amethyst, all held an audience.[27]

Twice since the disappearance of the empire in the West the senate had attempted to transform their patronage over church affairs into a direct control. The stakes were high for, local prestige apart, the Roman Church stood squarely in the way of renewed and uninterrupted communication with the East, the one source of legitimate political and social authority that the senate could recognize. The papacy, conversely, as recognized head and source of authority over the whole Church, had interests and concerns even in those parts which were in imperial hands, those parts were theology played a vital part in politics, where–such was the concept of the Christian empire–theology and politics over a wide area occupied the same ground. So it had been in the late fifth century; to recall to loyalty the dissident, theologically alert Syrian provinces, the Emperor Zeno had in 474 issued a decree of religious unity for the empire in which he assumed the right to amend and override the decisions of Church councils. In the executive sphere the Church had left much of the initiative and the routine in the hands of the civil authorities, but for this invasion into doctrinal matters the chief inspirer of the decree, the patriarch

[27] 'Passio SS. Rufinae et Secundae', (*AASS.* Iul. III, 30–1); 'Passio S. Marii et Socc'. (*AASS,* Ian. II, 1st ed., 216–9); A. Dufourcq, *Etudes sur les Gesta Martyrum romaines,* (Bibliotheque des Ecoles françaises d'Athènes et de Rome, 83, 1900), vol. I., pp. 311, 347.

Acacius of Constantinople, was excommunicated by Pope Gelasius, and religious schism entered to reinforce the political separation. The schism persisted, for Zeno's successor Anastasius was also of suspect orthodoxy. Gelasius was unable to excommunicate Anastasius himself for a powerful party persisted among the Roman senate and even among the clergy that looked in sentiment and law to the emperor as the true sovereign of Italy and the natural protector of all Christians. But Gelasius, uncompromising, wrote sternly to Anastasius: 'There are two powers which for the most part control this world, the sacred authority of priests and the might of kings. Of these two the office of the priests is the greater in as much as they must give account even for kings to the Lord at the divine judgment. . . . You must know therefore that you are dependent upon their decisions and they will not submit to your will.'[28]

Gelasius, perhaps African in origin, had already shown himself as a champion of the Roman Church's political, social and intellectual independence; as one of the makers of the medieval papacy. He had served as secretary to two of his predecessors, Simplicius and Felix III, and under them had already helped to shape papal policy.[29] It was on the death of Simplicius that the senate had tried to intervene in the succession, demanding that no election be made without senatorial consultation and insisting that Church property, which came largely from senatorial endowment, be declared absolutely inalienable.[30] This claim was not made fully effective, although later revived, and Felix III, aided by Gelasius, was able to maintain the

[28] P. Charanis, 'Church and State in the Later Roman Empire; the religious policy of Anastasius the First', (*University of Wisconsin Studies in the Social Sciences and History*, 26, 1939); S. Salaville, 'L'affaire de l'Hénotique, Les consequences de l'Hénotique, le Schisme acacien', (*Echos d'Orient*, 19, 1920); W. T. Townsend, 'The Henotikon Schism and the Roman Church', (*Journal of Religion*, 16, 1936); F. Dvornik, 'Pope Gelasius and Emperor Anastasius', (*Byzantinische Zeitschrift*, 44, 1951).

[29] H. Koch, 'Gelasius im kirchenpolitischen Dienste seiner Vorgänger Päpste Simplicius und Felix III', (*Bayer Akademie* Abt. 1935–6); E. Zeigler, 'Church and State under Gelasius', (*Catholic Historical Review*, 1942); P. Brezzi, 'Gelasio I e la nuova orientazione politica della Chiesa di Roma', (*Nuova Rivista Storica*, 20, 1936); J. L. Nelson, 'Gelasius I's doctrine of responsibility–a note', (*Journal of Theological Studies*, n.s. 18, 1967).

[30] See G-B. Picotti, cited n. 5.

independence of the papacy. But the advent of the Acacian schism, introducing a new factor into the delicate and personal relationships between East and West, reawoke the need of the senators for some control over the Roman Church.

Gelasius's protégé, Dionysius Exiguus, recalled his character in a letter to the priest Julian: 'He was animated by a saintly disposition. He accepted the highest place in the Church by God's will for the salvation of many. In this post he acted more as a servant than as a sovereign . . . this man who lived in prayer, reading and study and who would, when necessary, pen documents with his own hand.'[31] He had spent much effort in controverting the remnants of Pelagianism in the West; as pope he also overhauled the business arrangements of the Church, drawing up a comprehensive register of Church properties and revenues that was to be the foundation for much pastoral and charitable activity in the coming centuries; and he sought to free the Roman Church from over-dependence on its social and political environment.

Two major clashes occurred with the senatorial group. One concerned the condemnation of those unauthorized acts and passions of the martyrs that were beginning to gain currency as the staple of Christian literature for the masses, filling out the bare lists of names in the martyrologies with all the wonders of the novelette, and which the great families and political factions were to find a convenient *genre* for propaganda in internal disputes. The decree attributed to him, *de libris recipiendis et non recipiendis*, was most probably not of Roman origin but the product of some Gallic synod, yet it was adopted by the papacy and reflects the desire to retain an accurate and scholarly approach to Church history and to reduce the opportunity for doctrinal aberration. The decree, nonetheless, hit at popular entertainment and aroused a certain amount of opposition.[32]

The other major clash between Gelasius and the senatorial group concerned the antiquarianism of those Romans who maintained

---

[31] Dionysius Exiguus, *Praefatio ad Collectionem Decretorum*, (*PL.* 67, col. 231).

[32] E. von Dobschutz, 'Das Decretum Gelasianum de libris recipiendis et non recipiendis', (*Texte und Untersuchungen*, 38, 1912); B. de Gaiffier, 'Un prologue hagiographique hostile au Décret de Gelase?', (*AB.*, 82, 1964).

pagan customs unsuitable for a Christian city. It was against one such, Andromachus, and his associates that Gelasius in 495 issued his condemnation of the pagan festival of the Lupercalia, one of the oldest in the city, traditionally connected with Romulus's suckling by the she-wolf. To Andromachus, then leader of the senate and one of the festival's supporters, he wrote stressing the dignity of Christianity, the grandeur and sanctity of the Church and the disciplinary authority inherent in the papacy. The condemnation was in the nature of a counter-attack, for a group of senators—true to their conception of patronage in all things Roman—had apparently taken the pope to task for his tardiness in condemning a cleric found guilty of adultery. The pope's reply was based on the poor record of the Lupercalia as an averter of calamities in pagan times, and gives a Christian leader's view, without official or family sentiment, of Rome's republican and imperial history—it was the war-torn period described by Livy that had seen their celebration.[33]

Gelasius then had asserted the strength of the Roman Church at home and overseas; he had insisted that the sentimental attachment that Romans might feel for the Empire could not affect the Church's own championship of orthodoxy or the condemnation of doctrinal interference; he had improved the financial situation of the Roman Church, giving it a strength independent of government and social pressure and emphasizing its own corporate nature; and he had not hesitated to condemn, even to the proudest and greatest in the city, standards of conduct that might be associated with the origins of the city but which were unChristian. It was at the death of Gelasius's successor Pope Anastasius in 496 that the greatest struggle for control of the Roman Church and the shaping of its policies broke out. Two elections were made simultaneously; the friends of Constantinople, a majority of the senate, put forward Lawrence, the archpriest of Rome, whom they trusted to work for a closer religious and political union with the East. Liberius, the elder Cassiodorus and the senator Faustus, who had worked with the Gothic government and recognized the local advantages it brought, advanced a candidate whom they hoped would continue Gelasius's policy of doctrinal

[33] G. Pomarès, 'Gelase Ier; Lettre contre les Lupercales et Dix-Huit Messes', (Sources Chrétiennes, 65, 1959); R. Merkelbach, 'Zur Epistola Gelasii Adversum Andromachum', (Vigiliae Christianae, 9, 1955).

strength and independence of disruptive external pressures. This was Symmachus, a Sardinian who on his first arrival in Rome had not even been a Christian–Sardinia, backward and unhealthy, was at the end of the sixth century still the object of papal missions. More important to him was the support he had from the people, the Green faction, and the clergy. In addition, he had a considerable reputation for charity and generosity in building and endowment.[34]

On 22nd November 498 both men were consecrated pope. A virulent pamphlet warfare broke out and clashes in the street followed. The supporters of Symmachus sought to prove with pamphlets purporting to describe incidents in the papacy's history, none true, that the senate had always shown itself obdurate in the face of the Church's interests; that senatorial charges of avarice against Symmachus were dispelled by his generosity; and that the pope was above judgement even by a synod of bishops, for 'the disciple is not above his master'; and that any bishop, of however historic a see, was subject to trial and sentence by Rome. One such fabricated story tells of Pope Marcellinus, who was accused at the time of Diocletian of having sacrificed to the gods under compulsion, and appeared before an assembly of bishops: their declaration, 'You be judge and either sentence or absolve yourself: we are merely present, you are judge and accused', was followed by Marcellinus's confession. The pamphleteers in favour of Lawrence did not consider such essentials of the papal position but rather concentrated on the immediate and practical divisions between East and West, the separate dates observed for Easter and the legitimacy of the Eastern Empire, putting themselves forward as the party of unity. Counter-accusations flew between the parties, and Symmachus was accused–a standard practice–of adultery. The chief supporters of Lawrence, the senators Festus and Probus and the deacon Paschasius, exercised much violence to get their man in. The riots continued; Symmachus took refuge outside the city, across the river by St. Peter's, and a chronicler favouring his side reported on the disorder:

'Then Festus, the ex-consul and leader of the senate, and Probus the ex-consul, began brawling in the streets with other senators, in

[34] R. Cessi, 'Lo Scisma Laurenziano e le origini della dottrina politica della Chiesa di Roma', (*ASR.*, 42, 1919); A. Alessandrini, 'Teodorico e Papa Simmaco durante lo Scisma laurenziano', (*ASR*, 67, 1944).

particular with the ex-consul Faustus and in their hatred began to commit slaughter and murder on the clergy who correctly were in communion with the blessed Symmachus; with swords and publicly, they killed any they could find in the city. They also expelled consecrated virgins from their convents and houses; they stripped women of their clothes and wounded them with blows and stripes, and daily waged war against the Church in the heart of the city. Likewise they slew many priests, among them Dignissimus, priest of St. Peter's *ad Vincula* and Gordianus, priest of SS. John and Paul, whom they did to death with cudgel and sword; also many other Christians, so that it was unsafe for any of the clergy to walk abroad in the city, day or night. Only the ex-consul fought for the Church.' Rome had not forgotten the methods of Clodius and Milo.[35]

But Rome now had an external protector in the person of the king. Fulgentius, an exile from Arian persecution, had been amazed to witness an Arian German greeted and honoured by the clergy of Rome, but he was being welcomed for his tactful and firm conclusion to the Laurentian schism. His political interest lay with the party of Symmachus and Faustus, insistent on a strict orthodoxy that would continue the schism with Constantinople. But he had also a respect for the Roman Church and its influence, and a basic toleration in religious matters underlay his whole rule. 'We cannot give orders as to religious belief, since no one can be compelled to believe against his will'; a story was told that he had executed a sycophantic Catholic deacon who had adopted the court's Arianism. He now acted in Rome in a spirit of good order and of protection towards the Roman Church. A synod was summoned to meet at the Palmaris portico, at which Symmachus was declared the duly elected pope; Lawrence, being already consecrated, was compensated with the bishopric of Nocera. The settlement, conducted by Theodoric's special and saintly friend among the Italian episcopate, Epiphanius of Pavia, and aided by Ennodius as secretary, was not final. It won the favour of the largely pro-Gothic clergy, but rumblings of discontent continued for many years, and in 502 the Italian bishops rubbed

---

[35] *LP.* I, 260–1; *Gesta Liberii, BHL.* 4907; *Gesta de Xysti purgatione et Polychronii accusatione, BHL.* 7813; *Constitutum Silvestri, PL.* 8, 829–40; *Sinuessanae Synodi Gesta de Marcellini, PL.* 6, 11–20. W. T. Townsend, 'The So-called Symmachan Forgeries', (*Journal of Religion*, 13, 1933).

home their concept of the Church's place by declaring that laymen had no right of intervention in the disposal of ecclesiastical property. Ennodius himself was to spend much effort in propaganda on the synod's behalf; he recognized Gelasius's doctrines of the supremacy of the papacy above all other institutions: 'God no doubt consented to the affairs of men being settled by men; He reserves for Himself the passing of judgement upon the pontiff of the supreme see.' His efforts to secure full co-operation and accord between the senatorial party and the court continued; he urged the lady Barbara, who maintained a *salon* in Rome, supported poor scholars and had the *entrée* to the pope, to take up a post at the court of Ravenna and so to 'show the provinces that there was good in Rome'.[36]

This material and ideological consolidation of the Roman Church to which Gelasius had given direction shows it emerging with machinery, scholarship, laws and administrative powers of its own, parallel to those of the state and able, as the state waned, to sustain unity and learning of its own. The Roman Church drew scholars into its service who laid down principles which were to extend over Western Europe. The Scythian monk Dionysius Exiguus in his own person provided much of the impetus of the new papally-directed movement. Inheriting the tradition of Gelasius he codified, in the collection named after him the *Dionysia*, the synodal decrees of the West and, with Latin translations, those of the East; to these were added specifically papal decrees, ranging from those of Pope Siriacus in the fourth century to Anastasius. This work was undertaken at the instance of Pope Hormisdas; Cassiodorus summarized it: 'By the light of his eloquence, which is comparable to his moral authority, he composed the canons of the Church, for he was both a clear and fluent writer; the Roman Church honours these canons today with constant use.' Dionysius's work of codification marked an advance in the Rome-centred aspect of Western canon law. As with the legends and acts of the saints, and the calendars, the tradition of Gelasius insisted on the establishment of true texts and the

[36] Ennodius, *Epp.* VIII, 16; *Libellus*, in *Opera*, 287–330; G-B. Picotti, 'I sinodi romani nello scisma laurenziano', (*Studi Storici in onore di G. Volpe*, II, 1958); W. T. Townsend, *Ennodius and Pope Symmachus*, (Essays presented to E. K. Rand, 1938); E. Poma, *L'ingiudicabilità dello Romano pontifice*, (Scuola Cattolica, Milano, 1935).

elimination of apocrypha; the authentic codified texts, displayed the superiority of a general Roman discipline over the local canons and of written law over the variations of custom. The laws and decrees of synods were widely drawn, from Africa as well as Italy and Gaul, and completed with the translations of Greek canons, but the stamp of approval was Roman. As a mathematician and astronomer he was also well-respected, being employed in the computation of an accurate date for Easter and evolving the method of dating from Christ's birth, for he wished that the current era, from the accession of Diocletian, should not perpetuate the memory of a persecutor of Christians.[37]

Through the moderate government of Theodoric, Rome had been spared the worst effects of the vanishing of the Empire and had perhaps not yet come to terms with the changes in the Western world. But the peace of Theodoric was a fragile thing, for it was not conditioned by solely Italian factors. Two of the partners, the papacy and the senate, were involved on a wider plane and upon them external events could act. A major support to the unity of Gothic rule had been the discord between pope and emperor following the issue of Zeno's *Henotikon* decree, and against this discord, combined with Theodoric's own toleration, sentimental and cultural affinities with the East had been unable to prevail. Relations between Pope Hormisdas and the Emperor Anastasius had deteriorated, culminating in a final breach with the latter's message to the pope in July 517: 'Henceforth we shall suppress in silence our requests, thinking it absurd to show the courtesy of prayers to those who, with arrogance in their mouths, refuse even to be entreated. We can endure insults and contempt but we cannot permit ourselves to be commanded.' But a year later, in July 518, Anastasius died. From a welter of intrigue and bribery among the palace officials, courtiers and guards, his successor, the guardsman Justin emerged – a Latin-speaking illiterate from Illyricum who came of a firm peasant orthodoxy and was a strong supporter of Chalcedon. Close to him, possessing his family's brains, ambition and vision, stood his young nephew, the count Justinian.[38]

---

[37] See W. M. Peitz, 'Dionysius Exiguus – Studien', (*Arbeiten zur Kirchengeschichte*, 33, 1960).
[38] *Epistulae Imperatorum Pontificum Aliorum* (*Collectio Avellana*),

From the first, the policy of the new dynasty was the fierce enforcement of the Chalcedonian orthodoxy that Zeno and Anastasius had tried to amend, and reunion with Rome, the keystone in the suppression of heresy. Justin wrote at once to the pope, asking for his prayers; official letters followed, from the new emperor, the new patriarch John and from Justinian. Justin and John expressed pious hopes for the accomplishment of church peace; Justinian was more specific and autocratic, requesting Hormisdas himself to come to the capital. Instead, and with the consent of Theodoric, the pope sent legates, led by Bishop Germanus of Capua. Throughout their overland journey along the Via Egnazia, and from Durazzo across Thrace to the capital, they were everywhere accorded a triumphant welcome. In Constantinople peace was formally restored.[39]

To the ageing Theodoric this rapprochement seemed as if a ring was closing around him, as the events of the next few years would confirm. Never more than barely tolerated in the East, he was now becoming increasingly isolated in the West and his patriarchal standing diminished. In 516 his son-in-law King Sigismund of Burgundy was converted to Catholicism; in 523 his other son-in-law, King Eutharic of the Visigoths, died, leaving the succession an uncertain matter. In North Africa the Romanophil Hunneric, son of a Roman princess and grandson of the Western Emperor Valentinian III, succeeded to the throne and in 523 ended the persecution of the Catholics, while Theodoric's sister Amalafrida, widow of the late King Thrasamund, was no longer an influential link between the two courts. There was dissension within Theodoric's own court over the Romanizing tendencies of his daughter Amalasuntha, which were aggravated by the probability of her acting as regent for the young Athalaric. The delegation to Constantinople which had restored peace to the Church had brought the senators of Rome into renewed contact with an orthodox and legitimate régime for which they had an instinctive and traditional sympathy, and Justin had further marked reunion by massive donations of bullion to the Roman

(*CSEL*, 35, ed. O. Gunther, 1895), 138; on the accession of Justin, see A. A. Vasiliev, 'Justin the First; An introduction to the Epoch of Justinian the Great', (*Dumbarton Oaks Studies*, I, 1950).

[39] *Collectio Avellana*, 181, 182, 187. S. Salaville, 'L'affaire de l'Hénotique, IV; La réconciliation avec Rome', (*Echos d'Orient*, 19, 1920).

Church. Imperial orthodoxy had devolved logically into a persecution of the Arians of the East and this had extended itself into a bout of anti-Semitic feeling which reached Italy. In Rome, Ravenna and Verona synagogues were attacked, pillaged and burnt. Theodoric acted sternly; the perpetrators were arrested and flogged and in retaliation the church of St. Stephen at Verona was destroyed. The clergy of the whole kingdom denounced the act, but Theodoric went further in suppressing unrest. By decree all Italians were disarmed; each person was allowed only one small table knife, and even the martial heirlooms of the great Roman families were confiscated. Trust and confidence within the kingdom were evaporating.[40]

Then in 522 informers brought Theodoric word that senators, under the senate's leader Albinus, had been in treasonable correspondence with Constantinople. With age had come an increased savagery, a loss of that control instilled into him by his respect for civilization, and a bitterness at the disloyalty which could not extend to him the tolerance he had always shown. Albinus was arrested and Boethius, as president of the senate, summoned to Ravenna to explain its attitude. Boethius's exposure of corruption in Campania had already made him enemies within the administration. He had played a leading part in controverting Arianism, and further charges of witchcraft and of holding secret assemblies were thrown in to give added strength to the case. Boethius stood firm before Theodoric: the facts displayed no more than a sympathy to the orthodox Empire and, 'If Albinus is guilty, then so am I, and so is the whole senate'. Echoing Seneca he argued that, 'Even if I had known [of the conspiracy] you would not.' To Theodoric this was sufficient. At the age of seventy the strain of his long government was telling and one by one the tools he had chosen were slipping from his hand. Boethius was arrested; three shady senators, including the former consul Basilius, all in need of money, brought evidence, and Boethius was imprisoned in Pavia. His aged father-in-law Symmachus hastened to Ravenna to plead for him, and he too was arrested. In his cell in Pavia, Boethius resumed his philosophy and wrote the *Consolations* before being bludgeoned to death. Shortly afterwards Symmachus in his turn was executed.[41]

[40] Anon. Vales., 14, 82, 83.
[41] Anon. Vales., 14, 85–7; Procopius, *Bellum Gothicum*, I, 35. W. Bark, 'Theodoric versus Boethius', (*American Historical Review*, 1944) C. H.

The tension increased. In August 523 Pope Hormisdas, who had been in Theodoric's confidence, died. His successor was John, from Tuscany, a firm opponent of Arianism who, to Theodoric's great anger, set out to re-dedicate to Catholic use the Arian churches in Rome. He was associating in Rome with men of known imperialist sympathies, while in the East the persecution of Arians and the confiscation of their property was stepped up. Theodoric took certain precautions. In 524 he began re-arming, and using timber from the forests of Calabria he set out to remedy the sole deficiency of the Gothic state–the lack of a fleet. One last aim remained–to break the religious sympathy of a united Catholicism in East and West as he had thought to break the civil solidarity. Early in 526 Pope John, old and sick, was summoned to Ravenna and given his orders: 'Go to Constantinople, to the Emperor Justin, and among other things tell him to bring back [to Arianism] those he forced to accept the Catholic faith'. Pope John had the example of the senators before him; he could not permit his office to be used to obtain the toleration of heresy to assist an increasingly tyrannical king. Peace he would try to obtain: 'O King, what thou doest, do quickly; I stand here before you. I cannot promise to do this, nor shall I tell the Emperor of it. But as for the other matters which you charge me to obtain from him, with the help of God these I will accomplish.' He sailed from Ravenna to Corinth; there he was forced to borrow a horse (which in legend would never afterwards submit to carrying a woman) and so proceeded painfully to Constantinople. His welcome was royal; officials, including Justinian, met him at the twelfth milestone from the capital, 'for since the days of the blessed Pope Sylvester in the time of Constantine, they had wished to be accounted worthy to receive the Vicar of St. Peter in Greece'. John arrived on the 19th April, Easter Day, and celebrated the feast in the capital with full imperial splendour; then, as a climax, he crowned Justin. A month later he was back in Ravenna, worn out by his mission, and was immediately imprisoned by the king; in prison, mercifully, on the 18th May, he died. His body was brought back to Rome and as it passed he was hailed by the Italians as a saint and martyr for orthodoxy; miracles attended the passage of his bier and at his burial senators snatched pieces from

Coster, 'The Fall of Boethius; his character', (*Mélanges Henri Gregoire*, IV, 1953).

his vestments as relics of one dead in their cause. Three months later, at the end of August, Theodoric himself collapsed of a stroke at a banquet with, it was said, the face of Symmachus staring into his conscience and his strangled name on his lips.[42]

The death of Theodoric brought some hope to the cause of peace for Italy, for it was necessarily followed by the regency of Amalasuntha for her son Athalaric. Amalasuntha was perhaps the most ardent proponent of harmony between Romans and Goths, the most appreciative among the Goths of Roman culture, the most interested in its fostering. For this and not merely for her sex she was distrusted by those Goths who still looked on their rule in Italy as no mere commission from the Emperor but the reward of conquest. These had worked on the old king to remove the heir to the throne from his mother's influence, as well as from that of Cassiodorus and from the demoralizing effects of Roman culture. This accorded with Theodoric's dictum that a Goth could not be Romanized, or a Roman Gothicized, without ill-effects; and the example and warning of the king's nephew, Theodahat, also gave support to this view. For Athalaric was arranged the robuster education in arms befitting an Amal prince. It failed—perhaps Athalaric inherited too much from his father Eutharic, 'an excessively rough man, an enemy to the Catholic faith'. The prince, with the boon companions chosen for him, was soon drinking himself, first into sodden debauchery, and finally to death. But while he lived, for eight years from his grandfather's death, Amalasuntha managed to hold the government.

The battle for Italian sympathies was fought throughout in Rome. The new pope to succeed John was a Samnite, Felix IV, a man of great energy. He had been employed by Pope Symmachus on several embassies to Theodoric and under Hormisdas had been papal representative in Constantinople. The four years of Felix's pontificate

[42] W. Ensslin, 'Papst Johannes I als Gesandter Theoderichs des Grossen bei Kaiser Justinus I', (*Byzantinische Zeitschrift*, 44, 1951); H. Lowe, 'Theoderich der Grosse und Papst Johann I', (*Historische Jahrbuch*, 72, 1953); P. Goubert, 'Autour du voyage à Byzance du pape S. Jean I', (*Orientalia Christiana Periodica*, 24, 1958). For Justinian's view of Church–State relations, see M. Anastos, 'Justinian's despotic control over the Church as illustrated by his Edict on the Theopaschite Formula and letter to Pope John', *Zbornik nadova bizantinoloskog instituta*, II, *Mélanges Ostrogorsky*, II, 1964.

were a tug-of-war between the two factions. Felix, to secure his party and to prevent a clash, attempted to nominate his friend, the elderly Archdeacon Boniface, as his successor. When Felix died in 530 there was a double election. The majority of the Roman clergy supported Dioscorus, a deacon originally from Alexandria who had a high reputation in the East, having spent some years in Constantinople, and perhaps only seven out of nearly seventy supported the Gothic candidate, Boniface. Again two consecrations were made, Dioscorus within the Lateran basilica and Boniface in a hall of the Lateran palace. For a month the dispute raged and it was only ended by Dioscorus's premature death on 14th October. Even then Boniface had difficulty in asserting his authority; Constantinople had already been in communication with Dioscorus and now Boniface demanded a written declaration of loyalty from the clergy. This did not end his difficulties in securing a clear succession of policy in Gothic favour. He summoned a synod at which he in turn tried to nominate as his successor the deacon Vigilius, but the irate clergy refused to allow it, condemning the attempt as sacrilege and forcing Boniface to repudiate his acts and burn the decree. Through the tactlessness of two successive popes the clergy of Rome were firmly on the imperial side.[43]

Amalasuntha was in no position to intervene; as her son and the Gothic nobility were alienated from her, her authority steadily waned and she could exercise little power. When Justinian succeeded his uncle in the East in 527 events were already moving as he wished to recreate the unity of the Empire. Amalasuntha was putting out feelers towards Constantinople to ensure a safe refuge in case she was forced to flee, and in 533 Justinian found a pretext to invade North Africa. In one swift campaign his general Belisarius overthrew the Vandal kingdom and won great booty, a powerful fleet and the southern coast of the Mediterranean. After more than a century the provinces were reunited to the Empire. Belisarius' force had been small, less than 20,000 men, but the nerve of the Vandals, softened by the climate and the luxury they had adopted, had broken after two encounters and they succumbed with little resistance. The omens

---

[43] *LP*. I, 281; P. Ewald, 'Acten zum Schisma des Jahres 530', (*Neues Archiv*, 10, 1885); L. Duchesne, 'La succession du pape Felix IV', (*MAH*, 3, 1883).

seemed good; all that the legalistic and conscience-ridden Justinian needed was an occasion.[44]

It came soon. In 534 Athalaric died, worn out by the excesses the Gothic warriors had led him to. His mother's position was untenable, her life in danger; her regency had been barely tolerated, her direct rule would never be. But Theodoric's daughter recovered swiftly–the more prominent of her opponents were arrested and imprisoned and from Tuscany she summoned the last male Amal, her cousin Theodahat. Theodahat was an atypical Goth, a fatal result of that mixture Theodoric had condemned. He professed a keen studentship of philosophy, and especially of Plato; by character he was no warrior, but a coward, unstable and avaricious. He lived on his vast Etruscan estates and took no part in affairs, beyond seeking to extend his lands yet further. It was said of him that 'to have a neighbour seemed some kind of misfortune'. Amalasuntha promptly married him, giving him the title of king and a handsome allowance, and continued to rule in his name. But the elevation went to his head. In April 535 he had Amalasuntha arrested and imprisoned on an island in Lake Bolsena; shortly afterwards she was murdered. It was thought that Peter, the imperial envoy in Italy, 'a man of wide culture and special legal training', encouraged Theodahat in this crime at the instigation of the Empress Theodora who feared Amalasuntha's appeal to the susceptible Justinian. Peter was shortly after raised to the post of Master of Offices, head of the diplomatic service, for his work in Italy.[45]

Theodahat's action played directly into Justinian's hands. He had invaded the Vandal kingdom on just such a pretext, and now that Amalasuntha had placed herself under his protection he had ample justification for intervention. Although the sympathy and support of an imperial party in Italy was uncertain–Amalasuntha's murder had been the occasion for the retirement of many Romans, such as Arator, from the Gothic service–the northern Franks had been approached and, being orthodox Christians, were ready to accept imperial subsidies to act as allies. Peter was working on the unstable will of Theodahat, already panic-stricken at the consequences of his

[44] Procopius, *Bellum Vandalicum*, (Loeb ed.).
[45] N. H. Baynes, 'Justinian and Amalasuntha', (*English Historical Review*, 40, 1925): Procopius, BG. 11.

actions. Influenced by Theodora who had strong monophysite leanings, Justinian had that same year appointed the monophysite Anthemius to be Patriarch of Constantinople, in an attempt to reconcile where persecution had failed. The Emperor had promptly been condemned in Rome. To Theodora especially this was an affront to be atoned, and Belisarius, fresh from his African triumph, was ready with a trained army.

Justinian saw the war as one of liberation, restoring legal government to Rome and Italy, and giving back to Rome what was properly hers. It was also a necessary act in the completion of the majesty of the Empire that the ancient capital should be brought once more into the Empire's orbit. Above all, in his search for ecclesiastical and religious unity to underpin the Empire in the East he desperately required the authority and support of the papacy. Within the struggle for the old capital, therefore, lay the fight to secure a pliant papacy so that Justinian, with all founts of religious authority subservient to him, might fully dominate the church. He hoped for a quick and cheap victory, but the welfare of his future subjects was to be subordinated to his concept of empire, overridingly a concept of uniformity. Belisarius was ordered to sail for Sicily.

2

THE GOTHIC WARS

The army that Belisarius led into Italy had changed radically in composition and tactics from the former imperial army of heavy legionary infantry. This had finally disappeared from the line before the massed Gothic cavalry at the battle of Adrianople in 378, and even before then had suffered from the mounted Persian archers. The Western Empire had had little respite for military recovery and had been forced to engage whole tribes of barbarians and absorb them undigested into itself, but the East during the fifth century had evolved a new army which combined the shock of the Gothic cavalry with the firepower and mobility of the Persians. Specialist weapons demanded a small, trained field army, while manpower shortage left a perilously low margin of reserves. The Empire was beset on all frontiers; policy therefore demanded maximum use of the interior lines afforded, the hiring of mercenaries to take pressure off one frontier and for use on another, and a close reliance on effective diplomacy. In a process that culminated in Justinian's reign the frontier itself was stabilized by a series of fortifications to serve as an immediate centre for local militia and a base for the field army. Under Justinian Roman military architecture reached its height, and siege warfare—an essential strategy for the weaker party—assumed a dominant place in the operations of imperial generals. As a corollary the development of mechanical weapons had progressed; steel-sprung catapults and cross-bows provided a formidable artillery train. But numbers were always too low and the provision of reinforcements seldom adequate to risk open battle—the attrition of enemy supplies and morale was the normal approach. Later in the sixth century a handbook of military technique attributed to the Emperor Maurice, a successor to Belisarius in the line of scientific Byzantine soldiers, summed up what a general's aims should be; throughout the sense of inferiority in numbers and the over-extension of commitments dictate caution and the indirect approach

52

to victory, forcing retirement by avoiding a major pitched battle. 'A man must have taken leave of his senses who would wish, except in dire necessity, to gain a vain glory at the price of an expensive victory. War resembles the chase in which vigilance, nets, ambushes, drives, flanking movements and other stratagems contribute more than mere force to the best prizes. In war frontal attacks, even if certain of success, are not carried through without risk or loss.'[1]

This system of tactics, which operated closely within the context of an overall diplomacy, demanded above all great restraint and discipline on the part of commanders and troops. The core of Belisarius' army–the cavalry of his own household, 7,000 strong–was recruited, trained and paid for by the general himself. They accompanied him on all his campaigns and knew his methods as a leader. In addition there were 4,000 regular cavalry and 3,000 infantry, Isaurians from the Anatolian highlands. The remainder of the imperial army, mainly mercenary contingents, were Slavs and Huns from the Empire's northern and eastern borders and some Moors recruited in North Africa: in all perhaps 15,000 men. It was largely a cavalry army; two-thirds at least were mounted. But the role of the infantry contingents was not neglected; indeed, results were achieved by a combination of arms rarely paralleled in ancient or mediaeval armies, and no false reliance was placed on a doctrine of the dominant weapon. The bow was a weapon common to all and was supported by the admirable engineering and artillery train that made even the cavalry powerful in siege.

Weakness lay in indiscipline, among the mercenary troops and junior commanders alike. The troops, fighting for a pay always in arrears in a country totally foreign to them, could seldom be trusted to forgo the hope of plunder; the North African war had enriched most with the wives and estates of the conquered Vandals and new recruits wished to emulate in Italy the good fortune of the veterans. Closely controlled they were of excellent quality; when pressure relaxed they rapidly declined. The officers, gallant and intelligent under direct command, were prone to mutual jealousy, intrigue and avarice which weakened their combined efforts–even under Belisarius they could at times jeopardize the position by rash action,

[1] See F. Aussaresses, *L'armée byzantine à la fin du VIe siècle d'après le Strategikon de l'empéreur Maurice*, (1909).

53

disobedience or inertia. Suspicion on the part of Justinian cannot alone account for the failures of the high command which led to frequent reverses and near disaster. There was real difficulty in finding generals of the calibre necessary to co-ordinate the wide-spread detachments.[2]

The strength of the army lay above all in the abilities of its commander. Belisarius was still young; he was born in Thrace, the same province as Justinian, perhaps in 505. By the time of his arrival in Italy he had had six year's experience of high command in various situations: against the Persians on the Euphrates front, which he held against a great superiority of numbers; in suppressing, with tact and presence of mind, the Victory riots in Constantinople which threatened to dethrone Justinian; and in North Africa. He was able to command discipline and obedience through the respect afforded him as a fighting man, a tactician and a strategist, and through the confidence imparted by his endurance. He was the supreme exponent of the system of tactics outlined in the *Strategikon*, excelling in the indirect approach, but he had also an appreciation of the moment for direct, overwhelming action, as the brief Vandal war showed. Twice he caught the demoralized Vandal army at a disadvantage by swift, unexpected movements and broke it in a furious cavalry encounter. He had brought King Gelimer in chains to Constantinople with vast booty and had been rewarded with the last triumph to be celebrated. Coins were struck in his honour as the 'glory of the Romans', and he was given a consulship. His talent for quick decisive handling of cavalry, through a series of bugle calls devised by himself, was matched by his personal skill in arms and a singular inventiveness and ability in expedients. Personally he was a man of honour and principle; he had married Antonina, the friend and confidante of the Empress Theodora, who used him to further her own desires, but he himself remained aloof from palace intrigue. His wife was persistently unfaithful to him but he forgave and remained loyal to her. Politically she dominated him; militarily he was the only man who could handle the Roman army and its commanders on a major campaign.[3]

In the summer of 535 Amalasuntha was murdered on Marta

[2] K. Hannestad, 'Les forces militaires d'après la Guerre Gothique de Procope', (*Classica et Mediaevalia*, 21, 1960).

[3] L. M. Chassin, *Bélisaire, généralissime de Byzance*, 1957.

Island in Lake Bolsena and the envoy Peter conveyed the Empire's declaration of war. Theodahat, panic-stricken, again sued for peace. Pope Agapetus was summoned and sent to Constantinople but Theodahat was parsimonious and abrupt, and Agapetus was compelled to pawn church plate to provide his expenses. Justinian would not soften; Peter's reports indicated that Theodahat could be bullied at will into concessions. However, the presence of the pope in the capital provided an opportunity to secure approval for Theodora's support of the monophysites and confirmation of her new appointment of the suspect Anthemius as Patriarch. Justinian drew Agapetus into a theological discussion and hinted at exile. The aged, ailing pope remarked bitterly, 'I desired to come to the most Christian Emperor Justinian, but I have found Diocletian.' The pope again condemned Anthemius but Justinian's threats remained unfulfilled, for the pope died in the capital and his body was returned to Rome in a leaden coffin.[4]

The imperial attack continued. In Illyricum the general Mundus advanced against Salona, and Belisarius, in the year of his consulship, landed in Sicily. There was no resistance; a welcome was found on the estates of the Roman nobility and of the Church, while Catania and Syracuse opened their gates at once. Only in Palermo, where the natural strength of the site and its fortifications gave some encouragement, did a Gothic garrison show signs of holding out. But here Belisarius demonstrated his ingenuity in circumventing normal military obstacles. The sea walls of Palermo ran lower than the main landward wall, lower in fact than the masts of his ships. He accordingly had ships' boats slung between the masts and hoisted to the mastheads, and these improvised fighting-tops, manned by archers, were brought against the sea-walls. The Gothic garrison, seeing themselves outflanked from the start, at once submitted. So Sicily was reoccupied for the Empire, and on the last day of 535 Belisarius entered Syracuse and there formally laid down the insignia of his consulship.[5]

[4] W. Ensslin, 'Papst Agapet I und Kaiser Justinian I', (*Historisches Jahrbuch*, 77, 1958).
[5] The narrative of the wars follows Procopius, *Bellum Gothicum*; see also B. Lavagnini, 'Belisario in Italia–Storia di un anno', (*Atti dell' Accademia di Scienze, Lettere ed Arti di Palermo*, Ser. 4, vol. 3, 1948).

At the swift and effortless fall of Sicily Theodahat's never-strong resolution wavered. He had moved to Rome where his warlike preparations consisted only of advance instructions to the city officials to repair the Flaminian Way and to construct a pontoon over the Tiber to smooth his journey. They were also ordered to buy up all available delicacies for the royal table. Meanwhile Peter's pressure was maintained. At an interview at Albano the imperial envoy demanded sweeping concessions: the surrender of Sicily entire, an annual tribute of 300 lb. of gold, and the service of 3,000 Goths for the eastern front; senators and churchmen were to be immune to royal justice and taxation and the Emperor's name was to be included in all Gothic official acts. Theodahat agreed, then nervously recalled Peter to put before him a proposal that, if Justinian refused to ratify these terms, he should surrender all Italy in return for estates in the East. Peter continued to play on his nerves, finding consolation for him in a contrast of his and the Emperor's temperaments: 'Your great interest lies in philosophy, while Justinian's role is to be a worthy emperor of the Romans. There is this difference that, for one who has practised philosophy, it would never be seemly to bring about men's deaths, especially in such great numbers; this accords with the teaching of Plato, which clearly you have espoused, so that it would be unholy for you not to keep yourself free from all bloodshed. But for Justinian it is perfectly fitting to try to regain a land which of old belonged to his empire.' This appeal to his intellectual posturings gave Theodahat the excuse he needed; Peter and the Roman priest Rusticus were sent to Constantinople with an offer to Justinian of the complete surrender of the Gothic kingdom in return for estates in the East to a value of 12,000 lb. of gold. This offer, which was only to be revealed if Justinian refused the first, was naturally at once made known to the Emperor by his ambassador. They carried with them a letter from the king: 'From my earliest years', he wrote, 'I have been passionately addicted to scholarly disputations and have always devoted my time to this sort of thing. Consequently I have until now been far removed from the confusion of war. It is therefore absurd for me to aspire to the honours which royalty confers and so lead a life fraught with danger, when it is possible for me to avoid both.'

But now a new incident revealed the philosophical equanimity of the king's temperament. Early in 536 Belisarius was recalled to

Africa to quell a mutiny of the army stationed there. But the secondary imperial offensive in Illyricum continued. In a skirmish the son
of the imperial commander was killed and his father, judgement
overthrown by grief, rashly gave battle on unfavourable terms. The
result was a startling Gothic victory; Mundus was killed and the
imperial troops fell back in disorder. Theodahat's confidence surged
back; he refused to consider the terms the envoys brought back from
Constantinople. But the Gothic respite did not last. The general
Constantine was sent to reorganize the Dalmatian campaign and,
more important, Belisarius had returned from Africa. In the summer
of 536 he crossed the straits of Messina and entered the mainland of
Italy. Again there was effortless success; Messina and Reggio
Calabria yielded and the local Gothic commander Ebrimuth, a son-
in-law of the king, surrendered without offering resistance. He was
sent off to Constantinople and there loaded with honours and wealth
to demonstrate to the Gothic leaders their best and true interests.

Belisarius now marched towards Naples, the first major city on his
line of advance, and here the true anguish and dilemma for the
Italians was revealed. Hitherto Belisarius had operated through
country relatively unaffected by Gothic rule, which continued as it
had for centuries to accept the landlords in Rome: one isolated
garrison had been circumvented and had surrendered; one member
of the Gothic nobility had abandoned his command. But Naples was
a strongly fortified town of vast strategic importance as a naval base.
It had a large Gothic garrison and a mixed and articulate population.
Now traditional and sentimental attachment to the idea of the
Empire undivided came up against the fact of war on Italian door-
steps. As Belisarius approached, the Neapolitans sent out to him a
prominent citizen, Stephen, who begged him to consider that the
Neapolitans were not their own masters and that even the Gothic
garrison had families held as hostages by Theodahat. He pointed out
that the war did not concern Naples but had been forced on the
Italians by Justinian and suggested that Belisarius proceed straight
to Rome, by-passing Naples. Rome was the key to Italy and on its
fall Naples would naturally be gained, with no necessity for the
inhabitants to commit themselves in advance to a doubtful outcome.
The valid distinction between Italians and Greeks was already being
made, which the Goths were later to emphasize. It was expressed in

concrete form by a Jewish sorcerer to whom Theodahat, inert in Rome, turned for advice. This man, the story ran, penned up separately three groups, each of ten pigs; one group was labelled for the Goths, one for the Romans and one for the Greeks. After several days without food or water they were examined: of those named for the Goths, all were dead; half those representing the Romans had died and the rest had lost their bristles; of the Greek pigs, few had died and few lost any hair. The story summed up the forebodings of all in Italy.

On this occasion Belisarius replied to Stephen with the legal and sentimental justifications of the Emperor; he came only to restore true freedom and legitimacy to Italy, and Neapolitan patriotism and self-respect should lead the city to support the attempt. Stephen was won over and on his return to the city presented these arguments to an assembly of the people. Here he received support from one Antiochenus, a Syrian merchant long resident in Italy, a man to whom reunion would doubtless bring great commercial advantages and who had a wider knowledge of the world. A vigorous opposition was led by two schoolmasters, Pastor and Asclepiodotus, who were sensible of the advantages and peace afforded by Gothic rule, and personally friendly to the Goths. Significant support for them came from the Jewish community, alarmed at the treatment of their fellow-Jews in the East and at similar outbursts in Italy. They offered to man sections of the wall alongside the Goths. Above all the dangers of a premature decision were stressed: there was no assurance, now that the size of Belisarius's army was revealed, that he would win, and the Goths were nearer than the Emperor. Naples was accordingly placed in a state of defence, the walls manned and the aqueducts sealed off.

Belisarius was held before Naples for twenty days in mounting anxiety at the delay. He had no knowledge of Theodahat's measures and was anxious to press forward to Rome and force an early decision before the Gothic armies could be concentrated. He had finally accepted the necessity of leaving Naples and moving against Rome, despite the risk, in the event of defeat, of having so powerful a fortress and valuable a harbour at his rear, when fortune placed the city in his hands. The Gothic garrison had sealed off the aqueducts leading into the city with brickwork, but had neglected to break them entirely, and an Isaurian guardsman on patrol noticed that one water-channel, large enough for men to march along its entire length, led right through the walls. Belisarius again summoned the townsmen to surrender, informing them that he was certain to take the town and in the event of a sack would be unable to control his men. The offer was rejected and so, under cover of a diversion, an assault party moved along the water-channel, breaking down the flimsy brickwork and emerging behind the walls in an old woman's garden. A section of the wall, and then a gate, were won and the army entered. The sack was horrible, the Hun contingent especially excelling themselves, and left a mark on Italian memories—Belisarius, who finally succeeded in ending the slaughter, earned a rebuke from the pope. The Goths and Jews refused to submit and died, and the instigators of resistance were arrested. Pastor died of apoplexy when caught, but Asclepiodotus was brought before Belisarius. He pleaded the impossibility of complete loyalty in such a conflict and Belisarius released him. He was torn to pieces by the crowd which felt it owed its misfortunes to him.

No attempt had been made to relieve Naples, and its fall goaded the Goths into action. In Rome Theodahat had sat idle. His one activity had been to procure by force and bribes the election of a new pope in Agapetus's place: Silverius, son of the Gothic sympathizer Pope Hormisdas. But the gain, if it were a gain, of papal support could not counterbalance the disgust of the Gothic nobility at the king's character and inertia. He lacked all the qualities of a war-leader; his equivocal role and the precipitate surrender of his son-in-law Ebrimuth increased the conviction that he was prepared to betray the Gothic kingdom for eastern ease and wealth; in addition, his greed alienated the warriors who saw in him such a hybrid as Theodoric had always shunned. At a military assembly at Regesta, near Terracina to the south of Rome, the Goths raised on their shields a new king as war-leader. He was a veteran warrior and hero of Theodoric's Gepid wars named Vitigis, unconnected with the Amaling family. Theodahat fled north from Rome along the Via Flaminia for Ravenna. Vitigis sent agents to arrest him but he was overtaken first by one Optaris, whose betrothed the king had once given to a henchman. At the roadside Optaris dragged the king from his horse, then 'like a victim at the altar's foot' his throat was cut—antiquity's last sour joke on the theme of the philosopher-king.

Vitigis took immediate measures to strengthen his own position and the defence of Italy. The Gothic armies were unconcentrated so the garrisons in the North, in Provence and in Dalmatia were ordered to assemble at Ravenna. In Campania there were insufficient troops to confront Belisarius before Rome, and Vitigis merely garrisoned the city with 4,000 men under Count Leuderis whom he trusted to hold the imperial army until his own concentration was effected. With the rest of the field army he withdrew to Ravenna where, since the Amaling dynasty still commanded intense, almost religious loyalty, the new king hurried to ratify his position by marriage to the unwilling daughter of Amalasuntha, Matasuntha. Before leaving Rome he summoned pope, clergy and senate and harangued them on the debt of gratitude they owed to the rule of Theodoric and the peace of Italy.

Belisarius advanced northwards across Campania, travelling by the Latin Way and keeping in touch with the sea. Garrisons were left at Naples and at the natural strongpoint of Cumae on the north end of the Bay of Naples, which together dominated his land and sea supply-routes. In Rome, Leuderis now encountered the difficulties of defence; the great Aurelian Walls of the city, although recently repaired by Theodoric, extended for over twelve miles and he felt it impossible to cover the entire circuit adequately. Despite Vitigis's admonition the Romans were unreliable; led by Silverius and anxious to avoid the sack that would follow resistance, they came out to invite Belisarius to take possession. It was on the pagan December feast of the Saturnalia that the imperial army filed through the Asinarian Gate by the Lateran as the Gothic army left by the Flaminian on the retreat north. Only Leuderis remained in honour-bound at his post and was captured, to be sent with the keys of the city to Constantinople as another living trophy to Belisarius' success. After sixty years Rome was once more united to her Empire.

Immediate advantages were now realized from this advance. The Goths of Samnium, living on the Biferno and Sangro rivers, submitted under their leader Pizas, and the Italians of Apulia and Calabria, where few Goths were settled, also sent notice of their loyalty. By his movement on Rome Belisarius had won a measure of control over the whole of southern Italy at the price of one three-weeks' siege. He sought to strengthen that control by repopulating

Naples from the southern provinces and drafting colonists from North Africa into Sicily, Calabria and Apulia. But his position was still precarious; Vitigis had withdrawn only to assemble his forces and the imperial gains were dependent on holding Rome. Belisarius was too weak to risk an open engagement; instead the war must be one of siege and blockade, employing all the artifices of Byzantine military skill. Work was put in hand to strengthen the defences of Rome. Merlons were added to the walls to carry the siege engines and give them a maximum arc of fire; a dry ditch was dug before the walls and the aqueducts were broken. At the Milvian bridge where the Flaminia crossed the Tiber before entering the city, a tower was built denying the use of the bridge to the enemy. From Sicily and Cumae supplies were brought to Porto and up the river into Rome; all available provisions were brought in from the countryside. Then in the early months of 537 Belisarius sent detachments north to seize the towns commanding the northern routes. Bessas, a Goth in the imperial service, was sent to Narni, and Constantine into Tuscany and to Spoleto and Perugia. All towns fell easily, the inhabitants welcoming the imperial forces, and outside Perugia Constantine succeeded in destroying a considerable body of Goths. From the headquarters he had established in a palace on the Pincio, Belisarius considered these measures sufficient to delay the Gothic counter-offensive until reinforcements could arrive from the East.

The Romans themselves had reservations. Faced with the dilemma of dual loyalties, they had no more relished the prospect of a fight for Rome itself than had the Neapolitans. They also realized how scanty Belisarius's forces—reduced even further by the need to establish garrisons—were for the huge undertaking. A deputation waited on the general and pointed out the impossibility of holding Rome with so meagre an army: the vast extent of the walls could never be adequately covered, the flat terrain outside offered the easiest of approaches for siege-engines, and the supply position, with Rome distant from its harbours, invited famine. Vitigis was rumoured to have collected 150,000 fighting men. But Belisarius brushed aside these objections, confident in his strategy and ability to hold on.

In February 537 Vitigis marched from Ravenna. Belisarius recalled all but the necessary garrisons from the Tuscan and Umbrian towns, but Vitigis by-passed them, refusing to be diverted. Moving down the

Flaminia the Gothic host arrived early in March at the Milvian bridge and the new tower. Their arrival was reported to Belisarius who rode out next day with 1,000 cavalry to direct the delaying operation. But in the night following the Gothic appearance the detachment holding the tower, alarmed at the numbers of the enemy, had abandoned their post; some fled and some deserted to the Goths, allowing Vitigis an unhampered crossing. Belisarius unexpectedly came across the Gothic army; unhesitatingly he charged. A fierce cavalry action ensued in which he performed prodigies of valour; the deserters recognized him by his mount, a bay with a white blaze, and the Goths singled him out as a special target. By his leadership and example the Gothic cavalry was worsted and fell back until infantry support had completed the crossing. Belisarius, having obtained a limited delay and an unquestioned moral ascendancy, withdrew his men to the Salarian gate. Rumours of his death had reached the city and the guards on the gate failed at first to recognize him covered in dust; apprehensive of the approaching Goths and fearing a trap, they refused to open the gate. As dusk was falling and the Goths coming up fast, Belisarius was forced to prove his identity and win another respite with one more desperate charge. Again the Goths fell back and one champion, Visand–who received thirteen wounds at Belisarius's hands–was left for dead on the field. The garrison was convinced, the gates opened, and the cavalry admitted.

Rome was now invested. The Goths formed and fortified seven camps, one on the field of Nero by the river, and six stretching between the Flaminian and Prenestine gates. The extent of the walls now worked in the Roman favour, for the Goths had not resources enough to complete an encirclement of the city, and respect for Belisarius's activity restricted the distance between the camps. So the Gothic offensive was confined to one sector, about a third of the full circuit, and to a limited number of gates. One early panic arose when it was rumoured that the Goths had broken in by the St. Pancras gate, beyond St. Peter's; to prevent any repetition Belisarius appointed permanent commanders to each gate with instructions to ignore alarms at other gates–Belisarius alone, centrally placed at the exposed sector by the Pincio, disposed of the reserves. His judgement was sound for the main Gothic assault fell on the Eastern sector of the city. Some early-felt inconveniences were ingeniously countered.

The breaking of the aqueducts had stopped the water-mills powered by them on the Gianiculo, so to grind the harvest brought in from the countryside and the grain from Sicily, Belisarius caused wheels to be placed between barges moored across the river. The Goths tried to damage these by floating logs downstream into the wheels but chains above kept them clear and the logs were pulled out to fuel the bakeries.

The full assault opened against the Salarian gate on the eighteenth day of the siege. Vitigis first sent envoys demanding surrender, and the Romans urged Belisarius to accept. He was blamed for starting hostilities with insufficient forces and now the unaccustomed hardships of guard-duty into which Belisarius had drafted them completed the disillusionment begun by food-rationing. Lack of enthusiasm for active participation in the war was not confined to the masses; even senators joined in the pleas. Now Vitigis brought up the full range of Gothic siege instruments; bundles of faggots to fill in the ditches, followed by high ox-drawn wooden towers and, the chief weapon of all, four vast rams, each swung by fifty men. To counter these, the machines that the imperial army had mounted on the wall represented the finest mechanical skill of the time. *Balistae*, anti-personnel weapons which were powered by steel springs to discharge bolts were erected, and 'wild asses', small catapults firing stone missiles, were carefully positioned on the walls to give a wide angle for overlapping fire and mutual support. 'Wolves'–portcullis-shaped implements with spikes on the outer faces were poised on top of the wall itself; if ladders were placed against them they were levered out to fall, trapping the attackers underneath. Most important of all, every man of the imperial army was an archer. Even as the assault began Belisarius showed the place the bow was to hold in the war, for a shot by him brought down one of the oxen drawing a tower. Thus stimulated, the imperial troops and the Romans beat off the attack, with heavy losses for the Goths who then switched their efforts from the Salarian and Prenestine gates to the Mausoleum of Hadrian and the Aurelian gate on the other side of the river. Here the Goths temporarily found greater success; under covering archery-fire a party managed to creep along the roofed colonnade of St. Peter, running between the mausoleum and the river, and place their ladders against the mausoleum's wall. Again improvisation thwarted the attack. The guards of the mausoleum broke up the marble statues of gods, emperors and heroes that adorned it and threw the heavy fragments down onto the climbing Goths. This counter-attack succeeded and the Goths were scattered. Belisarius completed the work with sorties from the Prenestine and Vivarium gates which overran the retreating Goths, pursued them to their camps, and destroyed their siege-engines.

This serious reverse discouraged Vitigis from repeating direct assaults in the absence of replacements for the engines, and instead he settled to a blockade. Roman anxiety and opposition to the war was growing and superstitions were seized on for comfort. A group of old-fashioned senators tried to open the doors of the temple of Janus, traditionally left open when the republic was at war, but the hinges were stuck fast and the doors could not be moved. The Sybilline books were consulted; they revealed, falsely, that the danger would be over by July. Antiquarian exercises apart, Belisarius had enough to fear from internal unrest. All the useless mouths–women, children and old men–were sent either by land or sea into Campania, and the able-bodied Romans who remained were made to continue sentry-duty on the walls to relieve Belisarius's own men. No chances were taken; with Romans serving on the roster, guard duty was made irregular to prevent advance bribing and the locks on the gates were changed twice monthly.

The discontent also gave Belisarius an opportunity to carry out the instructions of Justinian–or rather of Theodora, transmitted through Antonina–to force the submission of the pope. Justinian had already given evidence of the control he wished to exercise over the Roman Church in a letter to Pope John. On the occupation of Rome another letter was handed to Silverius demanding in peremptory terms the recognition of the patriarch Anthemius. Silverius would not obey: 'Now I know', he commented on receiving the order, 'that this will cost me my life.' Theodora took action on his refusal, sending back to Rome the papal representative at Constantinople, the deacon Vigilius who had been Pope Boniface's own nominee as his successor and whom, as a political cleric, she hoped would be more malleable–with adequate funds and orders for his immediate appointment as archdeacon, the executive right-hand man to the pope. He carried with him instructions to Belisarius to find any excuse for Silverius's

Plate 1. Rufus Gennadius Probus Orestes, cos 530, the penultimate Roman consul of the West. A grandson of a member of Pope Leo's embassy to Attila, he was captured by Totila but released by imperial forces from Minturno. His escape to Sicily was however foiled through shortage of horses.

deposition. Silverius was arrested and brought to Belisarius's head-quarters on the Pincio, where he was keeping viceregal state, and there summarily tried; Antonina, as representative of the prime-mover Theodora, shared the judgement seat with her husband. Evidence was brought that he had plotted with Vitigis to open the Asinarian gate, near the Lateran, and admit the Gothic army. He had been appointed pope under pressure from Theodahat, and his father Hormisdas had been a confidant of Theodoric, but there is nothing to suggest that the charge was true; he simply shared the general Italian dissatisfaction and unease at the war. As a natural focus for Italian leadership he had to go. So Silverius was deposed, stripped of his pontifical vestments, forced into the rough habit of a monk and shipped off to the East. His first place of exile was Patara in Lycia, whose bishop protested at his presence: 'There are many kings in the world, but not one unique like the pope, who ruled the Church of all the world.' Indeed the contrast between the treatment of the pope and the other prisoners whom Belisarius had sent back was a portent of Justinian's intended rule in the West.[6]

The new pope was, naturally, Vigilius. The son of a consul and the brother of a senator, his niece married to a consul, he was a man of the Roman nobility. With the promises of support that he had given to Theodora, Belisarius could hope for his influential support in Italy. The general now went over to the attack as the Gothic offensive stagnated; regular patrols were maintained outside the walls and his Moorish auxiliaries, undetectable in their *djibbahs*, roamed at night cutting off foragers from the camps. To tighten his blockade Vitigis seized Porto but it was soon the Goths who were becoming isolated. The investment was incomplete, the Goths were increasingly reluctant to leave their camps and Vitigis made no attempt to use sea power; the fleet of one thousand ships that Theodoric had built was neglected in face of imperial command of the sea. Belisarius was able to run several overland convoys from his

[6] P. Hildebrand, 'Die Absetzung des Papstes Silverius (537)', (*Historisches Jahrbuch*, 42, 2, 1922): O. Bertolini, 'La fine del pontificato di papa Silvestro in uno studio recente', (*ASR*, 47, 1924); P. Batiffol, 'Justinien et la siege apostolique', (*RSR*, 1926); E. Schwartz, 'Vigiliusbriefe: Zur Kirchenpolitik Justinians', (*Sitzungsberichte der Bayerischen Akademie der Wissenschaft, Phil–hist. Abt*, 1940, 2).

base at Anzio which the Goths were unable to intercept. Their own supply situation was becoming critical; they had not the efficient commissariat service of the imperial army and the immediate countryside was devastated. In his weakness Vitigis turned to reprisals. Those senators not in Rome were arrested and executed–only Reparatus, Vigilius's brother, managed to escape to temporary safety in Milan. And now, in response to Belisarius's many requests, reinforcements of 1,600 Huns and Slavs–experts in ambushes and guerrilla war– had arrived in Italy, under the generals Martin and Valerian. Belisarius's offensive became more active against the Goths helplessly contained before Rome. Small cavalry detachments from the city lured parties of the Goths into range of fire from the walls while their retreat to the camps was cut off by roving patrols. The war developed into a series of isolated small encounters in heroic mould, reminiscent of the siege of Troy–a senator, watching the action from the walls, marvelled that 'one man's household alone was destroying all Theodoric's power'. Only once did Belisarius yield to the now enthusiastic Roman demands for a pitched battle, in spite of misgivings that attrition had not gone far enough. It was not a success; the initial cavalry encounter with the regular troops went, as always, in the imperial favour but the Roman contingents in support were insufficiently trained, disciplined and armed to sustain the attack. Pressure of numbers told and the army was forced back within the walls. Belisarius reverted to his strategy of limited offensives.

As spring arrived the full effects of a war of attrition began to be felt. Famine and plague were spreading through the two stationary armies and many of the external shrines of the city could not be visited on their anniversaries. The prayers that Pope Vigilius wrote at this time for the Mass indicate the fear and the sufferings of the Romans; the fear of the Goths roaming around the walls, destroying the cemeteries, and the sufferings from the plague and the shortage of food.[7] Within Rome baggage mules were being made into sausages but Belisarius preserved his cavalry intact by pasturing the horses on the open spaces and parks of the city. His men were still able to evade the blockade and reach the grain fields around the city, and his secretary, the historian Procopius, was sent to Naples to collect the

[7] A. Chavasse, 'Messes du pape Vigile dans le Sacrementaire léonien', (*EL.* 64, 1950; 66, 1952).

scattered detachments of troops throughout Campania and to load grain for transport to Ostia. More reinforcements, 3,000 Isaurians and a further 3,500 mixed troops, had landed at Naples and the commander Zeno had 300 men in Samnium. The encirclement of the Gothic army could now be completed. Local strongholds, Terracina, Tivoli, Albano—were taken and a strong encampment for the Hun contingent built near the basilica of St. Paul, dominating the route to the sea. Pestilence swept through the Gothic army and attacks on the city had virtually ceased. As high summer set in the besiegers' position became untenable, and proposals were made by Vitigis for an armistice. His first offer was to cede Sicily to the Empire in return for peace; as Sicily was no longer the Goths' to give away, Belisarius made a smiling counter-offer of another ancient province—Britain. A truce was arranged while Gothic emissaries went to Constantinople but it was not strictly kept. When the isolated and unsupplied Gothic garrison in Civitavecchia withdrew, Belisarius took over the port and gained another valuable base on the sea. Vitigis protested and made his last two attempts on the city. The first, along the channel of the Aqua Virgo, was foiled through Belisarius's vigilance and the second, involving a plot to drug the guards on one of the gates, also came to nothing.

Belisarius now struck out. The general John, with 2,000 cavalry, was ordered to Picenum on the east coast to ravage the countryside. There he encountered and defeated a Gothic force under an uncle of Vitigis, but the towns of Picenum, Osimo and Urbino held out and John had no siege equipment with him. A quick advance gave him Rimini, the metropolis of Picenum, and throughout the summer of 537 his operations brought him gradually closer to Ravenna until Matasuntha, Vitigis's wife, opened negotiations with him for the capital's surrender. In the north, Belisarius opened a new front at the appeal of Archbishop Datius of Milan, taking advantage of his sea-communications through Genoa. At last, after a year's siege which had worn down his army and achieved nothing, Vitigis was compelled to withdraw; in mid-March 538 he retreated towards Rimini. His withdrawal was not easy. Belisarius fell on his army as it crossed the Milvian bridge and inflicted savage losses; the remnant of the Gothic army was forced into detours round the towns—Narni, Spoleto and Perugia—still in imperial hands, and on arrival at

Rimini Vitigis was unable to retrieve the Gothic position. He fell back to Ravenna where he in turn was blockaded by the imperial armies but, although offers to partition Italy were rejected by Belisarius, he however hesitated to assault the almost impregnable city. Gothic disgust at Vitigis's failure now came to his aid. An offer which he agreed to consider was made by Gothic notables to support Belisarius himself as emperor of the West, and Ravenna was yielded to him. But his honour and loyalty did not allow him to take the idea seriously; Vitigis was sent to Constantinople and, with the Gothic kingdom in disruption, Belisarius was recalled to the Persian front.

The Gothic kingdom had been overthrown in a masterly campaign; now, to Justinian's cold mind, it must be paid for. During the next three years, from 538 to 541, Italy did just that. The troops, divided up into units throughout the country, were underpaid, for Justinian was unwilling to divert further resources to the West. They began to plunder from the provincials, the lead being taken by their commanders, Bessas, John and Constantine, who busily amassed personal fortunes. The declining morale and discipline of the army were further aggravated when a new financial officer, the *logothete* Alexander, was sent from Constantinople. Alexander, who had already won the nickname 'Clippings' from his expedient of shaving the edges of coins issued by the imperial treasury, began his mission by drastically cutting military expenditure – especially the ration allowances – and so driving the troops to further appropriations from the Italians. In addition, Alexander hunted out all debts owing to the defunct Gothic treasury and ruthlessly extorted them. Pressure was brought upon Pope Vigilius to fulfil his promise of recognition for Anthemius but this he resisted: 'I am, although unworthy, the vicar of the blessed apostle Peter, as were my predecessors the most holy Agapetus and Silverius who condemned him.' No immediate action was taken against him but Italian and Roman confidence in reunion with the Empire was weakened further. Worse, the Gothic war had not been finally ended and in the north count Ildibades held out around Verona with a small force; the imperial commanders, otherwise occupied and already quarrelling among themselves, did not think it worthwhile to eliminate him.

Over the years Ildibades's following grew with the miscontent of

Italy and early in 541 the imperial generals realized the necessity for action. A first move by Vitalian ended in a Gothic victory, but there was a brief respite following Ildibades's murder in the course of a feud and the seizure of power by a Rugian. Early in 542 Ildibades's nephew Totila, a younger, more vigorous and intelligent soldier, was hailed as the Gothic king. Once again the imperial army moved against Verona; 12,000 men of lowered morale commanded by twelve generals at loggerheads with each other. One sole competent and urgent voice, that of the Armenian Artabazes, urged decisive action and at his prompting Verona was entered. As the Goths were withdrawing and the generals already disputing over the distribution of booty, a sudden panic at possible ambush ran through their army; Totila attacked and the army dissolved in rout towards Faenza: Artabazes was killed in the retreat. More Goths rallied to Totila and outside Faenza he inflicted another shattering defeat on the imperial army.

With the death of Artabazes the only resolution in the imperial command had been extinguished, and the army now dispersed into garrisons holding widely-separated towns. Constantine in Ravenna, John in Rome, Justin in Florence, Cyprian in Perugia, Bessas in Spoleto, and Conon in Naples clung to their commands as independent lordships. None could communicate or co-operate with his fellows, and Totila controlled the open countryside. Towards the end of 542 he moved to besiege Florence, but the town resisted and he abandoned the attempt, determined not to be caught as Vitigis had been. In Aemilia, Cesena and Petra Pertusa fell to him and he then entered Tuscany and crossed the Tiber, avoiding Rome. Pope Vigilius' prayers reflect something of the relief as he swept past Rome into Campania and Samnium, taking Benevento and moving on Naples. Detachments entered Cumae and the southern provinces, Bruttium, Lucania, Apulia and Calabria; there they collected the taxes due to the imperial treasury and the rents of the absentee landlords to fill the Gothic war-chest. Against these moves the imperial commanders were neither able nor willing to unite.

Justinian took certain measures to restore the situation. A commander-in-chief, the praetorian prefect Maximinus, was appointed and provided with a fleet and an army of Thracians, Armenians and a few Huns. But he was inexperienced in war and timid; he delayed in Epirus while the Italian situation worsened. The commander in Sicily, Demetrius, acted more promptly in collecting and loading a fleet with supplies for Naples, but Totila–more flexible than Vitigis– had learnt from former errors and from Belisarius's success, and the capture of Cumae had given him a squadron of swift, light craft to patrol the coast. Demetrius's fleet was taken by this squadron and Maximinus, belatedly following, was lost in a storm. The haltered Demetrius was paraded round the walls of Naples, which surrendered after assurances, and again Totila showed that he had learnt the lessons of the earlier war. The walls were razed, so that the imperial armies could count on no sure base for operations and the war would be fought in the open field where Gothic superiority in numbers would tell.

The Roman armies, critically short of supplies and hemmed in to those towns they still held, continued their plundering of the provincials. Following the fall of Naples Totila wrote to the Roman senate, accusing it of grievously misleading the Italian people and of responsibility for the destruction of the prosperity of Theodoric's rule; again the Goths drew a distinction between Italians and Greeks, denying the fundamental unity of the Empire and claiming that this false conception of identity with the East had led to Italy's ruin. John, commanding in Rome, managed to prevent delivery of this letter but Totila was able to make use of the Roman habit of the *pasquinade*, the placard or lampoon stuck on walls by night, to make his terms known. John's suspicions fell first on those Arian priests still in the city who were expelled, but then it extended even to members of the senate. The leader of the senate, Cethegus, fled to Civitavecchia and his flight was symptomatic of the more bitter phase reached in the war–suspicion and savagery increased with opposition. Totila moved to Rome, where Bessas had joined John with 3,000 men, but he did not establish a close siege. At Tivoli four Isaurians of the garrison, demoralized like the rest of the army and at loggerheads with the townsmen, opened the gates to him but the ease of capture did not bring restraint; all the inhabitants, including the bishop, were murdered. From this base he ranged widely; Fermo and Ascoli fell to him, and he besieged Assisi and Spoleto; the latter, deserted by Bessas, surrendered. Having secured his rear against any possible concentration of imperial units he turned back to watch Rome.

There Bessas had assumed the command. He had not yet made the fortune he desired and was busy trying to do so; preparations for a siege were perfunctory—little more than savage attempts to quash internal dissent. Cethegus had fled; now Pope Vigilius was arrested on imperial orders and removed to Sicily. He had never been popular with the Romans and although his removal sprang directly from his opposition to Justinian's religious policy and the broken promises of his appointment, other pretexts were easily raised. He was charged by the Romans themselves with the murders of his secretary and his niece's husband, the consul Asterius, and as his ship left the Tiber wharves it was followed along the bank by the mob, yelling at him to go and take the plague with him.

Totila tightened his distant blockade. From Tivoli he controlled landward communications and the crossings of the Tiber, while his squadrons based on Naples and the Aeolian Isles swept the sea-routes. Soon there was famine once more in Rome; Bessas had hoarded available supplies and was selling them at hugely inflated prices. By now Belisarius had returned to the Italian command, but he had been delayed by the need to recruit in Thrace and landed at Ravenna with an untrained and ill-equipped army and consequently was able to carry out only limited operations around Bologna and Osimo. As soon as possible he sent reinforcements by sea to Porto under Valentine and Phocas. On disembarkation these made contact with Bessas and suggested a joint sortie, but Bessas was not eager to have his supremacy in Rome challenged and an early reverse had made him wary of sorties. Valentine and Phocas tried alone but were ambushed. The blockade remained unbroken; from Sicily Vigilius sent a convoy of grain ships under a Roman priest and bishop Valentine of Silva Candida, who were to take charge of ecclesiastical affairs in his absence. The convoy appeared off Porto but had been sighted by the cruising Gothic squadrons. The signals of the garrison from the harbour walls to the ships to make their escape were mistaken for a welcome; the convoy stood in and was captured. Bishop Valentine was taken to Totila who in an access of savagery had both his hands cut off.

The famine in the city grew worse. Bessas was now selling wheat at seven *solidi* a bushel, forty times the price in peace-time, and even so it was commonly mixed with three parts of bran. An ox cost fifty *solidi* and only the very richest could obtain them. Horses, dogs, cats and mice were all killed for food, yet when a deputation approached Bessas for permission to leave the city and take their chance from the Goths, he cynically refused it: the inhabitants, he remarked 'it was impossible to feed, but unsafe to dismiss and unlawful to kill, for they were the emperor's subjects.' Although he did, however, sell permissions to leave to the richer, the humbler people were soon reduced to eating grass and nettles from the waste areas, and such tragedies as that of the father who, unable to provide for his family, leaped to his death from a bridge, failed to move him. Private charity was boundless. Boethius's widow Rusticiana spent freely from her fortune for the common good, and so did the deacon Pelagius, now the leading cleric in the city. It was Pelagius who was chosen by the Romans to lead a delegation to Totila to urge that both Sicily, the prime source of Rome's provisioning, and the walls of Rome itself should be spared. Totila rejected both pleas; these alone had made Rome invulnerable and were responsible for the previous Gothic defeat, and Italy could not be held without Rome. Pelagius bore himself sternly and resolutely before the king and Totila was impressed by his firmness. But he still continued the distant blockade from Tivoli, not risking his army to action or to the unhealthy surrounds of the city. When at last Belisarius reached Porto, plague had been added to the famine and the Romans were dying by thousands. Relief operations were now pushed on with greater vigour. Totila had cut the river line with a barrier–a stout, heavily-manned bridge connecting two towers–and Belisarius prepared barges, some manned, others for use as fireships, to break this. Moving upstream with these, he left his subordinate Isaac with strict orders to hold Porto. Although the Gothic barrier was reached, attacked and destroyed by the fireships, at the moment of apparent success Isaac on his own initiative made a sortie from Porto, ran into an ambush, and was routed. Bessas also failed to make a preconcerted sally from the city and Belisarius, anxious for his base, was forced to withdraw.

At the time of the Roman siege, either late in 545 or early in 546– so later legend reported by Gregory I ran–St. Benedict was in conversation with Bishop Sabinus of Canusium, who ten years before had been Agapetus's legate to Constantinople. The bishop reflected common Italian foreboding: 'This city will be so utterly destroyed

that it will remain uninhabited.' Benedict corrected him: 'Rome will
not be depopulated by the barbarians but rather be worn out by
tempests, lightning, storms and earthquakes, and will decay of
herself.' The bishop's prophesies appeared, at the time, to be nearer
the mark.[8]

The failure to break the blockade was a final blow to Rome. Only
Belisarius could command the authority and effort required in a long
siege–Bessas had failed utterly. He had ceased to maintain a strict
and efficient guard and had lost the respect of his mutinous and ill-fed
troops. Once again it was some Isaurians who made contact with
Totila and offered to open the Asinarian gate; Totila accepted and
entered. Bessas and those senators who had most to fear from Totila,
the patricians Decius and Basil, fled to Civitavecchia; others,
including the senators Maximus, Olybrius and Orestes, took refuge
in St. Peter's. In all Rome only five hundred males had survived the
famine, the plague and the fighting, and these also took refuge in the
churches. The Goths stormed in and plundered the houses of the
patricians and the vast treasure of Bessas–which he had had to
abandon–winning rich booty for themselves. Fire spread, especially
in the Trastevere quarter, and raging unchecked, destroyed large
areas of closely-packed housing. Soldiers moved in on St. Peter's and
began to slaughter the pitifully few survivors–some eighty were
killed before Pelagius could intervene. Totila exulted at the proud
deacon's supplication but conceded his pleas. The Romans would
not be killed, merely reduced to beggary. They were: Rusticiana,
a special object of animosity to the Goths who held her responsible
for inciting the overthrow of Theodoric's statues, was seen begging
in the streets. The surviving senators were reproached for the in-
fidelity to the memory of Theodoric and to Italy's true interests.
Pelagius was sent with the orator Theodore to Constantinople with
Totila's terms for peace and his threat to massacre the remains of the
senate and destroy the city, making Rome a pasture for cattle. The
dismantling of the walls was ordered so that the imperial army should
have no stronghold, but here Belisarius intervened. Writing from
Porto he urged on Totila the antiquity and nobility of the city and
the name history would give him if responsible for its destruction.
Reluctantly and with the greater part of the wall still standing, Totila

[8] Gregory the Great, *Dialogues*, 11, 15.

agreed, but the senators and their families were removed under guard to Campania and the city abandoned. For forty days Rome lay empty.

Then, late in 546, Totila left Rome to subdue Apulia, and Belisarius at once issued from Porto to take possession of and repair the city. Stones, loose and without mortar, were piled into the gaps left by the incompleted razing. Supplies were brought in and the inhabitants of the surrounding area collected. There was no time before Totila's hasty return to replace the gates, but caltrops, three-pronged obstacles to cavalry, were scattered in the gateways. These were successful and Totila's first attempt at a quick sweeping-away of the defences failed; attacks on the next three days were also without result and once more, to avoid being drawn into a close static siege, he was obliged to withdraw to Tivoli and revert to blockade. Belisarius mounted subsidiary operations; in one John, moving up from Brindisi, sent a raiding party across Campania to release the captive senators in Minturno. All but two were brought safely to Sicily. Clementinus, who earlier had surrendered a stronghold to the Goths, preferred not to be rescued, and the former consul Orestes voluntarily remained behind when a shortage of horses was revealed. Valuable hostages had been removed from Totila's reach but the drawback of relying on one man to secure an empire was now realized again. Belisarius was recalled to the East.

At once the garrison in Rome mutinied and murdered their commander Conon: their pay was long in arrears, they suspected Conon of trafficking in grain and they trusted no one but Belisarius. Under pressure from Pope Vigilius and other Italian leaders in Constantinople, Justinian sent reinforcements. A new commander, Diogenes, was sent to Rome with 3,000 men as Totila moved in from Apulia. He proved stricter than Bessas, a firmer guard was kept, supplies were issued only from a central store and, in anticipation of a long siege, grain was sown in all the open spaces of the city. Totila's first attack was beaten off, but Porto fell. However, Totila was saved the necessity of a siege since the lowered morale of the imperial army readily produced traitors. Once more it was Isaurians who offered to admit him by the Ostia gate. Elaborate diversions were planned and the escape route to Civitavecchia was ambushed. Totila was determined to have Rome as his capital; recently his overtures for the hand of a Frankish princess had been rejected with the taunt that the king of

Italy had no claim to the title until he had received the acknowledgement of the Romans. This time, without mistake, he entered Rome,
and once more there was vast slaughter, both within the city and on
the road to Civitavecchia. Only one officer, the Cilician Paul, trained
under Belisarius, led any resistance; he held Hadrian's Mausoleum
and the bridge leading to St. Peter's for a day with four hundred
cavalrymen, but the tomb was unprovisioned and he was on the point
of leading out his men in one last death charge when Totila offered
terms. Paul's men promptly enlisted under the king while the officers
were permitted to leave for Naples. Soon after, Civitavecchia also fell.

Totila now had his capital, and in the eyes of neighbouring nations
his full title to kingship. There was no longer any question of Rome's
destruction, his tenure was secure and he concentrated on the
resettlement of the ravaged city. Some senators were brought back
and instructed to repair the damage. They had few resources left, of
money or of labour, their town houses had been sacked, their
estates devastated and their rents confiscated but, as Procopius had
noted, the distinguishing Roman quality was reverence for the past
and all its tangible memorials which surrounded them in their city—
memorials going back to the foundation of the republic and beyond—
the ship of Aeneas, the walls of the early kings, the temples. However, Rome was no longer to be left entirely to the Romans for
Totila planned to leaven the city population with a trustworthy
stiffening of Goths. Meanwhile as a sign of return to normality and
of his endeavour to rule Rome fittingly, he gave circus games, the last
ever held.

Before the departure of Pope Vigilius to face humiliation and
surrender in Constantinople there had been under his aegis one last
flicker of the leisured literary life that Rome had cultivated in the
days of peace. The subdeacon Arator, a pupil in Milan of Ennodius,
had during Totila's last siege of Rome been captured and held
prisoner in the Gothic camp; remembering the fate of Bishop
Valentine he had vowed that if he escaped with his life he would write
in the apostle's honour a metrical version of the Acts of the Apostles.
He survived and kept his vow and in April 544 presented his work to
Vigilius. 'Through the aid of the blessed lord Peter this book was
presented in the following manner by Arator, subdeacon of the Holy
Roman Church, to the holy and apostolic Pope Vigilius, and received

by him on 6th April in the sanctuary before the confession of the blessed lord Peter, in the presence also of many bishops, priests and deacons and of the greater part of the clergy. There it was recited, and afterwards the pope ordered it to be handed over to Surgentius, the venerable *primicerius* of the School of Notaries, to be placed in the church's archives. But all the learned men of letters present at once begged his beatitude to order a public recitation. So he gave instructions for this to be held in the church of St. Peter *ad vincula,* and a crowd of religious and noble laity and of all classes of people gathered there. And on separate days they listened to this same Arator reciting all four books; but on one day he recited only half the books because of the insistence with which the crowd begged for repetitions. The recitals were made on these days: the first on the 13th April, then 17th April; the third on 8th May, and the fourth on 30th May in the third proconsulate of Basil, *vir clarissimus,* being the seventh indiction.' It was an appreciable literary triumph, the last in Rome for many centuries.[9]

But Totila could not linger in his new-found capital; his kingdom would not be secure until Sicily was finally subject. A fleet of four hundred vessels was prepared and the island, hitherto untouched, was ransacked. Once more Justinian searched for a commander and a portent observed in Rome at this time indicated the result. A herd of cattle being driven through the Forum Pacis (itself an indication of the city's condition) passed the bronze statue of a bull, which one heifer attempted to mount. An Etruscan, so the rumour ran, belonging to the traditional race of Rome's soothsayers, interpreted the incident as foretelling the mastering of Rome's ruler by a eunuch. The interpretation may have followed the event for Justinian's initial appointments were nullified. Both were made to appeal to the Westerners; the first was the aged Roman patrician Liberius, who had been pretorian prefect to both Odoacer and Theodoric, but he was quickly replaced as being too old. Justinian's own nephew Germanus took his place, a competent commander who had had some success against the Persians; he had married Matasuntha, Theodoric's granddaughter and Vitigis' widow and it was hoped that the union of the dynasties would prove auspicious, that Roman

[9] Arator, *de Actibus Apostolorum,* (ed. A. P. Mckinlay, *CSEL,* 62, 1951) p. xxviii.

deserters in the Gothic army would rejoin one of the imperial family and that the Goths would be reluctant to oppose the last representative of the Amaling line. He gave a new impetus to the preparations for regaining Italy but tragically died before arrival. However, the command of the sea had been regained after a battle off the Adriatic coast; the coastal towns of Ancona and Croton were reinforced and Civitavecchia seized. An unusual appointment of the eunuch Narses, the palace chamberlain, was made to exploit this. He had had some experience of war, having led reinforcements to Italy during Vitigis's campaign, and had even presumed to dispute the commands of Belisarius. But now as supreme commander he acted firmly, refusing the appointment unless given adequate resources of men and money and proper authority. He got them all and, under the patronage of Our Lady, marched through Dalmatia and Istria into Italy. Besides the army collected by Germanus he had some 3,000 Herulian Huns, a contingent of Persians, and 5,200 Lombards–mercenaries from a German nation new to Italy. In 551 he entered Italy and Totila hastened north to meet him.

For nearly ten years Totila had fought his war with success in the open field; distrusting towns, he had sought to prevent the war being dominated by them. The weaker and divided imperial forces–compelled to shelter behind walls–had consequently been mopped up by the Goths. Now there appeared for the first time a sizeable imperial field army under unified command to meet the Gothic king on his chosen terms. Early in 552 Totila came up from the south through Rome to where Narses was gathering local units near Nocera. Each side was anxious for a speedy encounter; Narses realized that the army he had gathered was the last effort of a bankrupt state, and Totila feared an imminent Italian revolution. The king's first attempt to surprise Narses was unsuccessful and as the Gothic cavalry charged they were shot down by the concentrated fire of the imperial archers. Hemmed in and overwhelmed, the Gothic line broke and was pursued by Narses' cavalry. It never reformed, for Totila was killed in the rout. Gothic power was virtually at an end. For two years or more the kingdom of Theodoric was represented by desperate resistance, at first in the field and then in the fortress of Cumae, until at last it was extinguished. Italy lay exhausted, devastated but liberated.

3

THE ROME OF GREGORY THE GREAT

The purpose behind Justinian's reconquest of the western parts and his subsequent settlements was the desire to restore to Italy legality, the former unity of the Empire and the divine sanctions of legitimate government; and this he regarded as the only true freedom he could provide. He had, in the words of the eastern civil servant John of Lydia, wished to 'give back to Rome all Rome's privileges':[1] an attitude that was shared by Belisarius, and by Narses who, in the dedicatory inscription to a bridge he built over the Aniene stream near Rome, referred to 'the liberty of the City of Rome and the restoration of all Italy',[2] but these were Dead Sea fruit. The pragmatic sanction of 13th August 554, by which Justinian codified the restoration of Roman rule, had little realism; the restoration of the *annona*, of the educational system and of the organization of Rome's maintenance were all decreed, but the decree remained unsubstantiated, for they were to be re-established from endowments, and managed by a now impoverished class.[3] Some attention was paid to the pressing hardships of Italy—provision was made for a moratorium on debts, protection of fugitives' property, and the supervision of officials' actions by the Church authorities. But equally the conquest was to be made to pay for itself—the remaining Italian senators were given permission to withdraw from public life and from Rome, and the new officials to administer Italy were foreigners, Easterners. The return to an ordered administration was delayed: Gregory the Great, at the end of the century, was still exercising through his agents a strict protection of Italian rights.

The years following the death of Totila, the last dying efforts of the

[1] Johannes Lydus, *De Magistratibus*, III, 55.
[2] CIL. VI, 1199.
[3] Justinian, *Novellae*, (ed. R. Schoell, *Corpus Iuris Civilis*, vol. 3, 1899), App. VII, 22.

Goth race, filled Italy with a misery as far-reaching and as senseless as any that had gone before. Teias was elected by the remnant of the Goths to succeed Totila and, with the promise of the vast treasury of the dead king, secured an alliance from the Franks. His brother Aligern held the strong fortress of Cumae, where he was soon closely besieged by Narses. Teias set out to relieve him, coming south by forced marches, but before leaving Pavia, gave orders for the murder of three hundred noble young Romans, the sons of the senatorial families who had been held there as hostages by Totila. The two armies met on the Sarno in Campania. Two months of skirmishing gave the Goths no success and Teias withdrew to Monte Lattario where his army was surrounded; in the first combat Teias himself was killed, but his followers fought on until hunger and thirst compelled their surrender. A band of about 1,000 fought their way through the imperial encirclement and managed to reach Pavia. In Cumae, Aligern resisted for a year; the rock had been hollowed out into a series of caves, virtually impregnable to assault, but here too the hopelessness of the situation was realized and Aligern yielded.

But the alliance formed by Teias now bore fruit. Although the Frankish rulers had been reluctant to commit themselves, two brothers, Lothaire and Buccelin, led an independent marauding expedition into Italy. 75,000 descended into the plain of northern Italy; near Parma they defeated the advance guard of the imperial army—a contingent of Herulian Huns—whose commander, Fulcaris, sacrificed his life at the moment of defeat, exclaiming that death was preferable to the anger of Narses. The Frankish army poured through Aemilia into central and southern Italy; from Rimini Narses was unable to halt their progress for any length of time, but the surviving Goths in the area placed themselves under his command. Campania, Lucania and Bruttium were devastated by Buccelin and Lothaire ravaged Apulia and Calabria; Otranto and Reggio Calabria were sacked. But as they marched, disease and the climate reduced their strength, and in the spring of 554 they withdrew to the north. During the previous winter Narses had been building up his forces in Rome, and had ceaselessly drilled and trained his troops. At Casilino on the Volturno, through the skilful dispositions of Narses, the host was first trapped and then ridden to death by the imperial, Hun and Gothic cavalry. The war appeared to be over; the troops relaxed, and in all the cities of Italy gave themselves up to rejoicing, dancing and celebration.[4]

The damage to Italy had been enormous. Late in the fifth century the papal revenues from the rich province of Picenum amounted to 2,160 *solidi*; under Pelagius I they were reduced to 500 *solidi*.[5] The country people were reduced to eating acorns, and there were reports of multiple cannibalism.[6] It was impossible to estimate how many had died from famine, from the plague that had decimated the Frankish army and from the war itself, which had grown increasingly cruel, and agriculture had been totally disrupted. In December 556 Pelagius, now pope, wrote to Archbishop Sapaudus of Arles, begging for money and clothing to be sent, to be paid for from the Church's treasury in Provence: 'For the Italian fields have been so ravaged that no one can restore them'; the supplies should be sent by ship as quickly as possible because 'there is such poverty and destitution in this city that we cannot look without grief and anguish of heart upon men whom we know to be meritorious and born to an honourable position.'[7] In 561, he was writing to Boethius, the son of the philosopher who had joined the imperial service and was now praetorian prefect of Africa, asking for food to be sent to Rome from Africa and the islands, for as late as 559 estates belonging to the Roman Church on the Porto road were still out of cultivation and Pelagius was trying to get them resettled.[8]

Order had returned unsteadily to Italy. Narses held viceregal powers and used them sternly, and Justinian by the pragmatic sanction of 554 had settled the administration of Italy. This was liberal and local: officials and governors were to be appointed with the concurrence of prominent provincials, including the bishops, so that local circumstances could be regarded; a moratorium had of necessity been declared on all debts; weights and measures were to be standardized, under the inspection of the church authorities. But the task was made immeasurably more difficult by the almost total extinction of the curial classes of the municipalities, who had traditionally managed local affairs. For centuries they had been languish-

---

[4] Procopius, BG., 8, 35.

[5] Pelagius I, *Ep.* 83 (*Pelagii I Papae epistulae quae supersunt*, ed. P. M. Gasso and C. M. Batlle, 1956).

[6] Procopius, BG., 6, 20.   [7] Pelagius I, *Epp.* 4, 8.   [8] *Ibid.*, 76, 85.

ing under heavy taxation; the wars had given them the *coup de grâce*. John of Lydia, who was born about 490, writing in 550 could just remember town councils meeting in togas to transact business. The last official appearance in the West (Rome and Ravenna apart) was that of the Sabine town of Rieti in 565,[9] and even in Ravenna the council's function later appears to have been solely that of a bureau of legal registration, recording legacies and inheritance s. In a defensive world there was neither scope nor resources for the civil amenities in which local patriotism had expressed itself.

Rome itself found delay in returning to orderly government. Narses had carried out some rebuilding but from his administrative capital in Ravenna he had little opportunity for a real reconstruction. The papacy was going through stormy times–a legacy of the conflicting loyalties evoked by the wars and by Justinian's doctrinal experiments. Vigilius in Constantinople had finally faced the penalty of his broken promises and his refusal to confirm Justinian's religious policy, but he remained conscious of his failure as pope. 'Do with me as you will; I am receiving the rewards of my deeds.' He fled from the Emperor's supervision to the church of St. Peter by the Hormisdas Palace, was dragged out and finally forced to sign a form of approval of imperial policy after a rigorous imprisonment. At last, on petition from Rome, he was released and allowed to return, discredited, to the West; in June 555 he died at Syracuse.[10]

The Archdeacon Pelagius was his obvious successor; a man of business and charity, he was also a controversial figure. He had been legate in Constantinople, first for Pope Agapetus and latterly for Vigilius, and had been employed by Justinian in several missions to displace monophysite bishops in the East. He had come into further bitter conflict at the imperial court with the monophysite leader, Archbishop Theodore of Caesarea, and his manoeuvres to destroy Theodore's influence were, in Africa at least, held largely responsible for the disastrous schism of the Three Chapters.[11] His election caused

---

[9] J-O. Tjader, 'Die Nichtliterarischen Lateinischen Papyri Italiens aus der Zeit 445–700', (*Acta Instituti Romani Regni Sueciae, Ser.* 4, XIX, 1, 1955), n. 7.

[10] *LP.* I, 299; *PL.* 69, col. 53.

[11] Liberatus, *Breviarium,* (*PL.* 68, col. 1045); L. Duchesne, 'Vigile et Pelage. Etude sur l'histoire de l'Eglise Romaine au milieu du VIe siecle',

serious disputes in Rome and accusations were made that he had been involved in the death of Vigilius. The consequent difficulty of finding bishops willing to consecrate him was aggravated by the disorders of war which had left many bishoprics vacant. In 551 the clergy of Milan had written to Rome complaining that Bishop Datius had been absent in the East for twelve or thirteen years and that most of the bishops he had consecrated were now dead.[12] In Rome an ugly schism developed over Pelagius's accession and the suspicion that he like Vigilius was a political candidate. 'The monasteries and the majority of wise and noble devout withdrew from communion with Pelagius, saying that he was involved in the death of Pope Vigilius', but Pelagius swore to his innocence. 'I beg you to grant my request, that whoever deserves promotion in the city and is worthy of it, from doorkeeper even to bishop, should accept advancement, though not for gold or promises; you all know that is simony. But whoever is instructed in the works of God, and leads a good life, then him we bid, not by bribes but by honest conversation, to rise into the first rank.' A bishop was found to consecrate him, John of Perugia, and thereafter, until 561, he spent his pontificate working for the reconstruction of Italy and the prosperity of the Roman Church, 'scorning to be depressed by a failing world'.[13]

But Italy was not to be given the peace so desperately needed for recovery. Narses had governed well, if firmly, since Justinian's settlement, but Justinian died in 565, and his successor–his nephew Justin II–was an unstable man who finally lapsed into insanity. No such trust as had been accorded even to Justinian was felt for him, nor especially for his wife, the Empress Sophia. Corruption set in: Narses himself became a flagrant example of the Byzantine governor amassing a vast treasure that was to become legendary in the bankrupt province. In 567 delegates from Rome appeared before Justin and demanded Narses' dismissal: they declared that the tyranny of a Greek eunuch was worse by far even than their Gothic slavery. They

(*Revue des Questions Historiques*, 35, 1884); D. J. Constantelos, 'Justinian and the Three Chapters Controversy,' (*Greek Orthodox Theological Review*, 8, 1962–3).

[12] *MGH. Epp.* III, p. 438.

[13] *LP.* I, 303; inscription of John III in the basilica of the Apostles, *LP.* 1, 306, n. 2.

were listened to and Narses was relieved of his governorship. Legend added an insulting message from the Empress to the veteran that he should return once more to the employment fitting to his condition, the spinning of thread in the women's quarter of the palace. He retired to Naples with his great treasure; and there, it was said, proceeded to spin webs of intrigue in reprisal for the gratuitous insult. Certainly, in his conquest of Italy he had used Lombard mercenaries from the tribe of Germans who had been settled on the Danube for some decades, though his responsibility for their entry into Italy is more doubtful.[14] But in the year following his dismissal they appeared from the north–long-haired, tough Arian warriors, loosely federated into clans under their war-leader King Alboin–to plunder and to settle. Their appearance, burnt brick-red by the southern sun, with two long plaits of hair, was terrifying; and with only a loose political organization they quickly overran large areas of northern and central Italy. Here they set up semi-independent 'duchies', with a royal capital at Pavia. Only isolated garrisons of imperial troops, established by Narses, held out on the Alpine frontier, but beyond the walls they could retain nothing. Milan fell, giving the Lombards domination of the whole of north Italy and the Po valley. From this region, which was to take their name, they threatened Genoa and Ravenna and then penetrated southwards, establishing duchies at Spoleto, to cut Rome's communications with Ravenna, and at Benevento, to endanger Naples and all south Italy.[15]

In Rome few measures could be taken. Pelagius' successor, John III, went personally–and against the wishes of the Romans–to Naples to beg Narses to return. The old man, who may then have been in his eighties, did so and took up residence once more on the Capitol, but could achieve nothing. His successor as prefect of Italy,

[14] A. Haggerty-Krappe, 'La légende de l'arrivée des Lombards en Italie', (*Moyen Âge*, 44, 1934) gives a parallel legend from Persia.

[15] The early stages of the Lombard invasion are given in Paulus Diaconus, 66. HL. II and III; see also R. Cessi, 'Le prime conquiste longobarde in Italia', (*Atti della Reale Accademia d'Arte e Scienza di Padova*, 1922). For Spoleto, G. P. Bognetti, 'Tradizione longobarda e politica bizantina nelle origini del ducato di Spoleto, (*Rivista di Storia del diritto Italiano*, 26–7, 1953–4); O. Bertolini, 'I papi e le relazioni politiche di Roma con i ducati longobardi di Spoleto e di Benevento, I', (*Rivista di Storia della Chiesa in Italia*, 6, 1952).

Longinus, had nothing approaching the necessary military resources at his disposal. But when the Lombard King Alboin was murdered in 572, although Longinus may not have been directly implicated, the murderers fled to Ravenna.[16]

A temporary improvement came when Justin, having shown the first signs of insanity, was persuaded to appoint a Caesar as his deputy in government. Tiberius, the man chosen by the Empress Sophia, was a general of some reputation; tall, fair-haired, grey-eyed, he was noted for a liberality that contrasted with Justin's parsimoniousness, and showed a concern for the West. The same year, Alboin's successor Cleph was in turn murdered after a reign of eighteen months, during which he 'embroiled Italy and put to the sword so many important Romans and others'. No successor was chosen.[17] A three-year truce with the Lombards was arranged, but Tiberius had also succeeded in making peace with the Avars who were threatening the Danube frontier, and the troops so released were transferred to Italy under a new commander, Justin's son-in-law Baduarius. These were mercenaries; Tiberius, an Italian noted, 'hired the bodies of barbarians and formed them into regiments bearing his own name'.[18] But the anarchy of the Lombards' kingdom did not lessen their fighting power; Baduarius's counter-offensive in 575 was a disaster, the imperial army being annihilated in the field and its commander dying of his wounds.

Italy's situation in the mid-seventies was serious, for Tiberius had no more troops to spare. In 577, the most distinguished senator left in Rome, the patrician Pamphronius, leader of the senate and former praetorian prefect, went on an embassy to Constantinople with as much money as could be raised, 216,000 *solidi*, to beg for reinforcements. Tiberius could spare none; instead, he instructed Pamphronius to return with the money to Italy and to use it, either in bribing individual Lombard dukes to join the imperial service, or, if that failed, in hiring the intervention of Frankish mercenaries. Pamphronius attempted this. Some Lombard dukes took his money, but did not otherwise alter their conduct: duke Faroald of Spoleto in

---

[16] Paulus Diaconus, HL., II, 29–30.

[17] Cedrenus, I, p. 688 (ed. I. Bekker, *CSHB*, 24, 1838); Paulus Diaconus, HL. 11, 31.

[18] Menander, *fragg*, 63, 64 (*FGH*. IV, 263).

578 seized Classis, the port of Ravenna, and its rich treasures, and in 579 had moved to besiege Rome itself.[19]

Rome was under siege when the reigning Pope Benedict I, died, and his successor Pelagius II was elected without the customary imperial confirmation.[20] The new pope, himself of Germanic origin, was a vigorous man who determined to find an end to the wars devastating Italy. Early in 580 he wrote to Bishop Aunacharius of Auxerre to negotiate a Frankish intervention: the Franks were 'the divinely appointed neighbours and helpers of this city'; 'we urge you to hasten, as far as you can, to free from the pollution of the gentiles the shrines of those saints whose merits you seek.' New ambassadors from the pope and the senate had already been sent to Tiberius, now reigning as Emperor; representing the pope was a former prefect of the City, an aristocrat who had become a monk, the deacon Gregory. His instructions were contained in a letter brought to him by Bishop Sebastian, sent by the pope to reinforce the Italian mission. 'So great are the calamities and tribulations we suffer from the perfidy of the Lombards, in spite of their solemn promises, that nobody could adequately describe them. As to our brother Sebastian, you will learn from what he will tell you how we welcomed him. He has promised to portray to the most pious Emperor the necessities and the perils of the whole of Italy. Deliberate together over what you can do to relieve our distress promptly. The republic is in so critical a situation that if God does not inspire our prince's heart to show the pity he feels, and to grant us a general or governor, then we are lost. The territory round Rome is without garrison. The Exarch writes that he can do nothing for us, being himself unable to defend the region round Ravenna. May God bid the Emperor come to our aid at the earliest possible moment, in the perils that are now closing in upon us, before the army of that impious nation, the Lombards, shall have seized the lands that still form part of the Empire.'[21] Rome was still part of the Empire, and still felt itself, although neglected, an essential if despairing element in the constitution of the entire civilized world. Something of the anguish felt at the blows inflicted against the state

[19] P. Goubert, *Byzance avant l'Islam*; t. II, *Byzance et l'Occident*, pt. II, *Rome, Byzance et Carthage*, (1965), pp. 17–18.

[20] LP. I, 309.

[21] Gregory the Great, *Registrum*, append. II. (*MGH. Epp.* II, 440).

are seen in the inscriptions incorporated in the few works of adorn-
ment that Pelagius could afford to St. Peter's: 'May the Roman
sceptre be guided by the divine hand so that under the Empire the
true faith may have liberty'; 'May the enemies of the Roman
name be vanquished throughout the entire world by the virtue of
St. Peter, and peace be assured to the nations and to the Catholic
faith.'[22]

But Rome was not entirely deserted or thrown on its own resources. The disaster of 575 had prevented the fielding of another
imperial army in Italy, but the Empire under Tiberius, and from 582
under his chosen successor Maurice, was exerting its efforts to
relieve the pressure on imperial Italy. During the years Gregory spent
in Constantinople the imperial court was occupied in a wide-
ranging diplomacy, not merely to achieve the advice given to Pamphronius to secure Frankish intervention, but also to reaffirm the
concept of the republic, imperial and catholic, embracing the western
kingdoms under the suzerainty of Constantinople. The kingdom of
Burgundy, holding the Rhone valley, was the key to this: with a large
Gallo-Roman population it could be expected to sympathize with
the Empire, while its king, Guntram, was the most pious if the most
inert of the sons of Lothair I. Already his troops under the patrician
Mummolus had faced and defeated the Lombards. But Guntram
preferred the prospects on his Western frontier, and no alliance could
be formed. Other expedients were tried: the despatch of a pretender,
Gundowald, a bastard of the Merovingian line, who had fled from
his relations to Constantinople. But he was betrayed in 585 by the
instability of Frankish politics and the self-interest of the Gallo-
Romans, and Constantinople lost the chance of establishing at
Marseilles, as at Carthage, Ravenna and Cartagena, a sally-port into
the mainland.[23]

One tentative intervention had been achieved in 584 when Childebert of Austrasia on receipt of 50,000 *solidi* from Maurice entered
Italy with a strong army; the Lombards were reluctant to meet him in
the field, so he made a peace with them and withdrew. Maurice pro-

[22] LP. I, 310.
[23] P. Goubert, *op. cit.*, pt. I, *Byzance et les Francs*, (1956); W. Goffart,
'Byzantine Policy in the West under Tiberius and Maurice', (*Traditio*, 13,
1957) gives a truer appreciation of the Spanish involvement.

tested at this misuse of his subsidy, and another army was sent in the following year, equally ineffectively. Already Maurice had taken measures to adjust to defensive policy after the diplomatic failures. Under the style of Exarch a new official was created, a permanent commander-in-chief or viceroy with full civil and military powers, who from his seat at Ravenna was to control the united defence of the imperial fragments of Italy. The first to be sent, Smaragdus, succeeded in concluding a peace with the Lombards early in 586, to run for three years.

Before the truce was over Pope Pelagius was dead, in the course of a series of disasters that had struck the city in 589. The Frankish bishop, Gregory of Tours, received an eye-witness account of the catastrophic year: 'Now in the fifteenth year of King Childebert, a deacon arrived from the city of Rome with relics of the saints and reported that in November of the previous year the waters of the Tiber had overflowed Rome in such a flood that the ancient buildings had been destroyed and the granaries of the Church wrecked, containing some thousands of bushels of wheat, which had been lost. There then followed a plague called *inguinaria*; it broke out in the middle of January and first of all attacked Pope Pelagius, who quickly died of it; and after his death there was a great mortality among the people.'[24] Pelagius's successor, Gregory, writing five years after, stated that the flood was so vast that the water flowed over the city walls–although this was probably in the clumsily patched stretches that Totila had pulled down–and in a sermon referring to the plague said, 'With one's own eyes one saw arrows shoot from heaven and fell the people one by one'. War, massacre, and now flood and plague were reducing Rome to the narrowest possible margin and removing a whole way of life.

None appreciated this better than the new pope. Gregory was of an illustrious Roman family, perhaps connected with the Anicii, that for a century had served the city well in both civil and ecclesiastical office. His grandfather, Pope Felix III who had died in 492, was himself the son of the priest Felix of the present SS. Nereo et Achilleo, who had converted the temple of Romulus on the Via Sacra into a church dedicated to the Arabian doctors SS. Cosmas and Damian–the first Christian building in the old city, and the first dedication to

[24] Gregory of Tours, HF. X, 1.

non-Roman saints.[25] Gregory's father Gordianus, a rich man with a palace on the Coelian, in the centre of official Rome, was one of the district notaries of the city, charged with the administration of church property; his mother Silvia was well known in her lifetime for her piety, retiring in her widowhood to a retreat at Cella Nova, near the basilica of St. Paul's. The monastic vein was strong in the family: his father's sisters Tarsilla and Aemiliana founded and themselves lived in a convent within the city; they prevailed upon their youngest sister Gordiana to join them, but she, the gayest of the family, rebelled and eloped with the bailiff of her estates.[26] Gregory himself was born perhaps in 540, and certainly by 546, and shared in the general education of a noble Roman. Although Agapetus's plan for a papal university at Rome had been ended by the wars, Justinian had seen to it at the settlement that legal, medical and literary studies should flourish and that professors should be maintained from the public treasury. Gregory showed considerable aptitude for administration and for justice, and by 573 had risen to the highest civil post in Rome, that of prefect of the city. But that same disillusion with the continuance of normal conditions which sent so many of his relations and contemporaries into the contemplative or monastic life affected him also, and about 578 he abandoned the civil career and formed in his parents' house a monastic community.

To the Roman nobility this was nothing strange. Before the Gothic wars the monasteries of Italy were frequently under the patronage, as centres of learning, of the great men of the city. But this class was dying out, their estates had no heirs, and the last members of the families were turning themselves to the service of religion. Gregory himself described such an occasion when Galla, one of the noblest women in Rome—the daughter of the murdered Symmachus and sister of Boethius' widow Rusticiana—made this decision although she was the last heiress of an ancient family. 'During the time of the Goths there lived in this city a most noble girl, the daughter of

[25] A. Ferrua, 'Nuove Iscrizioni della Via Ostiense', (*Epigraphica*, 21, 1959), and 'Gli Antenati di S. Gregorio Magno', (*Civiltà Cattolica*, 1964, IV): amended by J. T. Milik, 'La famiglia di Felice III papa', (*Epigraphica*, 28, 1967). In general, F. Homes Dudden, *Gregory the Great*, (2 vols, 1905); P. Batiffol, *S. Grégoire le Grand*, 1923.

[26] *Hom. in Evang.* 38; *Dial.* IV, 16.

Symmachus, consul and patrician, who while still young had been given to a husband, but within a year was left a widow by his death. But she, though the fervent force of the world called her to a second marriage, both by reason of her age and her wealth, chose rather to join in a spiritual marriage with God, which, though she might begin in grief, she would complete in eternal joy, rather than a fleshly marriage, which always begins in joy, but leads finally to grief.' Her decision to enter the conventual life was against medical advice, but she lived for many years in a convent near St. Peter's, the later St. Stephen's and also called after her the *Cata Galla Patricia*, before dying of cancer of the breast. The dioceses and the monasteries to the north of Rome, Nepi, and St. Andrew on Monte Soratte, ascribed to her endowment from her vast family estates the foundation of many of the churches around Ponzano, on both sides of the Tiber Valley in the Sabine Hills, and on the Tregia.[27]

Galla's example was followed, as we have seen, by other leading members of Roman families. Gregory's decision to abandon his civil career and embrace the religious life was not unusual, therefore: his family estates, in Sicily and around Tivoli, were handed over to the Roman Church, and with a few companions he retired to the monastery he founded in his parents' house on the Coelian.[28] Rome could ill-afford his loss since the ranks of capable and experienced citizens were already thinned. Within two years Pope Benedict had ordained him as deacon of the seventh district, with responsibilities covering relief, charity and administration; then in 579 he was sent by Pelagius to Constantinople to secure aid for Italy.

His period in Constantinople, lasting perhaps seven years, was a personal success. The Emperor Maurice was involved in a war with the Persians, 'the ulcer of the state', over the possession of Armenia, and could spare little help for Italy, but in maintaining the Empire's wide network of diplomatic relations, extending to Spain and France, Gregory could supply advice from his vast interest in the Church universal. Constantinople remained the centre and many people came

---

[27] *Dial.* IV, 14; Benedict of St Andrew, *Chronicon*, (ed. G. Zucchetti, Fonti per la Storia d'Italia, 1920), pp. 25–6; also G. B. Proja, 'S. Galla, patrizia romana nei Dialoghi di S. Gregorio', (*Rivista Storica Benedettina*, 23, 1954).

[28] *Registrum*, append. I.

there who were to become his firm friends: Anastasius, the former
Patriarch of Antioch, and Leander, Bishop of Seville and brother and
tutor to Isidore, the encyclopaedic scholar of the following generation.[29] In purely religious affairs, concerning doctrine and the cure of
souls, Gregory had success and gained a reputation. While Tiberius
followed Justin's policy of repressing the dissident monophysites and
Arians, Gregory preferred persuasion and argument. One disputation
he held in the Emperor's presence with the patriarch Eutychius, who
maintained that at the Resurrection the bodies of the Elect would be
'impalpable and more subtle than the wind or air'. But Gregory prevailed and the patriarch on his deathbed shortly after recanted and
acknowledged orthodox teaching.[30] Gregory himself also fell ill,
perhaps–as recurrently afterwards–under stress of overwork for in
addition to his diplomatic duties he was preaching to his friends on the
Book of Job; a series of discourses later edited as the *Magna Moralia*.[31]

In 582, shortly before his death, Tiberius adopted as his successor
the Cappadocian general Maurice, a short, sturdy, round-faced man
of 43, who soon married Tiberius's younger daughter Constantia.[32]
To their first son Theodosius Gregory himself stood sponsor at
baptism, and his relations with the new court circle gained in
intimacy.[33] Some of its members were of Roman origin: the patrician
Rusticiana, a grand-daughter of Boethius, remained a faithful
correspondent whom he was always trying to lure back to her true
home, her native Rome. 'I remember writing to your Excellency
long ago, and frequently to have urged you to hasten here to see
again the dwelling of the blessed Peter, prince of Apostles. How
anyone can be seduced by Constantinople, and how anyone can
forget Rome, I do not know. . . .'[34] But Rusticiana preferred the

[29] *Ibid.*, I, 41; V, 53, 53a.
[30] Gregory I, *Moralia*, XIV, 72–4; Bede, HE., II, I; Paulus Diaconus,
Vita, 9; Johannes Diaconus, *Vita*, I, 28–30. John of Ephesus, 13 and 26,
shows that Tiberius was at this time recruiting Arian mercenaries from the
West but that popular outcry forced him to abandon this and institute a
persecution.
[31] *Magna Moralia*, (PL. 75).
[32] P. Goubert, *op. cit.*, 1, *Byzance et l'Orient; L'Empéreur Maurice*,
ch. I.
[33] Gregory of Tours, HF. X, 1; Johannes Diaconus, *Vita*, I, 40.
[34] *Registrum*, VIII, 22.

East; from Constantinople she went on pilgrimage to the Holy Land
and Mount Sinai, writing an account to Gregory on her return; the
pope chided her for her love of Constantinople which could draw her
from such places.[35] In the imperial family itself he had admirers:
Theoctista,[36] Maurice's sister and governess to his children; Philippicus, his brother-in-law; and his cousin Domitian, Bishop of
Mytilene. This last, a man of 'singular prudence and shrewdness,
distinguished both in speech and action, and well fitted to transact
business of the greatest importance', later played a major role in
negotiations with the Persian King Khosroes, which briefly gave rise
to hopes of the latter's conversion to Christianity.[37] To these, and to
friends in the army's high command, Gregory could as pope urge
with some familiarity the serious condition of Italy and the need for
help; all remained faithful friends after his recall to Rome, even when
matters of high religious policy clouded the accord between Emperor
and pope.

He returned to Rome in the spring of 586, to his monastery on the
Coelian, and there, while acting as Pelagius's secretary,[38] conceived
the design of converting the northern world into a new unity under
Rome, the unity of the Church. Here experience in Constantinople
took effect. He was aware of the Empire's concern in the West–
Maurice was even to contemplate the establishment of a son as
Western Emperor. But the diplomatic efforts he had observed from
the capital had foundered on the ambitions of the politician-bishops
of Gaul; the Christian foundation was not yet firm enough. Gregory
himself wished to go on a mission to the north, but plague and the
death of Pelagius intervened and he was summoned to the supreme
office itself.

An account of his appearance at this time has been given by
his biographer in the ninth century, the deacon John, who saw the

[35] *Ibid.*, V, 46.
[36] *Ibid.*, I, 5; VII, 26; XI, 45.
[37] *Ibid.*, III, 62; see also R. Paret, 'Domitianus de Mélitène et la politique
réligieuse de l'Empéreur Maurice', (*Revue des Etudes Byzantines*, 15, 1957)
and P. Goubert, 'Mystique et politique à Byzance; Domitien de Mytilène',
(*Ibid.*, 19, 1961). In the West the legend that Khosroes had become a
Christian under the influence of his wife Sirin is found in Fredegar,
Chronicon, IV, 9, (MGH. SS. Rer. Mer. II, 125–6).
[38] *Registrum*, III, 66.

fresco portraits in St. Andrew's: of medium height but good, well-proportioned figure, he had a large head, bald with a fringe of dark hair; his eyes were a light brown, his eyebrows long, thin, and arched; an aquiline nose, and red, rather thick lips; his complexion was swarthy and in later life flushed.[39] He was conscious of a lack of personal dignity of appearance, in contrast to the splendour of his office–'Strangers may smile at me', he wrote to a friend, 'because of the dignity of my priestly office', and he compared himself to an ape forced to play the part of a lion.[40] He suffered continuously from poor health–a weak digestion, gout and, the result of the progressive breakdown of Roman amenities, a slow periodic fever. He was an extremely hard worker and always seemed weighed down by the cares thrust upon him–the safety and maintenance of so many cities and refugees–and these added to his chronic physical weakness.[41] His ill-health forced him to be careful of his food: to settle his stomach he drank a wine, *retsina*, from Alexandria, called 'cognidium'; a correspondent was begged to procure some for him, since 'in Rome we get from the merchants a drink they call *cognidium*, but not the wine itself'.[42]

He too had his *familia*, a group of friends mainly from his monastery, whom he kept in his immediate service as pope. He disapproved of the custom that had grown up in the Lateran of the pope having lay chamberlains and pages to attend him, and always insisted on the service of monks. These included the deacon Peter, a friend from his youth who later managed the papal estates in Sicily and Campania, and was his particular confidant; the notary Aemilianus, who took shorthand notes of his sermons; the *defensor* John, later sent on a mission to Spain; Augustine and Mellitus of the English mission; Marinianus, whom he appointed Archbishop of Ravenna; Maximianus, who had joined him in Constantinople–he succeeded Gregory as Abbot of St. Andrew's, and in 591 was appointed Bishop of Syracuse and papal vicar for Sicily; and Probus, whom he sent to supervise the building of a hostel for pilgrims in Jerusalem.

[39] Johannes Diaconus, *Vita*, IV, 84.
[40] *Registrum*, I, 3, 5. Gregory was probably being popularly compared to pope Leo I.
[41] *Ibid.*, VII, 40.　　　　[42] *Ibid.*, VII, 37.

As pope, he is remembered above all for the English mission, when the Roman church first stepped outside the contracted bounds of the Empire into contact with peoples who had never been subject to its ecclesiastical jurisdiction; for writing the *Regula Pastoralis*, the key to a bishop's life, and so to civilization in the succeeding centuries; for welcoming the conversion of the Spanish Visigoths from Arianism to Catholicism; for his defence of Roman primacy against the pretensions of the see of Constantinople; for making himself pope of the emerging nations. But in Rome and Italy he was 'God's consul', under whose management came the whole care and preservation of the population of war-torn Italy–a frontier province since the Lombard invasions. The imperial authorities had no resources to spare for Rome in its almost isolated situation. The decimated senatorial families had vanished into exile in the East and had given their possessions to the Roman church, or–their estates bankrupt–existed on charity. The senate could not be renewed: Justinian's resettlement had left only four posts in the West which carried membership with them, and these were confined largely to existing members of the eastern senate.

In 593 a new Lombard king, Agilulf, resumed hostilities and moved to besiege Rome. While the city was surrounded and the countryside being devastated, Gregory, preaching from a text of Ezekiel, gave expression to the changes his lifetime had seen. 'Where now are those who exulted with joy over the glories of Rome? Where are their trains of attendants? Where is their pride?... Where, asks the prophet Nahum, is the dwelling of the lions, and the feeding-place of their cubs? Were not Rome's dukes and princes lions, who scoured the provinces of the world and seized upon their prey by violence and murder? It is here that the young lions had their feeding-place, for hither children, youths, young worldlings hastened from all parts of the world to make their fortunes. . . . The eagle has gone bald all over its body; growing old, it loses all its feathers, even those of its wings.' He also lamented, 'Where is now the senate, where are the people? It has gone, and the people vanish.'[43] The lives of the popes, in recording their donations and endowments to individual Roman churches, show something of this: although Gregory presented 100 lb. of gold (apart from the gift of

[43] *Hom. in Ezechiel.* II, 6, 22, 25. (*PL.* 76, 1010, 1011).

his family properties) no such other gift is recorded until Honorius I gave nearly 2,000 lb. in silver. This may have represented the estate of his father Petronius, a Campanian consul: the Roman church, drawing the best elements into its service, was also drawing upon their patrimonies. These were windfalls of capital, decreasing as established families decreased; until the death of Pope Sisinnius in 708, a total of 42 lb. in gold and 310 lb. in silver alone are recorded. When the father of a pope was demonstrably a great man, he was of the Byzantine civil service, such as Plato, father of John VII, who was a retired officer with military and naval experience, and caretaker of the imperial palace in Rome. Pelagius II, Gregory I, Boniface IV and Honorius I all turned family properties in Rome to religious or charitable uses which indicate that their families were without lay successors. One has to wait until Gregory II, in the eighth century, to find once more a pope with an established home in Rome. During the seventh century there was no great family in the city except for the *familia pontificis*, the household of the pope.[44]

The people had changed, but they had not gone; indeed the flood of refugees that now filled the city was to be the major concern of Gregory's domestic action. As the invaders swept the surrounding countryside, ancient towns fell abandoned and provision had to be made for spiritual and temporal needs. In the first year of his pontificate, Gregory wrote to Bishop Balbinus of Rosella: 'We have learned that the church of Populonia is so entirely destitute of clergy that the confessions of the dying cannot be heard or baptism given to infants. We therefore charge your fraternity, by the authority of these letters, to visit that church and to ordain there one cardinal-priest and two deacons, with three priests in the attached parishes'.[45] Similarly, depopulated dioceses were merged together: the diocese of Terni was joined to Narni, six miles away;[46] in 590, ruined Minturno was joined to Formiae;[47] two years later Cumae was combined with Miseno,[48] Tres Tabernae (where the Christians of Rome had gone out to meet

[44] Figures from *LP*; see also E. Stein, 'La disparition du Sénat à la fin du VIᵉ siècle', (*Bulletin de la classe des lettres et des sciences morales et politiques de l'Academie Royale de Belgique*, Ser. 5, 25, 1939).

[45] *Registrum*, I, 15.

[46] *Ibid.*, IX, 60.

[47] *Ibid.*, I, 8.

[48] *Ibid.*, II, 45.

St. Paul) with Velletri,[49] and Fondi with Terracina.[50] The following year Cures Sabinae (the modern Passo Correse) was joined to Mentana,[51] and Velletri itself moved its seat to higher and safer ground on the modern Rocca Massima.[52]

The inhabitants displaced in the upheavals that made these changes necessary poured into Rome as their only refuge to become a charge on the Church, the only body with the administrative capacity to deal with the problem. Gregory's biographer in the ninth century, the deacon John, gives a description of his activities in that field, based on the register drawn up by Gregory in the *scrinium* of the Lateran which contained the names of persons of every age, profession and of both sexes, in Rome and as far as the coastal cities who were in receipt of aid, the amounts to be received, and the dates when due:

'He converted into money the revenues of all the patrimonies and estates, in accordance with the ledger of Gelasius, whom he seems to have followed most carefully, and having collected all the officials of the Church, the palace, the monasteries, the lesser churches, the cemeteries, the deaconries, the hostels both within and without the walls, he decided from the ledger (according to which the distribution is still made) how many *solidi* should be given to each, out of the above mentioned payments in gold and silver. The sums thus decided upon were distributed four times a year, at Easter, on the feast of the Apostles (29 June), on the feast of St. Andrew (30 November), and on his own feast day (3 September). Also, early on Easter morning he used to sit in the basilica of Pope Vigilius, which was near his residence, to exchange the kiss of peace with the bishops, priests, deacons and other notables, and on these occasions he gave to each of them one *aureus*. On the feast of the Apostles, and on the anniversary of his own consecration, he gave them a sum of money and clothes of foreign material and make.

'On the first day of every month, he distributed to the poor in general that part of the Church's revenue paid in kind. So, in its season, corn, and in their several seasons, wine, cheese, vegetables, bacon, meat, fish and oil were with the greatest discretion doled out

---

[49] *Ibid.,* II, 50.   [50] *Ibid.*, III, 13.   [51] *Ibid.*, III, 20.
[52] *Ibid.*, II, 14; see also L. Duchesne, 'Les évêchés d'Italie et l'invasion lombard', (MAH., 23, 1903; 25, 1905; 26, 1906).

by this father of the Lord's family. Pigments and other more delicate articles of commerce were offered by him as marks of respect to citizens of rank, and so the Church came to be regarded as a source of supply for the whole community.

'To 3,000 handmaids of God (called by the Greek name *nuns*) he gave 15 lb. of gold for bed-clothes and bestowed upon them for their daily support 80 lb. in gold. Of these he wrote to the lady Theoctiste: "I believe that but for these women, not one of us could have survived for so many years in Rome amid the Lombard swords."

'Moreover every day he sent out by couriers appointed for the job cooked provisions to the sick and infirm throughout the streets and lanes of every district of the city. To those of higher rank who were ashamed to beg he sent a dish from his own table to be delivered at their doors as a present from St. Peter; and this he did before he sat down to dine himself. So not one of the faithful in Rome was without experience of this bishop's kindness in most tenderly providing for the wants of all'.[53]

A measure of the individual care of his charities is given in a letter written early in his pontificate to the subdeacon Anthemius, papal agent for Campania: 'I wish you, on receipt of this letter, to pay to my aunt Pateria forty *solidi* for shoes for her boys and four hundred *modii* of wheat; to the lady Palatina, the widow of Urbicus, twenty *solidi* and three hundred *modii* of wheat; to Felix's widow, the lady Viviana, twenty *solidi* and three hundred *modii* of wheat.'[54] It was a charitable undertaking to protect the individuals of a class whose position had been shattered and could no longer protect its own. Under the papal aegis came not only direct charity but also the safeguarding of inheritances and legacies. One recipient of charity was an itinerant organ-grinder with his monkey, another was a patrician of Sicily, Venantius, who had briefly become a monk; his return to the world and perhaps to a rather frivolous circle of literary friends grieved Gregory but did not impair their friendship. Venantius married a lady of some beauty, Italica, and they had two daughters, Barbara and Antonina. When Venantius fell ill and was harassed by creditors, Gregory wrote to the girls to assure them that he would fully protect their interests.[55]

[53] Johannes Diaconus, *Vita*, II, 24–8.   [54] *Registrum*, I, 39.
[55] *Ibid.*, I, 34; IX, 123; XI, 30, 35, 36, 78; *Dial.*, I, 9.

Other charges pressed heavily upon the Church: Pope Gregory was forced to buy peace from Agilulf with 500 lb. in gold, and even to provide pay for the few scattered imperial garrisons in the towns of the west coast of Italy.[56] The buildings and structures of Rome itself required constant and expensive attention. To the prefect of Italy, whose responsibility it now was, he wrote in concern at the condition of the aqueducts, cut and damaged in the sieges of the city: 'They are so overlooked and neglected that unless more care of them is taken they will shortly fall into complete ruin.'[57] In former days of peace, a large and complex organization had maintained them, the drainage of the city and the retaining walls of the Tiber banks; that organization had now vanished. Of the aqueducts, only the Aqua Virgo, which for much of its course ran underground, could now be relied upon. Vitigis had made his last attempt to take the city through this water channel, which could not be blocked up easily, and now its line determined the settlement of Rome's population. The others, patchily repaired after being frequently cut, and improperly maintained, leaked and formed marshes under their junctions; the drainage of low-lying parts of the city also became imperfect through neglect, and unrepaired embankments to the river allowed floods to overflow the streets. All these interruptions to the normal servicing that had hitherto kept them in good repair, and the insufficient resources to make good the damage, allowed the city to become a wetter, more unhealthy place. It is noteworthy that Gregory, whose lifetime spanned the Gothic wars and the sieges, should have suffered from a periodic low fever. There were further hazards: grain brought from Sicily could in flood time be ruined in the granaries as Rome became ever more at the mercy of the elements and its citizens had less control over their environment. These disasters could have repercussions. Gregory's successor Sabinian was forced in time of shortage to sell the Church's grain, an action which earned him great unpopularity and the stoning of his funeral cortege; the price he had fixed, thirty *modii* a *solidus*, was in fact twice the price of Theoderic's reign.[58]

From Gregory also we get the fullest picture of the desolation of Italy and of the Italian spirit during the cumulative disasters of the

[56] *Ibid.*, II, 45.   [57] *Ibid.*, XII, 6.
[58] LP. I, 315; Gregory of Tours, HF., X, 1; Paulus Diaconus, *Vita*, 2, 29.

sixth century. This is contained in the four books of the *Dialogues*, written between 593–4. In these, he pictures himself in a Roman garden, almost overcome by the temporal and spiritual cares so urgently thrust upon him, and there he encounters the Roman deacon Peter, a friend of his youth and former rector of the papal patrimonies in Sicily and Campania, a tried and trusted administrator. To him, almost as if to convince himself that God has not entirely deserted his country, he begins to talk of the saints who have lived and the wonders worked and the graces shown in Italy within the century. Peter has not heard the full tale; he appears as slightly slow and rather sceptical, a foil and a check to Gregory's rising enthusiasm. Following the military disasters of the century, it is an account of triumphs, of encounters with the Devil and his routing, of the courage of charity and of perseverance in prayer. It is the reverse of Procopius's story of the ambitions of Justinian, the jealousies of his generals and the self-defeating military conquests.

'I did not know', says Peter, 'that any had shone remarkably in Italy in the working of miracles so that I cannot know with whom you compare yourself. I have no doubt that there have been good men in this country but I did not imagine they had performed signs and wonders: if they have, then these events have been so hidden in silence that we cannot know whether they took place.' To which Gregory replies: 'If I should relate merely what I alone have come to know through the evidence of perfect and proved men, good men and orthodox, or from my personal experience, I should not finish before nightfall.' He then relates the wonders of the great upsurge of the monastic life that had overtaken Italy in the sixth century, an upsurge that embraced all walks of life from the nobles who gave estates and patronage to the religious houses to the peasants and Goths who turned to the service of God in a crumbling world–an upsurge whose dominant representative was St. Benedict.[59]

The *Dialogues* and the histories they present point to the changes in Roman thinking. By contrast to the Gelasian decrees of a century earlier, *de libris recipiendis et non recipiendis*, which presupposed a critical, scholarly society to receive the history and literature of the Church to the exclusion and condemnation of more popular forms, Gregory's encouragement and adoption of these same spontaneous,

[59] *Dial.* I, prologue.

uncritical, unintellectual literary forms which were to remain the staple of religious reading for centuries is marked. He was not directly responsible for this process towards a popular literature. Throughout the century–partly from the forgeries of the great Roman families and factions in the early electoral struggles, partly as a result of the decline in learning and partly through the introduction of new patron saints from the East–interest in the passions of the martyrs had been growing. But Gregory's work was to be the most perfect of the *genre*. Early in the seventh century it was to provide the inspiration for that classic of Greek spirituality, the *Spiritual Meadow* of the monk John Moschus of Sinai, who had lived in Rome; and when the *Dialogues* were translated into Greek they were sufficient to establish his name, alone of popes, in the Eastern church. The emphasis is on the triumphs growing out of the collapse of the old order and on the scenes of horror this brought in the provinces contiguous to Rome– Campania, Valeria, Tuscia, and Samnium–through the Lombard and Gothic wars. The monks, distinguished by their pallor and emaciation, and their homes became the natural refuges for the stricken *contadini*. At Sora in Campania the countrymen fled from the Lombards to a monastery; the abbot refused to surrender them and was butchered by the invaders.[60] Bishop Herculanus of Perugia was executed on the walls of his city for his part in leading the resistance.[61] No travellers were safe from wandering bands of troops of all armies; the monastery of Benedict's disciple Equitius in Valeria was sacked by the Lombards; in the same province they also captured two monks from the monastery of Abbot Valentio and hung them from trees.[62] Worse perhaps were the memories of Totila's deliberate atrocities: a certain monk Benedict was put to death by the Gothic king by being roasted in an oven.[63]

But it is not the martyrdoms and desolation that are Gregory's main theme: the stories of the Roman martyrs at the hands of the pagan emperors had gained hold on the popular imagination. Gregory's theme, for the first time, and as though even in this departing from the memory of the imperial past in Italy, is of the endurance of the confessor, the holy man who lives out his life in

[60] *Ibid.*, IV, 23.   [61] *Ibid.*, III, 13.   [62] *Ibid.*, I, 4; IV, 22.
[63] *Ibid.*, III, 18. See also B. de Gaiffier, 'Les Héros des Dialogues de Grégoire le Grand inscrits au nombre des Saints', (*AB.*, 83, 1965).

constant wrestling with evil, and is little concerned with the immediate decision needed for martyrdom. It was a struggle essentially hidden, permitting the deacon Peter's ignorance of events. Gregory was a man of intelligence and wide experience, and he himself intended the book to be documentary and factual. 'To remove all occasions for doubt among my readers' he says, 'I will in every individual passage that I write give my authorities clearly.'[64] Besides six stories from his own experience, the authorities he quotes include his predecessor Pope Pelagius and two bishops.[65] There survives also a letter he wrote while in the course of collecting his material; in July 593 he asked Bishop Maximian of Syracuse to send all the information he could gather on the Italian Fathers.[66] But most of his material is popular tradition, oral or written. 'What I am telling you is known to the people; and the priest and vergers of St. Agatha in the Suburra testify that they both heard and saw it.' 'Certain religious men in Apulia used to testify to this.' 'The marvels that are commonly told of him by our elders . . .'[67] These are the phrases Gregory used—and he had risen through the imperial service to be the highest judge in Rome. He had also served in the papal diplomatic service and had experience in sifting rumour from fact, and as pope he knew the men under him, having corresponded with and selected many of them.

Gregory was a realist; the *Dialogues* and his sermons testify to his grasp of the need to build up a strong Christian faith as the basis of society when the Empire—and with it, economic prosperity and military security—was fading in the West. Before his consecration he had led the people of Rome, grouped in their various orders, in a penitential procession of intercession, and in St. John Lateran had preached for special acts of contrition to remove the plague. To this end also, in the prayers he composed for public recitation, he emphasized the great weight of sin that was bringing the Lombard retribution.[68] Above all he preached to the people of Rome on his Stational visitations. Forty sermons on the Gospels have survived

---

[64] *Dial.*, I, prologue. [65] *Ibid.*, III, 16; 35; IV, 33.
[66] *Registrum*, III, 30. [67] *Dial.*, III, 30, 5, 2.
[68] See H. Ashworth, 'The influence of the Lombard Invasions on the Gregorian Sacramentary', (*Bulletin of the John Rylands Library*, 36, 1953–4) and 'The Liturgical Prayers of Gregory the Great', (*Traditio*, 15, 1959).

from the first three years of his pontificate, and from the years 593–4 another twenty on Ezekiel. The style was directly popular–using the method of allegory and mystical interpretation with the matter, as in the *Dialogues*, interspersed with anecdotes–in contrast with the mannerisms of the literary bishops earlier in the century; a pragmatic style directed to fortifying a sustaining faith in society, rather than a scholarly or literary exercise.[69] Care was taken that his writings should reach a wider audience: a collection of his homilies on the Gospels was dedicated to Bishop Secundinus of Taormina, and of his sermons on Ezekiel to his disciple Marinianus of Ravenna. As they were being preached inaccurate versions were in circulation–'people are eating this food only half-cooked'–and he placed an authoritative copy of the text of the homilies in the Lateran archives.[70]

The bishops to whom, among many others, Gregory sent copies of his sermons were those from whom he was hoping to create a new model episcopate and for whom he wrote the *Regula Pastoralis*. 'I do not care to observe the position, force or government of prepositions, for I think it absolutely intolerable to fetter the words of the Divine Oracle by the rules of Donatus.' A bishop was condemned for over-fondness of classical literature, but this was not philistinism: in these embattled days a bishop could have no time for Virgil.[71] The threat of paganism was never far off and in Sardinia and parts of France remained openly active; war, famine and plague might drive a Christian people into hysterical aberration. So while he strove to restore a uniform orthodoxy and reconsecrated the remaining Arian churches of Rome, he condemned an excessive puritan movement in the city that claimed the Jewish Sabbath as a second day of rest and sought to ban washing on Sundays. In the maintenance of this balance in western Christendom the bishop was the lynch-pin: 'Consider, brother, that the work you have been called to is one of toil, not of leisure,' ran the contemporary notice of appointment for

[69] F. Gastaldelli, 'Osservazioni per un profilo letterario di S. Gregorio Magno', (*Salesianum*, 26, 1964), and W. F. Bolton, 'The Supra-Historical Sense in the Dialogues of Gregory I', (*Aevum*, 33, 1959).

[70] *Registrum*, IV, 17a.

[71] *Ibid.*, III, 53a; XI, 34. See M. L. Laistner, 'The Church's attitude to pagan literature', (*History*, 20, 1935) and H. de Lubac, 'S. Gregoire et la grammaire', (*RSR.*, 48, 1960).

a bishop–not, that is, to the cultivated literary ease that had been the classical ideal and the distinguishing mark of the vanished nobility of Rome.[72] A sharp contrast to Cassiodorus's eulogy of the consulship earlier in the century: 'Your good fortune exceeds that of sovereigns since you wear the highest honours and yet have not the tedium of actually ruling.' Traditional social distinctions were also passing, as Gregory felt. He wrote that the regular use of the pallium by Archbishop John of Ravenna was not only contrary to ecclesiastical custom, it was also a civil and social distinction from which churchmen should be entirely free. The world that cared for Ciceronianisms, where a bishop was a politician and a social lion, the world of the Gallic bishops of his diplomatic experience in Constantinople, was passing; in speech and churchmanship the essentials alone remained.

Learning and the learned professions had not, of course, entirely vanished from Rome after the Gothic Wars. Legal studies were maintained, Justinian's Code was introduced, and the Greek additions translated into Latin by Julian in an adequate if unscholarly translation. Gregory himself knew the civil law well: his writings give over fifty references. Lawyers in Rome still practised the business of daily life–a document drawn up for a client contains this subscription and address: 'I, Theodosius, *vir honestis, tabellio* (notary) of the city of Rome, having my office in the portico in the Suburra, in the fourth region, drafted this document.' Doctors also still practised: the Byzantine physician Alexander was living in Rome about 560 and his works were translated into Latin. Gregory himself was interested in medicine, using medical terms in his correspondence and translating those in Greek, though this appears to have been the sole extent of his Greek. His entourage contained several doctors, one of whom had studied in Alexandria, and included the brothers Copiosus and Justin; Copiosus entered his monastery of St. Andrew on the Coelian. When his friend and disciple Marinianus, whom he had made Archbishop of Ravenna, fell ill, the pope summoned all the doctors of repute in Rome and ordered them to choose one of their number to attend the archbishop. But other professions were declining. There

[72] On Gregory's influence on the episcopate, see H. Hurtzen, 'Gregor der Grosse und der mittelalterliche Episkopat', (*Zeitschrift für Kirchengeschichte*, 73, 1962).

appears, for example, by the end of the century to have been only one banker in Rome.[73]

Gregory, it has been seen, had less time for the encouragement of purely literary or speculative studies. His genius was for administration, which the circumstances demanded, and he gave the papacy a pastoral cast, in contrast to the speculative theology still maintained in the East. This attitude prevailed: Pope Honorius in the seventh century, embroiled by the easterners in the questions of Christ's will, declared that the whole debate was one for grammarians, and his own answers show a parable-like approach, one that was pastoral and not purely academic. He, or his secretary John, later Pope John IV, compared philosophers to croaking frogs. But the study of theology and pure literature, and its teaching to the young, was not extinguished. The epitaph of a young Boethius, son of the notary Eugenius, who died in 578 at the age of eleven gives evidence of a precocious poetic talent. 'Your teacher saw his pupil in the first flower of song you undertook, and was amazed; young in years but mature, you were eager for instruction, and avid for poetry.'[74] The traditional centres still continued: Bishop Victor of Capua had in 547 produced a new edition of the Bible, with corrected orthography; Bishop Maximian of Ravenna, who died in 556, revised St. Jerome's version of the Old Testament 'so that ignorant or unskilled copyists cannot corrupt the text'. At the Lucullanum monastery a certain Facistus in 560 recopied an edition of Augustine's letters. Augustinian scholarship was strong in Campania: in 559 a rich layman near Cumae revised his *De Trinitate*; and in 582, even as the Lombards besieged Naples, the notary of the cathedral there issued a new edition of the *Excerpta* by Eugippius from Augustine's letters.[75] But little original was produced, and Gregory found difficulty in providing for an educated clergy. Many were over-occupied in secular affairs; the pope forbade the ordination of unlettered priests, and he found that deacons were being appointed for their fine voices rather than for their knowledge. The clergy of Rome were a corporation closely and

---

[73] Tjader, *op. cit.*, pp. 18–19; *Dial.*, III, 33, 35, IV, 57. G. Damizia, 'Il "Registrum Epistolarum" di S. Gregorio Magno ed il "Corpus Iuris Civilis" ', (*Benedictina*, 2, 1948): F. Ermini, 'La Scuola in Roma nel VI secolo', (*Medio Evo Latino, Studi e Ricerche*, 1938).

[74] CIL. VI, 8401.　　　　　[75] P. Riché, *op. cit.*

traditionally connected with city social life; young lectors and chamberlains of the Lateran still lived in their family houses, and it was only gradually that this dependence died out. Gregory provided a corrective to a certain extent by employing monks in key positions in his administration and by building up the pope's *familia* in distinction to the city clergy. One of his earliest acts was the removal from office of the archdeacon, holder of the most powerful post next to the pope, and often regarded as having a prescriptive right to the papal succession. In his place he substituted a new deputy, the *Vicedominus*, hitherto an occasional legatine appointment, to whom the supreme administration of the bishop's palace and the charities and provisioning were subordinated. The archidiaconate was not ended, but had suffered a grievous blow in prestige.

It was as a practical administrator rather than as a theoretical theologian that Gregory was remembered. His great books, the *Pastoral Care* and the *Dialogues*, were directed to the immediate ends of evangelization; the missions to the English and to Sardinia had a similarly practical purpose. His administrative achievements made possible the survival of Rome itself, by employing the vast wealth that the Church still retained to feed, maintain and defend the city. From the large quantity of his surviving *Correspondence*, the whole process of the Church's utilization of its estates and properties can be realized. So, too, can the habits and methods of Gregory's mind. No detail, however small, escaped his notice. Horse-breeding had become unprofitable in the absence of the Ostrogothic army, which had formerly provided a market to sustain the estate of the elder Cassiodorus, and was therefore abandoned on Gregory's instructions. He ordered the slaughter of cattle too old for milk or breeding and supervised the direction of individual charities. A constant preoccupation was the correct administration of legacies and the protection of the rights of heirs, especially minors; ominously, public administration—weakened by the wars and by the failures in the commissariat—was deteriorating in its respect for justice. The habits of the administrator can also be noted in Gregory's letters: his desire for an exact clarification of duties and accounts; his requests for lists of property, profits, and persons in receipt of charity to be drawn up. But through all appears the man who, as he so often and sincerely expressed to his correspondents, considered his pontificate a recall from the real life of his desire, in contemplation, and was spurred to his administrative exactitude by urgent love for his people.

Some properties were still privately owned; some were leased by the Church to individuals. The register of Pope Honorius's dealings in the first half of the seventh century in leasing land to private citizens has in part survived: among those who took estates were churches in the city, officers of the imperial administration, city officials and their widows. Gregory leased some estates near Rome– on long leases and for low rents–but most of these had been heavily devastated in the disorders and were largely unproductive. It was to the great properties under direct papal administration that Rome looked for sustenance.

These estates[76] were divided into units called 'patrimonies' and were administered overall by a Roman cleric, normally a subdeacon called the 'rector'. They comprised many individual properties, each managed by a bailiff or 'conductor'. Around Rome there were the patrimonies named after the great radial roads or the districts they covered–the Appian, Tuscan, Labican, Tiburtine, Sabine, and Caietine–and there were also separate properties in Provence, Sardinia and North Africa, the product of legacies or of outright donations by emperors from Constantine onwards. We have seen popes in correspondence with clerics and officials in France and Africa, begging for aid to be forwarded. But the most productive estates–the least ravished by war and in the richest agricultural areas –were in Sicily, the great grain producer that had supplied Rome for centuries, and in southern Italy. These provided Rome's main supplies, shipped to Porto to feed an almost destitute population, and the bulk of Gregory's correspondence is devoted to them. Instructions to conductors and rectors about the dispatch of supplies and the conditions of the peasants are frequent. Gelasius, a century before, had drawn up a register of the properties which Gregory brought up to date and employed, but his first consideration was to tighten control over the administration to prevent exploitation of his tenants

[76] See P. Fabre, *De Patrimoniis Ecclesiae Romanae*, (1892); E. Moresco, *Les patrimoines de l'Eglise Romaine*, (1916); E. Spearing, *The Patrimony of the Roman Church at the time of Gregory the Great*, (1918); L. Cracco– Ruggini, 'Vicende rurali dell'Italia Antica dall'età tetrarchica ai Longo- bardi', (*Rivista Storica Italiana*, 76, 1964).

(serfs, bound to their home estates, but gaining security thereby) and marginal profiteering by the officials over them. There were a considerable number of exactions upon the peasants: a one-*solidus* tax upon marriage, a land-tax paid three times a year, and certain death duties. An oppressive measure, which Gregory did his best to check, was the compulsory purchase of grain from the peasantry at fixed prices, and in certain annual quantities, leading to abuses as old as Verres; the pope insisted that even in times of shortage the current market price be paid. Abuses went further than this; some bailiffs employed a *modius* which contained eighteen *sextarii* as against the commercial *modius* of sixteen *sextarii*, and some even raised it to twenty-five. Officials were also taking a percentage from the peasants' taxes paid in cash. Gregory brought an end to these practices by insisting upon stricter supervision of officials. Clergy were employed where possible, and every official on appointment was presented with a form indicating his line of conduct. The central administration of the papacy was also tightened. The notaries were formed into a college under a *primicerius* (the chief clerk or chancellor) and a deputy (the *secundicerius*), and officials were appointed, as the treasurer and the accountant. All were, nominally at least, to be clergy; laymen appointed were to be tonsured and formally enrolled among the clergy. All were directly under the pope's vigilance.

The purposes behind this vast organization were the maintenance of Rome, the provision of funds for charity, and the payment of subsidies to imperial troops and peace-offerings to the Lombards. The estates nearer the city were normally reserved for supplying the city churches with the means to continue worship. Each rector kept a register of his properties, transferring on orders from the pope those granted in endowment or lease. So Gregory instructed the subdeacon Felix, rector of the Appian patrimony, on a papal grant made to St. Paul's-without-the-Walls: 'Therefore we instruct your Experience to delete from your brief the above-mentioned estate Aquae Salviae, with its named component farms, and to make this transfer.'[77] Local treasuries were maintained: in the Provençal estates, whose Gallic coin was not current in Rome, purchases were made locally to be forwarded to Rome–among them, specifically ordered, was the purchase of English slaves, to be sent to Rome for education. The

[77] *Registrum*, XIV, 14.

Sicilian estates ran two treasuries which dispersed aid direct to local bishops or institutions; on occasion there was extraordinary aid, in times of emergency. Gregory ordered Cyprian, the Sicilian rector, to send 1,000 *modii* of wheat to a bishop Zeno of Epirus as quickly as possible; this aid was limited only by the availability of shipping, for 2,000 *modii* were to be sent if possible.[78] Thessalonica and Alexandria also received supplies in time of hardship, and the Patriarchate of Alexandria in particular maintained a flourishing trade with the west. One of its grain ships, built from timber grown on the papacy's Calabrian estates, had a capacity of 10,000 *modii*.[79] Sicily remained one of Rome's important links with the East; the introduction of Sicilian saints such as St. Agatha, and the dedication of churches to them, emphasized these links and the island's importance to all of central Italy.

Pope Gregory established the pattern that the papacy was to retain in the succeeding centuries, shaping the Roman Church as the *de facto* authority of Italy in the provision of the essentials for Rome's continuance, ready and able to supplement the imperial administration itself in the preservation of a Roman Italy. His reign also marks the spread and intensification of the influence of St. Peter and of the Roman See which became the natural focus of the northern nations as the papacy recovered from the humiliations it had suffered under Silverius, Vigilius and Pelagius I, and from the suspicions aroused in the Three Chapters controversy. So although a good subject of the Emperor, bound up still in the context of Imperial Rome, Gregory as a realist adapted techniques and attitudes to new conditions which won for the Western Church explicit moral independence of the Empire.[80] The papacy towered in Italy, finding itself isolated from a social and political context in which it had first acquired its pre-eminence. It was therefore free of any stifling associations, and able to evolve its expression of moral authority standing apart from its milieu. Gregory himself was not fully aware of this; he lamented the passing of a whole society in Rome, although he emphasized the advantages that lack of trammels brought for the service of religion.

[78] *Ibid.*, VI, 4.   [79] *Ibid.*, X, 21.

[80] E.g. in defence of Rome's primacy against the patriarchate of Constantinople. See S. Vailhé, 'S. Grégoire le Grand et le titre de patriarche oecumenique', (*Echos d'Orient*, 11, 1908).

His successors, whom his name overshadows, continued his work, a work of endurance in the slow evangelization of the north, the gradual evolving of new themes of loyalty and unity, the painful resistance to the perversion of doctrine. The resources of the papacy, material and moral, represented the sole hope of Rome's survival and fashioned the shape of its future.

4

THE ROMAN CHURCH AND CLERGY

The civil administration of Rome in the years subject to the East was overshadowed in prestige, in quality and in effectiveness by the Church's own administration which through its management of charity, of its great estates and of a wide diplomacy, determined Rome's survival in the declining years of Byzantine power in the West. The Roman clergy formed a tight corporation with a common identity, a common interest and common privileges–the word 'cleros' retained its Greek connotation of a chosen group apart. Entry into the clerical ranks provided the sole opportunity for the realization of talent and ambition–whether spiritual or secular–and for learning. As a corporation the clergy retained a close family aspect, being in fact as well as in description the *familia*, the household of the pope. Recruitment was wide and service, except for episcopal promotion, lasted for life–Dioscorus in the sixth century, as a former deacon of Alexandria, was an exception. The members of the Roman clergy often joined in extreme youth and were of diverse origins, coming from Italy, Sicily, or the East.[1]

Their corporate nature was emphasized by their distinctive privileges. Chief among these was the use of the *mappula*, a white, fringed saddlecloth, the *campagi*, flat, black slippers, and the *udones*, white stockings, all inherited from the imperial senate.[2] These distinctions were jealously guarded; in 593 the clergy of Ravenna claimed the privilege of the *mappula* for themselves and Gregory the Great,

[1] Of the 23 popes who reigned from 604 to 715, seven were Roman-born, six came from the provinces immediately adjacent to Rome, two were Sicilian, four Greek, three Syrian and one from Dalmatia.

[2] M. Andrieu, *Les Ordines Romani de l'Haut Moyen Age*, (Spicilegium Sacrum Lovaniense, II, 23, 24, 28, 29; 1931–61): vol. 2, Ordo VIII; vol. 4, Ordo XXXVI. For the derivation of episcopal garb from that of the imperial magistrature which it largely replaced see Th. Klauser, 'Der Ursprung der bischöflichen Insignien und Ehrenrecht', (*Bonner Akademische Reden*, 1, 1948).

hesitating at first to allow it, finally conceded its use only to the senior deacons of that see.[3] The deacons of Messina also shared the right to the *campagi*, and complained bitterly to Gregory when it was usurped by the deacons of Catano.[4] Their removal was the symbol of degradation from or non-recognition of orders; Pope Martin was stripped of his after his trial in Constantinople before the senate, and in 769 the Roman synod removed the *campagi* from the usurper Constantine.[5] When Pope Constantine visited the East early in the eighth century, Justinian II provided *mappulae* for the horses of the imperial stable ridden by the pope and his entourage on their solemn entry into Constantinople,[6] and in the mid-eighth century the privilege was inserted into the Donation of Constantine by the Roman clergy as having been granted by Constantine I himself.[7] When Pope Conon stepped outside the ranks of the Roman clergy in appointing the Syracusan deacon Constantine as rector of the Sicilian patrimonies, the clergy's objections were as much to the permission granted the stranger to use this prerogative as to the loss of a profitable office to their number. It was a privilege rarely granted outside the Roman clergy; on occasion, to Frankish prelates.[8]

A boy could enter the ranks of the Roman clergy in a number of ways. His parents might present him at one of the city churches to receive minor orders and perform auxiliary services, or as a youth he might be educated in one of the various departments of the Lateran administration – the papal chamber in personal attendance on the pope, the office of the *vestararius*, or at the *schola cantorum*. These modes of entry and training tended to reinforce the corporate sense of the clergy who on several occasions were capable of closing their ranks to avoid any dilution of their unique status. Gregory I attempted to end the practice of employing young laymen in the papal chamber as *cubicularii*, which had been an honourable service for those of good family. His view was that it was inappropriate for the pope to be attended by laymen who took minor orders and filled the ranks of the ordained clergy with men involved in secular and family business whose aim was to be fashionable ministers only. Preferring his own companions from his monastery he chose monks from his household

---

[3] Gregory I, *Registrum*, III, 54, 66.   [4] *Ibid.*, VIII, 27.
[5] *PL.* 129, col. 595; *LP.* I, 472.   [6] *LP.* I, 390.
[7] *PL.* 8, 576–7.   [8] *LP.* I, 369.

instead. These came to hold the senior positions in the administration.[9] After Gregory's death there was, under Sabinian, a strong reaction away from this monastic trend, but Sabinian's successor Boniface, a disciple and admirer of Gregory, reverted to a monastic favouritism. In a synod he answered bitterly-voiced clerical criticisms that the pastoral nature of the papal administration was unsuited to monks who had withdrawn from the world and were not commonly in clerical orders, by pointing to the achievements of Gregory's missionaries, all monks, and to the great Martin of Tours. But the reaction was brief and Pope Deusdedit, himself the son of a sub-deacon, finally restored the secular clergy to their accustomed positions in the administration.[10]

With the reopening of Europe under the Carolingian dynasty the Roman clergy once more found their status threatened as Roman practices became more widespread. In the ninth century the deacon John expressed in his life of Gregory I the xenophobia that was becoming increasingly apparent among the Romans. Attributing to Gregory the compilation of the antiphonary and the organization of the *schola cantorum*, he spoke of the great Roman chant, made available to the northerners but corrupted by their native melodies and their inferior, barbaric skill. The Franks retorted with charges of deliberate obstruction by the Romans; that, when Charlemagne, seeking to unify the rites of his dominions, asked for and obtained from the pope twelve papal chantors, these clerics, jealous of the glory of the Franks, agreed among themselves to vary their teaching and so to preserve the pre-eminence of the Roman chant.[11] Again, it was the clergy of the Lateran who, in 826 when Radoin asked for the body of St. Sebastian, led the opposition to continued Frankish spoliation of the city's store of relics.

To serve as *cubicularius*, in immediate attendance on the pope, was a direct path to high office; popes Gregory II, Stephen II and his

[9] Gregory I, *Registrum*, V, 57a.

[10] *LP.* I, 315, 319; Mansi, 10, 504f; see also O. Nussbaum, 'Kloster, Priestermönch und Privatmesse', (*Theophaneia*, 14, 1961), p. 70.

[11] John the Deacon, *Vita S. Gregorii*, II, c. 1; Notker, *De Gestis Karoli imperatoris*, (*MGH. SS.* I, 734): see also S. J. P. Van Dijk, 'Papal Schola versus Charlemagne', (*Festschrift Smits van Waestberghe*, 1963) and, on Gregory as putative founder of the Schola, 'Gregory the Great founder of the Urban Schola Cantorum', (*EL.* 77, 1963).

brother Paul I, and Pascal I all served there. Service was not confined to the minor orders and there was some selective recruitment; Stephen III was a monk of St. Chrysogonus, placed there by Gregory III, when Zachary summoned him to the *cubiculum*. He continued to serve there even after ordination as priest of St. Cecilia, under Stephen II and Paul I, the latter of whom he nursed on his deathbed.[12] In spite of Gregory I's attempts, lay chamberlains continued to serve with clerics, while from the church of SS. Cosmas and Damian comes a ninth century epitaph of a certain Leo 'to whom the pope granted the honorary style of *cubicularius*'.[13] Other departments of the Lateran also provided avenues for promotion; Leo III as priest of St. Susanna continued to serve in the vestiariat.[14]

The *schola cantorum*, while retaining its prime functions to train and provide for the chant of the papal services, also served as a means of educating potential clerics from the boys who left. Institutions throughout the city–and especially the orphanages, which were closely protected by the Lateran–were combed for boys with suitable voices; of future popes, Sergius II, who was orphaned of both parents at the age of twelve, was brought up in the *schola*.[15] But it was not confined to the training of the young alone; the future Sergius I, who must have been a mature man on his arrival from Sicily at the time of Adeodatus only twelve years before his own election, was placed there by the reigning pope.[16]

The tradition of private education did not cease and, in the late eighth and ninth centuries acquired new vigour from the revived aristocracy. Hadrian I was brought up by his uncle, a *primicerius* in the papal service, while also serving in S. Marco in the Via Lata near his home.[17] Nicholas I was educated by his father, the *regionarius* Theodore who, against the advice of some holy man, delayed his son's formal entry into the clericate. Stephen V was taught by his uncle, bishop Zachary the papal librarian, and lived, like Hadrian, in his family's house in the aristocratic quarter of the Via Lata until Hadrian II took him into the Lateran as a subdeacon.[18]

[12] *LP.* I, 396, 440, 463, 468; II, 52.
[13] G. de Rossi in *Bulletin d'archéologie chrétienne*, 1870, p. 113; A. Silvagni, *Monumenta Epigraphica Christiana*, 1943, I, pl. xxxvi, n. 3.
[14] LP. II, 1.   [15] LP. II, 86.   [16] LP. I, 371.
[17] LP. I, 371.   [18] LP. II, 151, 191.

The minor orders, of doorkeeper, lector and exorcist, had from the fourth century become virtually functionless through frequent bestowal on children, but they retained a vestigial place to provide for junior clerics undergoing their training. A candidate was presented to the pope by his father or a relative or, if orphaned, by the head of the institution that had brought him up. The pope would thereupon name a day and a church for the boy's formal examination in reading proficiency—perhaps by reserving for him one of the lessons of the night office. This passed, he was enrolled among the clergy in a ceremony of blessing by the archdeacon: 'Almighty God, we beg that to this N., your servant, who has come here through love of Christ your son to lay down his hair, you may grant your Holy Spirit to guard in him for ever the religious profession.'[19] As the *mappula* was the especial insignia of the papal service in its closer sense, so the tonsure was the mark that set a man apart for a purely ecclesiastical career. Here there was a distinction to be made since the Roman style was to wear the hair short, in contrast to the Merovingian Franks or the Lombards—Gregory I refers to tenants of the Roman Church in Sicily as *tonsoratores*. In the eighth century when the inhabitants of the Lombard duchy of Spoleto commended themselves in loyalty to Pope Hadrian I, they symbolized this by cutting their hair off, in the Roman mode.[20] But the tonsure proper, a patch completely shaven, was the mark of the clergy distinct from the laity or the military. The Frankish monk Gotteschalk noted the secular fashions on his visit to Rome in 839: 'Noble Roman boys and even the youths among the Romans, both then and at this time, had long hair, coming down behind the ears to half-a-foot in length: and hence in admiration, or rather derision, are called *hypochoristicos*, "pretty things".'[21] Those who intended to live as clergy took the tonsure and then—perhaps a more decisive step—took orders as an acolyte which involved pastoral work in the various ecclesiastical regions as assistants to the priests and deacons. Promotion thereafter was limited by vacancies and age: the

[19] *Gregorian Sacramentary*, ed. H. A. Wilson, 1894, p. 139. See also M. Andrieu, 'Les ordres mineures dans l'ancien rite romain', (*RSR.*, 5, 1925); E. Josi, 'Lectores, Schola Cantorum, Clerici', (*EL.* 44, 1930).

[20] Gregory I, *Registrum*, IX, 22; LP. I, 496.

[21] Gotteschalk of Orbais, *Opuscula de Rebus Grammaticis, Opusculum II*, n. 3 (ed. D. Lambot, *Oeuvres Complets*, Spicilegium Sacrum Lovaniense, fasc. 20, 1945).

Quinisext Council of 692 formally laid down the rules which had long been traditionally observed concerning the interstices of the subsequent grades; subdeacons were to be at least 20 years of age, deacons 25, and priests 30.

The collegiate nature of Roman administration that had marked the republican offices of the consulate and pretorate, and latterly the imperial dignity itself, was perpetuated in the papal service among lay and clerics alike. The seven deacons, each in charge of one of the seven regions into which Rome had been ecclesiastically divided, and the priests, formed colleges under the archdeacon and archpriest respectively. In the seventh century, the lesser orders of the subdeacons who served in each region as deputy to the deacon, and the acolytes–perhaps six to each region, giving the deacon seven assistants altogether–were also grouped into a college, controlled by the archdeacon who had jurisdiction in any disputes or suits affecting them and any layman.[22] The archpriest, nominal head of a similar college of priests, did not have such authority, for the priests had no such collective functions as the lesser orders.

Gregory I extended the collegiate system to the (lay) regional notaries and the *defensors* of the Church, advocates charged with the administration of property; each of these new colleges was headed by a *primicerius*, with a deputy, the *secundicerius*.[23] The *primicerius* of the notaries was one of the senior officials of papal Rome, ranking as a chancellor and having the direction of the papal offices in the Lateran, the *scrinium*, where he managed the correspondence and the records and was responsible for their production when needed. Here pride in a formal Latin was longest preserved. The deacon John, a leader of the ninth century resurgence of Roman pride and antiquarianism, exaggerated when he wrote in his Life of Gregory I that in the Lateran (the 'palace of Latium' in his play on words) everyone spoke good Latin and wore the toga, but a fresco of the most articulate and stylistically flexible of the Latin Fathers, Augustine of Hippo, presided over the *scrinium*, with an inscription pro-

---

[22] OR. vol. 2, Ordo 1.

[23] Gregory I, VIII, 16; on the origin of *defensores*, see F. Martroye, 'Les "Defensores Ecclesiae" aux Ve et VIe siècles', (*Nouvelle Revue historique du droit français et étranger*, 1923): B. Fischer, 'Die Entwicklung des Institutes der Defensoren in der romische Kirche', (*EL.*, 48, 1934).

claiming him the patron of *romanum eloquium*.[24] It was the department of the *primicerius* that drew up, perhaps for the training of junior clerks, the collection of standard *formulae* used in papal correspondence, the *Liber Diurnus* of the Roman Church.[25] As the name implies, it presents the general scope of the regular Lateran correspondence: the reception of notices of the election of new bishops, their declarations of orthodoxy, and the issue of papal approbation;[26] permissions for the building of new churches and the translation of relics;[27] exchanges with private persons of land belonging to the Roman Church when full details of the land had to be entered;[28] notification of the deaths of popes to the exarch and the emperor, and to the archbishop and city council of Ravenna, to use their influence for a rapid confirmation of a successor;[29] the summoning of Italian bishops to the annual synod held in Rome on the anniversary of the pope's consecration, and receipt of the accepted reasons, illness or extreme age, for non-attendance;[30] the appointment of rectors and stewards of patrimonies, and of wardens of charitable institutions within the city.[31] The *primicerius* was therefore a person of high consequence in the Roman Church; his importance was recognized in that, with the archpriest and archdeacon, he was normally an administrator of the Church in an interregnum or the absence of the pope.[32]

The work handled by his office extended over most of the daily business of the Church and was especially important in the unsettled seventh century. From his office bishops were warned of accepting unattached clergy; refugees in the main from the Arab raids in North

[24] See Ph. Lauer, 'Les fouilles du Sancta Sanctorum au Latran', (*MAH*, 20, 1900); a list of those recorded as having worked in the papal *scrinium* is in L. Santifaller, 'Saggio di un Elenco dei funzionari, impiegati e scrittori della Cancelleria Pontificia dall'inizio all' anno 1099', (*BISI*, 56, 1940): see also N. Ertl, 'Diktatoren frühmittelalterlichen Papstbriefe', (*Archiv für Urkundenforschung*, 15, 1937–8).

[25] *Liber Diurnus Romanorum Pontificum*, ed. T. Sickel, 1889.

[26] *LD*. form. 1; form. 2; form. 3–5; form. 6; form. 73–6.

[27] *LD*. form. 10; form. 11; form. 12; form. 16; form. 17–22; form. 21–6.

[28] *LD*. form. 33.

[29] *LD*. form. 58, 59, 60–3.

[30] *LD*. form. 42–4.

[31] *LD*. form. 51–6.

[32] *LD*. form. 59; Martin I, *Epistola II*, (*PL*. 87, col. 201).

Africa, where the memories of many ancient heresies still lingered. Since they might be, for example, Manichees or even Donatists with a tendency to rebaptism, a full inquiry must be instituted.[33] Other letters dealt with recruitment to the Roman clergy itself: the wardens appointed to the orphanages maintained by the Church must be rigorous in avoiding loss from endowed lands, for the orphanages supplied most of the cantors.[34] Managers of hostels for pilgrims were given full instructions on appointment: 'That you zealously prepare their beds, with bedclothes, to receive the sick and needy, and provide them with care and all necessities; an annual ration of oil for the sick and poor, and anything else their sickness requires. Provide also doctors and nursing . . .'[35] Under the *primicerius* came also the maintenance of a postal service; he was to ensure that papal notaries or other emissaries were given mounts from city to city – the bishops of towns *en route* were to be informed of this.[36] The Roman Church probably did not have the means to keep up a postal service of its own: Gregory I had ended the Church's horsebreeding on Sicilian properties when he found it did not pay.[37]

The *scriniarii* were tonsured but did not normally proceed to major orders. For those who did there were two distinct channels – the priesthood and the diaconate. The diaconate was not (although the subdiaconate was) normally or necessarily a step towards the priesthood, or a bar to subsequent direct promotion to the papacy itself. There were insurmountable barriers to admission into the major orders – commission of unnatural vice, of adultery or of the violation of nuns.[38] The higher ranks were not yet formally known as cardinal-priests or cardinal-deacons; the term *cardinal* was in the late sixth century confined in use to clerics temporarily seconded to other sees in times of emergency or shortage following the Lombard invasions.[39] Only by the eighth century was it beginning to be used, unofficially, of the clergy of Rome (and, in imitation, of the clergy of other great sees, such as Ravenna), and thereafter more frequently. The epitaph of one deacon, who as archdeacon attended the synod of 721, has

---

[33] *LD*. form. 6. [34] *LD*. form. 97.
[35] *LD*. form. 46. [36] *LD*. form. 49.
[37] Gregory I, *Registrum*, II, 38. [38] *OR*. vol. 3, Ordo XXXIV.
[39] See Stephan Kuttner, 'Cardinalis: the history of a canonical concept', (*Traditio*, 3, 1945).

survived in the crypt of St. Peter's. He calls himself cardinal in the looser sense, then coming into use; his name, Moschus, implies his Eastern origin: 'The tomb in this church of Christ's venerable martyr Cecilia, is where Moschus, humble deacon of the Apostolic See, lies at rest; I ask you to pray for me to the Lord that, by the intervention of that same most holy Virgin, I may deserve to receive indulgence for all my sins: a cardinal, living in the time of Gregory III, a.d. 735.' St. Cecilia's was the *titulus* of a priest, never of a deacon, and at this period the regionary deacons did not have *tituli* – the eighteen deaconries of the later cardinal-deacons had a separate origin.

In earlier centuries and still in the sixth, the archdeacon, who was the pope's right-hand man in administration and also his chief theological adviser, had come to acquire an almost presumptive right to the succession. Early in the seventh century a patriarch of Constantinople could still regard the Roman archdeacon as the natural heir, and the seventh century *formula* of notification of an election also assumed the archdeacon's election.[40] But Gregory I weakened the archidiaconate by the regular appointment of a new deputy, the *vicedominus*, and from Pelagius I to Valentine in 827 no archdeacon was elected. Deacons however were, for it was in their hands that experience of the higher administration, especially that of the patrimonies and of diplomatic missions, was concentrated; of the priests who succeeded to the papacy, most appear to have been selected on a reputation for charity.

One extremely influential post, normally held by a deacon, was that of *apocrisiarius*, the papal representative in Constantinople. It was a post demanding considerable secular and ecclesiastical ability as well as theological acumen, and Pelagius II commented that the *apocrisiarius* was one 'who could never be more than an hour away from the palace'. By virtue of the qualities required and experience gained, several holders rose to the papacy: Vigilius, Pelagius I and Gregory in the sixth century: and Sabinian, Boniface IV and Martin in the seventh. The *apocrisiarius* had an official residence, the *domus Placidiae*, which was perhaps bequeathed to the Roman Church in the sixth century by Placidia, granddaughter of the Western Emperor Valentinian III. The clergy of the papal mission served two

[40] *LD*. form. 58.

neighbouring churches with the Latin rite, SS. Sergius and Bacchus and SS. Peter and Paul. Vigilius, as pope, had lived there under virtual house arrest.[41]

The *apocrisiarius*, as a subject of the Empire, was not an ambassador and could play a considerable part in the affairs of the East, according to his aptitude and the personal relations he established. So Vigilius was a protégé of Theodora, Pelagius had great influence with Justinian and was employed by him in ecclesiastical missions, while Gregory was intimate with the family and court of Maurice. Scholarship was required to comprehend and guide the theological speculations of the East. Pelagius wrote in defence of the Three Chapters, and Gregory preached and held disputations.[42] In the seventh century as the monothelite controversy intensified discord between Rome and Constantinople, the position of the *apocrisiarius* and his staff became correspondingly hazardous. It was in Constantinople that Martin had acquired experience of the issues and personalities involved and during his trial was able to make allusions to equivocal episodes in the careers of his accusers. The *apocrisiarius* Anastasius, one of his immediate successors, was also active against monothelitism; he edited a series of extracts from the Roman scholar Hippolytus and perhaps also a *Doctrina Patrum*, a *florilegium* from the anti-monophysite fathers. Like Gregory he also had a following in Byzantine society, led by two rich young men, sons of the chief imperial quartermaster. His anti-monothelite activities brought first the closure of the nunciature's chapel by the patriarchal authorities and then in 647 his arrest and that of his friends. He was exiled to the Caucasus, where he died in 666, but he remained active in exile, writing to inform the West of the sufferings of the confessors and even undertaking plans for the fuller evangelization of the Caucasian principalities.[43] Later in the century two papal representatives,

[41] Pelagius I, *Epistulae, ed. cit.*, p. 192: A. Emereau, 'Apocrisiaires et Apocrisiariat: notion de l'apocrisiariat: ses variétés à travers l'histoire', (*Echos d'Orient*, 17, 1914–15); R. Janin, 'Constantinople Byzantine', (*Archives de l'Orient Chretien*, 4a, 1964), p. 135.

[42] Liberatus, *Breviarium*, c. 22: R. Devreesse ed., Pelagii, 'In defensionem Trium Capitulorum', (*Studi e Testi*, 57, 1932).

[43] Mansi, 10, 853; *MPG.*, 90, 171–94; *LP.* I, 336; on authorship of the *Doctrina Patrum*, (ed. F. Diekamp, 1907) see E. Stiglmayr in *Byzantinische Zeitschrift*, 1909.

Bishop John of Porto and the counsellor Boniface were held under arrest by Justinian II, and regular representation appears to have ceased from about 730 when Leo III, after his excommunication, caused papal envoys to be detained in Sicily.[44]

Ordinations to the priesthood and diaconate were made only as replacements were necessary and, by a ruling made under Gelasius, at certain times of the year only, the four Ember weeks (the first week of Lent, the week after Pentecost, the week between 16th and 27th September and, the preferred period, in December after the third Sunday in Advent).[45] On the Wednesday, after the Epistle of the Mass at S. Maria *Maggiore*, the priests-elect were brought forward into the sanctuary; there a *scriniarius* read out the names for formal approval by the congregation. The same ceremony was repeated on Friday in the basilica of the Apostles. On Saturday Mass was said by one of the suburbicarian bishops in St. Peter's, after which the ordinands were again brought forward, vested now in dalmatic and *campagi*, and the bishop read out the names and *tituli* to which they were assigned. The domestic character of the Roman clergy was emphasized by the withdrawal of all *forenses*, non-Roman clergy who might be present, and the inclusion of some Roman priests in the laying on of hands. After ordination they were conducted in procession, attended by candles, by a *mansionarius*, or warden of their *titulus*–like a magistrate amid the acclaim of the people–to their church; there, accompanied by an older priest, they said their first Mass.[46]

Some ordinands were already married at the time of taking orders; in such cases at the ordination their wives were also blessed, being in future referred to according to their husband's grade, as *presbyterissa* or *diaconissa*, and wearing a distinctive dress. But priests and deacons were to be celibate and if widowed no *diaconissa* or *presbyterissa* might remarry. The Roman synod of 721 condemned 'the deaconess Epiphania, who after taking the vow, has lapsed and eloped with

[44] *LP*. I, 373, 416.
[45] Gelasius I, *Epp.* 14, 15 (Thiel, *Epistolae Romanorum Pontificum*, I, 368, 380); on ordinations in general see *OR*. vol. 3, pp. 541–99; B. Kleinheyer, 'Die Priesterweihe in römische Ritus', (*Trierer theologische Studien*, 12, 1962).
[46] *OR*. vol. 3, Ordo XXXIV; vol. 4, Ordines XXXV, XXXVI, XXXIX.

Hadrian, son of Exhiliratus.'[47] Other pious women, who helped in works of charity, might also be granted the style of deaconess; and these, with the Roman matrons of noble family, and nuns, had a special place in church. Some protection against instances such as that of Epiphania was provided by a rule that no deaconess might be blessed before the age of forty.

The churches of Rome were of several classes, of which the ancient foundations, the *tituli*, which dated from the early years of established Christianity, alone carried the full status of priesthood in the Roman Church. They had previously been known by the names of their founders, such as *titulus Pammachii* and *titulus Vestinae*, founded respectively by the senator Pammachius in the late fourth century and the matron Vestina by will in the early fifth century. But by the sixth century the origins of the churches were already being forgotten along with the families that had founded them, and as the cult of the saints became more prominent they received the dedications by which they are still known; the basilica of St. John Giovanni and St. Paul, and St. Vitalis. In the fourth century their number appears to have been fixed at twenty-five; by the end of the fifth there were twenty-eight, a number that remained constant until the twelfth century. These alone were the parish churches of Rome, distinct from the chapels and oratories that served private institutions and the great basilicas that served the papal court.[48]

The activities of priests were naturally restricted in the main to their own churches, for instruction for baptism had traditionally a larger part in the priest's work in Rome than elsewhere.[49] Rules of guidance for their conduct have come down from a synodal admonition, probably derived from a Frankish original but reissued in Rome by Leo IV during his general reforms of clerical discipline.[50] Slipshod performance of the liturgy was to be shunned: the sign of the Cross in particular must not be sketchily made, the sacred vessels might not

[47] Mansi, 12, col. 263–4; LP. II, 6.

[48] See L. Duchesne, 'Les titres presbyteraux et les diaconies', (*MAH*, 7, 1887); F. Lanzoni, 'I titoli presbiterali di Roma nella storia e nella leggenda' (*RAC*, 2, 1925); J. P. Kirsche, *Die römischen Titelkirchen im Altertum*, (1918).

[49] *OR*. vol. 2, Ordo XI, pp. 366–447.

[50] *PL*. 96, 135 and *PL*. 115, 1929: see also G. Morin, 'L'auteur de l'admonition sur les devoirs du clergé', (*Revue Benedictine*, 9, 1892).

be of base metal and must be washed by the priest himself. He must live near his church, an important point for the Romans were devout–Bede reports on the frequency of lay communion in the city.[51] He must possess certain books, including the rite of exorcism by salt and water, the night and day offices, a penitential, a martyrology and a sermonary. The reading of the martyrology announcing the daily commemorations to be made gave rise to the popular need to expand the bare names into the legendary or hortatory acts of the saints.[52] The sermonaries, indicative of the derivative nature of intellectual life in the seventh and eighth centuries, were selections of extracts from the sermons of the Fathers; in Rome those ascribed to Leo I were especially drawn upon. One sermonary, compiled early in the eighth century by the priest Agimund of SS. Philip and James has survived, with another of the ninth or tenth century from St. Peter's.[53]

The seven deacons of Rome originally had no churches. With their seven subordinate subdeacons, the acolytes and the regional notaries and *defensors* they had custody over charity and property in the seven ecclesiastic regions, and were named after their region; the later identification with the *diaconiae* was an artificial one. Their pastoral functions, in earlier centuries at least, had largely been concerned with the administration of the sacrament of penance,[54] but from the sixth century onwards the deacons were primarily attached to the papal court and administration. For around the pope had grown up the complicated administrative body necessary to handle the increased papal burden; this included, besides the deacons and subdeacons, various officials in charge of separate departments who may themselves have been in orders. The most senior of all was the *vicedominus*, who had a staff of notaries of his own; originally an *ad hoc* appointment, it was made permanent by Gregory I. The *vicedominus* was normally a bishop–for example, Bishop Benedict under

---

[51] Bede, *Epistola* II, (*PL.* 94, 666).

[52] B. de Gaiffier, 'De l'usage et de la lecture du martyrologie', (*AB.*, 79, 1961).

[53] G. Low, 'Ein stadtrömisches Lektionar des VIII Jahrhunderts', (*Römische Quartalschrift*, 37, 1929) and 'Il più antico sermonario di S. Pietro in Vaticano', (*RAC.* 19, 1942); A. Chavasse, 'Le sermonaire des saintes Philippes-et-Jacques et le sermonaire de S. Pierre', (*EL.*, 69, 1955).

[54] F. Bussini, 'L'assemblée des Fideles et la réconciliation des pénitents', (*RSR.*, 41, 1967).

Zachary and Bishop Theodore under Stephen III.[55] The *vestararius* had charge of the papal sacristy and altar furnishings–a responsible task since many of the articles, like the great Gospel Book sent by the Emperor Constantine IV, were jewelled and of considerable value. Later *vestararii* were given outside tasks as well–Miccio was given charge of the affairs of the abbey of Farfa in the Sabine hills by Hadrian I–and, perhaps by virtue of being in custody of what were in effect Rome's principal capital reserves, the vestiariate when held in the ninth century by Roman magnates became a foundation for dynastic ambitions.[56]

Two financial officers were also in close attendance on the pope; the *arcarius* or general treasurer and the *sacellarius*, in charge of disbursements. Gregory II had been *sacellarius* under Sergius I and combined this with the care of the library before his promotion to the diaconate, but it was as deacon and theological adviser to Pope Constantine that he visited the East and impressed Justinian II with his conversation.[57] Also connected with the *arcarius*, and possibly under his department, was the *nomenclator*, whose function was to receive petitions and issue answers, and also to control the papal guest table.[58] Finally, in the eighth century the offices of *bibliothecarius*, the papal librarian, who was normally a cardinal-bishop, and of *superista*, military governor of the Lateran palace, were developed.

This court grew rapidly from the personal, monastic *familia* of Gregory I. Constantine's journey to the East shows us the pope by imperial orders being accorded full imperial honours; the circumstances were unusual, for Justinian was playing for support, both from the papacy and his own subjects. But it was an example of the change that had come to the papacy, the elaboration of the symbols of a sovereign court, marked by the ceremonial adapted from the imperial court itself, whereas, before, so many of the episcopal trappings had been derived from the Roman magistracy. Leading in

[55] *LP*. I, 470.

[56] *OR*. vol. 2, Ordo I, n. 22. See also P. Galletti, *Del Vestarario della S. Romana Chiesa*, 1758.

[57] *LP*. I, 396; a list of *sacellarii* in L. Halphen, *Etudes sur l'administration de Rome au moyen-age*, pp. 135–9.

[58] A list of *nomenclatores* in Halphen, *op. cit.*, pp. 131–4.

this symbolism was a court music. Byzantine inventiveness in the mechanical arts had developed the organ to a high degree of performance, and the imperial ceremonial was accompanied by hidden choirs singing the praises and achievements of the Emperor. A high, almost religious ceremonial surrounded his sacred person: the strictly ordered grades of functionaries, the succession of ante-chambers to the presence, the profound *proskynesis* or bow at the throne's foot. Artifice was added to the splendour; in the tenth century, following the reign of Constantine Porphyrogenitus to whom the court ceremonial was a paramount and central interest, the Italian Bishop Liutprand of Cremona, as envoy at the court, described the mechanical lions by the throne that roared at subjects' approach, and the throne that rose by invisible machinery to increase the height and impressiveness of the imperial aspect.

In the latter half of the seventh century something of the magnificence of these trappings of sovereignty penetrated under strong Eastern influence into the Roman Church. The process is most probably to be linked with the pontificate of Pope Vitalian who in contrast to his predecessors John IV, Theodore, Martin I and Eugenius I, embarked on a policy of co-operation with the Empire and the restoration of religious unity. He received Constans II in Rome, and helped assure the succession of Constantine IV following his father's murder. The lives of the popes following Vitalian, Leo II, Benedict II and Sergius I, stress the importance of music in their education: Leo II, a Sicilian, was 'learned in both Greek and Latin, outstanding in both chant and psalmody, and most practiced in the exercise of these subtle senses.' Benedict, a Roman who was brought up by the Roman Church, 'from boyhood, by his application to the Scriptures and the chant, as in the priestly dignity, showed himself worthy of his name'. Sergius, a Syrian from Antioch who had come to Rome from Palermo little more than ten years before his election and was appointed priest of S. Susanna by Leo II, was 'extremely studious and skilled in the office of the chant, and was handed over for his education to the Prior of the Cantors.' Later mediaeval authorities on church music associated Vitalian's name with the extended use of the organ, and it is likely that he, rather than Gregory the Great as is traditionally supposed, reorganized the *Schola Cantorum* to provide this fundamental expression of the papacy's position. It was from the *Schola* that the imageries of sovereignty spread in the eighth century to the Frankish kingdoms.[59]

Other expressions of the papacy's sovereignty in the West were adopted in the latter part of the seventh century: the use of the *phrygium* or *camelaucon*, a tall white head-dress from which the tiara was to develop and which, in legend, had been accepted by Sylvester from Constantine I in lieu of a temporal crown which would obscure his clerical tonsure; the *laudes*, the acclamations from the people, adopted from the court ceremonial of appointment; and the service of the suburbicarian bishops in the Lateran.[60] The pope's position as more than a leading bishop is above all seen in the accounts of the great papal ceremonies in the city, ceremonies peculiar to the papacy and standing apart as a court ceremonial from the normal liturgy of the city churches. These, as later adapted by Frankish bishops, have survived in the *Ordines Romani*, essentially the handbooks of papal masters of ceremony, compiled to ensure the smooth performance of a complicated court and religious function. Here also the collegiate nature of the Roman clergy found expression. In the ordering of papal ceremonies, which–unlike those of other bishops–were not essentially confined to the cathedral church of the Lateran but stood outside it and the normal parochial system, it was the ecclesiastical division of the seven regions that had the prime significance. Each region in turn took the responsibility for the ceremony and the reception of the pope; and the clergy of the duty region were bound, under pain of censure, to attend.[61]

[59] E. Jammers, 'Die Musik in Byzanz, im päpstlichen Rom und in Frankenreich', (*Abhandlungen der Heidelberger Akademie*, 1962, I), S. J. P. van Dijk, 'The Urban and Papal Rites in 7th and 8th century Rome', (*Sacris Erudiri*, 12, 1961).

[60] *LP.* I, 390; Constantine Porphyrogenitus, *De Administrando Imperio*, c. 13 (ed. and trans. Gy. Moravcsik and R. J. H. Jenkins, 1949). E. Muntz, 'La tiare pontificale du VIIIe au XVIe siècle', (*Mémoire de l'Académie des Inscriptions et des Belles-Lettres*, 36, I, 1897). H. W. Klewitz, 'Die Krönung des Papstes', (*Zeitschrift für Savigny-Stiftung für Reichsgeschichte*, 61, *Kanonische Abteilung*, 30, 1941). On hebdomadary service of suburbicarian bishops, *LP.* I, 478; *OR.* vol. 2, Ordo I, 8, 13.

[61] L. Duchesne, 'Les circonscriptions ecclésiastiques de Rome', (*Revue des Questions historiques*, 28, 1878) and 'Les régions de Rome', (*MAH.*, 10, 1890). On the liturgical stations, J. P. Kirsche, 'Les origines des Stations Liturgiques du Missel romain', *EL*, 41, 1927; *id.*, 'Origine caratteri

The entire papal court was assembled together in the procession to the appropriate stational church.[62] The pope rode, attended by lay grooms, from the Lateran palace at daybreak: before him went the regional *defensores*, the regional subdeacons, the two regional notaries, the *primicerius* and the deacons, keeping their ranks separate. Then a gap, and the mounted pope immediately preceded by an acolyte of the duty region carrying the Holy Chrism wrapped in his cloak. Behind the pope came the rest of the court, the *vicedominus*, the *vestararius*, the *nomenclator* and the *sacellarius*. The whole procession was directed by the acolyte preceding the pope and was an opportunity for any Roman to present a petition to him; as the procession passed a petitioner dismounted to receive the papal blessing, and his business was attended to by the *nomenclator* or the *sacellarius*, who reported later to the pope. At Easter, on his way to S. Maria *Maggiore*, the pope also received a report from the regional notary on the number of infant baptisms performed, the notary receiving a fee of one *solidus* from the *sacellarius* for the duty. Before the procession the vessels and the Gospel Books to be used in the papal Mass had been obtained from the Lateran sacristy where they were kept under the sacristan's seal, and brought to the stational church; one of the lay *cubicularii* had also brought the portable chair, ready for the pope's arrival.

Within the church the bishops of the suburbicarian sees, with any others in Rome, and the priests were waiting; outside, at the spot where the pope would dismount, were the regional officials and acolytes, the priest of the *titulus* and his assistant priests, and any prominent laymen associated with the church. The head verger (*mansionarius*) was also there, with a thurible of incense to greet the pope, a gesture of respect to his person adopted from the Byzantine court for it was not at this period used in the ceremonies of the Mass proper or for censing the altar. On entering the church the pope went

primitivi delle stazioni liturgiche di Roma', *Pontificia Accademia Romana di Archeologia, Rendiconti*, 3, 1925; *id.*, 'Die Stationskirchen des Missale Romanum', *Ecclesia Orans*, 19, 1926; R. Zserfass, 'Die Idee der römischen Stationsfeier und Ihr Fortleben', *Liturgisches Jahrbuch*, 8, 1958.

[62] *OR.* vol. 2, Ordo I; English translation by E. G. C. F. Atchley, *Ordo Romanus Primus*, 1905; an illustration of the architectural setting for a papal ceremony is given by T. F. Mathews, 'An early Roman Chancel arrangement', (*RAC.*, 38, 1962).

immediately to the sacristy to vest; there the vestments were brought to him by the regional subdeacons in their order of seniority, the *primicerius* and *secundicerius* standing by to adjust the folds. The final vestment, the pallium, was presented by a deacon or subdeacon chosen for this honour, and the regional subdeacon thereupon informed the pope of the names of those reading the Epistle and singing in the choir. The choir took up its position, men outside the sanctuary and boys within, and as they began the Introit the pope entered escorted by the archdeacon and the next senior deacon. The Mass proceeded to the choir's accompaniment and at the Offertory the pope, attended by the two senior lay officials of the court, the *primicerius* and the *primicerius* of the *defensors*, went down to the place reserved in the church for the lay notables, the *senatorium*, and accepted the offertory loaves from them in their order of rank; the archdeacon followed, accepting the cruets of wine they offered. The suburbicarian bishop of the week received the offerings of the rest of the congregation. At the communion the pope himself administered the sacrament to the court and the archdeacon to the rest of the people, and afterwards announced the station for the next day. Meanwhile the *nomenclator*, the *sacellarius* and the notary of the *vicedominus* went to the papal throne and there received the names of those who were invited to dine afterwards at either the pope's or the *vicedominus*'s table, and then delivered the invitations. At the conclusion of the Mass all–bishops, monks, laity and soldiers with their banners–processed out as the pope retired to the sacristy to unvest.

The *Ordo Romanus* for a papal Mass presents us with a fully articulated ceremonial, carefully planned and executed, whose splendour was directed towards the person of the pope, on the model of Byzantine court usage, rather than the sacramental Mass itself. It is in effect a state function of the city, surrounding the pope's person with the mystique of sovereignty, ecclesiastical and civil. The attendance of the junior clergy, the court officials, the leading laymen and the *militia*, and the carefully arranged choir and use of incense heightened the effect of sovereignty which, above all else, impressed northern visitors to Rome. The *Ordines* were taken north with papal approval, and they and the chant adapted from Lateran usage were absorbed into the Frankish church.

126

The Roman administration, operating in the main through the deacons, kept the city in immediate contact with most of western Europe and with Italy in particular. The deacons and subdeacons who acted as rectors of the papal patrimonies were also charged with overseeing the work of local bishops on behalf of the pope, their metropolitan. Roman influence was also spread by the appointment of these men, trained in the Roman service, as bishops themselves. Bishops were elected by the people of the vacant diocese under the supervision of the local civil authorities and a representative of the pope, the visitor, who was usually a neighbouring bishop appointed by the pope for the vacancy. He also reported to the pope on the fitness of the bishop-elect and the election was then confirmed at Rome. We have information of some elections during the pontificate of Gregory I. In 592 the see of Rimini fell vacant; the Bishop of Cervia was appointed visitor, and the Roman cleric Ocleantinus elected. For some reason, now unknown, Gregory refused his confirmation to Ocleantinus, and at a second election the Roman subdeacon Castorius, who was already in that area, was proposed. Again Gregory was unwilling to confirm, for Castorius had been seriously ill some time before—Gregory had written to Bishop John of Ravenna to thank him for visiting Castorius and removing him to Ravenna for treatment—but he agreed and Castorius was consecrated. But Gregory's doubts were proved right. Castorius came back to Rome to convalesce while Bishop Leontius of Urbino administered his diocese; four years later, still not sufficiently recovered to perform his duties, he resigned the bishopric.[63]

The visitor appointed was not necessarily a bishop; he might be a priest or even a layman. From 591 the priest Honoratus administered the diocese of Bevagna while no election could be held; finally Bishop Chrysantus of Spoleto was ordered as visitor to end the vacancy.[64] When Bishop Demetrius of Naples was deposed for his scandalous life and his involvement in politics, Bishop Paul of Nepi was sent as visitor. A section of the Neapolitans wanted Paul himself for their bishop but this Gregory would not allow, telling Paul to remain in Naples and ordain priests until a suitable candidate could be found; meanwhile the administration of Nepi was put in the charge of a

[63] Gregory I, *Registrum*, I, 55; III, 24, 25.
[64] *Ibid.*, I, 78; IX, 166.

127

local layman, Leontius. Neapolitan politics proved too much for Paul; a faction in the city opposed him and he was ambushed and severely wounded. Gregory at once sent a legation of Roman clergy to investigate conditions there and one of these, the subdeacon Florentius, grandson of St. Benedict's old enemy, was elected bishop; but to Gregory's disgust he fought shy and fled the honour.[65]

The consecration of Italian bishops took place in Rome, as the pope was metropolitan over all save the suffragans of Ravenna and Milan. This was a ceremony usually performed in the chapel of St. Martin near St. Peter's, and was not so strictly tied to liturgical seasons as the ordination of priests and deacons. On confirmation of the election the bishop-elect came to Rome and deposited before the *confessio* of St. Peter his affirmation of orthodoxy and adherence to the Councils, and his acceptance of the canons, especially those regarding the disposition of church revenues. These, traditionally, were divided four ways–the *quadripartitum*–among the bishop, the clergy, the poor and widows, and for providing for the upkeep of church buildings. The archbishops of Ravenna, as metropolitans for Pentapolis and Emilia, consecrated their own suffragans, but they themselves were meant to come to Rome for consecration. Archbishop Maurus obtained from the Emperor Constans II, on his visit to Italy, imperial confirmation of Ravenna's autonomy; but internal dissension over the revenues with the clergy of his diocese led to his submission to Rome once more. The diocese of Ravenna, which had endowments and properties second only to Rome's in wealth and organization, had long been bedevilled by the feuds between archbishop and clergy; Pope Felix IV in the sixth century had enjoined a strict adherence to the *quadripartitum* but in the late seventh Archbishop Theodore refused to honour it. By taking advantage of a local famine and buying up all available supplies of wheat he was able to blackmail his clergy when they appealed for assistance for their flocks; they were forced to surrender their right to a share in diocesan revenues, and the contracts and conditions of office of all officials were burnt. He in turn submitted to Rome and abandoned Ravenna's autonomy, hoping to strengthen his hand against his clergy, but it was a conditional surrender only. The archbishop would receive consecration in Rome but could not be compelled to linger

[65] *Ibid.*, II, 5, 13, 14, 18; III, 2, 15.

there or attend synods: instead he might be represented by a priest.[66]

For the focal point in Roman and Italian national life, which provided the sole opportunity for representatives from the peninsula to meet, was the annual synod of Rome. All suffragan bishops of the pope were expected to attend. The synod was normally held on the feast of the Apostles and transacted, besides matters of international moment such as the rejection of the *Ecthesis* and the *Typos*, a wide range of church, social and economic matters; the episcopate was recognized as expressing Italian sentiment, as the imperial instructions to Olimpius show.[67] Not merely Italian, but specifically Roman as well, for attendance was not confined to the bishops. The Roman priests, deacons and all the clergy attended, as well as the laity, who stood outside the circle of the clergy and gave their approval to the proceedings; Bishop Wilfrid noted this when, in the course of one of his appeals to Rome, a lector read his plea 'in a clear voice and, as the Roman custom is, in the presence of all the people'. In the synod of 649 the notaries, under the supervision of the *primicerius*, read the relevant texts, translating from the Greek where necessary.[68] Gregory III's synod in condemnation of Iconoclasm was attended by 'Antoninus, Archbishop of Grado, John, Archbishop of Ravenna, ninety-three other bishops of these Western parts, and the priests of this Holy Apostolic See, with the deacons and all the other clergy standing by, and the nobility, the consuls and other Christian people also standing'.[69]

The synods dealt with a wide variety of business, hearing appeals from foreign bishops, such as Wilfrid of York, debating the doctrinal interventions of the emperors and considering matters of clerical discipline. The synod of 721, for example, besides condemning Hadrian, son of Exhiliratus, who had eloped with the deaconess Epiphania, laid down that the clergy were not to go out of doors without wearing the *opitergum*, a great all-enveloping mantle; while the distinctive mark of clerical status was not to be abandoned in the dictates of fashion: 'If any cleric allows his hair to grow, let him be

---

[66] Agnellus Andreas, 'Liber Pontificalis Ecclesiae Ravennatis', (*MGH. SS. RR. Long. et ital.*), c. 60, cc. 110–14, cc. 117–24.

[67] *LD*. form. 42; LP. I, 337.

[68] Eddius, *Vita Wilfridi*, c. 53; cf. also cc. 29–32.

[69] *LP*. I, 416.

condemned.' The Church's interest in reconstructing the agriculture of its estates and in finding the oil for the many church lamps was also reflected by the same synod: 'If anyone, in any district, shall have spurned the orders already issued by the Apostolic See concerning olive groves and other places, and has not in every respect observed them, let him be condemned.'[70] The Roman synod, referred to as the *synodale collegium*, also granted permission for the restitution of lands lost by poorer houses and for the endowment of new foundations.[71] Two and a half centuries after Gelasius's decree a substratum of paganism could still be found; even the archdeacon Paschal had been found guilty of witchcraft.[72] The synod of 721 condemned 'those who follow fortune-tellers, omen-interpreters and spell-casters, or who use phylacteries', and in 743 the synod banned the celebration of *cappodanno*: 'None shall presume to celebrate the first of January, nor hold the pagan winter rites; nor prepare tables for feasts in their houses; nor prance through the streets and piazzas with songs and choruses, for it is a very great evil in the sight of God.'[73]

The synod, as a common focus of expression in Italian and Roman life, was more than matched by the greatest event of the Roman Church, the election of the pope. This was not yet confined to the clergy, but as the choice of their chief magistrate as well as spiritual father, was something in which the whole city, sometimes too vigorously, participated. First the death of the pope was formally announced to the emperor and exarch by the regents, the archpriest, archdeacon, and *primicerius* of the notaries; and following the election, a formal request was made for permission to consecrate. 'Although most grieved at the death of our supreme bishop under God, let it be known that the votes and the general consensus of all have concurred in the choice of a man, so that none was found opposed; therefore we, your servants, must pour out our prayers in petition to your most serene and pious Lordship, who should assuredly concede what we all ask of you, that your Clemency may rejoice in the accord of your subjects. For N., our pope of most blessed memory having died, the assent of all fell, through the will of God, on the election of N., the venerable archdeacon of the Apostolic See; who from his earliest years has served this church, has shown

[70] Mansi, 12, 261–6.   [71] *LD.* form. 96.
[72] *LP.* I, 372.   [73] Mansi, 12, 382–90.

himself solicitous in all things, so that by divine aid he was not unworthy to be placed in a position of authority in ecclesiastical affairs: especially, when appointed to such a post, he inspired the mind of our most blessed pope N. in conversation with him, in his desire by Christ's help for heavenly joys, and in the display of the so great merits that this bishop of holy memory knew to adorn him. Therefore, whatever good we have lost in the former, we are confident and without doubt we have gained in the latter. Therefore with fear we, your servants, beg that the piety of your servants' Lord may deign to hear our request and, conceding the desires of your petitioners, order through your Piety's command that we may perform his consecration: so that, through the sovereignty of your sacred Clemency, we may be established under this Pastor to pray for the life and empire of our most serene Lords to Almighty God and the blessed Peter, Prince of Apostles, for whose Church you may deign to order a worthy governor:

'I, N., by the mercy of God a priest of the Holy Roman Church, subscribe and consent to this decree made by us, concerning N., the venerable Archdeacon of the Holy Apostolic See and our pope-elect.

'I, N., your Piety's servant, subscribe and consent to this decree.'[74]

So ran the official formula of the Lateran *scrinium*, signed by both clergy and laity, who had combined in the election. At its most formal, the mode of election may best be seen in 769 when, following the usurpation of Constantine, the authorities were scrupulously legal in the election of Stephen III; the participants were the priests 'and all the clergy, the leaders of the army and the army itself, the more substantial of the citizens, and the general populace itself'.[75] But elections by the entire Roman people were not always as unanimous and peaceable as diplomatic usage assumed. There were first the natural difficulties caused by a spontaneous form of election; the dangers of two groups meeting in different parts of the city and electing simultaneously–the assembly was usually held in the Lateran basilica and the square outside. In 686 on the death of John V, there was such a disputed election between the candidates of the clergy and the army, the archpriest Peter and the priest Theodore; the army barred the entrance of the basilica to the clergy while their leaders met in the basilica of St. Stephen nearby. The deadlock was

[74] *LD*. form. 58. [75] *LP*. I, 471.

resolved after several days of discussion by the clergy proclaiming a third candidate, Conon, from the patriarchal palace.[76] On Conon's death within a year there was again a disputed election between the archpriest Theodore, perhaps the candidate of the previous year, and the archdeacon Paschal. This time each party had its own followers among clergy and army, and there was no such clear divide of interest. The senior clergy, magistrates and officers on this occasion took the initiative in selecting a third candidate by meeting in the imperial palace on the Palatine, for Theodore and his supporters held the interior of the Lateran, and Paschal some of the surrounding chapels. On the selection of Sergius, Theodore submitted but Paschal called in the exarch to support him.[77] This was the last occasion of attempted force in an election until in 768 the landed nobility of the duchy of Rome invaded the city to foist one of their number, Constantine, on to the papal throne. The attempt, an indication of a revived nobility with strong political awareness as well as of the increasing temporal attractions of the papacy, was defeated and strict rules prohibiting the wearing of arms or the admission of rustics to the city laid down in synod to prevent a recurrence.[78]

On election the pope was ceremonially inducted into the Lateran palace, and there gave a banquet for the leading clergy and laity of the city. His consecration took place on the Sunday following receipt of imperial approval; accompanied for the first time by the singing of the papal choir and with the ceremonial candles carried before him, he came from the sacristy and took his place on the throne. The bishops of the senior suburbicarian sees performed the ceremony; the Bishop of Albano giving the first prayer, followed by the Bishop of Porto: the senior Bishop of Ostia performed the actual consecration. If any of these sees were vacant the place was filled by the next senior, the Bishop of Velletri. When finally the archdeacon placed the symbol of supreme authority, the pallium, upon him the pope rose and reseated himself on his throne, while the choir sang the 'Gloria' and the people shouted the imperial *laudes*.[79]

The Church to which he had been elected was a large organization. Its universal commitments in spiritual and temporal matters made necessary participation in affairs throughout Europe and the East as

[76] *LP*. I, 368. [77] *LP*. I, 369, 371.
[78] See ch. 7, pp. 221–4. [79] *LD*. form. 57.

THE ROMAN CHURCH AND CLERGY

well as the protection of Italy and Rome. Gregory I, it has been seen, overhauled its organization, relying on the monks and companions of his own household and monastery who were trained in his own methods, and supervising everything by his attention to detail. But in the latter years of the seventh century there are indications that this machinery was suffering from a lack of sufficiently trained and educated recruits. The intellectual life of this period was dominated by Easterners–Greeks and Syrians from the East or Sicily–who made their mark through the increased Hellenism of the Church at this time; rising swiftly over the less educated native Roman clergy they formed a preponderance of influence and learning. Pope Agatho encountered this shortage of competent indigenous assistants early in his reign for, contrary to the normal custom, he made no appointment to the office of *arcarius* but himself acted as treasurer, issuing orders through the *nomenclator*, until with declining health he was forced to give up routine administration.[80] Something of this difficulty was expressed by him and by the synod of Rome in the letters they sent to accompany the Roman legates to the Trullan Council summoned by Constantine IV to achieve church peace:

'In the hope of consolation in our profound straits, I have chosen persons of such quality as this failing and subject province can provide in such times as these, to make their inquiries under obedience. Therefore we send them in dutiful obedience rather than in confidence in their learning. For how can men surrounded by barbarians and hampered by constant physical activity, which is a cause of great misgiving, be able to acquire a complete knowledge of the Scriptures unless we maintain them regularly, as was laid down by our holy and apostolic predecessors and by the five venerable councils, in simplicity of heart.'

To the council of 680–1 the pope and synod repeated their excuses for the lack of learning in Rome: 'If our concern were with secular learning, we think that no one in these times could be found who boasts of the highest erudition; since here the fury of the various barbarians burns daily, now flaring up, now ebbing and dying down. For this reason our whole life is absorbed in cares and our whole effort goes into restraining the barbarian bands surrounding us.'[81]

[80] *LP*. I, 350.   [81] Mansi, 11, 234.

And yet the legates sent to the East were the most distinguished available; the bishops of Paterno and Reggio (both from southern Italy) and of Porto, the priest Theodore (perhaps the later archpriest, twice unsuccessful candidate for the papacy), the deacon John (later Pope John V) and the subdeacon Constantine (perhaps the later pope).[82] It was Agatho's successor Leo II, a Sicilian, who translated the *Acts* of the Council from Greek into Latin for dissemination through the West.[83]

A few years later Pope Conon encountered similar difficulties in providing for the normal administration of the Church's estates. He had been brought up in Sicily before joining the Roman Church, his father being a soldier of the Thracesion regiment of the imperial army which was perhaps stationed in Sicily at the time of Constans's residence there. Conon found it necessary to appoint as rector of the Sicilian patrimonies a Syracusan deacon, Constantine, to whom also he conceded the privilege of the *mappula*. It was an appointment that aroused the bitterest of opposition from the Roman clergy as an act 'beyond custom, without the clergy's consent, on the advice of evil men and contrary to the feelings of churchmen.' Conon may have been inspired by a former friendship from his Sicilian days, or have made the appointment in the absence of any available talent in Rome, but to the Roman clergy this represented the loss of a profitable office.[84] A striking example of the gains of office is provided by an incident a few years earlier in the Church of Ravenna which also possessed considerable estates and trading interests in Sicily, as well as in Pentapolis and Emilia. Archbishop Maurus had attempted to remove from office the deacon Benedict, manager of the diocese's business in Sicily, and to appoint his own valet in his place. But Benedict retained his appointment by bribing the valet with a considerable quantity of merchandise and 300 *solidi* in gold. Thus he was able to continue his trading activities in large quantities of wheat, spices, wool and textiles, and Syrian metalwork which gave him an annual turnover of more than 300,000 *solidi*. Each year he paid 15,000 *solidi* into the imperial treasury, and 16,000 *solidi*, as well as considerable supplies of foodstuffs for the archbishop's household, to the diocesan treasury. The Ravenna historian's figures may be suspect but the scale of operations had left its mark. It was a profit-

[82] *LP*. I, 350.　　　[83] *LP*. I, 359; Mansi, 11, 1052.　　　[84] *LP*. I, 369.

able trade and a profitable office – and the papal properties were more extensive yet.[85]

The monasteries of Rome were originally small, independent foundations, created in the houses of those Roman families – such as that of Gregory I – whose members entered the church. The Rule of St. Benedict, while the common basis for monastic observance, was not followed exactly; individual divergences grew up among the houses and some, especially that of Gregory I, had constant interruption to their life of seclusion from the secular world through the calls put upon them by the Roman Church. During the Lombard invasion the numbers of monks and nuns in the city were increased by refugees from the country, especially the hill regions of Sabina, and from Latium and Campania, the original centres of the Italian monastic movement. Gregory described how the Roman Church was at the end of the sixth century supporting three thousand nuns alone, and begged his correspondents to send clothing for them.[86] The seventh century saw another influx of monks into the city, Easterners this time, refugees from monothelitism and the Arab conquest in Africa and, later, from Iconoclasm.[87] Abbot Maximus the Confessor, who was arrested and tried at the same time as Pope Martin, lived for a period in Rome with his disciples. Earlier the monk of Sinai, John Moschus, had lived in the West, having been driven from Palestine with his friend Sophronius, the later saintly Patriarch of Jerusalem; in Rome Moschus first read the *Dialogues* of Pope Gregory which inspired him to write that classic of Greek spirituality, the *Spiritual Meadow*. The Eastern monks took their full part in the life of the Roman Church; their abbots attended Roman synods, giving advice especially on those matters of which they had cognizance, the thorny theological matters arising from the East, on which a Roman decision was urgently required.

In this influx there was a danger of loss of discipline. Just as in the seventh and eighth centuries bishops in Italy and France were

[85] Agnellus Andreas, LPR, c. 111.

[86] See T. Leccisotti, 'Le conseguenze dell'invasione longobarda per l'antico monachesimo italico, (*Atti Io Congresso di Studi Longobardi*, 1952).

[87] See F. Antonelli, 'I primi monasteri di monaci orientali in Roma', (*RAC*, 5, 1928).

135

warned of the introduction of heresies–of Manichaeism and Dona-tism–from North Africa, so the refugee monks in Rome sometimes clung to some forgotten eastern divergence of the faith. Pope Donus discovered in the Boethiana monastery a community of Nestorians, perhaps Syriac-speakers from Iraq, who had for some time lived undetected; the community was broken up, the monks dispersed among other houses and a community of Romans settled in their place.[88] To bring the monasteries more closely into the life of the city the papacy began to group them around the basilicas, to perform there the perpetual divine office. So in the Lateran the choir services, the special papal ceremonies apart, were performed in rotation, by the communities of the monasteries of St. Pancras, the *monasterium Honorii* (taking its name from the pope), SS. Sergius and Bacchus, and St. Stephen by the Lateran; those in the Vatican basilica, St. Peter's, were conducted by the monks of St. Martin, SS. John and Paul, St. Stephen Major and St. Stephen Minor. Monasteries were also founded near some of the titular churches to maintain the divine office there, but independent of the normal parish services, and of the jurisdiction of the priest of the title. Gregory III, who carried out considerable improvement and decoration to the title of St. Chryso-gonus, founded a monastery nearby dedicated to SS. Stephen, Lawrence and Chrysogonus, which he and private individuals en-dowed with lands, to perform the office in the church.

Houses were small and fell easily into decline; much papal care was concerned with the re-establishment of houses that had decayed both in structure and in community life, or had proved incapable through poverty of performing their liturgical duties. Gregory III restored the life of St. Pancras, one of the communities serving the Lateran, whose numbers had fallen. Other houses in the city had failed to support it and over a period its lands had become alienated. Gregory revived the community by drafting in monks from other houses and instal-ling an abbot to give guidance, and the alienated lands, to their original value, were given back.[89] Pope Adeodatus, a former monk of S. Erasmo, rebuilt the monastery, re-endowed it and gave to the community a new state of discipline; Adeodatus was a Roman but by the next century S. Erasmo had been turned into a house of Greek observance.[90] Foundation from private houses revived in the

[88] *LP.* I, 348. [89] *LP.* I, 418–9. [90] *LP.* I, 346.

THE ROMAN CHURCH AND CLERGY

eighth century with the re-emergence of a strong native-born clergy: Gregory II on the death of his mother Honesta turned her house into a monastery dedicated to St. Agatha and endowed it with lands, cells and additional rooms which were added to the building itself.[91]

The prominence of monasteries and churches dedicated to St. Stephen was a marked feature of the seventh and eighth centuries; Stephen was not merely the proto-martyr of the Church but also the first deacon, representative, with the Roman martyr and deacon Lawrence, of the charitable and administrative aspects of Church life. This was reflected in Rome, constantly preoccupied with its food supply and material support, by the growth in the seventh century of a new institution of Eastern provenance–the *diaconiae*, or centres of distribution for supplies to the city.[92] Derived from a Greek word connected with *deacon* and with the implication of service, the *diaconiae* were in origin and function separate from the office of the regional deacon. They may not have been at first purely charitable organizations; their connection may rather have been initially with the quartermastering needs of the imperial *militia* which in the time of Gregory I was already beholden to papal resources–of the twenty-four *diaconiae* at the end of the eighth century, nine were dedicated to Eastern military saints. This same influence can be seen at Ostia, which still served as the principal port for traffic with the south, in the similar dedications of known Ostian churches: St. George and St. Theodore were likewise Eastern military saints and St. Vitus, a Sicilian saint, commemorated the source of the grain supply. All three dedications are to be found among the Roman *diaconiae*.[93] Although their foundation was made under papal encouragement, they quickly gained the patronage of wealthier Romans; by the late eighth century the nobility of Rome closely connected with the papal

[91] *LP.* I, 402; in general on monasticism, see G. Ferrari, 'Early Roman Monasteries, from the V through the X century' (*Studi di Antichità cristiana*, 23, 1957).
[92] J. Lestocquoy, 'Administration de Rome et diaconies du VIIe au IXe siècle', (*RAC.*, 7, 1930). H-I. Marrou, 'L'origine orientale des diaconies romaines', (*MAH*, 57, 1937). P. Romanelli, 'Le diaconie romane', (*Studium*, 40, 1940). O. Bertolini, 'Per la storia delle diaconie romane nell'alto Medio Evo sino alle fine del secolo VIII', (*ASR*, 70, 1947).
[93] P. A. Février, 'Ostie et Porto à la fin de l'Antiquité', (*MAH*, 70, 1958).

court had taken over their management and endowment as a work of charity.

The *diaconiae* were founded close to suitable abandoned public buildings of the imperial age, convenient for storing foodstuffs and for transporting them from the wharves of the Tiber bank. S. Maria *Antica* and St. Theodore were founded as deaconries next to the *horrea Agrippiniana*, the imperial granaries by the Forum, S. Vito *in Macello*–a *diaconia* founded early in the ninth century–was built in the ancient meat market, the *macellum Liviae*, and S. Maria *in Cosmedin*, an early *diaconia*, was in the *Statio Annonae*, the head-quarters of the imperial food supply system. Small oratories for the monks who usually performed the distribution were attached, but from an early date the management was under the care of a rich and philanthropic layman, the *pater diaconiae*. An inscription surviving from the eighth century lists the donation of the patron of one *diaconia*, the duke Eustathius, whose endowment included one whole estate, the *fundus Pompeianus*, as well as the houses, vineyards and olivegroves of two other farms. Later in the eighth century the family of Pope Hadrian was prominent in this charitable work, made so necessary after the confiscation of the Sicilian properties.

The resources of the papacy–which paid for city charities, for the upkeep of crumbling buildings and aqueducts, for tribute and levies to the Lombards, and for the stipends to its own clergy–cannot be accurately assessed. Theophanes estimated the value of the southern estates at the time of their confiscation in 729 as 250,000 *solidi*; but these properties were larger, more closely worked, untouched by war –although heavily taxed–and in closer commercial contact with the East than those in the neighbourhood of Rome. The sixth century had seen a heavy drop in the productivity of the properties in peninsular Italy; at the end of the fifth century, under Pope Gelasius, the estates of the Roman Church in Picenum were estimated at a value of 30 lb. in gold *per annum*, or 2,160 *solidi*–under Pelagius I, at the conclusion of the Gothic War, they were worth 500 *solidi per annum*. The Gallic patrimonies are not heard of after 613. Gregory I described them as a 'little patrimony', but an instalment of only one year's income was 400 *solidi*–nearly equal to the entire income of the Church of Naples.[94] Figures for the rents of papal lands to individuals, military

[94] Gregory I, *Registrum*, VI, 6; Boniface IV, *Ep*. See also A. H. M.

or church officials, or to their widows, are seldom given in the surviving records from the reigns of Honorius, Gregory II and Zachary; Gregory II, however, leased the island of Capri for 100 *solidi* and 100 *megarici* of wine.[95] The windfall accumulation of family estates granted to the Church declined sharply in the seventh century. Gregory I presented the Church with his family estates and 100 lb. of gold, 7,200 *solidi*, and Honorius gave nearly 2,000 lb. of silver, but from then until the reign of Sisinnius donations totalled a meagre 42 lb. of gold and 310 lb. of silver.[96] At least that amount was spent in Church ornament during this period, yet–despite the plunderings of exarchs and the stripping of Church treasuries–funds remained available. Gregory I found 12,000 *solidi* to secure peace from the Lombards, in addition to other commitments, including the distribution of donations, *roga*, paid to the clergy and ecclesiastical institutions. This custom became more extensive during the seventh century. Benedict II could spare 30 lb. of gold, 2,232 *solidi*, in his *roga* to the Roman clergy; if this represented a strict *quadripartitum* it indicates that the available income to the Church was nearly 9,000 *solidi*, but the *roga* was more likely an additional largesse. John V gave a *roga* of 1,900 *solidi*, and Conon one of 2,232 *solidi*.[97] Gregory II found over 5,000 *solidi* for the reclamation of Cumae from the Lombards as well as quantities of silver for church ornament, and 2,160 *solidi* in *roga*.[98]

Throughout the seventh century agricultural conditions were on the whole favourable; the first two decades of the century saw some famine, drought and floods, but none recurred worthy of note until the beginning of the eighth century. Indeed, in 672–6 exceptional rain was followed by a double harvest of the vegetable crops, and three years' famine in the reign of Constantine were followed by harvests of exceptional prosperity.[99] More important, the price of grain had stabilized after the disorders of the previous century. Pope Sabinian, facing a famine early in the century, opened the Church's granaries but was forced to sell the wheat at a price of 30 *modii* a *solidus*, twice

Jones, 'Church Finance in the 5th and 6th centuries', (*Journal of Theological Studies*, n.s. 11, 1960).

[95] *Liber Censuum Ecclesiae Romanae*, (ed. P. Fabre, 1910) I, p. 352, n. 56.
[96] *LP*. I, 312, 323.   [97] *LP*. I, 364, 367, 369.
[98] *LP*. I, 400, 402–3, 410.   [99] *LP*. I, 347.

the price prevailing a century earlier. This earned him considerable unpopularity; in legend, a vision of a disapproving Gregory appeared to him, and his funeral cortège was stoned, yet Gregory himself had complained of rising prices.[100] The price charged by Sabinian was not exorbitant; wheat prices had fluctuated between 25 and 40 *modii* per *solidus*. In seventh-century Egypt 30 *modii* a *solidus* remained the standard price, and in the East, where prices tended to be higher, it oscillated between 22.4 and 60 *modii*. The patriarch Nicephorus of Constantinople, late in the eighth century, regarded the price of 60 *modii* a *solidus*, induced by Constantine V's hoarding of bullion, as dangerously low.[101]

The active expression of Roman life during the seventh century was focused solely through the agency of the Roman Church whose institutions and functions supplied the prime and central means of civic activity and representation. The secular life of Rome continued but was muted in comparison with the growing power and splendour of the papacy; the *senatorium* in the church, still so called, was no longer occupied by senators but simply by the *archium*, the authorities. The civilian population, more localized than it had been in the sixth century, was drawn into the orbit of the Church as it forgot its original connection with the Empire and saw the papacy increasingly as the proper leader of the city. In the eighth century the nobility was to grow again, drawing strength from its association with papal offices in the city, and with the ending of formal imperial rule in the countryside. Contact with Lombard influence was to weaken the city's hold on the countryside and to redevelop a new scheme for politics, with the papacy and papal offices as the prize. The Roman Church alone, with its corporate officials, had survived to transmit the ideas of the ancient city to the kingdoms of the north.

[100] *LP.* I, 315; Paul the Deacon, *Vita S. Gregorii*, 29; *Anon. Vales.* 73.
[101] See in general, L. Ruggini, *Economia e Società* . . . (cit.).

5

ROME AND THE BYZANTINE EMPIRE

From the second half of the sixth century Rome was technically a duchy under the imperial exarch, or viceroy, of Italy with his seat at Ravenna.[1] The ducal office in Rome appears to have paled into insignificance beside the practical, moral and administrative ascendancy of the Roman Church. No duke is mentioned or known by name until early in the eighth century, and then his position is a permissive one only. Gregory I is seen advising, and on occasion immediately supervising, the subordinate military and civil functionaries of Tuscany and Campania; and he acted directly for the emperor and exarch over a large range of public business. 'In short, I will say this: in the region of Ravenna, His Piety the Emperor has, attached to the first army of Italy, a paymaster who oversees the daily expenditure. Well, at Rome it is myself who is the paymaster.'[2] At times of stress Gregory may have helped to pay local military units out of the Church's own resources, but it seems that the papacy was used directly by the imperial authorities as an agency for payments and a large variety of other business. When, in 640, the exarch's chancellor Maurice planned to enter the Lateran and remove the treasure accumulated by Pope Honorius he won over the local contingents by asserting that Honorius had failed to pass on the sums remitted to him by the emperor: 'What is the use of all that money hoarded in the Lateran by Pope Honorius, if the army gets none of it? For he has hidden there even the donatives that the lord Emperor ordered to be distributed.'[3] This was a pretext only but a reasonable one to assume that the papacy acted for the emperor in this way.

[1] Ch. Diehl, 'Etudes sur l'administration de l'Exarchat byzantin de Ravenne', (*Bibliotheque des Ecoles françaises d'Athens et de Rome, fasc.* 53, 1888): A. Guillou, 'L'Italia Bizantina: Δουλέια ε οἴκειωσις' (*BISI*, 78, 1967).

[2] Rome was not alone in providing this service which was undertaken by the patriarch Gregory of Antioch; see M. Higgins, 'Notes on the Emperor Maurice's Military Administration', (*AB*, 67, 1949).

[3] *LP.* I, 328.

In 556 Justinian had intended a reversion to a municipal form of administration giving a large share of control to the leading men and to the bishops of the provinces. But the impoverishment of the curial classes rendered this impossible to achieve, while the advent of the Lombards demanded a new concentration of military and civil power in the same hands. By the end of the sixth century, in a process that was to be extended through the organization of the themes to the whole Empire by Heraclius in the seventh, the local imperial commanders, counts, dukes and tribunes, had gathered control of municipal finances, as well as some authority in testamentary matters. The process reached culmination in the establishment by Maurice of a permanent supreme authority in Italy, the exarch.[4] The basis of the new exarchal system lay in providing for a home-based militia centred on the new duchies into which the exarchate was divided; a militia which, by withdrawing detachments, could provide a field army for the whole of Italy. The seventh century saw this militia army absorbed into the full social and political framework of the Empire; in its efforts to maintain unity the imperial government associated in its acts the army as well as the clergy, to give one collective expression, religious and political, to the imperial ethos. Herein for Italy lay the possibilities of dissent and separatism; from early in the seventh century the militia on whom the Byzantine authorities relied were closely identified with the interests of the provincials and the Italian churches. Service was hereditary and both the Churches of Rome and Ravenna leased lands to members; they also accepted patronage for them.[5] Decisions, such as fixing of taxation levels, were carried out by a remote government in Constantinople, which easily gave rise to suspicions of exploitation by the East.[6] Above all, Italy was the seat of the papacy, whose encouragement and

[4] G. Ostrogorsky, 'L'Exarchat de Ravenna et l'origine des Themes Byzantins', (*VII Corso di cultura sull' Arte Ravennate e Bizantina*, 1960).

[5] *LC*. p. 351, nn. 34, 43, 44: Tjader, n. 36: see also G. Cencetti, 'Il contributo dei papiri alla conoscenza di Ravenna nei secoli VI e VII', (*IV Corso di cultura sull' Arte Ravennate e Bizantina*, 1957); P. Rasi, *Exercitus Italicus e milizie cittadine nell'alto Medio Evo*, 1937, and A. Guillou, *Régionalisme et Indépendance dans l'Empire byzantin au VIIe siècle. L'exemple de l'Exarchat et de la Pentapole d'Italie*. (Istituto storico per il Medio Evo, Studi Storici, fasc. 75–76, 1969.)

[6] *Ephemeris Epigraphica*, 8, 1899.

approval of any scheme for religious unity in the Empire as a whole was vital to the government; but the papacy, wielding territorial influence in the sensitive Sicilian provinces as well as in peninsular Italy, was a potential obstacle to the creation of a firm area of defence for the central Mediterranean region. The course of Byzantine rule in Italy was, therefore, a series of clashes; the maintenance of the Roman order in face of the Lombards was desired by both sides, but the papacy, with the people and army of Italy increasingly behind it as their champion, was too often pressured to pay an over-high price in doctrinal or political compliance, and frequently had to defer to problems alien to Italy itself.[7]

In the duchy of Rome, mention is made of subordinate officers of the imperial service being at Civitavecchia, Miseno and Terracina in the seventh century, and in the eighth at Alatri and Anagni, and possibly at Civita Castellana and Nepi as well. The *Liber Diurnus* indicates that the election of new bishops was supervised by the local tribune on behalf of the central government, implying that a tribune was stationed in every episcopal town. But there is no sign of any effective intermediary authority between the local commanders and Ravenna; there seems to have been no administrative or military machinery at Rome directing the local officers–instructions were issued only from Ravenna. The officers were appointed by the exarch and took oath before him; they received instructions from him and reported to him, and they were paid from Ravenna. Events of political importance were managed by officers of the exarch's staff sent to Rome for the purpose. Rome does not appear as the administrative centre of its duchy but on a level with the towns of southern Etruria and Campania, the papal administration providing the sole connecting channel. Of the quality of the lesser officials there is little indication; in the time of Gregory I there was certainly a flood of fortune-seekers from the East, who bore heavily upon the province and its remaining nobility. Of one official we have a tantalizing picture; when Abbot Maximus and his disciple Anastasius were on trial in

[7] See O. Bertolini, 'Riflessi politici delle controversie religiose con Bisanzio nelle vicende del secolo VII in Italia', and P. Lemerle, 'Les repercussions de la crise de l'empire d'Orient au VIIe siècle sur les pays d'Occident', (*Caratteri del secolo VII in Occidente*, II: *Congresso Internazionale sull'Alto Medio Evo*, 1958).

Constantinople, the latter scoffed at an official witness: 'Do you bring Constantine into the secretariat of the palace? He is no priest or monk, but a buffoon of a tribune, and all Africa and all the Romans know how many girls he has left with child since he came there.'[8]

Constantine was not perhaps typical of the imperial civil service in Italy: indeed, the quality of the early exarchs was such that with only limited resources at their disposal they were able to stabilize the Italian situation after the first Lombard onslaught. The work of Romanus, especially in his campaign of 590, was crucial. An alliance with the Franks drew off Lombard strength to the north, and Romanus was able to recapture Parma, Piacenza and Reggio Emilia, commanding the Flaminian Way, so that the provinces of Emilia and Pentapolis, which were ruled direct from Ravenna, formed a barrier that denied the Lombards the eastern routes into southern Italy. This block of territory remained substantially intact for more than a century and a half, and was cohesively welded together as its later names–the Romagna and the exarchate–imply. Communications across Umbria to connect Ravenna and Rome were maintained by the possession of Perugia, the seat of an imperial duke; although changing hands several times in the nineties, the peace of 598 finally stipulated its tenure by the Empire. But Rome itself remained ringed by Lombard states: Spoleto passed at an early date to duke Faroald, whose possession of Rieti blocked the Via Salaria, and to the north-west Viterbo on the Via Cassia was the seat of a Lombard duke. Only to the south, through Latium and Campania to Naples, was the frontier comparatively safe; Byzantine command of the sea, with naval bases at Civitavecchia, Caeta, Amalfi, Anzio, Terracina and Naples, gave reasonable security, while the threat from the Lombard duchy based on Benevento, which later isolated Rome from Naples, had not yet developed. Gregory bitterly disputed the strategic dispositions of Romanus, accusing him of neglecting the defences of Rome in order to assure Perugia to the Empire; but they were sound and stood the test of time. Around the duchy of Perugia grew up a new strategic highway protected by the imperial-held towns: Nepi, Orte, Todi, Perugia, Tadino, and, at the entry into Pentapolis, Petra Pertusa holding the twenty-five mile pass between Perugia and

[8] *Relatio motionis* . . ., *PL.* 129, col. 604, 599.

Fossombrone. Rome itself was sheltered on the north by a ring of strongholds, retaken and organized by Romanus: Blera, Sutri, Bomarzo, Ameria, Narni, and to the east, Tivoli and Palestrina. These frontiers endured and as with the exarchate, formed the duchy of Rome into a cohesive whole.[9]

This concentration of the imperial possessions was emphasized under one of Romanus's ablest successors, the exarch Isaac. As his epitaph in Ravenna proclaims, he was responsible for preserving Rome and the Western parts for the Empire against the last onslaught of the Lombards, under King Rothari, before the eighth century. For eighteen years he built up the resources of his viceroyalty and was able to resist successfully the Lombard drive from 636 to oust the imperial government from Italy. The remoter possessions of Byzantine Italy, the Maritime Alps with their isolated garrisons and the western coast to the Magra, were lost. Isaac himself was defeated and killed on the Panaro in 643, but his work of protecting the major blocs was completed.[10] It was achieved in spite of inadequate military support from the East and political instructions that served to divide Italy.

The rule of the Emperor Phocas ended in 610 when Heraclius, the son of the exarch of Carthage, seized the throne, but the damage of his reign continued. The Avars had broken through the Danube frontier, and in the East the Persian King Khosroes overran Syria in 611; Damascus was captured two years later, and Jerusalem followed in May 614 when, to the horror of Christendom, the True Cross preserved there was removed in triumph to Ctesiphon. In 619 the Persians overran Egypt, cutting off the capital's grain supply, and, in conjunction with the Avars, were able to besiege Constantinople itself. Heraclius was unable to make a counter-attack until 622 when, with the full support of the Church under the patriarch Sergius, he left Constantinople to its own defences and by a bold strategic outflanking movement struck through Armenia at Persia itself. He entered it in 627 and won a great victory at Mosul, forcing a peace by

[9] P. Goubert, *op*, *cit*., *Rome*, *Byzance et Carthage*: see also D. A. Bullough, 'La Via Flaminia nella storia dell'Umbria, 600–1100', (*Atti del IIIe Convegno di Studi Umbri*, 1965).

[10] O. Bertolini, 'Il patrizio Isaacio esarca d'Italia', (*Atti del 2° Congresso internazionale di Studi sull' Alto Medio Evo*, 1953).

which he was able to obtain the restitution of the Eastern provinces and the restoration of the True Cross. His conclusive triumph over the ancient Eastern enemy was celebrated by the adoption of the style *basileus*, great king, and on the feast of the Holy Cross, 14th September 628, solemnly and barefoot, he carried the True Cross back to Jerusalem.[11]

But the long struggle had cost the East dear. Under Persian occupation the dissident provinces of Egypt and Syria had been stripped of their veneer of Hellenistic unity and loyalty to the Greek world. A notable resurgence in Syrian and Egyptian particularism resulted, which found expression in a revival of the Syriac and Coptic languages in liturgy and literature, and in an endemic monophysite theology opposed to official and orthodox Trinitarianism. Heraclius's first attempts to regain solid unity were obstructed by resentment of his officials' harsh methods. The emergence of a new religious force in Arabia–unitarian, simple and Arabic-conveyed, and at first scarcely distinguishable from monophysitism–found ready support in these provinces. Mahomet fled to Medina from Mecca in 622, and Islam did not expand from its homeland until after his death in 632. Yet before Heraclius died in 641 he had seen the Eastern provinces once more swept away. In 634 the Arabs entered Palestine, taking Jerusalem in 637, Syria was overrun by 639 and Heraclius, struggling against ill-health, was unable to repeat his earlier military successes or to rally the threatened provinces by theological concession. Immediately the offensive was launched against Egypt and the entire country was occupied by 642. In the following decades the Arab expansion continued by land and by sea, for in Syria they found themselves in possession of a littoral with a long sea-faring tradition, a plentiful supply of seamen and ships, and on Lebanon the timber required to construct a navy. In 648 an Arab fleet seized Cyprus and subjected it to tribute to Damascus; thereafter raiding expeditions from Syria or Egypt reached as far as Sicily, while land forces entered the North African provinces.

The repercussions of these events on Italy included, besides limitations on the amount of help available from the East, involvement in the consequences of the imperial government's attempts to underpin political with religious unity. To find a common ground

[11] A. Pernice, *L'Imperatore Eraclio*, 1905.

between the partisans of one will in Christ and official Dyophysitism, the patriarch Sergius, with Heraclius's approval, issued a pilot compromise urging the recognition of 'one energy' in Christ, avoiding commitment on the question of His will. The divergence in approach between West and East was seen in Pope Honorius's reception of this formula; the East still retained intact the full apparatus of scholarship and education which were being eroded in the West. Honorius followed the pastoral tradition established in the West by Gregory and, perhaps through insufficient knowledge of Greek, failed to understand the implications of Sergius's thought; he congratulated the patriarch on his attempts to achieve unity and harped on the necessity of the human will remaining in accord with the divine; he used the dispute almost as a parable, while considering the argument itself to be rather a matter for the grammarians.[12] In 638 Sergius extended his argument in the imperial publication of the *Ecthesis*, expounding a doctrine of one will in Christ. In the East it failed, largely through the opposition of the Patriarch Sophronius of Jerusalem; in the West, and especially in North Africa which still retained a vigorous theological tradition, it aroused bitter dissent.

The papacy was less forthright in its condemnation. A copy of the *Ecthesis*, together with the minutes of a synod held in Constantinople by Sergius's successor Pyrrhus, was sent to the Exarch Isaac, to be forwarded to the pope. Honorius was dead and the imperial authorities were attempting to bring greater pressure on the Roman Church by delaying the legates sent to Constantinople to ask permission for the consecration of his successor Severinus. Isaac saw an opportunity to gain added resources for his defence against the Lombards and to strengthen the unity of the Italian provinces. The Exarchate was undoubtedly hard-pressed financially; in the reign of Pope Deusdedit

[12] Honorius, *Ep.* IV, (*PL*. 80, 470, 474) P. Galtier, 'La première lettre du pape Honorius: sources et éclaircissements', (*Gregorianum*), 29, 1948: L. Pargoire, *L'Eglise byzantine de 527 à 847*, (1925). On the early stages of monethelitism, see: V. Grumel: 'Recherches sur l'histoire de monethelisme: I: Decrets monothelites d'Heraclius avant l'Ecthese II: Les premiers temps de la monthelisme III: Du monoergisme au monothelisme: Action et role d'Honorius', (*Echos d'Orient*, 28, 1928; 31, 1931) and *id.*, 'Après l'Ecthese', *ibid.*, 29, 1930: on Honorius's posthumous reputation see R. Baumer, 'Die Wiederentdeckung der Honoriusfrage im Abendland' (*Römische Quartalschrift*, 56, 1961).

the army of Naples under a local commander John of Conza had rebelled and been suppressed by the exarch Eleutherius, who was immediately forced to pay a donative to the troops: this action, the papal biographer noted, 'brought peace throughout Italy'. Perhaps Eleutherius considered this donative sufficient and unexpected enough to earn him popularity, for a few years later he declared himself emperor and marched on Rome, but in camp his contingents from Ravenna mutinied and murdered him, sending his head to Constantinople.[13] Isaac, his successor, saw in the enforced interregnum of the papacy an opportunity to secure himself against such dissidence and to fill the military chest. His chancellor Maurice was sent to Rome to organize the looting of the Lateran of the treasure accumulated under Honorius; he found *agents provocateurs* to approach the garrisons of the *castra* in the region of Rome, spreading rumours of the Lateran's fraudulent wealth. The troops were concentrated in Rome, then 'with spirits inflamed, all who could be gathered in Rome, old men as well as boys, marched armed to the Lateran'. The papal household resisted for some days but the army battered its way in and Maurice entered with his officials. Seals were placed on the treasure chambers and on the arrival of the exarch they appropriated the accumulated pious offerings of several centuries 'bequeathed to the blessed Apostle Peter by so many Christian emperors, patricians and consuls, for the redemption of their souls, the support in perpetuity of the poor, and the ransoming of captives'. All was removed under the supervision of the exarch who 'sent some of it to the Emperor Heraclius in his capital'.[14]

Precedent for this was provided by the Emperor himself – Heraclius had been obliged to lay hands on the church plate of Constantinople to finance his wars. But perhaps the motives of Isaac and Maurice were not so pure, for within three years Maurice was in rebellion against his master. Again it was the army around Rome that supplied the means; Maurice approached each unit in turn, putting out that Isaac, like Eleutherius before him, was aiming to establish himself on the throne, and eliciting from the troops an oath never to serve the exarch. Isaac acted promptly, sending the general Donus with troops and a large sum of money to Rome. On his approach the army of Rome deserted Maurice and returned without a fight to their allegiance; Maurice himself fled into the city and took sanctuary in the church of S. Maria *ad Presepe*, but he was dragged out, placed in chains and with his accomplices sent to Ravenna. At Cervia, some miles from the exarch's capital, he was executed, for Isaac had sworn he should never again enter Ravenna alive; his head was placed on a spike in the circus there as a warning.[15]

Severinus, at last consecrated, died without accepting or formally condemning the *Ecthesis*. But relations between papacy and government did not improve. On the death of Heraclius his widow Martina –suspected of having poisoned Heraclius's elder son by his first wife– tried with the support of the Patriarch Pyrrhus to establish a regency for her son. A *coup* was staged by the generals in favour of the heir's sons, Constans and Theodosius, and Martina was removed from the regency. Her colleague Pyrrhus was attacked in Hagia Sophia but managed to escape to North Africa, by now the main centre of opposition to and refuge from monothelitism. In Carthage, he made contact with the exarch Gregory of Africa, a cousin of Heraclius and a reputed anti-monothelite who was considered to have designs on the throne. He also met the abbot Maximus, Heraclius's former secretary who was the leading intellect in the fight against monothelitism. In May 645 they held a series of debates on the problem of the wills of Christ, and Pyrrhus pronounced himself convinced of the Dual Will, saying that he would condemn his monothelite predecessors 'if this condemnation is necessary; but first I must visit the tombs of the Apostles and the pope, to whom I will submit a written account of my errors.'[16] Pope Theodore had refused to extend recognition to his successor Paul, on the grounds that a bishop can only be deposed by a synod, and he had reiterated his condemnation of the *Ecthesis*. Pyrrhus was received with honour in Rome as legitimate patriarch, but his hopes of reinstatement soon vanished when Gregory rebelled and proclaimed himself emperor in 646. The Arabs of Egypt took the opportunity for an extended raid into the province and Gregory was killed in battle against them. Pyrrhus at once withdrew his submission to the pope and was excommunicated by Theodore.

The court of Constantinople now faced the almost complete loss

[15] *LP.* I, 331.
[16] *Disputatio cum Pyrrho, PG.* 91, 287–354.

of its Western provinces: the rebellion of Gregory and the Arab invasions came at a time when close contacts between the religious opposition in the West and Rome were being forged; the papacy was sending funds to Arab-held regions for the relief of refugees; moreover loyalty in Italy itself was clearly uncertain. Greater pressure was applied. In 647 the papal representative in Constantinople, Anastasius, was arrested and exiled to the Caucasus; the following year a new document, the *Typos*, was issued by Constans II forbidding any further discussion of the question of the Wills. The *Ecthesis* was withdrawn and drastic penalties against infringement of the document were laid down. Recognition was once more refused to a pope-elect in succession to Theodore, the Tuscan Martin, who, as a former legate in Constantinople, was well aware of the personalities and issues involved, until his attitude could be better known. He was consecrated without imperial permission and, further increasing imperial suspicion, took steps to reorganize the Church structure of Palestine, left in ruins after the Arab conquest. A papal vicar was appointed and a wide tolerance shown in re-admitting monothelite clergy to unity to care for the population. The Greek leaders of the religious opposition were now assembling in Rome and with their aid, in October 649, Martin assembled a synod at the Lateran of 105 bishops and also 37 abbots, priests and monks, refugees from the East. The result was the condemnation of monothelitism and the *Typos*, and anathemas directed against the patriarchs Sergius, Pyrrhus and Paul.[17]

Constans resolved immediately on firm measures to bring Italy and the papacy into line. The chamberlain Olimpius was appointed exarch, with specific instructions to secure papal co-operation; but Constans' advisers, the former exarch Plato and another former high official in Italy, Eupraxius, counselled a cautious approach. Olimpius was first to see what local support could be found for the *Typos*; if this was sufficient, then the bishops, the administrators of Church property and other Church leaders who had attended Martin's

[17] Martin, *Ep.* V (*PL.* 80, 897, 154): Mansi, 10, 883; E. Caspar, 'Die Lateransynod von 649', (*Zeitschrift für Kirchengeschichte*, 51, 1932). W. M. Peitz, 'Martin Ier und Maximus Confessor. Beiträge zur Geschichte des Monothelitenstreites in Jahre 645–668', (*Historisches Jahrbuch*, 30, 1917).

synod, were to be arrested. But Plato and Eupraxius warned that public support might well be for the pope, in which case the army must be used – although even the army, according to these officers of recent experience, might be unwilling to obey such orders: Olimpius should proceed slowly until he was at least sure of the armies of Ravenna and Rome. The exarch sailed for Italy and immediately paid a state visit to Rome, his formal capital, where he was received with all due honours. Here he found the Italian episcopate firmly united behind Martin, and his initial attempts to create a schism failed. So he resorted to assassination, arranging for one of his aides-de-camp to murder the pope at High Mass in S. Maria *ad Presepe*. The attempt failed; the soldier was blinded (Martin's supporters claimed by a miracle) and confessed to the orders he had received. Olimpius, abashed, also revealed the Emperor's instructions to him and made his peace with the Church. Shortly after he was called away to Sicily to counter an Arab attack, sustained a defeat, and died there of fever.[18]

An instance of the pressure now being placed on the Italian clergy by imperial officials comes from Sardinia; the island, administratively under the exarchate of Carthage, showed resistance to monothelitism, for both Bishop Deodatus of Cagliari and Bishop Valentine of Turres were present at the synod of 649, and it was to some monks of Cagliari that the *apocrisiarius* Anastasius wrote from his Caucasian exile to encourage them in steadfast orthodoxy. In an Athonite manuscript is preserved the profession of faith of a Sardinian bishop, Euthalius of Sulcis, made perhaps after 668, during the slight improvement of relations on the succession of Constantine Pogonatus. After the usual act of adherence to the great councils, Euthalius continues:

'In addition to all these I assent to the holy council summoned in Rome by the most holy Pope Martin of apostolic memory for confirmation of the orthodox apostolic teaching of our unimpeachable Christian faith, and to condemn audacious innovations ... I anathematize and reject all heresy, of ancient or recent provenance, and condemn also that profession which in unhappy malice John, *exceptor* of the ducal administration, drew up in contempt of the abbot Maximus, of blessed memory, and which I myself, in my simplicity and not suspecting the malignity and calumny of the man,

[18] *LP.* I, 387–8.

was in secret constrained to sign, in respect of the books received by us, which had violently and by force been stolen from the abbot Maximus, of blessed memory.'[19]

Olimpius's reverse in Rome merely stimulated the imperial court to harder measures. Theodore Calliopas, who had already served a term as exarch, was sent as replacement; his instructions were simply to end papal opposition. He arrived in Rome with the army of Ravenna on Saturday, 15th June 651, and went straight to the imperial palace on the Palatine, where he was waited on by a delegation of the Roman clergy. This explained to him that Martin, who had been an invalid since the previous October, would be unable to make his official welcome until the following day. But on the Sunday Calliopas was suspicious of the crowds gathering before the Lateran for Mass, and assumed that the Romans were preparing to defend their bishop. He therefore sent a message to the pope, postponing his welcome until Monday, alleging tiredness after his journey. He did not come on Monday but on Tuesday sent his chancellor with other officials to the Lateran, who accused the pope of having prepared arms and stones to defend himself. Martin sent them on a tour of inspection and nothing was found; he spoke to them afterwards, saying that the rumours of resistance were false and pointing to the previous impossibility of defence against Olimpius.[20]

His arrest was imminent and Martin himself described it in a letter to a friend from his exile in the Crimea. 'I had my bed set up in front of the altar in the church and there slept; but just after midnight these men entered with the army, fully armed with spears and swords, their bows and shields at the ready—an unspeakable action. For, just as the leaves are torn from the trees and fall in the winter storms, so with their weapons they overturned the candlesticks in the church and smashed them on the pavement; and we in the church heard the din, like thunder, from the clashing of their armour and the breaking of the many candlesticks. The moment they entered an order from

[19] Letter of Anastasius in *PG*. 90, 133: B. R. Motzo, 'Barlumi dell' età bizantina in Sardegna: II: La professione di fede di Eutalio vescovo di Sulcis', (*Studi Cagliaritani di Storia e Filologia*, I, 1927).

[20] *PL*. 87, 119–98; E. Michael, 'Wann ist Papst Martin I in Exilierung nach Constantinopel gekommen?', (*Zeitschrift für Katholische Theologie*, 16, 1892).

Calliopas was read to the priests and deacons, containing much abuse of my humble self: that I had illegally and uncanonically seized the bishopric, that I was unworthy of the Apostolic See, and that I was to be taken to the capital, by any means necessary, and there questioned on my episcopal status (something that has never been done before and, I trust, will never be done again), and that in the absence of the pope, the archdeacon, the archpriest and the *primicerius* should exercise his authority.' By now a crowd had gathered, which began to shout abuse at the exarch and his troops, maintaining that Martin had always been orthodox. Calliopas stepped forward and tried to persuade the Romans that he himself was orthodox and that Martin's arrest was not for doctrinal reasons; and indeed the charges later brought against him were, beside that of harbouring the Emperor's enemy Pyrrhus, of implication in Gregory's rebellion, and of sending money to the Arabs in North Africa. The clergy, whom Martin had ordered not to resist to avoid bloodshed, now clamoured to be taken with Martin; Calliopas, feeling things slipping from his control, hurried the pope off to the Palatine.[21]

The following morning, Wednesday, the palace was beseiged by clergy and laity alike, with their baggage hastily packed into hand-carts, ready to accompany the pope into exile. Again Calliopas became alarmed; in the early hours of Thursday morning Martin with only six attendant clerics, was bundled into a river-barge with all the possessions he had with him, for Calliopas gave no time for selection, and taken down to Porto; the city gates were double locked behind them. They sailed at once, first to Miseno where they transhipped on 1st July; then on the long, slow, painful voyage to Constantinople. Winter came on; at Naxos they were delayed by storms which lasted for a month, giving Martin the first relief since leaving Rome: he was allowed ashore to stay in a local hospice, and granted the comfort of a bath and a rest. Not fully recovered from his previous illness, he was still very weak, the ship's provisions did not agree with him, and he suffered from dysentery. At Naxos, too, there were signs of sympathy and loyalty from the local priests and faithful who brought food and comforts to him in considerable quantity; but these the guards would not allow

[21] *PL.* 87, 119–98.

him, destroying them, and threatening his sympathizers with arrest for showing kindness to a traitor. They reached Constantinople on 17th September and here, as Martin disembarked, the crowd proved hostile, heaping abuse on him as an enemy of the state. For three months he and his companions were kept in strict confinement in the palace guardroom; then he was brought for trial before the Senate.

The trial was a farce; Martin, feeble as he was, was refused a chair, and no discussion of theological issues was permitted. Among the official witnesses were senior soldiers from Olimpius's command, and the former exarch's secretary. Dorotheus, a former governor of Sicily, gave evidence on oath: 'If Martin had fifty heads he ought not to live, for singlehanded he had subverted and overthrown the whole of the West, by raising it in rebellion; he had been like a brother to Olimpius, a murderous enemy to the Emperor, and to the Roman state.' At this point Martin begged the presiding senators that witnesses might be excused giving evidence on oath, so as not to imperil further their souls; his spirit remained unquenched and his humour flashed out. Some soldiers who had served under Olimpius were brought in: 'They spoke against the holy man, as they had been instructed to do beforehand, and their evidence was prepared and arranged. But some of them, who had not been so adequately briefed, began to tell the truth, as is usual: this aroused the organizers of the trial, who swore at and threatened them, and so influenced them into saying what suited the holy man's condemnation. The pope, as he watched them go up to give their evidence, laughed and said: "Are these the witnesses? They are well drilled!" Once only was Martin permitted to make a statement of his own. He began "When the *Typos* was issued and sent by the Emperor to Rome ..." ': the prefect Troilus interrupted him, saying that theology was not under discussion, that they were all perfectly orthodox and that Martin was on trial for his involvement in a rebellion by Olimpius. It was a mistake; Martin had been papal legate in Constantinople and he perfectly illustrated the folly and uselessness of resistance to a man with supreme military power by reference to some equivocal incidents in Troilus's past at the time of the overthrow of Martina and Heracleonas. The secretary Sagoleva hastily rose and announced that no more witnesses would be heard as the presidents were tired; and the court adjourned.

Martin was removed to a courtyard of the palace, where he was stripped of his vestments; then, in fetters, he was led through the crowded streets to the prison of the prefect of the city. There he was kept in great discomfort, chained to an armed warder, with inadequate coverings for the bitter winter that set in. Although his sufferings were soon alleviated at the intercession of the Patriarch Paul who, on his death-bed, persuaded the emperor to lighten his treatment, he was kept in prison in the capital for more than two months and subjected to renewed interrogations, for the irrepressible Pyrrhus had returned on the death of Paul to claim his patriarchal throne. Martin was cross-examined on Pyrrhus's activities in Rome, on his submission to Pope Theodore and his writings on the matter of the *Typos*. At last orders came for his removal to the Crimea. After a tearful parting from the faithful band of clerics who had stayed with him through all the torments of his voyage, trial and imprisonment, they exchanged the kiss of peace. The lamentation grew louder and Martin, unquenchable still, asked smiling, 'Is this the peace I asked for?' He was taken to Kherson in the Crimea, where he spent the remaining two years of his life in great hardship, subject to petty restrictions and insults from the local authorities. His sole means of communication was by the infrequent merchant ships, trading salt for wheat; in a letter that he wrote to his clergy still in Constantinople he complained of the shortages of food and money; the merchants were willing to sell supplies only at an exorbitant rate, four *solidi* being their price for a single *modius* of wheat.[22]

The news of Martin's sufferings spread through the West; his own letters, written to one Theodore, were received there, and a full account of his trial and imprisonment was sent by one of his companions for publication in the West. Opposition became more widespread and articulate among the Italians and Romans themselves. Martin's successor, Eugenius I, was a gentle man, who had been brought up from youth in the Roman clergy; he received the customary synodic letter from the new patriarch of Constantinople, by which patriarchs were used to inform each other of their appointment, with assurances of orthodoxy. To the Roman mind this letter was unsatisfactory and vague on the patriarch's exact stand on the Dual Will. It was spontaneously rejected by the people, who besieged

[22] *Commemoratio eorum quae saeviter* ... Mansi, 10, 853.

Eugenius and his clergy in S. Maria *ad Presepe* after Mass, not allowing them to leave the church unless he promised to reject it.[23]

The preoccupation of the imperial government with the security and loyalty of the Western provinces was well attested in the contemporary trial of the abbot Maximus, who had also been arrested in Rome and brought to Constantinople. Officials from Africa and Rome were introduced to witness to his political activities: by dissuading the governor of Numidia from defending Egypt when invaded by the Arabs, for 'co-operation with Heraclius was displeasing to God,' he had betrayed all Africa to the Saracens. Further allegations were made that he had encouraged Pope Theodore to support the patrician Gregory in establishing himself as an independent, orthodox emperor by a vision of angelic choirs in East and West singing 'Gregory, Augustus, you will conquer', the sound of the Western angels drowning that of the Eastern; to which Maximus properly replied that his dreams were involuntary.[24] But the bitterness between the two halves of the Empire was such that the summons was almost for a new Constantine; and the government was insisting on an absolute surrender of conscience and intellect to its own *politique* schemes for unity.

The self-sufficient and integrated nature of the army envisaged in the exarchal and thematic organization of the Empire was now seen to have been achieved and to have worked against imperial unity. It had to be wooed, flattered and bribed to make its interests conformable with imperial policy, and those interests tended to become more exclusively Italian and Roman. It was emerging as a distinct stratum of Roman society; its officers were in receipt of papal grants or leases of land, and it took its part in purely domestic issues—in the *formulae* of notification of a papal election the army magnates signed with the clerical regents. A generation after the arrest of Pope Martin, the army was taking a full and influential initiative in the elections themselves. So in 686 on the death of John V the military put up a candidate in opposition to that of the clergy and refused to stand down until a compromise candidate was proposed. Imperial civil affairs were largely outside the immediate consciousness of

[23] *LP.* I, 341.

[24] Anastasius apocrisiarius, *Relatio motionis factae inter domnum Maximum et socium eius et principes in secretario*, (*PG.* 90, 109).

Roman life in the latter part of the seventh century; when they did impinge on the life of the city, it was as an alien intrusion, often disruptive and disastrous.

One such occasion–the last visit of a Roman Emperor to his capital in the West–profoundly affected the aspect of the city. By the seventh decade of the century the war against the Arabs in the East had calmed down; both sides were beset by domestic difficulties. But the incursions of Arab raiding fleets into the central and Western Mediterranean continued, and Constans II planned to move his capital temporarily to the West and reorganize the defences of the central Mediterranean on a sounder basis. In this he was following the predilections of the Heraclian dynasty for the West; Heraclius had at one moment thought of transferring the seat of government to Carthage, and North Africa had long been under the governorship of a member of the imperial family. Pope Vitalian, Eugenius's successor, had achieved a certain reconciliation with the emperor, who had confirmed Rome's privileges as senior church and sent jewelled and gilded copies of the Gospels to St. Peter's treasury. But Constans could not feel secure about the West; North Africa, under continual Arab raid, had a record of dissent and rebellion; the Lombard duchy of Benevento was a threat to Sicily and southern Italy where the imperial administration was strongest and must be the key to a successful Mediterranean strategy; in Sicily too the Roman Church by virtue of its extensive estates had a dangerous influence and was not in imperial eyes entirely reliable.

Financial and military measures were to be taken to create of Sicily a strong fortress and bulwark dominating the sea and holding Africa. Accordingly, in 664 with a large fleet and 20,000 men from the Asiatic armies, Constans sailed to Italy, by way of Athens and Taranto. A campaign in the south against Benevento achieved some temporary successes and an imperial progress was undertaken to review the naval bases of the Campanian towns, Naples and Amalfi. Then Constans paid a state visit to Rome. He arrived on 5th July; Pope Vitalian and the entire clergy went out to the sixth milestone to greet him with all proper solemnity; the following day Constans visited St. Peter's on foot to pray and make offerings, and there was similar ceremonial, in which his whole army joined, at S. Maria *Maggiore*. The visit lasted twelve days and in that time Constans

157

managed to strip the buildings of Rome of all metal parts, the bronze tiles, clamps and ties with which they were bonded; the remaining statues were also removed and the great mass of metal transported to Syracuse, for shipment to Constantinople to be used for armaments. They never arrived, being intercepted off Syracuse by an Arab raiding fleet and taken to Alexandria. It was a savage blow against the survival of the imperial aspect of Rome; the buildings were weakened and opened to the weather, and it was an encouragement to their further spoliation by the Romans themselves.[25]

Constans remained in Sicily until 668, when he was murdered in Palermo by one of his officers. His presence, although a great stimulus to the united defence of the central Mediterranean area, was a bitter burden to the provincials and institutions of Italy.[26] Heavy taxation, including new poll-taxes and shipping dues, were imposed throughout Calabria, Sicily, Sardinia and Africa. Measures were taken to reduce the potential influence of the papacy, an opportunity seized by the ambitious Archbishop Maurus of Ravenna. It had long been his aim, as of several of his predecessors, to achieve independence of Rome; he had approached Constantinople on many occasions to negotiate this autonomy and the historian of Ravenna, Agnellus Andreas, who was abbot of Maurus's former monastery and had the documents preserved, hints at bribery. Now he presented to Constans a document, said to have been issued in the fifth century by Valentinian III, granting autonomy to Ravenna. This Constans willingly confirmed; henceforth archbishops-elect of Ravenna were to be elected by the clergy of the diocese, their election approved in Constantinople and their consecration to be, not in Rome, but by three of Ravenna's own suffragan bishops, as was the pope's. This it was felt would weaken the papacy in Italy and prevent its domination of the exarchate becoming as marked as the domination it exercised over the duchy of Rome.[27]

[25] *LP.* I, 363.
[26] *LP.* I, 344; J. B. Bury, 'The Naval Policy of the Roman Empire in relation to the Western provinces from the 7th to the 9th century', (*Centenario Amari*, 1910); H. Ahrweiler, *Byzance et la mer*, 1966.
[27] *LP.* Eccl. Rav. cc. 110–14: on the growth of Ravenna to metropolitan status and its claims to autocephaly, G. Zattoni, 'Origini e giurisdizione della metropoli di Ravenna,' (*Rivista di Scienze Storiche*, 1904–5); R. Massigli, 'La creation de la Metropole ecclesiastique de Ravenna',

Constans's murder was planned by one of his officers, Mezezius; one account implicates the son of Troilus, Constans's agent in the persecution of Martin, in the crime. Mezezius aimed at the throne for himself, supported by the Eastern army that had accompanied the emperor. In suppression of the rebellion, and assuring the succession to Constans's son Constantine IV, Vitalian, true to his policy of conciliation and service to imperial unity, took a leading role; he mobilized the detachments of the army of Italy and concentrated them with African and Sardinian units against the usurper.[28] The initiative in preserving Italian unity with the Empire came now increasingly from the papacy whose forebearance outweighed the exasperation of the provincials themselves. The exarchs and other officials were showing themselves more and more irresponsible in their activities, and their rule was increasingly burdensome. In 687, following the death of Pope Conon there was a disputed election, the two candidates being the archpriest Theodore and the archdeacon Paschal, each party holding a different part of the Lateran. Neither would yield, until the city magistrates with the senior officers and the priests met and proclaimed a third candidate, the priest Sergius, a Syrian whose parents had settled in Palermo and who now held the title of S. Susanna. Theodore submitted to this choice but Paschal was defiant; secretly he wrote to the exarch John Platyn in Ravenna, offering him 100 lb. in gold to come to Rome and ensure his election. Again the greed of Byzantine officialdom at the expense of Italy, the Church and its own authority prevailed; John hastened to Rome, only to find Sergius fully accepted by the Romans. He did not intervene on behalf of his protégé Paschal, but merely delayed Sergius's consecration until he had collected the bribe Paschal had offered. Sergius protested that the Church could not bear the imposition but John insisted, and Sergius was forced to strip the ornaments from

---

(*MAH*, 31, 1911); A. Testi Rasponi, 'La nomina dei Vescovi suffraganei della metropoli ravennate sotto l'amministrazione bizantina', Bologna, 1911; K. Brandi, 'Ravenna und Rom: neue Beiträge zur Kenntnis der römisch-byzantinischen Urkunden', (*Archiv für Urkundenforschung*, 9, 1924); E. Dupre-Theseider, 'La questione dell' autocefalia della Chiesa di Ravenna', (*Corsi d'Arte Ravennate e Bizantina*, 1957, *fasc.* 2).

[28] *LP*. I, 346, and n. 1; for another account, P. Peeters, 'Une Vie Grecque de S. Martin', (*AB*. 51, 1933).

St. Peter's until the full weight was made up. The exarch thereupon left Rome, leaving the archdeacon to his fate. Paschal was tried and found guilty of, among other things, witchcraft, incantations and the casting of lots for fortune-telling, and was imprisoned in a monastery where he died a few years later, still unrepentant.[29]

The swing of the now thoroughly naturalized army towards Italian and papal interests, and resistance to pressure from its nominal master the Emperor, became yet more pronounced in Sergius's reign. In 692 the Emperor Justinian II summoned a synod to Constantinople to enact severe measures to control the Church, to establish the usage of the see of Constantinople as the canonical norm, and to place severe restrictions on future doctrinal enquiry. Papal legates were sent to this synod, Bishop John of Porto and Sergius's counsellor Boniface; the patriarchs of Constantinople, Antioch and Alexandria subscribed to the canons, and the papal legates, perhaps through insufficient knowledge of Greek or more likely through compulsion, also signed, but Sergius refused to ratify the acts when they were sent to him for confirmation or to regard the synod, as Justinian did, as ecumenical. Justinian, a brilliant but unstable man subject to outbursts of great cruelty, undertook reprisals; Bishop John and Boniface were arrested and an officer, Zachary, was sent to Rome to arrest the pope and bring him, like Martin, to Constantinople. However, when the purpose of Zachary's mission leaked out, the armies of Ravenna and the Pentapolis which he was leading to Rome mutinied outside the city. Zachary escaped from his own troops into the city, had the gates barred and ordered Sergius's arrest. But his nerve broke at the sight of contingents from every region of Italy, all seemingly determined to have his life in defence of the pope. One refuge alone seemed secure – the Lateran, and within the Lateran itself, the bedroom of the pope. There he fled and tearfully begged for Sergius's protection. The army of Ravenna had entered Rome through the St. Peter gate and had moved up to the Lateran with much blowing of trumpets; there they shouted for the pope to show himself, for a rumour had already spread that he had been abducted. The Lateran gates remained shut and the troops threatened to storm them if they were not speedily opened; inside, Zachary, almost senseless with panic, had hidden under the pope's bed.

[29] *LP.* I, 371–2.

Sergius tried to comfort him, assuring him that his life would be protected; he then went out in front of the basilica of Theodore and showed himself to the army. He received a rapturous welcome but when he asked the army to disperse, it insisted on remaining on guard through the night.[30]

This was an example of a national and religious assertion against imperial rule in Italy which reached serious proportions under Justinian II. In 695 Justinian was deposed and, his nose cut off, exiled to the Crimea. Some citizens of Ravenna were apparently implicated in his deposition, for when he regained his throne ten years later, his anger fell first on that city. Prominent citizens were arrested, including Archbishop Felix and Johannicius, a renowned scholar and an ancestor of Agnellus Andreas, who was executed. A fleet was sent to Ravenna under Theodore Monstraticus to complete the subjection of the rebellious province but the citizens of Ravenna, electing Johannicius's son George as their captain, prepared to resist. Units of the militia were summoned from all the towns of Emilia and Pentapolis. 'He rode out on his dun horse beyond Ravenna to observe Italy's preparations, and on his return at the ninth hour said to his companions: "... We must provide a guard, for I have had news from the Sea of Marmora of the bitter drink preparing for us. We will not show our backs to these boastful Greeks. Be confident!... The whole assembly of Ravenna must give battle ... and when they see this our allies will be ready to give fight. Your right hands must be brave in defence of our city walls; the allies from the surrounding cities will join you to defend our citadel and save our city. The coasts must be kept safe and the watch kept at their posts. Sarsina must keep guard; let Cervia also keep guard on the Po, at Nones on the Cesena bend. The men from Forlimpopoli must station themselves at the Port of Savio, where the tides flow; the countrymen from Decumana must guard the Candiano harbour. Forli holds the curve of the shore, the men from Ronco are

---

[30] On Justinian's Trullan Council (Mansi, 11, 921), P. P. Joannou, *Discipline Generale Antique*, (1962) I, I: V. Laurent, 'L'Oeuvre canonique du Concile in Trullo (691–2), Source primaire du droit de l'Eglise Orientale' (*Revue des Etudes Byzantins*) 23, 1965; in general on Justinian's relations with the papacy, F. Gowes, 'Justinian II und das romische Papstum' (*Byzantinische Zeitschrift*), 17, 1908. *LP.* I, 372–3.

to watch the fortress of Faenza by the old river bed, behind Port Lacherno, and the banks of the Po. The battalion from Imola are to hold the fields of Coriander, and the surrounding area; the contingents from Bologna, across the Po, are to be stationed at Porto Leone." ' So George's descendant Agnellus, with conscious heroic echoes of Virgil, described the preparations a century later. His work, including the division of Ravenna into twelve militia companies, proved permanent. Monstraticus was defeated and the anniversary, 14th July, was kept as a holiday in Ravenna.[31]

This twelve-fold division of the militia was not confined to Ravenna, and may not have been initiated by George. The seven ecclesiastical divisions of Rome each had their banner, a cross, which were stored in the church of St. Anastasia when not in use. On stational occasions, they were carried in procession but were left by the *ambo* of the church and not brought into the *presbyterium*. From the seventh century however there was a distinction; the military banners, the *bandora*, were also paraded on these occasions, and their bearers, the *milites draconarii*, were permitted into the sanctuary. Both groupings of the people were present on important civil occasions, such as the reception of Constans or of the exarch, and at the reception of Charlemagne in 774, the return of Leo in 799 and the welcome to King Louis in 844. On each of these occasions the military chiefs with their standards rode out thirty miles to make the first welcome; nearer home, because presumably unmounted, were the contingents of the *scholae*, with their patrons and the children they supported, and those of the ecclesiastical regions behind their crosses; but all collectively were the army and militia of the Romans. The appointment of officers remains in doubt, but probably they were elective or hereditary; certainly each of the Byzantine circumscriptions of Italy retained a lively control over its affairs and an exclusive community spirit, which was recognized by Church and State and later used in negotiation with the Franks. This may have made a distinction –certainly it did in some parts of Italy–between the Church's sphere of influence and the civil, but at the beginning of the eighth century the full weight of the local civil authority was thrown behind the papacy in defiance of imperial government.[32]

[31] *LP*. Eccl. Rav., cc. 139, 140.
[32] P. S. Leicht, 'Il termine "communitas" in una lettera di Gregorio II',

Imperial authority still existed in Italy but was permissive only and, in spite of provocation, maintained through the exercise of all the papacy's peace-keeping powers. A rebellion in the army broke out when the exarch Theophilact, whose authority was largely limited to Sicily, tried to visit Rome; but through the good offices of Pope John VI the mutineers were calmed down.[33] Pope Constantine went further in his efforts to restore good relations; receiving an invitation to go to Constantinople he went accompanied by a large staff of advisers. His reception was an honourable one; wherever the papal ship put in to land, Constantine was received by Justinian's orders with full imperial honours. At Constantinople Justinian's son Tiberius, with the entire senate, court and senior clergy, came out seven miles to greet him. He entered the capital on a horse from the imperial stable and was lodged in the Placidia palace, the normal house of papal legates. Justinian was at Nicaea and he wrote suggesting a meeting at Nicomedia, the mid-point. The meeting was successful; Justinian exhibited every reverence and courtesy to the pope, attended his Mass and received communion from him, and confirmed once more the privileges of the Roman Church. Constantine then returned to the West, reaching Gaeta a year after his departure. It had been a meeting at which both the principals had genuinely concerned themselves with unity within the Church, even if Justinian hoped by his display of reverence and humility to regain some of the loyalty he was fast losing again. But the Italian aspect had been less happy; there the administration had once more settled into a form of brigandage that eroded its capabilities as a responsible government. As Constantine's ship passed Naples on its outward voyage, it encountered that of the new exarch, John Rizocopus. Once the pope was safely on his way, he headed for Rome, landed and caused the murders of several high papal officials, including the deacon Saiulus who was acting as Constantine's vicar in his absence, and the papal treasurer Peter.[34]

Justinian failed to obtain any advantage from Constantine's visit; three months after the pope's return he was dethroned for the second time and murdered. His successor was one Philippicus, reputedly of

(*ALMA*, 1, 1924); F. Arnaldi, 'Ancora sul significato di "patria" ', *ibid.*, 3, 1926.

[33] *LP*. I, 382.　　　　[34] *LP*. I, 389–91.

strong monothelite tendencies, who instituted a reaction from Justinian's careful orthodoxy of doctrine. Again the Romans spontaneously rejected his authority: they would not acknowledge his effigy on the coinage, or his name on documents; his official portrait was not hung in the churches and his name, at popular insistence, went uncommemorated in the Mass. It was at this stage of imperial authority that the office of Roman duke first specifically appears; one Peter was sent in Philippicus' name from Ravenna to assume the duchy of Rome. The Romans refused to recognize him and a party gathered round the previous duke, Christopher; a clash developed in the Forum and the Sacred Way, just below the imperial palace, and on either side about thirty men were killed or wounded. Constantine intervened, sending priests carrying the Gospels and the Cross who managed to separate the combatants when duke Peter's faction was on the defensive. There was a lull for some days, until the news came of Philippicus's own deposition in a mutiny of the Thracian army and of the elevation of the first secretary Flavius Artemius to the throne. The exarch Scholasticus himself brought the imperial letters to Rome assuring the pope of the new Emperor's orthodoxy. The civil war was ended, Peter holding the duchy on a promise not to interfere in Roman affairs.[35]

A story has come down of these events which serves to show the bitterness of feeling aroused and the sense of triumph felt in Rome at the overthrow of the heretic. In a text dated 30th September 713 is told how a Syrian bishop arrived in Rome with his young daughter whom he placed in the convent of St. Cassian. There in consequence of a love intrigue she became possessed by a devil, and her distressed father took her to the shrine of St. Anastasius *ad Aquas Salvias*, near St. Paul's, to obtain an exorcism. The cult of this Persian martyr of 627 had spread to the West and assumed, partly perhaps through memory of the two Anastasii, the papal legate and the disciple of Maximus, something of the nature of a symbol of resistance to imperial tampering with doctrine—Flavius Artemius, on his elevation to the throne, chose to reign as the Emperor Anastasius. The Syrian girl's devil, as the relics were brought forward, cried out in anguish: 'Why do you lead me to Anastasius, that dog-eater? He was mine, but he gave his body to be crucified for the Nazarene. I cannot be

[35] *LP.* I, 392.

cast out, for I am an Emperor, and have a diadem and troops and patricians.' But Philippicus had been cast out, and the devil blamed orthodoxy; when threatened with the major relics of St. Peter and St. Paul, he cried, 'O, this old man, Peter, what has he done? I would have arranged for Philippicus to reign, for he was my friend; but at Pentecost this person strolled in and established another. This is what he has done to me.' Roman influence may not have been as great as this Roman text implies, but the victory of orthodoxy was firmly ascribed to St. Peter.[36]

This succession of ephemeral emperors seriously weakened the Empire at a crucial time for the Arab war, after a period of quiescence, was flaring up again and neither Philippicus nor Anastasius were figures to command firmly. Imperial policy had imposed an economic blockade on the Arab dominions and in consequence a grand assault was opened by the Arabs on the capital itself, when an army crossed Asia Minor and closed the straits. In 717 a leader of real ability appeared, Leo, governor of Anatolia, who marched to Constantinople, destroyed the besieging Arabs and proclaimed himself emperor. A vigorous programme of reconstruction was set afoot; the Arabs were driven from Asia Minor over the next ten years and the financial and agricultural recovery of the Empire undertaken. With the total loss of the ancient provinces of Syria and Egypt, Anatolia became the main centre of Roman economic strength and manpower, and Leo III's great work lay in creating and encouraging a strong, free peasantry which would ensure a permanent and adequate supply of recruits. He was also vitally interested, as all emperors were, in securing unity in the Church as a reinforcement of unity in the State; but here his own predilections caused further schism. He was in origin from Northern Syria, and there, either as a result of the influence of Islam which was at this time developing its doctrine of opposition to human representation in art, or through some lingering taint of monophysitism which had always distrusted religious art as emphasizing physical and human characteristics in the Trinity, he had acquired a strain which developed into Iconoclasm. This policy brought him some advantages; Islamic artistic influence had been growing within the Empire, even in Constantinople and—concerned as he was with the fluid border regions—there was a strong hope of appeal to uncommitted frontier areas. It was combined with an attack on the Greek monasteries, which had always provided the most vociferous opposition to imperial activity in religious matters; these had grown, in wealth and numbers, through the previous centuries. Leo aimed, not only at reducing a formidable body of opposition to the government, but at utilizing land confiscated from them for distribution to his peasant soldiery and, by restricting entry to the monastic houses, at stopping the drain on potential military recruits. The Iconoclast movement, which lasted for more than a century from Leo's first decree in 727, split the Empire; rebellion accompanied the first decrees in the island province of the Aegean and in Italy. A new influx of refugees from the East entered Italy and heightened the opposition there to Iconoclasm.[37]

Pope Gregory II condemned Iconoclasm, following the example of the patriarch of Constantinople. Leo wrote sternly to him, claiming an absolute power in both Church and State: 'I am both king and priest.' Gregory, a sound theologian who had accompanied Constantine to the East and made a good impression on Justinian II, refused to give way; he was also able to point out how small was imperial power in Italy, for simply by moving a few miles from Rome he would be out of its reach. The normal methods of countering papal opposition were tried. Byzantine officials in Rome formed a plot to murder Gregory, and secured the co-operation of a subdeacon, John Lurion; a new duke, Marinus, was sent to supervise the operation. It failed; Marinus was dismissed for dissoluteness of character and no other opportunity of reviving the plan could be found until the arrival of a new exarch, Paul. But it was discovered by the Romans, and the conspirators were killed or imprisoned.[38]

Now even the pretence of imperial control over Rome was almost at an end. As Lombard ambition once more revived with the weakening of the Empire, the papacy realized that a more powerful and trustworthy protector must be found for the scattered Roman provinces. Yet loyalty persisted and none demonstrated it more than Gregory II. When the Lombards of Benevento seized Cumae, the strongest point on the Western coast linking Rome to Naples and a

[37] L. Bréhier, *La Querelle des Images*, 1904; E. J. Martin, *A History of the Iconoclastic controversy*, 1930.
[38] *LP.* I, 403–4.

potential naval base, it was the pope who organized the combination of Roman and Neapolitan armies that retook it, and the Roman subdeacon Theodimus, rector of the Campanian patrimony, who accompanied the troops and arranged the ransoming of prisoners. As Leo's efforts to enforce Iconoclasm increased so did Italian opposition, checked only by the pope. Throughout the imperial possessions in the peninsula the armies gathered and elected their own dukes; a proposal was made to nominate an emperor and lead him to Constantinople but this Gregory restrained. When the duke Exhiliratus held out loyally for Leo in Campania, trying to collect forces to take Rome and arrest the Pope, the Romans marched out and put him and his son Hadrian to death. Finally duke Peter also met his fate, being blinded by the Romans on suspicion of treachery towards Gregory. At Ravenna the army mutinied and murdered the exarch Paul; his replacement, Eutychius, still tried to enforce the coercion of Rome. From Naples he sent men to murder Gregory but they were detected by the Romans, while throughout Latium and Campania the Italians were arming with weapons obtained from the Lombards and gathering to defend Rome. Eutychius tried once more, this time in formal alliance with the Lombard King Liutprand, who was taking advantage of these disorders to annexe the border-districts of the duchy of Rome. By the terms of the alliance Liutprand was to be allowed to bring the dissident duchies of Spoleto and Benevento to heel, as the exarch reduced Rome.[39]

Exarch and king marched on Rome and encamped in Nero's Field. But under Gregory's personal pleas Liutprand's determination waned; he came to St. Peter's to pray and before the tomb of the Apostle made an offering of his cloak, his gilded sword and scabbard, his breastplate and baldric and his crown. He then effected a re-conciliation between pope and exarch. Once more Gregory demon-strated the willingness of the papacy to support the imperial administration even against the incompetence of the imperial officials themselves. Immediately after Liutprand's withdrawal another rebellion rose in Tuscany; a certain Tiberius Petasius gained a following from the countryfolk around Bieda and Luni and pro-claimed himself emperor. Eutychius, timid and distrustful of the loyalty of the local troops, hesitated to take action, but Gregory

[39] *LP.* I, 404–5.

spurred him to it, sending him off accompanied by leading churchmen and citizens of Rome. The rebellion was crushed without difficulty and Tiberius executed; his head was sent to Constantinople.
Yet Leo remained unmollified by these proofs of papal co-operation,
and Gregory's opposition on the religious front continued; Leo's
nominee Anastasius, patriarch of Constantinople, was excommunicated.[40]

In 729 Leo took the final step that was equivalent to abandoning
Rome and excluding it from the Empire. Since the visit of Constans II
the attempts to make a bastion of Sicily and Southern Italy, where
imperial authority was strongest, to control the central Mediterranean had been accompanied by hardship and heavy taxation for
the inhabitants. The reigns of Constantine IV and Justinian II, with
the temporary restoration of good relations between Empire and
papacy, had led to some alleviation; Pope John V, who as deacon
had been a papal representative at the Council of Constantinople in
682, obtained from Constantine a relief of the poll-taxes and the
compulsory state purchase of wheat levied on the Calabrian and
Sicilian patrimonies. This had weighed heavily on the Roman
Church, and his successor Conon obtained the cancellation of a
further two hundred dues and levies on these properties, as well as the
release by the imperial authorities of those families imprisoned for
inability to pay their heavy taxes.[41] But the disorders that preceded
Leo's accession and the spread of Arab power along the African
coast and into Spain forced a tightening of control upon the Empire;
the papal estates in the South were just such vast properties that Leo
in the East was confiscating from Church houses and laity alike for
the establishment of his small-holding peasantry. Stringent fiscal
measures were tried first; the exarch Paul had arrived in Italy with
instructions to complete new tax assessments for all Byzantine Italy
and when promulgated they were found to be far more severe than
any formerly raised–in all doubling the previous rates. The rebellions
that broke out were as much in protest against these as against
Iconoclasm, and Gregory, appalled by the inequity they involved,
issued general instructions forbidding their payment.[42] In reprisal
and to buttress imperial authority where it could be maintained, Leo
responded with a drastic confiscation of all the papacy's holdings in

[40] *LP*. I, 408.   [41] *LP*. I, 366, 368–9.   [42] *LP*. I, 404.

Southern Italy and Sicily, then estimated at a value of 252,000 *solidi*, while Sicily and Illyricum, admittedly now predominantly Greek in complexion, were transferred from the Roman to the Constantino-politan patriarchate.[43]

Since the first major endowments to the Roman Church by Constantine I these properties had provided the bulk of the papacy's income, spent on multiple charitable purposes; from the Gothic Wars and the devastation of the Lombard invasion they had served also as the primary means of victualling Rome itself and of ensuring its continued existence as a city. Through Sicily Rome had traded with the East and had maintained contact with the world, avoiding the danger of slipping into an isolated village economy and mentality, which its own meagre resources would have dictated. Through Sicily also had come latterly many of Rome's leaders, men of a wider outlook and learning than Rome of itself could produce. Now the city was thrown back on its resources alone. During the previous century Rome and Italy had been increasingly sacrificed to imperial policies that had little domestic meaning and now, as the Lombard threat reawoke, the Empire was failing in its primary function of defence. The imperial territory—made up of scattered, isolated fragments—could not survive by itself; an outside protector as well as internal leadership must be found. The imperial connection was not formally ended; in Ravenna the exarchate was to survive another twenty years, and for even longer than that the Emperor in the East was still regarded as the fount of sovereignty. But in practice and spirit Leo had cast Rome out of her Empire, and Sicily was to be a barrier rather than a channel for communication. The common tradition and continuity of the Roman towns was to survive, materially and politically, through the efforts of the papacy alone.

But Rome still remained an imperial city, imbued with the Greek and Latin spirit of the Empire. The Greek area of the city, below the Aventine, was the first that any traveller arriving from down-river

[43] V. Grumel, 'L'annexation de l'Illyricum, de la Sicile et de la Calabre au Patriarchat de Constantinople: le temoignage de Theophane le Chrono-graphe', (*RSR*, 40, 1952): M. V. Anastos, 'The Transfer of Illyricum Calabria and Sicily to the jurisdiction of the patriarchate of Constantinople in 732–3', (*Studi bizantini e neoellenici, Silloge in onore di S. G. Mercati,* 9, 1957).

saw; and here were reminders of the East, churches dedicated to saints familiar at home, SS. Cyrus and John, St. Alexis, St. George and St. Maria *in Cosmedin*–this last reflecting, as so often, a piece of Constantinople transported and set down as a reminder of the city in the East. Above was the Palatine, reserved for imperial officials with its imperial chapel of S. Cesario, where the portraits of the reigning emperors were kept, a mystical presence even in the Westernmost city of the Empire. Yet even in this centre consecrated to imperial sovereignty there had latterly grown up signs of a rival papal sovereignty. John VII was the son of Plato, a retired officer of the imperial service with military experience both at sea and on land, who had been given the curatorship of the almost desolate imperial palace; his son, as pope, made a move to transfer the papal seat to the old civil centre. A new bishop's palace was built on the Palatine slopes, and the walls of the nearby church of S. Maria *Antica* were adorned with frescoes of John receiving the symbols of the papacy from a Virgin crowned and robed as an empress–the papacy, secure in divine patronage, needed little from earthly authority. However, the techniques of expressing this idea still displayed continued contact with the East; Alexandrian experts, refugees or imported, lent a new subtlety and brilliance to the native Roman tradition.[44]

S. Maria *Antica* shows the high tide of Eastern influence reached in Rome towards the end of the seventh century–the concept of the Virgin, crowned as the Queen of Heaven near to the source of sovereignty, was matched by liturgical developments. Pope Sergius had borrowed from the East the Marian liturgical cycle of the Annunciation, the Dormition and the Nativity of the Virgin, to-

[44] L. Duchesne, 'Notes sur la topographie de Rome au Moyen-Age; VII, Les légendes chrétiennes de l'Aventin', (*MAH*. 10, 1890); III, 'S. Anastasie', (*ibid.*, 7, 1887); P. Verzone, 'La demolizione dei palazzi imperiali di Roma e di Ravenna nel quadro delle nuove forze politiche del secolo VIII', (*Festschrift Gierke*); M. Avery, 'The Alexandrian Style of S. Maria Antiqua', (*Art Bulletin*, 1925); E. Kitzinger, *Römische Malerei vom Beginn des 7. bis zur Mitte des 8. Jahrhunderts*, Munich, 1934; N-J. Nordhagen, 'Nuove constatazioni sui rapporti artistici tra Roma e Bisanzio sotto il pontificato di Giovanni VII', (*Atti del III Congresso di Studi sull' Alto Medio Evo*, Spoleto); id., 'The Mosaics of John VII: The Mosaic Fragments and their Techniques', (*Acta ad Archeologiam et Artium Historiam Pertinentia, Institutum Romanum Norvegiae*, 2, 1965).

gether with the *hypopanti*, the combined feast of the Purification and of St. Symeon; a procession in her honour was the occasion for prayers giving a new emphasis to her bodily assumption. He also adopted in the Mass the invocation of Christ under the figure 'Lamb of God', a Syrian liturgical practice that was banned by the Quinisext Council of 691-2 in its attempt to impose the local and Greek rite of Constantinople on the universal Church–this Council, never recognized in the West as authoritative, marked one stage in the separation of the Churches. Sergius I again emphasized the independent nature of papal authority by his translation and re-burial in the centre of St. Peter's of the body of Pope Leo the Great who, far more than Gregory I, was regarded as the sustaining creator of the papacy in its championship of Christological and Petrine orthodoxy.[45]

Rome also continued throughout the eighth and ninth centuries to provide a congenial and useful refuge for those who fled from the doctrinal disputes of the East. These were principally monks who kept alive a strong tradition of Greek monasticism in Rome.[46] The Greek colony also took the lead in the production of books, so that Paul I was able to present to King Pepin works on grammar, geometry and orthography, as well as the writings of Aristotle and Dionysius the Areopagite, laying the foundations for the Carolingian revival of learning. Late in the ninth century there is evidence of a Greek scholar working in Rome, the archpriest John of St. George *in Velabro*. He had been educated by his father, who was a lay professor in Constantinople, perhaps a colleague of Photius at the university established there by the Caesar Bardas. So Roman society continued to span the bitterest controversies.[47] Indeed,

[45] See Ordo XX, (Andrieu, *OR*, 3, pp. 231–6); B. Capelle, 'L'Oraison "Veneranda" a la Messe de l'Assomption', (*Ephemerides theologicae lovanienses*, 26, 1950). The Quinisext Council, text in Mansi, 11, 921–1006, and P. P. Joannou, *Discipline Generale Antique*, Rome, 1962, I, 1, 98–241; see also V. Laurent, 'L'oeuvre canonique du Concile in Trullo (691–2), source primaire du droit de l'Eglise Orientale, (*Revue des Etudes Byzantins*, 23).

[46] F. Antonelli, 'I primi monasteri di monaci orientali in Roma', (*RAC*, 5, 1928); E. Binon, 'Greek monasteries and churches in Rome', (*Studi bizantini e neoellenici*, 5, 1940).

[47] P. Batiffol, 'Inscriptions byzantines de Saint-Georges-du-Velabre', (*MAH*. 7, 1887) and 'Les libraires byzantines à Rome', (*ibid.*, 8, 1888).

controversy was basic to a community of refugees; a manuscript from Rome of 759 contains *opuscula* of St. John Damascene, the greatest of the opponents of Iconoclasm. But Greek monks went even further than this. Theodore of Studion was able in the ninth century to make an appeal, dangerous to a Greek, to Petrine authority against imperial heterodoxy, and equally the Greek monks of Italy and Rome made a formidable contribution to the legend of St. Peter. The dioceses of southern Italy and Sicily, although for long Greek in speech and rite,[48] resented their forcible transfer to Constantinople's authority; the burden of many of the lives of the legendary founders of these sees, Pancratius of Taormina and Marcianus of Syracuse for example, looks back to a Petrine foundation, whether from Antioch or Rome, to demonstrate their independence of the imperial Church.[49]

The imperial connection, while it had at times cost Rome and the papacy dear, had nevertheless moulded the political thought and the culture of the city; henceforth settlements to achieve stability and freedom from external domination, demanded in the name of St. Peter, would only be conceived in the framework of the Roman Empire. The papacy, almost alone in Italy, had fought against great provocation to sustain the ideal of Christian and imperial unity and had, against its will, been virtually ejected from one form of this; but this form had been consecrated by tradition and the Fathers, and was to be reconstituted under whoever should prove worthy.

[48] Lynn White, 'The Byzantinization of Sicily', (*American Historical Review*, 41, 1936).

[49] E. Patlagean, 'Les moines grecs d'Italie et l'apologie des thèses pontificales', (*Studi Medievali*, 5, 1964).

6

ROME OF THE PILGRIMS

By the beginning of the seventh century Rome, the *communis patria* of the legal and political world, had ceased to exist. Gregory I wrote to Rusticiana in Constantinople, urging her to return to her native city and wondering how anyone could forget Rome: but Gregory was the last of his generation in the west and was speaking to the last of his generation in the east. Those who now came to Rome came with different memories, different eyes, to be in contact with the mystique of St. Peter and the martyrs; and Rome's influence was henceforth to be that of the power and patronage of Peter, the key-bearer of the kingdom of heaven.

This pilgrim spirit of the *romipetae*, those who came to the city for its associations with the apostles and martyrs, and not as those young men to whom Gregory had referred, to seek their fortunes, was nothing new. In the fifth century Sidonius Apollinaris, the son-in-law of a western emperor and a future praetorian prefect, described his entrance into Rome from the north, by the imperial *Via Triumpalis* 'Before allowing myself to set foot in the outer boundary of the city itself, I sank to my knees at the triumphal threshold of the Apostles'; and the tradition of the Christian holy city antedated him.[1] Fulgentius also, before visiting the persons of influence whom he had come to see in Rome, went the rounds of the holy places to pray, the prime and transcendent meaning of any visit to Rome.[2] But it was over the northern nations that the purely Christian and Petrine elements were to exert their influence, to whom the histories of the emperors were dark and diabolical legends, whose knowledge of the past and education by the past came from the stories of the martyrs and to whom physical contact with the past was to be found in their

[1] Sidonius Apollinaris, *Ep.* 5. See also: J. Giraud, 'Rome ville sainte au Ve siècle', (*Revue d'histoire et de litterature religieuse*, 3, 1898) and G. Bardy, 'Pelérinages a Rome vers la fin du IVe siècle', (*AB*, 67, 1947).

[2] *Vita Fulgentii*, c. IX.

shrines and at the scenes of their sufferings. As the staple of literature these acts of the martyrs prevailed; the Gelasian decree was the product of a period when critical scholarship still flourished, but within a century Gregory had issued his *Dialogues*, with an inordinate amount of the fabulous, for Gregory was a pragmatic who saw that the world had left behind the appreciation of scholarship and that the faith and morals of Christendom must be sustained by less sophisticated means.[3] And for that, not deliberately but in the spontaneous acceptance of the new primacy of Rome, the cult of St. Peter grew as a new imperial theme.[4]

The awe in which the apostles and saints of Rome were held is testified by Gregory the Great; writing to the Empress Constantina, wife of Maurice, he told her of the impact of their shrines. 'The bodies of the apostles Peter and Paul glitter with such great miracles and awe that no one can go to pray there without considerable fear. When my predecessor of blessed memory wished to change the silver which covers the sacred body of the blessed apostle Peter, although this is fifteen feet away from the body he received an apparition of considerable horror. I myself in the same way wished to carry out some repairs near the most sacred body of the apostle St. Paul; as it was necessary to dig to some depth near his tomb the foreman found some bones, which had no connection with the tombs. He dared to lift them and move them elsewhere; he died suddenly with horrifying symptoms. Again, my predecessor of holy memory wished to make some improvements not far from the body of St. Lawrence, whose burial place was unknown; excavations were undertaken in search of it and suddenly his tomb was uncovered. Those working there, monks and servants of the church, saw the martyr's body which, indeed, they did not dare touch; all died within ten days.'[5] Gregory's missions to England carried the patronage of the apostles with them; to St. Peter was dedicated Paulinus's church at York; to St. Peter and St. Paul, Augustine's first monastery at Canterbury and to St. Paul

[3] See W. F. Bolton, ch. 3, n. 69.

[4] See F. Susman, 'Il culto di S. Pietro da Leone Magno a Vitaliano', (*ASR*, 84, 1961); E. Ewig, 'Der Petrus- und Apostelkult im spatrömischen und fränkischen Gallien', (*Zeitschrift für Kirchengeschichte*, 71, 1960). For the influence of Roman cults in Byzantine Italy, see A. Dufourcq, 'La passionale occidental du VIIe siècle', (*MAH*, 26, 1906).

[5] Gregory I, *Registrum*, IV, 30.

Mellitus's cathedral in London.[6] Bishop Palladius of Saintes, in Provence, also built a church dedicated to St. Peter and St. Paul and received from Gregory relics of the shrines of the apostles and also of St. Lawrence and St. Pancras.[7] St. Amandus, a frequent and ardent pilgrim to Rome, was typical of the seventh century prelate in naming his foundations in his diocese of Maastricht after the princes of the apostles out of reverence for the city and its patrons.[8] But although these were visible reminders scattered throughout Europe of the loyalty and devotion owed to the new founders of Rome, they were only substitutes for a visit to the city of the apostles and to the possession if possible of some tangible association with them and their confrères, the martyrs, the new heroes of Europe's past.

In the time of Gregory I Agilulf, a deacon of St. Gregory of Tours, was sent by his bishop to Rome to collect relics; the bishop set down his description of the cults. 'St. Peter is buried in a church called from ancient times the Vatican. . . . His sepulchre, which is placed under the altar, is very rarely entered. However, if anyone wishes to pray the gates by which the spot is enclosed are opened, and he enters above the sepulchre; then he opens a little window there and puts his head inside, and makes his requests according to his needs. Nor is the result delayed, if only his petition be a just one. If he desires to carry away with him some blessed memorial, he throws inside a small handkerchief which has been carefully weighted and then, watching and fasting, he prays most fervently that the apostle may give a favourable answer to his devotion. Wonderful to say, if the man's faith prevails, the handkerchief when drawn up from the tomb is so filled with divine virtue that it weighs much more than it did before; and then he who has pulled it up knows that he has obtained the favour he sought. Many also make gold keys to unlock the gates of the blessed sepulchre; then they take away those previously in use as a sacred treasure, and by these keys the infirmities of the afflicted are cured. For true faith can do all things.'[9]

[6] Bede, HE (ed. Plummer), I, 33; II, 3, 14.

[7] Gregory I, *Registrum*, VI, 48.

[8] E. de Moreau, 'La "Vita Amandi Prima" et les fondations monastiques de S. Amand', (*AB*, 67, 1949).

[9] Gregory of Tours, *De Gloria Martyrum*, (*MGH. SS. Rer. Merov.*, II), 1, 28.

These keys were sought-after keepsakes of the shrine; Gregory I sent them to Theoctista, the sister of the Emperor Maurice and governess to the imperial children, to King Childebert of the Franks and to Anastasius, patriarch of Antioch.[10] A later pope was to send them to a Frankish king in appeal for the liberation of Rome from the Lombards. Other relics, too, were sought, above all filings from the chains worn by St. Peter in prison; Gregory of Tours described the process of obtaining them: 'A priest stands by with a file; in the case of some seekers a portion comes off from the chains so quickly there is no delay', but for others, presumably of less worthy intentions, it was found impossible to obtain any filings at all.[11] These keys were deeply reverenced; Pope Gregory tells a story of an Arian Lombard who was struck dead because he impiously tried to extract the gold content of one to sell.[12]

Rome was prepared for visitors and a whole organization of hostels and guide books grew up to meet their needs. From the time of the persecutions, the Roman Church had been concerned to preserve the bodies and memories of the saints. The greatest work had been undertaken in the mid-fourth century by Pope Damasus who had collected the bodies of the martyrs in the catacombs and clearly marked in verse of his own composition the names and facts of each; notaries had also been instructed, in each ecclesiastical region, to compile the Acts of the martyrs from official records or tradition. The work at the cemeteries was continued; Pope Vigilius, after the Gothic sieges of Rome, was compelled to undertake major reorganization. But the literary record soon became contaminated; too many external influences, the love of the amazing, parallels with secular stories or names, and the pride of the great families who wished to incorporate themselves in the Christian as well as imperial past of Rome, intervened. But they stood as a lively source to stimulate the minds of emerging Europe. Europe knew of the martyrs and wished to visit them.[13]

[10] Gregory I, *Registrum*, VI, 6; I, 25; VII, 23. The impact of the image of St. Peter as door-keeper of Heaven (as for example on king Oswy at the synod of Whitby, Bede, HE, 3, 25) was a powerful one; see Th. Zwolfer, *Sankt Peter, Apostelfürst und Himmelsförtner. Seine Verehrung bei den Angelsachsen und Franken*, Stuttgart, 1929.

[11] *Ibid.*, IV, 300.   [12] *Ibid.*, VII, 23.

[13] A. Ferrua, 'Epigrammata Damasiana', (*Sussidi allo studio della*

From the catacombs and the shrines had grown the custom of removing oil from the lamps, sealing it in small *ampullae* or phials and labelling it with the source, so retaining a memorial of the saints by whose bodies the pilgrim had prayed. A number of these labels have survived, in copy, from a visit made late in the sixth century by John, chaplain to the Lombard queen Theodolinda at Pavia. It is apparent from their listed order that John made a consistent tour of the sites of veneration in a clockwise direction round Rome from St. Peter's.[14] All the cemeteries where the bodies and shrines of the martyrs lay were naturally outside the city, lying on or near the great arterial roads that radiated from it. The pilgrims, therefore, like John, moved round the city on the perimeter, either clockwise or anti-clockwise, to visit all the shrines.[15] That was the order in which the pilgrim guides of the seventh century came to be compiled, following a definite, logical sequence: compiled perhaps by some Roman cleric and taken north and copied by rich pilgrims. There is no more telling illustration of Rome's changed fortunes and status in the world of realities than the new centres and objects of interest; where the author of the passage inserted into Zachary's work emphasized the height of the blocks of buildings, the splendour of the princely palaces, the great public buildings, little more than a century later all these are ignored. The two earliest pilgrim guides, the *Notitia Ecclesiarum Urbis Romae* from the middle of the seventh century and the *De Locis Sanctorum Martyrum quae sunt foris Civitate Roma* of the same period, (but probably revised from an earlier edition of the time of Pelagius II) makes no mention of the antiquities or the imperial remains; as the title of the latter implies, they are concerned with something that imperial Rome noted only in an administrative context. Now guides were being published to bring the faithful to the graveyards.[16]

Considered simply as guides they are remarkably detailed. An entry from the *Notitia* dealing with a group of cemeteries on the Via

antichità cristiana, II, 1942) and 'Antichità cristiana. I lavori del papa Vigilio nelle catacombe', (*Civiltà Cattolica*, 118, 2; 1967). A. Dufourcq, *Etudes*, *cit*. ch. 1, m. 27.

[14] Valentini and Zucchetti, *Codici topografici*, vol. 2, pp. 29–47.

[15] *Ibid.*, vol. 2, pp. 49–66 for a catalogue of the cemeteries, probably of the late 7th century.

[16] *Ibid.*, vol. 2, pp. 67–99, 101–31.

Salaria Vecchia runs as follows: 'Then you proceed eastwards (i.e. from the Via Flaminia) until you come to the church of the martyr John on the Via Salaria: here rest the martyr Diogenis and, in another alcove, the martyr Bonifacianus and, underground, the martyr Festus and, also underground, the martyr Blastus. Then come the martyrs John and Longinus. Then proceed south along the Via Salaria until you come to St. Hermes; in the basilica there, the first at rest is Bassilla, virgin and martyr, then the martyr Maximus, and the martyr St. Hermes, who is deep underground. In another tomb there are the martyrs Protus and Hyacinth, and further on the martyr Victor. Then further along the same road you come to the holy martyr Pamphilius, underground: you go down twenty-four steps here.'[17] There was therefore little chance of losing one's way, or of subsequent regrets that one had missed anything; the itineraries of Rome provided a complete list of what people wanted to see.

Those who came were of all kinds: the ordinary pilgrims, usually clerical; bishops or their clergy with business to transact with the papacy, or to collect relics, manuscripts and privileges of confirmation for their foundations: envoys or exiles from the east concerned in the religious troubles of the Empire. Pyrrhus, a deposed patriarch, and Maximus, an exiled monk in opposition to his government, came in the mid-seventh century; later the deposed Macarus of Antioch, in exile for obdurate monothelitism, was sent to Rome with his disciples, and there on papal orders the counsellor Boniface engaged him in controversy. Early in the ninth century, Methodius, a future patriarch of Constantinople, spent some time in Rome, either as a semi-official envoy or as a refugee: 'Never', it was said, 'had the tomb of St. Peter had a more fervent and assiduous visitor.' Appeals were sent to Rome as the frontiers of Latin Christendom expanded in Germany and England during the seventh and eighth centuries. Bishops came to attend synods–those from central Italy, of the province of Rome itself, came three times a year. Kings came: the Saxon kings Ine and Offa, and Caedwalla who was baptized as Peter by Sergius I, settled down and lived the pilgrim life in Rome until they died in the shadow of the apostles.[18] These Anglo-Saxon kings

[17] *Ibid.*, pp. 74–5.
[18] Mansi, 12, 1035; L. Pargoire, 'S. Methode de Constantinople avant 821', (*Echos d'Orient*, 6, 1902); J. Zettinger, 'Die Berichte über Rompilger

founded for their own nation, who were the most eager of all for the Roman pilgrimage, their own hostel or series of hostels, near St. Peter's, which they called in their own tongue their borough (in Italian 'borgo'); there they lived as a separate community, the *Schola* of the Saxons, just outside the limits of the city.[19] Other national communities followed, the *Scholae* of the Greeks, the Lombards and the Frisians, and all these served with the Romans in defence of the city and as units on ceremonial occasions.[20] National characteristics persisted; twice in the ninth century fires, which spread and threatened St. Peter's, broke out 'through the carelessness of some Saxons' in the Borgo, the result perhaps of their preference for the wooden houses of their home country in what was still a city of brick and marble.[21]

Apart from the national foundations there were papal hostels set apart for pilgrims; the *xenodochia* or homes for foreigners. One was founded by Belisarius near the present Trevi Fountain; others took over the great houses of the defunct nobility and all received endowment, support and maintenance from the papacy. The papacy itself directly helped the poorer or the more unfortunate pilgrims and visitors, such as the refugees from persecution in the East. The wardens of these hostels, appointed by the pope, were enjoined to take the greatest care of visitors; they were to provide not merely food and beds, but bed-clothes, and medical attention for the sick.[22] When Pope Martin was on trial in Constantinople, he was questioned by the secretary Demosthenes on the visit of the deposed patriarch Pyrrhus in the time of Pope Theodore and the welcome accorded him by the pope. Martin explained: 'Of his own accord Pyrrhus came to Rome, in the footsteps of the blessed Peter: so why should not my predecessor receive and honour him as a bishop?' Demosthenes replied: 'Yes, that is so. But where did he get the necessities of life, to support himself?' The blessed pope replied, 'Openly, from the patriarchal palace in Rome.' His examiner asked 'What quality was

---

aus dem Frankenreiche bis zum Jahre 800', (*Römische Quartalschrift, Supplementum XI*, 1900).

[19] W. J. Moore, *The Saxon Pilgrims to Rome and the Schola Saxonum*, 1937.

[20] *LP*. II, 6 and n. 27.   [21] *LP*. II, 53–4, 111.

[22] *LP*. I, 296: see also ch. 4, p. 116.

the food given to him?' 'Do you not know the Roman Church, my Lord? I tell you, that whenever some unhappy man, it does not matter who, comes for hospitality, then everything is laid out for his use, and St. Peter sends no arrival away without his gifts; but bread of the finest and several wines are given not only to him but to all his company. If this is the reception of the unfortunate, what sort of treatment is given to one who comes honourably as a bishop?'[23] Private lodgings were also available; the founder of Farfa Abbey visiting Rome early in the eighth century with his disciples stayed in the house of a pious widow; the families of his disciples, looking for them, searched the more usual hostels and monasteries, before running them to earth.[24]

One bishop who received, on occasion, less than episcopal respect was Amandus of Maastricht. He visited Rome on several occasions, in 627, 630 and around 650; he became a close friend of Pope Martin and took back with him a deep respect for the cult of the princes of the apostles. But he also appears as an early victim of a certain habit of mind of minor Italian officialdom: 'One day, towards evening, this holy man of God was sitting in a small church after everyone had left, and the *custodi* were as usual tidying up, for he wished in his devotion to pray through the night: but one of the *custodi*, finding him there, ejected him from the church with contempt and blows.'[25]

In the uncertain state of Italy a normal method of travelling was by sea from Marseilles. So Amandus on his third pilgrimage sailed to Civitavecchia on the coast north of Rome; and Hadrian and Theodore on their voyage in 668 also took a merchant ship to Marseilles.[26] The legates of the apostolic see, the envoys of the Empire and the Frankish kings normally also travelled by sea when Rome was isolated by the Lombards, but in the ninth century, with the union of the Frankish and Lombard kingdoms and the growth of the Saracen menace at sea, the land route again became safe and popular. Even so this had its trials; in the mid-ninth century Bishop Ansovinus of

[23] Mansi, 10, 859.

[24] *Constructio Monasterii Farfensis*, lectio VIII, in *Il Chronicon Farfense di Gregorio di Catino*, (ed. U. Balzani, 2 vols., 1903), vol. 1, p. 11.

[25] Baudemundus, *Vita Amandi*, (*MGH., SS. Rer. Merov.*, V, 431). This was the paraliturgical ceremony of the *diligentia*, *OR*, vol. 4, *ordo* 44.

[26] Bede, HE, IV, 1.

Camerino, travelling to attend a synod in Rome, stopped for the night at a hostelry. Becoming suspicious of the wine served, he blessed it and to the discomfort of the *padrone* it separated in the cup into its component wine and water. An eighth century archbishop complained of another aspect of the English vogue for pilgrimages; the towns of northern Italy were overrun with English prostitutes.[27]

Rome was without a fleet or merchant marine of its own; under the Byzantines a fleet stationed in Sicily served the Tyrrhenian Sea and the merchant ships of the Byzantine trading towns, Amalfi, Gaeta, Salerno and Naples, carried the produce of the Sicilian estates, the real centre of Roman and papal trading. Through Sicily arrived most of the oriental visitors to Rome, mainly Greeks and Syrians, some of whom had settled in Sicily as a result either of imperial persecution or of the pressure of the Arab conquests in the East and South. Rome remained a meeting point for the nations; the Cilician Theodore of Tarsus, in Rome, was unexpectedly appointed Archbishop of Canterbury, and he was accompanied to England by the North African abbot Hadrian.[28] When, about 633, the envoys of the Irish abbot Cummian came to Rome to seek a solution to the question of the date of Easter, they found staying in their hostel a Greek, a Hebrew, a Scythian and an Egyptian; all celebrated Easter together in St. Peter's.[29] But there were other visitors to Rome, merchants of less reputable aspect. In the mid-eighth century Pope Zachary found that 'many Venetian merchants arrived here in Rome, and they were active in an unmentionable trade, buying a great number of slaves, both male and female, whom they attempted to transport to the pagans in Africa. When he discovered this, the most holy father had it forbidden, judging it not right that those who had been washed in Christ's baptism should be slaves to pagans; he paid the Venetians the price they could prove to have spent in their purchase, and so ransomed them all from the yoke of slavery and set them free as his children.'[30]

Rome also drew travellers from all over the Western world as the

---

[27] *Vita Ansovini*, (*AASS*, Mart. II, 322–7) cc. 9–10; Boniface, *Ep.* 78, (MGH. Epp. 111).

[28] Bede, HE, IV, 29.

[29] *Vita Cummiani*, (*PL.* 87, 972).

[30] *LP.* 1, 433.

possessor of libraries to which scholars flocked to research, copy and borrow books–an important service to a faith that was built largely upon patristic commentaries to its texts, and needed good copies of its authorities. That was what Cassiodorus had attempted to provide at the Vivarium and the tradition, if not the great bulk of the library of Vivarium, had passed to Rome. This constant need for authorities and for care in accepting received texts was illustrated in the course of the sessions of the Third Council of Constantinople, when the patriarch Macarus referred to texts in support of his monophysite teaching to be found in the letters exchanged between Pope Vigilius and the patriarch Menas of Constantinople. At the insistence of the papal legates, these volumes were brought in from the nearby archive of the patriarchate, and the relevant passages were found to be blatant forgeries.[31] In Rome, the *scrinium* provided a similar service; during the synod of 649 'it was found necessary to bring a copy of this Doctor. . . . All manner of documents and books are provided by the *scrinium* and the library at once, for it is nearby,' and the *primicerius* was on hand to bring them.[32] People borrowing or copying rare books caused a heavy strain on the Lateran's resources; Pope Martin wrote to his friend Bishop Amandus 'Our library is being ransacked for books, and so we have none to give away.'[33] The deacon Taio of Saragossa, who visited the Lateran in 642 to consult on behalf of his bishop the works of Gregrory the Great, shows something of the great hunger for texts that there was in less endowed parts. It was reported that he encountered a common difficulty in being unable to find the texts he required and that a vision of Gregory himself supplemented the librarians' efforts.[34] Under Pope Martin there was a reorganization of the facilities in Rome–inspired largely by the doctrinal disputes of the seventh century, and encouraged by the presence in Rome of so many Eastern and African refugees. In 649 there was an adequate service for compiling dossiers and a system for translation, but the native scholarship of Rome was not flourishing. Boniface, the counsellor of Benedict II, translated an

[31] Mansi, 11, 583–602.
[32] Mansi, 10, 863.
[33] Mansi, *Ep.* 2, (*PL.* 87, 138)
[34] *MGH. AA.* XIV, pp. 287–90; Mansi, 10, 773; E. Madoz, *Tajon de Zaragoza y su viaje a Roma*, (Mélanges De Ghellinck, 1951).

encomium by Sophronius of Jerusalem of St. Cyrus and St. John with an account of their miracles,[35] and under Gregory III a Greek version of the Life of Martin was produced.[36] Knowledge of Greek was common under the Eastern popes of the late seventh century[37] and Greek libraries existed, producing, indeed, in contrast to the Latin texts, more volumes than could be employed locally.[38] The Hellenized aspect of Rome was indicated by Wilfred's reception before a Roman synod: 'They (the Roman clergy) sat there, laughing among themselves and chatting in Greek.'[39] Throughout the greater part of the seventh century, then, the resources in Rome for scholarship were utilized in the main by northern or Eastern scholars, such as the English priest Nothelm, who examined the archives and made copies of letters of Gregory I concerning the English mission, which he transmitted to Bede for inclusion in his History.[40]

Devotion to the saints of Rome gave rise to another traffic, which grew in popularity as a result of the more settled conditions following the establishment of Carolingian power and the growth of the French and German Churches. This was the acquisition of whole bodies of the Roman saints, translated to old or new foundations, to grant an added lustre by their presence. Gregory I had frowned on the removal of saints' bodies; and supernatural fates followed archaeological research. There was also the danger of false ascription – Gregory himself supplied one instance: 'Certain Greek monks who came here more than two years ago dug up in the silence of the night, near St. Paul's Church, the bodies of dead men lying in the open field, and kept their bones in their own possession until their departure. But they were arrested and examined with care on their reasons for this, and they confessed that they were going to transport these bones to Greece, to pass off as relics of the saints.'[41] The reality of the

---

[35] *PG*. 87, 3379–3422; 3423–3675.

[36] P. Peeters, 'Une Vie grecque du pape S. Martin', (*AB*. 51, 1933).

[37] H. Steinacker, 'Die römische Kirche und griechischen Sprachkenntnisse des Frühmittelalters', (*Mitteilungen des Instituts für Oesterreichische Geschichtsforschung*, 62, 1954).

[38] P. Batiffol, 'Les libraires byzantines à Rome', (*MAH.*, 8, 1888); Cod. Carol., 24.

[39] Eddius Stephanus, *Vita Wilfridi*, (ed. and Eng. trans. by B. Colgrave, 1927) c. 53.

[40] Bede, HE, preface.   [41] Gregory I, *Registrum*, IV, 30.

saint's power in the vicinity of its remains was strongly held, and something more than symbolism dictated men's attitudes to them. For instance, in the ninth century Pope Paschal received a vision of St. Cecilia which at first he refused to credit, since it was believed in Rome that Cecilia's body had been removed fifty years before by the Lombards and taken to Pavia—she could not appear at such a distance. The saint insisted and her body was found where she indicated and where it had been hidden. Another example is provided by the devotion of the Carolingian house to St. Petronilla, believed to be the elder daughter of Peter. At Pepin's request she was moved from the shrine on the Ardea road to the Vatican, nearer her father; there she was placed in one of two tombs built in the fifth century for the Theodosian family, and there the baptismal cloth of Pepin's daughter Gisela, for whom Pope Paul stood sponsor, was placed in offering.[42]

The Roman Church attempted to control this traffic and provide some means of authenticating the relics; the frequent requests of Frankish pilgrims, although unpopular to the Romans who felt that they were being denuded of their store of treasure, their reserve of spiritual patronage, could hardly be resisted at times when the papacy was in close political dependence on the Frankish Empire. But even among the Romans there naturally arose unscrupulous agents; and Frankish clerics were not above underhand means to obtain illustrious patrons to obtain prestige since the corporate sense of a diocese or religious community was expressed as a function of its patron saint.

The monk Radoin, sent in 826 by Abbot Hilduin of Soissons in search of relics, ran directly into a political controversy. He arrived armed with letters of introduction from the Emperor Louis, and Pope Eugenius, whose authority in Rome was still unsure, was in no condition to dispute his demands. However Eugenius was ill at the time and Radoin was forced to await the return to Rome of the pope's all-powerful advisers, the *superista* Quirinus and the *nomenclator* Theophylact. To them Radoin presented his letters and made his request—for no less than the body of St. Sebastian. The two ministers paled; they told Radoin that St. Sebastian was, after St.

[42] *LP.* II, 56; I, 455; Cod. Carol., 14; P. Danglefort, *S. Petronille, patronne de France*, (1911).

Peter and St. Paul, the third patron of Rome, that he had been named by Pope Gaius as *defensor* of the Roman Church and that the transfer was therefore impossible. Radoin again mentioned the interest the Emperor had in the translation and was taken by the two ministers to an audience with the bed-ridden pope. Eugenius was also astonished at the request and, after consulting with the senate, refused it, but in private conversation with Quirinus and Theophylact, Radoin was able to put to them the advantage of pleasing the Emperor. Opposition remained strong and vociferous; many of the clergy and secretaries of the Lateran assembled in the papal apartments and a violent argument broke out in the pope's very chamber. Instances were brought up of the attempts of Eugenius's successors to move St. Sebastian–Popes Hadrian, Leo III and Paschal had all tried but signs had frustrated each attempt, and there was a strong sentiment that any renewal would bring misfortune on those responsible. However, political pressures proved too strong, and Eugenius sent Bishop John of Silva Candida to obtain the body for Radoin. John brought the body to the Lateran to be sealed with the pope's personal signet, the normal guarantee of authenticity; it was then taken temporarily to St. Peter's. There the Romans made a last attempt to save their patron; gathering together they taunted the pope with exceeding his predecessors in cruelty in allowing so great a saint to be taken from them, and persuaded him to remove the body from its casket, leaving only one arm. Abbot Ingoald of Farfa, a strong Frankish supporter, foiled the attempted fraud and Eugenius, with no room for further manoeuvre, could not prevent the saint's removal to Soissons, to redound to the glory of that town.[43] But perhaps the Romans succeeded in part; a few years later, in the time of Gregory IV, at least some relics of Sebastian were still in Rome.[44]

Eight years later, in 834, Bishop Hitto of Freising came to Rome on a similar relic-collecting expedition. Pope Gregory IV showed him his storehouse of immediately available relics but none of these was sufficiently impressive for the bishop of an increasingly important see, and the pilgrim offered the Pope a 'noble and weighty pile of precious

---

[43] 'Translatio S. Sebastiani', (*MGH. SS.* XV, 379–91); see also B. Pesci, 'Il culto di Sebastiano a Roma nell' antichità e nel medio evo', (*Antonianum*, 20, 1945).

[44] *LP.* II, 74.

things' in return for the remains of the Pope St. Alexander and the Roman priest Justin. The request was unpopular: 'The citizens at once came running together in amazement, for the rumour had quickly stirred up the city, especially concerning St. Alexander . . . The people were accustomed to visit his tomb with solemnity as they maintained that he cured the sick. They were also extremely grieved at the removal from Rome of the holy priest Justin, who is mentioned in the *Passio* of the deacon Lawrence, who actually buried the priest.' There were scenes of protest as Hitto left Rome with his acquisitions but divine favour for the translation was shown when the relics cured Gerald, the head papal groom, of a fever.[45]

Although the papacy attempted to control the unpopular whole-sale translation of relics, the documents of authentication which were carried away with the relics increased still further the place of Rome in the European consciousness of its past. When Abbot Marcuard of Prum came to Rome in 844 and was granted the relics of St. Chrysantius and St. Darius by Sergius II, the pope sent Bishop Marinus, his librarian, to him, with 'a book of the Passions of the Saints', and told Marcuard to copy from it the Passions of his acquisitions.[46] But inevitably there was abuse and lack of proper documentation; a priest of Mainz, Liutolf, writing in about 860 of St. Severus's translation there, said 'There was at that time a cleric from the Gallic regions called Felix (though whether he was happy in deed is not for me to judge). I can remember seeing him when I was a boy. It was his custom to wander through the various provinces in search of any relics, which he stole whenever he could.' In fact he stole some relics from the monastery of St. Severus in Ravenna and the monks instituted a hue and cry throughout Italy for him, alerting all magistrates to secure his arrest.[47]

A prominent victim of unscrupulous trading in relics was the scholar Einhart. In about 826 he had planned to retire from the court and had founded at Seligenstadt a small community. 'When according to my powers and means I had built there not only houses and other places for permanent habitation but also a small church of suitable design, I began to wonder in what saint's or martyr's name it

[45] 'Translatio SS. Alexandri et Iustini', (*MGH. SS.* XV, 286–8).
[46] 'Translatio SS. Chrysantii et Darii', (*MGH. SS.* XV, 374–6).
[47] Luitolf, 'Translatio S. Severi', (*MGH. SS.* XV, 289–93).

186

had best be dedicated. When I had spent a long time in indecision, it chanced that a certain deacon of the Roman Church, called Deusdona, came to court, wishing to request help from the king in some private needs. After he had stayed there for some time and the business he had come on was settled, he was preparing to return to Rome and was invited by us one day, as a matter of courtesy, to our frugal dinner; there was a good deal of conversation at table, and we chanced in our talk to mention the translation of the blessed Sebastian and the neglected tombs of the martyrs, of which there are many in Rome. Then the talk turned to the dedication of our new church and I began to ask him how I could arrange to obtain some bit of true relic of the saints, now at rest in Rome. Here at first he hesitated a moment and replied that he did not know how it could be managed. But when he saw that I was in earnest and anxious he promised to give me an answer some other day.'

Some days later Deusdona slipped Einhart a note, to be opened privately; in this he undertook, in return for Einhart's influence at the Frankish court, to help him obtain relics: he told Einhart to send a trusted servant, with a mule, back with him to Rome. So Einhart sent his secretary Ratleig with him; they went by way of the monastery of St. Medard at Soissons, for Deusdona had undertaken to get for Abbot Hilduin the body of St. Tiburtius, and Hilduin sent with them 'a certain priest, a crafty man, called Lehun'. The party went together to Rome, but Ratleig received one warning of his companions' quality—a few day's journey from Rome his servant fell ill of a fever and in his delirium had a dream of a man, dressed as a deacon, who warned him not to trust Deusdona. He was also shown a vision of Rome, and a church in the centre of the city was pointed out to him where relics could be found.

'So arriving in Rome, they took up residence in the house of the deacon who had come with them, near the church of the blessed apostle Peter, called "ad Vincula"; and they stayed with him for some days, waiting for him to fulfil his promises. But he, being quite unable to make good his agreements, excused himself for not doing so with various pretexts and delays. At last they spoke out to him and asked why he chose to trifle so with them; he must no longer put them off, disappoint them and prevent their return with vain hopes. He listened and realized that he could no longer impose this kind of trickery on them, so he told my secretary that he could not have the promised relics since his brother, to whom he had entrusted his house and possessions when he left Rome, had gone on business to Benevento and he had no idea when he would return; and that since he had given him the relics and his other portable property for sake-keeping, he could not tell what he had done with them for they could not be found anywhere in the house.' He then suggested taking them to see other tombs, but in his usual fashion kept postponing the expedition.

So the two Franks found one of the regular guides of Rome, who took them to the church of St. Tiburtius on the Labico road; there they examined the tomb and came to the conclusion that they could open it in secret. But their visit was discovered by Deusdona who joined them: 'First they attempted to open the altar over where the body is supposed to lie . . . but the monument, being of a very hard marble, easily resisted their unskilled hands as they tried to open it.' They therefore abandoned that tomb and crossed over to the tomb of St. Marcellinus and St. Peter; they managed to get the top off and 'then saw the most holy body of St. Marcellinus in the upper part of the tomb, and close by his head a marble tablet with an inscription on it, giving clear proof of whose martyr's limbs lay there. So with the greatest reverence, they lifted out the body and wrapped it decently in clean white linen; they then handed it to the deacon for him to take and look after for them. They then replaced the stone, so as to leave no trace of the body's removal, and returned to their lodgings in the city.'

Their host urged Ratleig to return to France at once with St. Marcellinus, but Ratleig thought it inconsiderate to part the saint from Peter after so long and determined to obtain the other saint as well. 'But how he was to effect this he was uncertain, for he knew that he would find no Roman who would help him and none even in whom he could confide. While puzzling over this, he chanced to meet a certain foreign monk called Basil, who had come from Constantinople two years before, and lived with four disciples on the Palatine, in a house with other Greek monks of the same persuasion as himself.' Basil gave him every encouragement in the project, and a few nights later Lehun and Ratleig returned to the church of St. Tiburtius. Ratleig managed easily enough to remove the body of St. Peter, but Lehun could find no trace of St. Tiburtius; however

'Ratleig found in the tomb where the bodies of St. Marcellinus and St. Peter had laid a certain round hole, a full foot across and at least three feet in depth, and in it some quantity of very fine dust–it seemed to both of them that this could have been left from the body of St. Tiburtius, if his bones had been removed: and the body might have been placed just so between the blessed Marcellinus and Peter, in the same tomb, to make it harder to find; and so they agreed that the priest should take it away as a relic of St. Tiburtius.'

They then returned to their lodging and recovered Marcellinus from Deusdona, who now produced a bundle of relics, anonymous but of whose authenticity he assured them, as a final bargain, which they accepted. There remained the problem of removing the relics from the city undetected; it was agreed that after packing and sealing them up, Lehun and a brother of Deusdona, Luniso, should take them as far as Pavia, while Ratleig stayed a further week in Rome to see whether the removal had been detected, and then catch them up in the north. All went well; the advance party reached Pavia unchecked and deposited the bodies in the church of St. John the Baptist where a night vigil was kept in their honour, and there later Ratleig joined them. There was one further alarm, a rumour that papal envoys had been sent north to intercept them, but the two parties separately reached their destinations in safety, Lehun and Luniso carrying the dust they called St. Tiburtius to Soissons, and Ratleig returning in triumph with Marcellinus and Peter to Seligenstadt.

A few days after welcoming the remains of his new patrons, Einhart was in attendance in the ante-chamber of the Emperor Louis' palace, and there encountered Abbot Hilduin. The abbot began talking of the quality of the wrappings that had contained Marcellinus and Peter, and Einhart, alarmed, asked him how he knew of them. Reluctantly Hilduin told him that Lehun had confessed to switching the relics during their vigil in Pavia; that night all the clergy and laity present had drowsed off and 'he, Lehun, had fallen to pondering, that it seemed to some great purpose that so deep a slumber should have overcome so many men and, deciding that he ought to avail himself of the offered opportunity, he rose and with a lighted taper made his way silently to the caskets. He burnt the cords of the caskets with the flame of the taper held close, and so quickly

189

opened them without a key; then, taking a portion of each body, he refastened the seals together with the ends of the burnt cord, so that they appeared unbroken and, still unobserved, went back to his place.' This disturbed Einhart, especially when he found rumours already spreading through the countryside impugning the quality and authenticity of his patrons, and hence the prestige of his foundation, so he summoned Ratleig and Luniso and cross-examined them further. It became clear that Luniso and Lehun had deceived Hilduin as well, and that the theft had not taken place in Pavia. Rather it had been in Rome, while the relics were in Deusdona's house in the care of Luniso. Lehun, disappointed at his failure to secure St. Tiburtius, had bribed Luniso with four gold and five silver pieces; the latter had opened the caskets and Lehun had taken from the ashes of Marcellinus 'as much as a vessel of a pint-and-a-half capacity could hold.'[48]

Other sounder and more reputable borrowings were made from Rome by the North in the fields of liturgy, monastic rule and canon law.[49] The great glory of Rome in the seventh and eighth centuries, as it appeared to pilgrims, was the stational procession when pope, papal court, clergy and people all combined in a splendid communal service and a vivid expression of the new papal sovereignty. The characteristic chant adopted from the Byzantine court ceremonial by the Lateran *Schola Cantorum* made a strong impression on the resurgent Frankish Church and monarchy. Bishop Chrodegang of Metz was sent by Pepin as ambassador in 753 to invite Stephen II to France; in the city he saw the majesty of the papal service and the *cantilena*, the chant, and adopted it for his own diocese: 'He ordered his clergy, imbued with the divine law and Roman chant, to follow the Roman custom and order, which up to then had hardly been done in the Church of Metz.'[50] Stephen II's visit in 753-5 introduced the Roman chant to a wider Frankish audience, especially when he anointed Pepin and his sons at St. Denys; the 'sweet chant' became ever more the ideal of the Frankish Church and its impact was

[48] Einhart, *Translatio SS. Marcellini et Petri*, (*MGH. SS.* XV, 238–64); M. Bondois, 'La translation des saints Marcellin et Pierre', (*Bibliotheque de l'école des Hautes Etudes, fasc.* 160, 1907).

[49] C. Vogel, 'Les échanges liturgiques entre Rome et les pays francs jusqu'à l'époque de Charlemagne', (*Le Chiese nei regni dell' Europa ocidentale, Congresso Internazionale sull' Alto Medio Evo*, Spoleto, 1960).

[50] *MGH. SS.* II, 260–70.

described by Walafrid Strabo: 'It was Stephen II, on coming to France to seek justice for St. Peter against the Lombards from Pepin, the father of the Emperor Charles the Great, who brought here by the agency of his clergy and in the presence of Pepin himself the perfection of knowledge of the chant, which has since been used so widely.'[51] Ten years later, Pepin's brother Bishop Remedius of Rheims sent some of his monks to Rome to receive instruction at the *Schola* itself. Pope Paul I reported to Pepin on their progress and the reasons for delay: 'We stated in our letters that it was our duty to hand over your brother Remedius's monks to Simeon, the Prior of our choir-school, for him to instruct in the chanting of the psalms; so that they may learn this, at present unknown in your dominions, which is, as you say, a source of sorrow to your brother, in that he cannot perfectly instruct his monks. So now, most benign king, we can satisfy your Christianity; it was only because of the death of George, the former head of the *Schola*, that we sought to withdraw Simeon from your brother's service. Simeon succeeded to George's post on his death, and so we recalled him to teach in our *Schola*. . . . Accordingly we have handed over your brother's monks to Simeon for him to instruct frequently, with the utmost diligence, in the chant of the psalms, so that when they have been taught to perfection we will send them to maintain the singing of the church's rites to full effect and the complete delight of your most excellent and noble brother.'[52]

This adoption of the 'divine law and the Roman chant' was necessarily accompanied by the growing influence of the Roman liturgical texts in the North. Later in the eighth century Pope Hadrian sent to Charlemagne at his request a copy of the book of Sacraments current in Rome which was then traditionally ascribed to the composition of Gregory I. Internal evidence suggests that it was an early eighth century compilation from earlier material. It was not a complete Missal; it contained for example, besides the Ordinary of the Mass, none of the Propers for ordinary Sunday but only those for the major festivals and the solemn stations and no other liturgies, as for dedications or burials. By its inclusion of the Roman stations and of special services for the ordination of popes and Roman priests it was designed entirely for a Roman context. However it served as a basis

[51] *Liber de exordiis*, (*MGH. Capitularia* II, 508).   [52] Cod. Carol., 41.

for expansion, initiated under Charlemagne by Alcuin who added the necessary features; editions of this Gregorian Sacramentary and its supplements spread rapidly through France. It was not the first Frankish import from Rome since it combined with a sacramentary introduced from Rome probably in the seventh century to which Frankish scholars–eager in papal and liturgical history–had ascribed the authorship of Pope Gelasius.[53] Other Roman rites and especially those of the *Ordines*, the functions of the papal court distinct from the parish services of Rome, were also eagerly adapted for use by Frankish dioceses and monasteries, and here the influence of Rome continued as a corrective to the divergencies that naturally arose with time. The Frankish scholar Amalarius, who spent a lifetime devoted to liturgical studies, was slavish and prolix in his adherence to Roman practice. He twice visited the city, and on the first occasion, exploring at dawn, caught a glimpse of Leo III slipping off for his daybreak Mass. His second visit, in 831–2, was primarily devoted to liturgical research in preparation for a new edition of his *Liber Officialis*; Pope Gregory IV was unable to lend him a copy of the Roman antiphonary for the Emperor Louis, as the Abbot Wala, Charlemagne's cousin, had already borrowed it and removed it to France–an indication of the extent of Frankish borrowing. But the pope placed at Amalarius's disposal the archdeacon Theodore who was subjected by the Frankish enthusiast to a rigorous session of questioning on Roman practice; the fruits emerged in his new edition, and scholars and prelates continued to draw on the city for their authority in service books and chant.[54]

By the close of the eighth century the axis of the city to which the pilgrims came had changed. The Forum and the Palatine, with the imperial buildings and the palace of Byzantine officials, had ceased to be the centre of papal Rome. The administration was now firmly bound to the Lateran but this shared its sovereignty with the Vatican area, across the river and outside the old city limits, where–more than in Rome itself–the new spiritual capital of the Western Empire

[53] E. Bourque, *Etudes sur les sacrementaires romaines:* I: *Les Textes primitifs,* (1948). II: *Les textes rémaniés,* (i) *Le Gélasien du VIIIe siècle,* (1952), (ii) *Le Sacrementaire d'Hadrien: le supplément d'Alcuin et les Grégoriens mixtes,* (1958).

[54] A. Cabaniss, *Amalarius of Metz,* 1954.

was growing. The Vatican, approached by all the main routes from the north and lying as a complex of shrines before the city, was in the eyes of the kings–the last and most important group of pilgrims to Rome–the foremost reason for Rome's prestige; to the Romans, with their intervening city walls, it still allowed for a certain exclusion of their own concerns as Rome became more involved in the affairs of Europe. The Vatican and the shrine of St. Peter had their own administrations: the former was served by a separate branch of the *Schola Cantorum* under an archcantor; a *praepositus*, assisted by *custodes martyrum* or *mansionarii*, served the shrine and the pilgrims. Late in the eighth century repairs to the aqueducts running from the Gianicolo ensured amenities for the pilgrims as did the *diaconiae* and hostels established on the north bank.

This, then, for kings as for the permanent colonies of foreigners in the *scholae*, was the natural focus of life or rule in Rome. Here the Lombard King Ratchis settled after his abdication in 749 and before his entry into Monte Cassino, followed three years later by Hunald, the deposed duke of Aquitaine. Hunald was killed in 756 in a conflict that developed when the Lombard King Aistulf visited the Vatican; Aistulf himself, like Liutprand before him and Desiderius afterwards, could not enter the city itself but could still pay homage to the prince of the Apostles. Pepin's envoy Fulrad of St. Denys on his embassy of 757 took over Ratchis's old house and from this perhaps developed the Carolingian palace in Rome, a palace specifically for a monarch accredited, not to the old imperial Rome, but to St. Peter. The *domus Aguliae* had possibly been a temporary lodging of the popes for use during prolonged ceremonies at St. Peter's, and was extensively rebuilt, with a ceremonial *triclinium*, by Leo III. This was where Louis II gave judgement in 855, and where Louis III stayed in 901; entry into the city was by invitation only for a northern monarch.[55]

The growth and fortification of the Vatican with its monasteries

[55] L. Duchesne, 'Notes sur la topographie de Rome au moyen-age, X: Vaticana', (*MAH*, 22, 1902); XII, (*ibid.*, 34, 1914); XIII, (*ibid.*, 35, 1915). C. R. Bruhl, 'Die Kaiserpfalz bei St. Peter und die Pfalz Ottos III auf dem Palatin', (*Quellen und Forschungen aus Italienischen Archiv und Bibliotheken*, 38, 1958). C. Cecchelli, *Saint-Pierre et les Palais du Vatican*, 1927. F. Ehrle and H. Egger, *Der Vatikanische Palast*, 1935. C. Jurgen, 'Der Anfiss von

and shrines as a distinct city outside Rome was part of a general shift in the pattern of the old city in the ninth century. The low-lying centre near the river was becoming unhealthy as the complex organization that under the emperors had maintained the banks and drainage disappeared; on the outskirts of the city the aqueducts, broken in the wars and sketchily repaired, dripped and formed stagnant, fever-carrying swamps. But the hills, the healthier region of the city, were losing the greater part of their population through the breakdown of the system of internal water-supply operating off the main aqueducts. The Aventine, which in republican times had been a plebeian quarter and under the Empire was only sparsely built on by a few noble families, became in the eighth and ninth centuries a quarter where some prominent Roman families congregated. The bulk of the population shifted to follow the remaining water supply, even if this involved a move into the more unhealthy parts. The line of the Aqua Virgo, entering the city from the East and running underground for much of its course, provided for growth in the Campus Martius, formerly uninhabited and devoted to public buildings into which – north and west of the Corso – most of the mediaeval population of Rome was now concentrated. Even the greatest families, such as that of Hadrian I in the eighth century and of Theophylact in the tenth, lived on the swampy lower ground, open to flood from the river and from springs beneath the surface. It was this concentration that made mediaeval Rome a death-trap, especially for unacclimatized visitors from the North; both Otto II in 983 at the age of twenty-eight, and his son Otto III in 1002 at the age of twenty-one died of malaria in the city. Nor were the traditional refuges of the Roman nobility – their villas in the surrounding countryside – still extant; not until the mid-ninth century do we read of Pope Gregory IV building for himself a summer villa between Rome and Ostia, which with the imminent Saracen raids can have had only a short existence. Rome too had shrunk within its walls; the parks of the imperial city were possibly cultivated and there are later references to city farms, distinct from the suburban immediately around the city.[56]

Alt–St. Peter, (*Römische Quartalschrift*, 62, 1967). J. H. Jonkees, *Studies on Old St. Peter's*, 1967.

[56] *LP.* II, 82; see F. Castagnoli, C. Cecchelli, G. Giovanni, M. Zocca,

The wars, the breakdown of the aqueducts and of a city administration with the resources for constant maintenance, thinned and moved the population. The buildings also suffered and altered; the action of Constans II in removing the metal tiles, cramps and ties from the public buildings hastened the process of decay, leaving them open to the elements. Of these, the flooding of the Tiber, which before its embankment and upstream damming was a swift-rising river, was the most destructive. There was a serious flood, lasting some days, in the pontificate of Gregory II, when the river burst through the Flaminian Gate, filling the piazzas and the Corso to a depth of eight feet; houses, the tall *insulae*, or blocks of flats, were undermined and crashed.[57] A more serious one occurred in 791. Again the water entered by the Flaminian Gate, ripping the gate from its hinges; at points it swept over the walls, perhaps at the lower sections weakened by Totila's destruction; the Corso was flooded, deeper than before, and the flood stretched down to and damaged the Aurelian bridge at the river bend above Tiber Island. Large areas of the Corso and the Campus Martius regions were cut off, and Hadrian organized a ferry-service of punts to carry food to the stranded.[58] Each flood, with a heavy flow of water, weakened yet further the remaining aqueducts. Hadrian, an indefatigable builder and engineer, grew concerned for the health of the inhabitants of the low-lying areas by the river; he embanked a stretch with more than 12,000 blocks of *tufa* along the St. Peter's side of the river, using this as a foundation for a road, the first *lungotevere*.[59]

But the city was also changing shape through deliberate works of building. The new complexes, like the Lateran and St. Peter's, were the most obvious additions to the city, but the records of the eighth century popes show a continuous programme of repairs and rescue of decayed churches and monasteries–although the chances of decay were increased by shortage of suitable building material. In the sixth century Calabria had provided beams of an imposing length suitable for building the largest merchant ships afloat; Gregory I supplied them to the patriarchate of Alexandria, the only limit to size being the capacity of the ships to take them. Gregory II obtained roof-beams

Topografia e Urbanistica di Roma, (Istituto di Studi Romani, Storia di Roma, 1958); G. Matthiae, *Le chiese di Roma dal IV al X secolo*, (1962).
[57] *LP*. I, 399. [58] *LP*. I, 513. [59] *LP*. I, 507.

from the Calabrian forests, but by the end of the eighth century this source was removed from the papacy's sphere and Hadrian was negotiating with Charles to draw on the forests of Spoleto.[60] Supply was always limited and it was the frequent decay of roof-beams that necessitated most of the repairs. There was no purpose in preserving the ancient public buildings; the Colosseum itself, although proverbially renowned, had no place in the cult of Christian Rome.[61] Monuments were deliberately destroyed or their materials plundered if Christian necessity demanded. In the time of Pope Hadrian, 'the deaconry of the holy Mother of God, the Ever-Virgin St. Mary *in Cosmedin*, was a frail building standing under some ruins, a great monument of Tiburtine *tufa* which overhung it: about New Year he [Hadrian] assembled a large crowd and set fire to a pile of wood, demolishing it. He then had the rubble collected, and rebuilt the basilica from its foundations, larger and longer, with three apses; and so he repaired the Cosmedin.'[62] Hadrian appears to have taken a practical and personal interest in most of the building and engineering work required, personally devising some of the means; the sacristan Januarius is also mentioned, chosen as a 'suitable person' to oversee rebuilding, but Hadrian appealed to Charles for a *magister* as well to give help.[63]

The ancient buildings that were preserved owed their survival to their adaptation to Christian uses. The Pantheon was granted to Boniface IV by the Emperor Phocas in 608 and was dedicated by that pope as the church of S. Maria *ad Martyres*; its roof was stripped by Constans II but its use as a church saved it from utter decay– Gregory II reroofed it with lead. It may have been dedicated on 1st November 609, an ancient feast of Isis and the later feast of All Saints. The collective dedication was an innovation in the West of Syrian origin, and the use of a circular structure for a church, also new to the West, may have been suggested by a foundation of the Emperor Maurice near Jerusalem.[64] In the Forum the senate house

[60] Gregory, *Registrum*, X, 21; *LP*. I, 397; Cod. Carol., n. 65.

[61] See 'L'Amphithéatre Flavien et ses environs dans les textes hagiographiques' (*AB*, 16, 1897).

[62] *LP*. I, 503.   [63] *LP*. I, 505, 506; Cod. Carol., n. 65.

[64] *LP*. I, 317, 343, 419; see J. Hennig: 'The Meaning of All the Saints', (*Medieval Studies*, 10, 1948); R. Krautheimer, 'Santa Maria Rotonda', (*Arte del Primo Millennio, Turin*, n.d.).

was similarly saved by Pope Honorius who converted it into the church of St. Hadrian and added an apse; by the late eighth century the curial secretariat nearby was also a church, dedicated to St. Martin.[65] However, the majority of new churches were small, possibly limited in size by the shortage of available material. They were not built on the exact foundations or structures of former buildings, but drew on them for their framework and materials.

From the sixth century onwards there was a proliferation of new dedications as the cults of saints originally strangers to Rome were introduced by successive immigrants or outside influences.[66] At this time the presence of large numbers of foreign troops in the city was responsible for the cult of soldier-saints, especially SS. Theodore, Hadrian, George, Boniface, Sergius and Bacchus. Dedications to St. Apollenaris of Ravenna, St. Lucy of Syracuse and St. Agatha of Catania represented those places of importance to the political and economic life of Byzantine Rome. Other churches adopted the pagan associations of their site and neighbourhood; in the seventh century, S. Maria *Antica* which stood close to the former site of the temple of Castor and Pollux, a frequent pagan resort for healing, celebrated in its frescoes the doctor saints of the East: SS. Cosmas and Damian, and SS. Cyrus and John of Egypt; St. John the Baptist and St. Euthymius of Melitene, both with established therapeutic reputations in Armenia; and St. Sebastian, also a therapeutic saint whose cult may have been established in Rome after the plague of 680. All these dedications reflect a strong eastern, possibly Armenian, influence. On Tiber Island the church of St. Bartholomew carried on the reputation of the ancient temple of Aesculapius as a hospital, the name finding its way ultimately to London.

S. Maria *Antica* shows also the high tide of Greek influence reached towards the end of the seventh century in Rome; close to the imperial palace, it was a favourite church of Pope John VII whose father had been curator of the palace, and near which John built a second bishop's palace. The frescoes with which he adorned the church, and his mosaics in St. Peter's, reflect not only the popularity of Greek saints in this official quarter, but also the growth

[65] *LP*. I, 324, 517, n. 43.
[66] E. Donckel, *Ausserrömische Heilige in Rom von dem Anfang unter Liberius bis Leo IV* (1938).

of Eastern and specifically Alexandrian art-forms and techniques, brought by refugees from the Arab invasions. There the representation of two former popes, and perhaps the contemporary portrait series of popes in St. Paul's-without-the-walls, indicated also the independent continuity and sovereignty of papal Rome. The churches of attendant saints, given the status of courtiers in the hierarchy, were endowed by the popes with the trappings of a Constantinopolitan palace; the jewels and the frescoes, and the shimmering, gauzy veils, purple and white silk that hung between the columns; the glow of the silver and gold ornaments, the lamps, altar-rails, crowns, candlesticks and plate that the popes dedicated; the crosses and bindings of the liturgical books studded with jewels; and–in a resurgence of an art-form that Italy was to adopt as its own–the walls ablaze with mosaics, of gilded iron, coloured glasses, gold, *lapis lazuli* and enamel. All this reached its peak late in the eighth century as Hadrian and Leo III gave new expression to an imperial Rome in their vast building programmes in a renaissance of art unparalleled at the time. The shrine and sovereignty of Peter, with the churches of his satellite saints arrayed within 'the glittering colonnades of Rome'[67] continued to draw pilgrims in wonder to the city.

[67] See ch. 5, n. 44 and J. Croquison, 'L'Iconographie chrétienne à Rome d'après le Liber Pontificalis', (*Byzantion*, 34, 1964).

7

ROME AND THE LOMBARDS

The eighth century opened with the papacy at a high point of popularity in Italy; it had become the focal point for provincial dissatisfaction with harsh taxes, administrative inefficiency and unorthodoxy in religion. The imperial authorities in Italy were proving incapable of defending the imperial provinces and–even worse to Italian thinking–the exarch Eutychianus had allied himself with the newly-assertive Lombard monarchy under Liutprand to bring down the pope. On this occasion it was Liutprand himself who in laying down his regalia before the confession of St. Peter demonstrated universal belief in the apostle's continuing influence and authority. The ancient churches of the west were conscious of their foundation by disciples of Peter and now under pressure of persecution the Greek churches of southern Italy were also discovering in him a champion of orthodoxy.

In the north the ties with Rome were being strengthened. The Arabs who entered France across the Pyrenees from Spain were met on the Rhone by duke Eudo of Aquitaine and Charles Martel, the mayor of the Merovingian palace. Eudo wrote to Gregory II announcing his victory in which 375,000 Saracens were said to have been slain with the loss of only 1,500 Franks; the previous year, Eudo reminded the pope, he and his subjects had sent as a mark of their devotion three sponges for use at the papal table, and of those Franks associated in the gift not one had been harmed in the battle. In 722 the Englishman Boniface received episcopal consecration and took a special oath of allegiance to the papacy in preparation for his mission to convert the continental Saxons and ultimately to reform the Frankish Church: the terms used by Gregory II and his successors, the 'unity' of the mission to Rome, and Boniface's 'membership of the household and service' imply that on both sides his activities were seen as an extension of the Roman Church.[1]

[1] *LP.* I, 401; Boniface, *Epistolae*, 108; O. Bertolini, 'Il dramma di

Gregory II died in 731 and his successor, a Syrian also named Gregory, was a man of learning and charity; he was extremely popular in the city and was elected by acclamation at the funeral of his predecessor. He continued Gregory II's opposition to imperial Iconoclasm, and immediately on accession summoned a synod attended by the greatest prelates of Italy, the archbishops of Milan, Ravenna and Grado and ninety-three other bishops, at which the persecution of images was condemned. The sequel revealed the split between East and West; the detention of the papal emissaries in Sicily prevented them from delivering the acts of the synod, and Leo III followed this by confiscating the papal properties in the south.[2] The split was all the more dangerous to Rome since from about 713 the Lombards under Liutprand had been moving towards a unification of Italy, beginning with the independent southern duchies of Spoleto and Benevento, and then advancing on the imperial possessions. Duke Faroald II of Spoleto had patronized the refounding of the abbey of Farfa in the Sabine Hills in 705, and from there successive endowment and settlement by the abbey's tenants were encroaching on the eastern boundaries of the duchy of Rome itself. Liutprand himself took Narni, an essential link in the communications between Rome and Ravenna, and then invaded Pentapolis itself. He besieged Ravenna for some days and took its port of Classe, with immense plunder and many prisoners. His concerted drive against Rome in company with the exarch failed as the southern duchies rallied to the Romans but he retained possession of Sutri, a bare thirty miles from Rome itself.

The pontificate of Gregory III covered years that were uneasy for Rome in the absence of a strong external protector. A dispute broke out, leading to conflict with the duchy of Spoleto over the town of Gallese on the frontiers of the Roman duchy. Gregory was only able to save it by paying subsidies to duke Transamund, Faroald's son, but an indication of the increasing withdrawal from the concept of Empire was shown when Gregory ordered the redeemed town to be incorporated into the 'holy republic and body of the beloved army of Christ'. The papacy was groping towards a new concept of the

Bonifacio', (*BISI*, 78, 1967); also L. Spatlung, 'Die Petrus-Verehrung in den Bonifatius–Briefen', (*Antonianum*, 42, 1967).
[2] *LP*. I, 416–17.

sovereignty of Christ and the Prince of His Apostles. The renewed
Lombard threat also prompted Gregory to undertake repairs to the
walls of Rome, supplying the lime needed and the mason's pay from
his own resources; the walls of Civitavecchia, the main port for the
north and the west, were also put into repair.[3] But the chief hope of
Rome's preservation lay in obstructing Liutprand's attempts to
stamp unity on his ramshackle kingdom. Gregory concluded treaties
with Spoleto and Benevento for mutual respect of boundaries, and
when in 739 the dukes refused Liutprand's summons to attack
imperial territory, Gregory stated that it was out of respect for their
treaty and for the Church.

Liutprand invaded the duchy of Spoleto, chasing Transamund into
refuge in Rome; his demand that he be surrendered was rejected
by Gregory and the duke and patrician Stephen, and the Roman
army. The Lombard king proceeded to take four of the border towns
of the Roman duchy, Ameria, Orte, Bomarzo and Bieda, in retaliation before returning to his capital at Pavia. Duke Transimund swore
to the Romans that on recovery of his duchy he would return these
towns to Rome; the Roman army thereupon assembled with
Gregory's approval and, reinforced by Lombards from Benevento
and some of Transimund's own followers, advanced in two contingents
up the Salaria into the Sabine hills. The lesser towns of the Spoletan
duchy, Furcone, Valve and Penne, surrendered without resistance
and the country-people also submitted; the army then proceeded to
take Rieti, and on to Spoleto itself. But now disputes with the Lombard
contingents over permitting Roman troops to garrison the newly-
won towns rent the alliance and, with success so near, Transimund
repudiated his bargain, refusing to return the captured towns and
neglecting other articles in the agreement. As the pope died, the duke
was in his turn preparing to invade the Roman duchy.[4]

During the short campaign the Roman army had been under a dual
leadership; on the one hand Gregory, and on the other the patrician
Stephen, directing the army, presumably as one of the elected Italian

[3] *LP*. I, 420–1.
[4] *LP*. I, 426. O. Bertolini, 'I papi e le relazioni politiche di Roma con i
ducati longobardi di Spoleto e di Benevento, III', (*Rivista di Storia della
Chiesa in Italia*, 9, 1955); A. Crivellucci, 'Stefano patrizio e duca di Roma
(727–754)', (*Studi Storici*, 10, 1901).

dukes who had emerged from the Italian revolt, representing the whole
Byzantine duchy of Rome. These two elements, the ecclesiastical and
the civil, worked in harmony in the delicate situation facing the city.
But of itself the duchy could not survive and could not rely upon maintaining a favourable balance of power throughout Italy. Already
before the Roman counter-attack and Transimund's defection, and
while Liutprand was still pressing against the borders of the duchy of
Rome, Gregory had appealed to Charles Martel for intervention. His
request was couched in the only terms that could have any meaning
north of the Alps; the devastation caused by the Lombard armies
around Rome and Ravenna had destroyed 'all St. Peter's farms and
carried off what livestock remained'. 'And so far from you, most
excellent son, whom we had appointed our refuge, we have received no
consolation; we observe that since you have not actually given the
order to march against these kings, you have believed their lies rather
than our truth. We fear that yours may be the guilt when these kings
reply from their present camp to our protests: "Let Charles, whom you
have made your refuge, come with the army of the Franks; let them, if
they are strong enough, help you and deliver you from our hands." ...
So we exhort your Goodness ... that you may support the Church of
St. Peter and its special people, that you at once refute these kings,
drive them away from us and force them to return to their own
territory. Do not despise my appeal or turn deaf ears to my entreaty,
that the Prince of Apostles may not shut the heavenly kingdom against
you. I conjure you by the True and Living God and I send you the
keys of the Confession of St. Peter, not to contemplate friendship
with the Lombard kings.' Again the themes and practices of St. Peter,
sovereign among saints, are brought to bear: the keys of his confession, which had long been a reminder to pilgrims of the new centre
of the world and of the office of the key-bearer to the gates of
Heaven; so too, the insistence on Peter's 'special people' who now in
truth had no other patron or champion. This concept and that of
Peter's rights and possessions were to grow in northern and Lateran
thinking until they ousted the real origins of the Byzantine successor
territories.[5]

Gregory's letter was written in the last year of his life and the
change of pope was fortunate; his successor was a Greek, Zachary, a

[5] Cod. Carol., 2.

man of supple mind and in secular matters not so closely committed to the alliances of Gregory. His prime concern in face of Transimund's threatened invasion was the safety and integrity of the Roman duchy; those towns which had under the long Byzantine defence been welded together as a part of the duchy, whose inhabitants lived by the Roman law and which were essential safeguards against Rome itself being absorbed into a Lombardic Italy, must be regained. Once more Liutprand was assembling his army; as before, he had little fear of Frankish intervention for Charles had received support from the Lombards against the Arabs and might need it again. Zachary's envoys met him and offered an alliance with the Roman army, which had recently shown itself an effective instrument, for the return of the four towns. Liutprand assented and the Roman army on Zachary's instruction moved off to co-operate with the king. It was a bloodless campaign for Transimund surrendered at once. But again there was trouble; once in possession of the duchy of Spoleto, Liutprand was reluctant to yield towns which so drastically impaired the unity of the kingdom he was trying to create.[6]

Zachary thereupon took the step–courageous in itself and a portentous precedent–of interviewing the king himself. Leaving Rome with an entourage of his clergy he went on foot to Terni, within the duchy of Spoleto, where Liutprand was in residence. His coming was announced and Liutprand sent his dukes to meet the pope at Orte. These conducted him with honour to Terni, which he reached on a Saturday; Liutprand and his court were waiting for him on the steps of the basilica of St. Valentine. After a friendly welcome Zachary addressed his appeal to the king and again the next day continued his exhortations for peace, for a cease to bloodshed and for the restitution of lawful boundaries. Liutprand, impressed by the courage, sincerity and eloquence of the Pope, ordered the restoration of the four towns to the duchy of Rome and confirmed a peace treaty between duchy and kingdom, to last twenty years. He also returned Narni and the cities of the exarchate, Osimo, Ancona and Umana, taken in his previous campaigns, and instructions were sent throughout Lombard Tuscany and beyond the Po ordering the return of all captives from the Roman regions. In addition the lands of the Sabine patrimony, annexed nearly thirty years before by Spoleto,

[6] *LP*. I, 427.

were to be returned. All this stemmed from the powerful impression of Zachary's personality; in celebration of the new accord he consecrated a bishop in the king's presence, and the papal preaching and the music of the papal court worked strongly on the Lombards. The Sunday Mass was followed by a banquet to which the Pope invited the king; their personal encounter went so well, with such pleasantry and hilarity, that Liutprand later declared he could not remember a meal like it.[7]

The convention of Terni showed much of the attitudes of the two parties. Liutprand, working towards a united Italy, was impressed by Zachary's courage and authority and by the fact that the cities remaining within the imperial provinces had so continuous a tradition of association as to form a unity not readily absorbed. But the impression was a personal one; Liutprand felt no respect for the weak, divided authority of the imperial government in Italy, and what he had negotiated with the pope was relevant to the pope and the apostle alone. The agreement did not alter the fact that the Roman cities formed a barrier to a united Italy and a constant temptation. On his part Zachary can be seen as arguing within the framework of Roman law and imperial administrative practice. To Zachary and all Romans imperial Italy still remained one, the constitutional and legal identity remained unbroken, the common heritage and political link still binding, however meagre its military expression. The agreement was tripartite, concerning the towns taken two years previously from the duchy of Rome, the return of the captives and towns of the exarchate, and the restoration of the papacy's own patrimonies in the Sabine region. This last was a Roman legal claim, for under Roman law barbarian squatters' rights to uncultivated land became absolute after thirty years' uninterrupted tenure. This period had by 742 almost elapsed and Zachary had at least won an acknowledgement of continued ownership, if not actual possession; the claim had been kept alive but was as yet unsettled, and the Sabine problem was to occupy the papacy for many years. But at the moment all was friendliness. Zachary was escorted back to Rome by Liutprand's dukes and officials, making a circuit of the duchy and receiving the

---

[7] *Ibid.*, I, 427–8. For Liutprand, see M. Roberti, 'Liutprando, re longobardo', (*Rendiconti dell' Istituto lombardo di scienze e lettere, classe di lettere e scienze morali*, 85, 1952).

cities formally from the king's representatives; then he returned to Rome, to be acclaimed as in a triumph.[8]

Liutprand did not regard it as treachery, therefore, to attack the exarchate the following year. The exarch, the patrician Eutychius, had no resources to counter the Lombard attack and when Ravenna was actually under siege he sent an appeal with Archbishop John and the citizens of Ravenna and Pentapolis to Zachary. An embassy of the *vicedominus*, Bishop Benedict, and the *primicerius* Ambrose failed, so once more Zachary, leaving the city in the care of the patrician Stephen, set out on a personal mission. He was met at L'Aquila, nearly fifty miles from Ravenna, by the exarch and a great throng of citizens who acclaimed him as 'the shepherd who leaves his sheep to rescue those that perish'. It was a formidable acclamation for it impressed upon the Roman clergy at least the fact that the imperial provinces were one, and that Ravenna under stress recognized its place among the 'special people' of St. Peter. From Ravenna the Pope sent Ambrose and the priest Stephen to interview Liutprand in person, but once in Lombard territory they lost heart and instead sent letters to the king. So Zachary himself went. Ashamed, Liutprand tried to put him off for he now realized the extent of the Roman legal and political bonds from which he had been trying to create an Italian kingdom; but the pope persisted and arrived in Pavia. There honourably received, he begged for peace and the restoration of the territory of Ravenna. Once more the magic of his office and personality achieved his ends and the king gave back the cities he had taken. It was his last act, for just as Zachary once more arrived back in Rome in triumph the Lombard king died after a reign of twenty-seven years in which he had tried, and failed, to unite the Italian pensinula under him. The waning imperial power had been an easy opponent but the papacy was more durable. His successor Ratchis was by repute a peaceable man and it seemed that Italy could expect its first tranquillity for twenty years.[9]

Italian hopes were disappointed. The lure of easy conquest was too much for the Lombards, and Ratchis embarked on the capture of Perugia, the key to central Italy, and of Pentapolis. Once more Zachary preserved Roman Italy; subsidies and entreaties combined to work on the Lombard king–so well in fact that he was persuaded

[8] *Ibid.*, I, 429. [9] *Ibid.*, I, 429–31.

to abdicate and, with members of his family, enter the monastic life. Once more the *confessio* of St. Peter saw a king kneeling and divesting himself of his regalia, but again the respite was temporary; Ratchis' successor was Aistulf, the most bloodthirsty and the most untrustworthy of the Lombard kings.[10]

Aistulf became king in 749; three years later Zachary died. His portrait in S. Maria *Antica* reveals him as a small, slender, balding man with a reserved, almost diffident air. But he had fought toughly to preserve Roman Italy and had been successful; and he had not neglected the universal Church itself or the practical details of economic life. In the north he had continued his predecessors' patronage and encouragement of Boniface's great missionary movement and had, besides seeing the growth of a new Christian nation, established by his authority a new Christian monarchy when Charles's son Pepin was permitted to set aside the shadowy Merovingian dynasty and with Christian unction and military acclaim call himself king. In the East approaches had been made to heal the Iconoclast dispute, Zachary shared the reluctance of Gregory II for outright condemnation, hoping for the conversion of heretics. In the year of Gregory III's death his old enemy Leo III had also died; his successor Constantine V, his son, had been responsible for the intellectual development of Iconoclasm. But his accession was not smooth; his brother-in-law Artavasdes who opposed Iconoclasm rebelled and for two years was in possession of the capital. Zachary recognized Artavasdes as emperor and saw the final end of Iconoclasm in sight, but Constantine regained his throne, forcing on the pope a reconsideration of relations with the East. Constantine did not at first pursue matters; he perhaps recognized the present ineffectiveness of imperial authority so far north as Rome and had no wish to antagonize so soon the leadership of the Iconodule party. Indeed, he made some restitution for his father's confiscation of papal property by presenting to Zachary two properties still belonging to the imperial fisc, Ninfa and Norma, south-west of Rome in the plain of Lazio.[11]

[10] *Ibid.*, I, 433–4: *Chronicon S. Benedicti Cassinensis*, (*MGH. SS*. Rev. Lang. *et*. p. 487).
[11] See O. Bertolini, 'I rapporti di Zaccaria con Costantino V con Artavasdo nel racconto del biografo e nella probabile realtà storica,' (*ASR*, 78, 1955).

This gift fitted well with Zachary's domestic plans to rescue Rome from the economic results of the losses in Sicily and to resettle the Roman countryside, devastated since the first arrival of the Lombards. Then the tale of abandoned or amalgamated bishoprics had shown the loss of inhabited centres as the peasants took to the high ground or to Rome; Zachary set out to reverse the process and to make Rome self-sufficient. The death of a leader of the Roman militia, Theodore eldest son of Megistus Cataxanthus, provided an opportunity; he left to St. Peter in his will his paternal farm, five miles from Rome on the Via Tiburtina, called from a chapel it contained, St. Cecilia. Zachary used this as the nucleus for an enlarged estate with new buildings, formed by purchase of neighbouring land; under the name of *domusculta* he settled these as the perpetual property of the Roman Church. The word indicates the nature of the settlement, for it was used by the abbots of Farfa in the Sabine hills to describe those properties they reclaimed and resettled. Agriculture and resettlement went together, and to serve religious needs a chapel dedicated to St. Cyrus was built. Another *domusculta* fourteen miles to the north of Rome was established with a legacy from Anne, widow of the former *primicerius* Agatho; estates near the sea, at Anzio and Formiae, were acquired and *domuscultae* established there, and a fifth at Lauretum, between Rome and the sea, was formed by the amalgamation of the great Fonteiana estate with another. Constantine's gift of the two estates was also made use of in the same way, and the near-by bishopric of Tres Tabernae, on the spot of the Appia where the Christians of Rome had met Paul, was re-established after a century and a half. The *domuscultae* were reserved strictly in perpetuity and under pain of anathema to be used and controlled by the Roman Church; there was to be no alienation. Colleges of priests were formed to serve them and the rebuilt basilicas of the *campagna*. Produce was to be directed immediately to Rome.[12]

On Zachary's death in 752 a priest, Stephen–perhaps Zachary's envoy to Liutprand–was elected pope but died before consecration. His successor, another Stephen, was a deacon, unanimously elected. He was the son of the Roman Constantine and since his father's early

[12] O. Bertolini, 'La ricomparsa della Sede episcopale di Tres Tabernae nella seconda metà del secolo VIII e l'istituzione delle "domuscultae" ', (*ASR*, 75, 1952); *LP*. I.

death had been educated in the Lateran. He enjoyed a great reputation for charity and had an especial concern for the Roman churches and for the pilgrims' hostels, whose provisioning he reorganized. But external affairs soon called him away from domestic charity; his first task was to confirm the peace with Aistulf for a term of forty years. Within four months Aistulf had broken it, advancing to the borders of the duchy and claiming the levy of a poll-tax on the Romans of one *solidus* per head. Stephen's protest, carried by two senior abbots of houses in Lombard territory, was ignored and the abbots were instructed not to report back to Rome. Negotiations appeared to be deadlocked, Ravenna had fallen in the last year of Zachary's life and Aistulf was encouraged to complete the conquest. But the extinction of the exarchate had at last aroused the Empire to take some action; an envoy, the chamberlain John, arrived in Rome to appeal for its return. He was received by Stephen and sent on to Pavia accompanied by the Pope's brother, the deacon Paul. Aistulf could safely ignore the imperial threat for John could follow no stronger line than to plead his case; and he and Paul reported back to Rome that their embassy had been fruitless. On John's return to Constantinople, however, Aistulf attached one of his own officials to him to carry on negotiations independently of the papacy.[13]

Envoys continued to pass between pope and king with gifts and entreaties for the return of the exarchate; in Rome Stephen organized solemn prayers and processions in which Aistulf's dishonoured treaty was carried on a processional cross. But the king continued his aggression, demanding the submission of all imperial Italy and threatening universal slaughter. He advanced once more into the Roman duchy, penetrating as far as Ceccano, and Stephen, despairing of effective aid from the Empire, turned like his predecessors to the Franks. A Frankish pilgrim carried a message to Pepin, who at once sent the Abbot Droctegang as his representative to take stock of the situation; at the same time the chamberlain John returned to Rome, carrying with him meaningless instructions to the pope to receive on the emperor's behalf the lost cities of the exarchate.

[13] *LP.* I, 441–2. See also O. Bertolini, 'Il primo "periuria" di Astolfo verso la Chiesa di Roma, 752–3', (*Studi e Testi*, 125, *Miscellanea Giovanni Mercati*, 5, 1946).

Stephen at once sent to Aistulf asking for a safe-conduct to visit Pavia and re-open the whole question. The papal messengers joined up with a Frankish embassy under Bishop Chrodegang of Metz and duke Autchar which had been sent to conduct Stephen, as he had requested, to France – the first results of Droctegang's mission.

On 14th October 753 Stephen, escorted by the Franks and with a full staff of clerics and leading members of the Lateran secretariat, set out from Rome; the Romans and citizens of other towns of the duchy followed him as far as they were allowed, weeping for fear of his death. But signs of heavenly approval were noticed; the weather was favourable and as they reached the Lombard frontier forty miles from Rome, a fireball was seen in the sky, rising from the northern, Frankish territory and sinking over the Lombard kingdom. Duke Autchar preceded the party, preparing the way with full Frankish authority, but messengers from Aistulf continued to arrive saying that the king would listen to no more pleas concerning Ravenna. The pope replied that he would persist in his demands, and the party continued on to Pavia. Once there he presented his demands as strongly as he could, and the imperial envoy John also handed over letters from the Emperor, but Aistulf's response was wholly negative. The Frankish envoys then intervened to tell Aistulf that their master would tolerate no hindrance to the pope's journey into France; Aistulf pleaded with Stephen not to go and was enraged by Stephen's unbending refusal.[14]

On 15th November the party left Pavia and proceeded through the Alpine passes, a difficult winter journey in the course of which the *primicerius* Ambrose died. Pepin was at his palace of Ponthion near Paris when he heard of Stephen's approach and at once sent his son and senior officials to meet the pope. By the feast of Epiphany they had reached Ponthion and Pepin, with his wife and court, came out three miles to greet him. The king himself took the bridle of the pope's horse, like a groom, and led him to the palace. There Stephen addressed his appeal to Pepin for aid against the Lombards and for the protection of the Church and St. Peter's special people.

The Frankish monarchy of the Carolingian line was well-placed by temperament to receive this appeal. In 741 Pepin and his brother Carloman had succeeded their father Charles as joint mayors of the

---

[14] *LP.* I, 444–9; Cod. Carol.

palace and had continued his policy of encouraging the papally-founded mission of Boniface; they had also, with Boniface's advice, undertaken through a series of synods a thorough reform of the Frankish Church, designed to restore discipline and a guaranteed revenue to Church institutions despoiled by magnates over the previous fifty years. In 747 Carloman abdicated his position to become a monk. He had journeyed to Rome with the intention of rebuilding the monastery of St. Andrew on Monte Soratte immediately to the north of Rome and had provided some endowments but, receiving the tonsure from Pope Zachary, abandoned this plan and entered Monte Cassino. Pepin the Short, left sole ruler of France, in 750 sent to Zachary asking formal permission for a change of dynasty; for whoever held the power should also hold the title. Zachary approved and commissioned Boniface to anoint Pepin as king. The last Merovingian, Childeric, was placed in a monastery and at Soissons Boniface as papal legate, with the Frankish bishops, anointed Pepin, as Samuel had anointed Saul. Traditional Frankish ceremony was added to the new church rite by the hoisting of Pepin on the warriors' shields.

At Ponthion Stephen probably asked only for generalized aid and protection of the Church's interests in Italy–Pepin's answer, in which he swore to force full restitution of all Lombard conquests, far exceeded the immediate papal request. But it was a justified promise by Pepin and could justifiably be accepted by the pope; he was the leading elected official of imperial Italy and he and his ministers had inherited the trappings of the Roman senate; Ravenna and the exarchate had seemingly placed themselves under his predecessor as being part of St. Peter's special people and of the pope's flock; and Stephen was in possession of the vague imperial commission to receive back all imperial Italy. But this promise of Pepin's was, in the course of the following two generations, to be hardened in the mind of the Lateran clergy until, as the Donation of Constantine, it was to be provided with a full historical and legal background to form the basis of papal government throughout the Middle Ages. In its fullest developed form the Donation maintained that Constantine I, in return for his cure from leprosy by Pope Sylvester and for his baptism, had granted the pope the Lateran palace, wide estates and sovereignty over the whole Western Empire; the pope and his clergy were to receive the insignia of the imperial senate and court and Constantine himself withdrew from the West to his new capital named after him. By the middle of the eighth century, many of these privileges could be seen as operative; the *Liber Pontificalis* and the papal registers in the Lateran recorded the generous endowments of Constantine and his family, while earlier in the same century Justinian II himself had recognized the sartorial privileges of Rome and had sent his court out to meet the pope, as Pepin had now. In addition, the person of Sylvester had been surrounded by an acquired significance; in Diocletian's persecution he was thought to have taken refuge under the Monte Soratte recently endowed by Carloman, and –perhaps under Gelasius and certainly in the 630s–his legend had been used as a vehicle for the expression of orthodoxy against imperial interference with the faith. The profession of faith by Constantine in the Donation contained a reproach to heretical rulers; and Sylvester was patently a figure from the papacy's history endowed with a special interest for the founders of a new, Christian and orthodox dynasty.[15]

Stephen remained in France the whole winter, taking up residence with his court at St. Denys; exhausted by his journey and the severity of the winter he fell seriously ill and for a time his life was in the balance. On his recovery Pepin summoned an assembly of the Frankish nation at Quierzy and associated them with himself in his resolve to do justice to St. Peter and fulfil his promise. On this occasion Stephen, who had repeated the anointing of Pepin and his two sons as kings of the Franks, conferred upon them a new title,

[15] See W. Levison, 'Konstantinische Schenkung und Silvester–Legende', (*Miscellanea F. Ehrle*, II, *Studi e Testi*, 39, 1924); E. Griffe, 'Aux origines de l'Etat pontifical: A propos de la Donation de Constantin et de la Donation de Quierzy, (753–755)', (*Bulletin de littérature ecclésiastique*, 53, 1952); W. Gericke, 'Das Constitutum Constantini und die Silvester-Legende', (*Zeitschrift für Savigny-Stiftung*, 44, 1958), and 'Konstantinische Schenkung und Silvester-Legende in neuer Sicht', (*ibid.*, 47, 1961), and, 'Wann entstand die Konstantinische Schenkung?', (*ibid.*, 43, 1957), and, 'Das Glaubensbekenntnis der Konstantinischen Schenkung', (*ibid.*, 47, 1961); W. Ohnsorge, 'Die Konstantinische Schenkung, Leo III und die Anfänge der Kurialen römischen Kaiseridee', (*ibid.*, 37, 1951); R. Bork, 'Zu einer neuen These über die Konstantinische Schenkung', (*Festschrift A. Hofmeister*, 1955); E. Petrucci, 'I rapporti tra le redazioni latine e greche del Costituto di Costantino', (*BISI*, 74, 1962).

that of Patrician of the Romans. This was strictly speaking a high grade of the Byzantine court nobility whose owners were normally invested by the Emperor with the insignia of their rank and acclaimed as patrician by the people. It had frequently been held by barbarian chiefs, as had other imperial honours; Odoacer and Theodoric had been patricians, Clovis of the Franks had received the insignia of consulship. Nor was it new in application to Carolingian power; Gregory II, writing to Boniface in 724, had referred to Charles Martel as patrician, as well as duke, *princeps* and *subregulus*, though none were strictly correct terms. But in Italian eyes the style patrician had a more immediate meaning; it was the rank normally held by the exarchs of Ravenna, and by some dukes of Rome and governors of Sicily; in common parlance their office was often omitted and they were simply referred to as patrician of Sicily. As conferred by Stephen on Pepin and his sons it was an evocative title, implying a general championship and patronage rather than a specific office or function; by virtue of the style, the Frankish patrician had a protectorate and place in Roman life and would wear the Roman clothes of his rank.[16]

Aistulf made one attempt to interrupt this accord between pope and king. Pepin's brother Carloman was summoned from Monte Cassino and sent to dissuade his brother from supporting Rome. The attempt failed and Pepin ordered that Carloman be placed in a Frankish monastery under the royal eye. Frankish envoys were sent to Aistulf, reminding him of his peace treaty and demanding the restoration of the exarchate; Aistulf ignored them but at the instance of Stephen who wished to avoid an armed clash, second and third embassies were sent. On the failure of these and the gifts they carried, Pepin ordered the mobilization of the Frankish army. Accompanied by Pepin and the pope, it marched towards Italy; but even at this point, on Stephen's urgings, appeals were addressed to Aistulf both by Pepin and the pope. The distinctive views of their aims may be seen in these; for while the Romans maintained that it was the

[16] See F. L. Ganshof, 'Notes sur les origines byzantines du titre patricius Romanorum', (*Melanges H. Grégoire*, II, 1950); W. Ohnsorge, 'Patricus-Titel Karls des Grossen', (*Byzantinische Zeitschrift*, 53, 1960); J. Deer, 'Zum Patricius–Romanorum–Titel Karls des Grossen', (*Archivum Historiae Pontificae*, 3, 1965).

integrity of the republic that must be restored, the Frankish sources refer only to the rights of St. Peter. Aistulf remained obdurate, replying with threats and insults, and moved north to try to catch the Frankish van in the Alpine passes. But the van achieved a swift victory in advance of the main army, the Lombards broke and the Lombard plain with its promise of rich plunder lay defenceless. Pepin kept his men in hand and pressed on to the siege of Pavia; this was vigorously pursued until Stephen once more interposed to end bloodshed, and peace proposals were put forward. A tripartite pact was made, between the Lombards, Franks and Romans; Aistulf swore to return the cities of the exarchate, to surrender hostages to Pepin and to preserve peace with the imperial territories. His oath was accepted and Pepin and Stephen returned to their capitals.[17]

Aistulf was not slow to prove himself a perjuror; he made no move to hand over the cities and within a few months of Pepin's departure from Italy had marched against Rome itself; for three months he besieged the city, inflicting terrible damage on the surrounding countryside. Stephen sent an appeal to Pepin, carried by Bishop George of Ostia, the Roman tribunes Thomaricus and Comita and Abbot Warneharius, Pepin's own ambassador in Rome; they were forced to travel by sea. Stephen's letter described the full fury of Aistulf's siege and his animosity against the person of the pope.

'On 1st January last the entire army of this Aistulf king of the Lombards marched out of Etruria on Rome and encamped before the St. Peter's gate, the Porto gate and the St. Pancras gate; then Aistulf himself joined this army with forces drawn from other regions and encamped by the Salarian and other gates. He then wrote to me in these words: "Open the Salarian gate and I will enter the city; hand over your bishop and I will spare you, otherwise I will overthrow your walls, I will slay you with my own hand, and then we will see who can save you from my clutches." He was then joined by the Beneventans who encamped before the city by the St. John, St. Paul and other gates.

'Far and wide outside the city they ravaged all the farms with fire and sword, burning all buildings, destroying them right to the ground. They burnt the churches of God, impaled the images of the saints on their swords and threw them on the fire; they desecrated the sacred vessels that carry the Oblation of the Body of Our Lord Jesus Christ by eating from them, bloating themselves with vast meals of meat. . . . Those of God's servants, the monks, who had stayed behind in their monasteries to perform the divine office they beat up and severely injured; the nuns and cloistered women who had given themselves to the cloister from infancy or youth for the love of God, they abducted and most savagely misused; some were murdered as well as raped. They burnt all St. Peter's estates and those of the Romans as well, it is reported; they have burnt all houses on the outskirts of the city, removed the livestock, torn down the vines to the roots, torn up the crops and devoured all. . . . They yoked together the servants of St. Peter and of the Romans and led them off as captives; innocent babes were snatched from their mothers' breasts, the mothers raped, the babes sold by the Lombards. For certain they did more evil in this province of Rome than any pagan race has ever done; so that, so to speak, the very stones join us in weeping as they see our desolation. For fifty-five days they besieged this afflicted Rome, day and night surrounding us entirely; day and night fierce battle raged with fury before the walls. . . .[18]

Stephen's envoys reached Pepin and supplemented the papal letter with their eye-witness account; Warneharius especially had earned the pope's commendation for he had donned armour during the siege and stood guard with the Romans on the walls. Pepin assembled his army again and marched for Italy; the passes of the Alps were seized without difficulty. At the same moment the chamberlain John with another official, the First Secretary George again arrived in Rome. Stephen informed them of Pepin's campaign but they refused to credit the news so Stephen sent them with a papal envoy to Marseilles. On landing in France they heard of Pepin's rapid successes; their mission was in serious jeopardy if they could not reach Pepin before he made some irrevocable settlement contrary to imperial interests. They tried to delay the papal agent in Marseilles but failed; George therefore hurried ahead to reach Pavia first. On arrival he begged Pepin to restore the exarchate to the Empire and offered great gifts, but Pepin had little knowledge of the Empire; his loyalty was to St. Peter and the pope and he regarded these territories as already belonging to St. Peter. When Aistulf surrendered Pepin took mea-

[18] Cod. Carol., 8.

sures to ensure the handing over of the territories; Fulrad, abbot of St. Denys, was summoned from France as commissioner and with Aistulf's representative made his way through Pentapolis and Emilia to each town in turn, receiving the keys of each together with hostages from their leading citizens, and proceeded to Rome. In the presence of the pope he placed both the keys of the cities and the written document listing them as being in the perpetual possession of the pope with Pepin's guarantee before the *confessio* of St. Peter.[19]

There seemed some hopes that this arrangement would prevail, for shortly afterwards Aistulf died in a hunting accident. The succession was disputed. The majority of the Lombard nobles stood for Aistulf's brother Ratchis, but the duke of Tuscany, Desiderius, also claimed the throne. The latter, with the greater part of the Lombard nation against him, sought papal support, promising to confirm the peace and in addition to hand over the former imperial cities, Faenza, Castel Tiberiaco, Gavello and the whole duchy of Ferrara—districts that had not been included in Aistulf's surrender. On Fulrad's advice Stephen opened negotiations, sending his brother Paul and the counsellor Christopher to Desiderius. The pact was made, the Roman priest Stephen was sent to Ratchis while Fulrad, at the head of some Frankish detachments and units of the Roman army, marched to reinforce Desiderius. Stephen wrote to inform Pepin of these events, of his hopes of Desiderius who seemed a peace-loving man, and of his joy at the reunion of those towns 'which have for so long been associated under one dominion and jurisdiction'. It was the last official act of his pontificate for in 757, after an illness of some length, he died.[20]

His five years' pontificate had achieved much; the formal recognition by the Western powers of papal rule over central Italy, the exclusion of imperial claims, the discovery of a formula sufficient to provide protection without too close a domination, and the accession of a Lombard king with professedly peaceful intent and good cause

---

[19] *LP.* I, 452–4: see O. Bertolini, 'Il problema delle origini del potere dei papi nei suoi presupposti teoretici iniziali; il concetto di 'restituto' nelle prime cessioni territoriali (756–7) alla Chiesa di Roma' (*Miscellanea Pio Paschini, Lateranum*, 14, 1948).

[20] *LP.* I, 455; Cod. Carol., 11.

for gratitude. But the wording of his last letter to Pepin gave indication of a papal theory of reclamation that was not necessarily shared by the other inhabitants of imperial Italy. In particular the archbishop of Ravenna had cause to suspect many of the acts of Stephen and Pepin; the Church of Ravenna had long been jealous of its rights and assertive of its independence of Rome, receiving recognition of this in the previous century from Constans II. In Emilia and Pentapolis it boasted of an administrative structure and properties comparable only to those of Rome. In 743 Ravenna had only temporarily when under pressure from Liutprand welcomed Pope Zachary as mediator and hailed him as their shepherd; the subsequent settlements – by which it became clear that the exarchate and with it Ravenna's capital status would not be restored – pointed only to a large increase in the authority of St. Peter and Rome. If imperial authority were to be put into commission in this manner, St. Apollenaris and the archbishop of Ravenna had an equal claim to inherit local government to that of St. Peter and the pope. The position was complicated by the person of the archbishop who had been elected in 744. Sergius was a young man and married when he won a bitterly disputed election; he had received consecration from Zachary but his episcopate was spent in disputes with his clergy over revenues, a besetting sin of Ravenna's archbishops. The Ravenna tradition of relations with Rome is confused since there is some duplication of incidents and names, but the prevailing impression is that Rome was seeking to extinguish her independence. On Stephen's return from France he had passed through Pentapolis and stayed at the monastery of S. Ilaro which he granted to Ravenna's jurisdiction, but Sergius, annoyed at the terms of Pepin's settlement, ostentatiously ignored him. In implementing these terms Stephen also appointed papal agents, the priest Philip and the duke Eustachius, for the exarchate. They were both Romans, and this aroused Ravenna's suspicions still further. Finally, by reason of Sergius's own lack of support among his clergy, Stephen was able to have him arrested and brought to Rome to be tried before a synod charged with improperly holding the see. Here he was accused, as a layman, of using the Church of Ravenna for worldly ends, a symptom of the marked intrusion of the laity of Pentapolis into the church. Sergius defended himself by declaring that he had been openly elected and had been consecrated by Zachary. He had not received sentence when Stephen died.

The papal election of 757 was disputed; one party favoured the archdeacon Theophylact and, even before Stephen was dead, had gathered round his house to acclaim him. But the majority, including the more responsible officials, selected Stephen's own brother, the deacon Paul, who was in the Lateran nursing his brother; only on Stephen's death did he emerge, to be acclaimed pope during the funeral in St. Peter's. It was a wise choice; Paul had been closely associated with his brother, had served as legate in missions to Aistulf and Desiderius, and had the knowledge of political affairs necessary if Stephen's gains were to be consolidated. He immediately announced his election to Pepin as being by 'the whole senate and the general populace of the God-guarded city of Rome', and sent Bishop Wilcharius of Mentana to be his representative at Pepin's court. He also reported that he had restored Archbishop Sergius to Ravenna; the Ravenna tradition asserted that Paul had only done this in return for the promise of the archdiocese's entire treasure, and that it was merely another move to weaken Ravenna's independence. In 758 Paul visited Ravenna, perhaps to extract the payment of his price, for the clergy of the city at this time feared for the safety of their treasure and formed a plan to murder the pope before he could lay his hands on it – the *vicedominus* of Ravenna planned to drown him. But, according to the Ravenna tradition, less drastic methods advocated by the archdeacon Uviliaris prevailed; as much as possible of the diocesan treasury was hidden and Paul obtained only what could not be removed. Sergius was determined to exercise as much civil authority as the pope now did; relying on his diocese's wealth and organization, on bribes to the local nobility and on a pact with Venetian merchants, he assumed direct rule throughout the former exarchate 'travelling round giving justice, from the borders of Persiceta through the whole of Pentapolis, as far as Tuscany and the Volano, dispensing justice just like an exarch and discharging business in the Roman manner'. Paul had taken hostages from Ravenna's leading citizens, including the great-grandfather of Agnellus the historian of Ravenna, who were kept in Rome until their deaths.[21]

[21] *LP. Rav.*, cc. 154–9; O. Bertolini, 'Le prime manifestazioni concrete

Paul's pressing need for money perhaps compelled him to grant Sergius delegated powers, for the early hopes of the pontificate were proving false. Within a year he was reporting to Pepin that George, the imperial first secretary who had remained in Italy, had concluded an alliance between the Empire and the Lombards; an imperial fleet was to land troops in conjunction with a Lombard army and planned to overrun Ravenna, Pentapolis and Rome itself. But Desiderius had not openly committed himself to renewing the reconquest or the quarrel with Rome; in that same year, 758, he visited Rome in person to pray at the tomb of St. Peter. Paul pressed him for the surrender of Imola, part of the price for Roman aid in his accession, but evidently formed a good opinion of his intentions, since he wrote asking Pepin to return the hostages taken from Aistulf and to confirm the peace treaty.[22]

Desiderius, however, promptly threw off all hesitation. He marched through Pentapolis, causing considerable destruction to the harvest, and entered the duchy of Spoleto. Duke Alboin and his *gastalds* were arrested and Desiderius moved south into the duchy of Benevento; the duke fled to Taranto and Desiderius set up his own nominee, Arichis. George, who had accompanied him, went to Naples and organized imperial co-operation for the reconquest of the exarchate and the Roman duchy, while the Byzantine fleet stationed off Sicily sailed to blockade Taranto in conjunction with the Lombard army. In a letter sent secretly to Pepin to avoid interception by the Lombards, Paul stated that his requests for the return of Imola, Bologna and Osimo had been refused and that Desiderius himself demanded the return of the hostages. In 760 Pepin's envoys forced an agreement on Desiderius that all would be restored–cities, patrimonies and full rights–before the end of April; but the situation steadily worsened. News arrived in Rome and was transmitted to Pepin that an imperial fleet, three hundred vessels strong and commanded by six patricians, had sailed to link up with the Sicilian

del potere temporale dei papi nell' esarcato di Ravenna (756–7)', (*Atti dell' Istituto Veneto di Scienze, Lettere ed Arti*, 106; *Classe di Scienze morali e lettere*, 1947–8), and 'Sergio, arcivescovo di Ravenna, 744–769', (*Studi romagnoli*, I, 1950); M. Baumont, 'Le Pontificat de Paul Ier', (*MAH*, 47, 1930).
[22] Cod. Carol., 16.

fleet. In addition, Desiderius had attacked Sinigaglia in the exarchate and devastated the countryside, as well as sending foraging expeditions throughout Campania. Disaffection was also noted in the ranks of the Roman clergy; the priest Marinus, at present in France, whom Paul had appointed titular of S. Chrysogonus with generous endowments, had been found intriguing with George. Paul asked that he might be consecrated to a Frankish see, to check possible imperialist sympathy in Rome.[23]

For the remaining six years of his pontificate the Italian situation remained unstable under the threat of a full-scale imperial invasion. A warning of what might befall Rome, now that the temporary accord of Zachary and Constantine V had ended and with the Iconoclast dispute still raging, came from Naples where Bishop Paul was compelled to spend the first five years of his episcopate, from 762 to 767, in hiding from the imperial authorities in the catacombs outside the city.[24] Throughout these years Pope Paul was seeking to strengthen the ties between Rome and the Franks; donations of Greek books were made to the royal court and with some symbolism the monastery of SS. Silvester and Andrew on Monte Soratte was granted to Pepin. Bishop Wilcharius of Mentana served as an indefatigable envoy between the two courts and Paul constantly urged the establishment of a permanent Frankish ambassador in Rome. His attention was also given to repairing the damage done to the countryside by Aistulf's siege which had retarded much of Zachary's work. In synod on 4th July 761 Paul decreed the foundation and endowment of a monastery dedicated to Sylvester into which many bodies of the saints from the suburban cemeteries were moved, for the cemeteries themselves were in decay: 'So it has transpired,' the decree ran, 'that many of the cemeteries of Christ's holy martyrs and confessors, of such antiquity, sited outside the walls of Rome have for many years been fallen into a state of neglect and now through the devastations of the impious Lombards are totally in ruins. For these most sacriligiously desecrated them, digging up the graves of the martyrs and removing the bodies of the saints as plunder. Since then the respect due to them has been entirely lacking

[23] Cod. Carol., 20, 21, 24, 25.
[24] D. Mallardo, 'Il calendario marmoreo di Napoli', (EL, 58–60, 1944–6, pp. 40, 53, 194–6).

and neglected. What is worst of all, animals of various sorts are even herded in some of the saints' cemeteries so that they have become mere cowsheds, filled with farmyard muck.'[25]

Envoys, Frankish and papal, had been sent to negotiate a peace with Constantine V; their arrival in 764-6 was delayed by winter storms but it increased the internal divisions on policy within the Roman Church itself, for they brought back with them Byzantine envoys, the eunuch Sinesius and the *spathar* Anthius. In Roman circles, dominated by the descendants of imperial office-holders who still bore their titles, there had been a resurgence of sympathy with the East and reluctance at the irrevocable dissociation from the Empire. This opinion had been enraged by Pepin's rejection of the imperial envoy George in his negotiations with Aistulf and by Paul's continuation of close Frankish dependence. Now the *primicerius* Christopher was accused of negotiating independently with the imperial envoys and perhaps of having tampered with the translation of imperial letters; but Paul, in reply to Pepin's charges, emphasized the trust he placed, as his brother had, in the *primicerius*. A servant of the Roman Church, one Saxulus, fled for unknown reasons to Desiderius; Paul petitioned Pepin for his influence in securing his return. He asked that the Greek envoys he had forwarded to France should be cross-examined, presumably on the state of military preparations, and Bishop George of Ostia and the Roman priest Peter were sent to Pepin to act as interpreters. Permission was given for a lengthy stay and Paul gave assurances that 'it will be our duty to see that George's diocese and the church entrusted to Peter do not fall into neglect from lack of supervision during their absence'.[26] But the threat of a major imperial assault on the east coast continued; Paul received letters from Archbishop Sergius enclosing others from certain Venetians and from an imperial official which seemed to indicate that such an attack was under preparation. Pepin was asked to arrange for Desiderius to send aid if necessary from the Lombard duchies of Spoleto, Benevento and Tuscany 'to the maritime towns of Ravenna and Pentapolis to combat any invasions by the enemy'.

In the summer of 768 Paul paid a visit to St. Paul's basilica and

[25] V. Federici, 'Regesto del Monastero di S. Silvestro in Capite' (*ASR*, 22, 1899).
[26] Cod. Carol., 16.

was taken ill there; carried back to the Lateran, he lay for some time in extreme weakness. His pontificate, with that of his brother, had seen the emergence of the papacy as the recognized residuary legatee of imperial authority in central Italy, but this had been achieved at the cost of a too-sharp separation from the Empire and a dependence on the Franks that was not to the taste of many elements in Roman life. The internal order of the new state was not yet established; there were many outstanding problems in connection with the duchies of Spoleto and Benevento and many claims for compensation for damage inflicted by the Lombard kingdom. Furthermore, the assumption of the Franks that rule belonged to St. Peter was not universally shared; Ravenna had its own equally sound claims to civil independence, and in the duchy of Rome there were many imperial office-holders who could claim that the reversion of civil authority rightly belonged to them rather than to the papacy. But the papacy by its leadership and organization had emerged as the only practical central authority, and political activity could not, as in Ravenna, aim at achieving independence of the papacy but only at controlling it.

Even as Paul lay dying, one of the magnates of the Roman country-side, duke Toto of Nepi, was planning to stage a *coup d'état*. With his brothers Constantine, Passivus and Paschal, he collected a small army from Nepi and other Etrurian towns and from the *contadini*, armed them and brought them into Rome by the St. Pancras gate, establishing his headquarters in his town house. Hearing of this assembly the *primicerius* Christopher with other officials summoned Toto to his own house and urged him not to attempt so monstrous a crime: 'After these talks in my house,' he said later in evidence, 'we swore together on Christ's four Gospels and on the holy chrism and on the other mysteries of God that we would not make trouble in a papal election but that we should elect our pontiff according to the traditional methods of this holy see . . . from among the priests and deacons.' Paul died on the 29th June and Christopher led the magnates, rural and urban, to the basilica of the Apostles where he announced the terms of the oath to the people. But when the crowd had dispersed Toto seized the Lateran and proclaimed his brother Constantine, a layman, as pope. In the Lateran they found Bishop George of Palestrina, the *vicedominus*; by threats of violence they prevailed on him to give Constantine clerical orders, despite his pleas that they forgo this sacrilege. The next day, Monday, Constantine was successively ordained subdeacon and deacon in the chapel of St. Lawrence in the Lateran where he had taken up residence: the whole population was summoned to swear loyalty to him. The following Sunday he was consecrated bishop by George, Eustratius of Albano and Citonatus of Porto.

One person was absent from the swearing of loyalty and the consecration: the *primicerius* Christopher, head of a powerful family of papal office-holders, whose support was essential to Constantine. The notary Constantine was immediately sent to Christopher's house, intimating to him the grave dangers of his opposition, but he and his son Sergius, the *sacellarius* of the Roman Church, fled for sanctuary to St. Peter's. Constantine applied pressure; the duke Gregory, a friend or relation of the *primicerius* living in Campania, was murdered, but Christopher would not move under any threat or persuasion. Instead he told Constantine that he and his son wished to become monks in the monastery of S. Salvatore outside Rieti, in the duchy of Spoleto. Constantine came down to St. Peter's in person and swore that they should have safe-conduct to Rieti, and permission to live under house-arrest in Rome until Easter. On the conclusion of the Easter festivities they were permitted to leave Rome, but once in Lombard territory hastened to duke Theodicius of Spoleto and urged his help. Theodicius took them to Desiderius in Pavia who promised them his aid. In July 769 they returned to the Sabine area; Sergius and a Lombard priest Waldipert, Desiderius's appointed agent, recruited troops from the region around Furcone and Rieti and from other Lombards of the duchy. On 29th July they seized the bridge over the Aniene and on the following day the Ponte Milvio; then, skirting the Vatican, they came to the St. Pancras gate.

Allies within the city opened the gates to them and they entered Rome but, uncertain of Roman feeling, remained on the Gianiculo summit. Toto had been informed of their entry and with his brother Passivus and their allies, the *secundicerius* Demetrius and the *chartularius* Gratiosus, hastened to the gate to eject them. However, Toto's party was divided; Demetrius and Gratiosus, of the papal service, were undoubtedly resentful of this dominance by non-Roman magnates and were in touch with those allies of Christopher who had opened the gate. The engagement at the Gianiculo's foot was brief; a celebrated Lombard warrior, Racipert, charged Toto but was killed, and the Lombards recoiled. Demetrius and Gratiosus, behind Toto, seized their chance and stabbed him in the back with their lances. Toto's brother Passivus fled to the Lateran where he broke the news to Constantine; then, with Constantine's newly-appointed *vicedominus* Bishop Theodore (for George had died of a stroke immediately after Constantine's consecration) they took refuge first in the Lateran basilica and then for greater security in the chapel of S. Cesario whose doors they shut behind them. A few hours later officers of the Roman militia came to arrest them.[27]

There now followed a second *coup*. The priest Waldipert who had accompanied Sergius, acting on instructions from Desiderius to secure a favourable pope, went with several Romans but without informing Sergius to the monastery of St. Vitus and took from there the priest Philip whom they acclaimed as pope: 'St. Peter has chosen Philip.' They brought him to the Lateran and installed him with the usual ceremonies–the prayers offered by a bishop, the kiss of peace, followed by a banquet for the leading men of the Church and army. But that same day Christopher reached Rome and was horrified at an appointment he had not managed; before all the Romans he swore he would not remain in Rome if Philip stayed in the Lateran. Gratiosus thereupon hastened forward with an escort and, not violently but with reverence, Philip was returned to his monastery.[28]

The following day a new election was made; Christopher assembled the clergy, the army and the citizens in the church of Tribus Fatis and there, with punctilious legality, the choice fell upon Stephen, priest of St. Cecilia, who was brought from his church to the Lateran amid acclamations. He was a Sicilian who had come to Rome in the time of Gregory III, who had placed him for his education in the newly-founded monastery of St. Chrysogonus. His scriptural learning attracted the attention of Zachary and he was brought into the Lateran service, remaining there, even after his appointment to St. Cecilia, during the pontificates of Zachary, Stephen II and Paul, whom he nursed on his deathbed. Mild and charitable by nature, he was at first unable to exercise authority. The feud continued; a band

[27] *LP*. I, 468–72; Mansi, 12, 717.
[28] *LP*. I, 470–1.

of Christopher's supporters seized and blinded Bishop Theodore and Passivus; Theodore's tongue was also split. Passivus was taken to the monastery of S. Silvestro, and Theodore to the Clivo Scauro where he died a few days later, tortured by thirst, crying out for water. Constantine was also dragged out, placed side-saddle on a horse with weights fastened to his feet, and taken to the Cellanova monastery.

Before his consecration Stephen ordered an inquiry into the *coup* and Constantine was brought before the synod in the Lateran to be degraded from his orders. Following Stephen's episcopal consecration a general confession was made by clergy and people of their sin in having acquiesced in his usurpation. The rooting out of his supporters continued; the Roman army with contingents from Tuscany and Campania marched to Alatri whose tribune, Gracilis, had been an ally of Toto; the town surrendered and Gracilis was brought under heavy guard to Rome. The following night Gratiosus with a band of Tuscan and Campanian toughs dragged him from prison as though to transfer him to a monastery, but near the Colosseum they blinded him and cut out his tongue. A few days later they raided the Cellanova monastery at dawn and, after blinding Constantine, left him lying in the *piazza*. Waldipert was then accused of conspiring with the duke of Spoleto and some Romans to murder Christopher and regain control of Rome in Lombard favour; when Christopher set out with a posse to his house, he fled for sanctuary to S. Maria *ad Martyres* but was dragged out still clutching the image of the Virgin and locked up under strictest custody in the Ferrata prison. A few days later he was taken out and in the *piazza* before the Lateran was viciously blinded and mutilated. He was then sent to the Valeria hostel where he soon died of his injuries.[29]

In April 769 Stephen held a council in the Lateran to consider the fate of Constantine and the control of papal elections. Sergius, now as *secundicerius* his father's deputy and *nomenclator*, went to France with invitations to the new kings, Pepin's sons Charles and Carloman, to send bishops from their dominions. Twelve attended with thirty-four Italians and representatives of five others. Constantine was brought before them and cross-examined on his seizure of the papal throne; blind, he lay prostrate before the synod and begged pardon

[29] *LP*. I, 471–2.

for his great sins, pleading in extenuation that others, such as Sergius of Ravenna and Stephen of Naples, had been consecrated direct from lay status; but these instances merely exasperated the fathers. His acts were condemned and copies burnt, and the synod proceeded to the problem of his ordinations. The bishops created by Constantine were to revert to their former grades, priest or deacon, but if they had already proved acceptable to the people of their sees they might be elected anew and presented in regular form to the Roman see for reconsecration by Stephen. It was decided that priests and deacons of Constantine's ordination were also to revert to their previous grade–they might be reordained but were never to be promoted to higher office. However, Pope Stephen swore before the whole college of priests that he would never reordain them, and he proved as good as his word for while all the bishops were re-presented, the rest stayed in their former states.

A decree was also passed governing future elections:

'So we decree under sanction of anathema that no layman or person of any other status shall presume to attend a papal election in arms; but the election shall be in the hands of the known priests and leaders of the Church and of all the clergy. And when the election is made and the elect conducted to the patriarchal palace the leaders of the militia and the whole army, the leading citizens and the whole population of this city of Rome shall go to greet him as their Lord. And so in the customary manner drawing up a decree and all consenting to it, they shall sign it. . . .

'Furthermore no one from the settlements of Tuscany or Campania or elsewhere shall be invited or brought into the city. And no servants of clergy or military shall be found taking part in the election: and no one shall be armed.'[30]

Christopher's party now seemed in full control; they had ousted their rivals, the lords of the neighbouring towns and of the Tuscan and Campanian countryside, and had established papal elections as the prerogative of the clergy and Lateran officialdom alone. As a clan they dominated the Lateran. Christopher remained *primicerius*; Sergius was his father's deputy and as *nomenclator* controlled access to the Pope; Christopher's nephew Gratiosus was duke of Rome.

[30] *Concilium Romanum*, a. 769, in *MGH. LL.* Sect. III; *Concilia Aevi Karolini*, I, i, pp. 86–9.

They pressed their policy forward; Christopher went on an embassy to Desiderius to obtain the cities in Pentapolis that were still unrestored, but Desiderius–bitterly opposed to Christopher since he had ousted his agent's candidate for the papacy–plotted his removal. He made contact with Christopher's enemies within the papal household and especially with the chamberlain Paul Afiarta, an avaricious man, jealous of Christopher's ascendancy and reputedly pro-Lombard in sympathies. To bring about their downfall Desiderius came to Rome on the pretext of a visit *ad limina*. Christopher heard of this and, with few illusions, hastily armed the city; contingents were brought in from Etruria, Campania and the duchy of Perugia and were organized for the defence of Rome.

On his arrival Desiderius camped outside the city by St. Peter's on the far side of the river; he then requested that Stephen come for an interview. While pope and king discussed reparations owed to the Roman Church, Paul Afiarta by a preconcerted plan attempted to rouse the Romans to overthrow Christopher. When Stephen returned, Christopher and his son, with armed followers, burst into the Lateran and demanded the arrest of Afiarta and his followers; they had with them King Carloman's envoy, Dodo, and some armed Franks. To Stephen, perhaps under Afiarta's influence, it appeared as though they planned to murder him; the pope later wrote to King Charles: 'With Dodo and his Franks and with some of his wicked followers, they collected a force and broke in upon us here, in the sacred patriarchal palace of the Lateran: in arms, breaking down the doors and slashing all the curtains with their spears they entered the basilica of the lord Pope Theodore, which no one has ever dared to do with even a sword; but they did in mail and with lances, to where we sat.' Stephen sharply rebuked Christopher for this breach of etiquette and then with his clergy managed to slip across the river to St. Peter's. Christopher now held the whole city and maintained a strict guard; but Stephen, hoping at least to save his life, sent the bishops of Palestrina and Segni to him and urged that he either join him in St. Peter's or enter a monastery. The pope was still under the impression that Christopher and Sergius had tried to murder him and that he owed his life to Desiderius's protection, but Christopher understood the trap Afiarta had prepared and preferred to keep the river between himself and the king; he replied to the bishops that he would rather be handed to the Romans, brothers and fellow-citizens, than to foreigners. His followers however, hearing the papal proposals, began to desert him; duke Gratiosus, on pretext of returning to his own house, slipped out of the Porto gate with some companions and made his way to St. Peter's. Then Sergius abandoned his father; that night he climbed over the wall and tried to reach sanctuary in St. Peter's, but Lombard sentries patrolling the steps arrested him and took him to Desiderius. The following day Christopher in turn surrendered; but as the pope was still in St. Peter's his and Sergius's safety was temporarily assured. Stephen ordered them both to be given the tonsure and the monastic habit as a basic safeguard, then left them in the basilica, intending to have them quietly smuggled back into the city by night for their own protection.[31]

But Paul Afiarta had not completed his vendetta; the following events involving the deaths of the *primicerius* and *secundicerius* were unearthed in an investigation conducted by Stephen's successor, Pope Hadrian. On Stephen's return to the city Paul collected some Lombards, took Christopher and Sergius from their sanctuary and blinded them; Christopher was taken to the monastery of St. Agatho where three days later he died, while Sergius was removed to the cellars of the Lateran and placed under the guard of the cellarers. When, eight days later Pope Stephen died, worn out by the horrors of his pontificate, Sergius had vanished. Hadrian examined the cellarers who stated: 'In the first hour of the night the chamberlain Calventzulus came with the priest Lunisso and the tribune Leonatus, both of Anagni, and these took Sergius away; this was about eight days before the death of the lord Pope Stephen. So he was handed over to these Campanians.' Calventzulus was then cross-examined as to the authority by which he had removed Sergius; he replied that he had been given these orders, in the presence of the Campanians, by Paul Afiarta and his associates, the regional *defensor* Gregory, Pope Stephen's brother duke John, and the chamberlain Calvulus. Orders for the Campanians' arrests were given and when brought to Rome they confirmed Calventzulus'

---

[31] See O. Bertolini, 'La caduta del primicerio Cristoforo', (*Rivista di Storia della Chiesa in Italia*, 1, 1947), and M. G. Mara, 'Una pagina di Storia Langobarda', (*Studi Romani*, 9, 1961).

evidence; moreover they took officers of the papal household down to the Merulana, the street leading to S. Maria *Maggiore,* and showed them the spot where they had buried Sergius. The grave was opened and his body found, lacerated with wounds and with a rope still round its neck; it was clear that he had been strangled and then buried while still half-alive.

Paul Afiarta now seemed supreme; Christopher and Sergius were dead, he himself took the post of *superista* or military governor of the Lateran; his rivals, city and military officials and clerics, were exiled from Rome; he was secure in the friendship of Desiderius and in his dominance over the feeble Pope Stephen, whose brother was his associate. But it was a fragile ascendancy, depending on the life of the pope and the division of the Carolingian power. Pepin had died in 768, leaving the kingdom to his two sons, Charles and Carloman; these had been unable to co-operate and Carloman had intrigued in Rome to gain a preponderant influence. But he died in 771, leaving Charles as sole ruler, and his wife and children fled to Desiderius for protection. When Pope Stephen died, Afiarta's position became yet more precarious, but he had hopes of dominating the new pope and inducing him, by force if necessary, to a pro-Lombard policy. Early in the pontificate he went on an embassy to Pavia and there promised Desiderius that he would bring the pope to Pavia to consecrate Carloman's sons as Frankish kings and so disrupt for ever the Frankish alliance. 'He will come even if I have to hobble him with a rope round his feet; I will bring him to your presence by any means I can contrive.' But Paul had underestimated his man; Hadrian was no tool, like Stephen, to be used by others, but a vigorous man well able to take charge of Rome's fate.[32]

[32] *LP.* I, 489–91.

8

ROME AND THE FRANKS

The unhappy pontificate of Stephen III had shown Rome and the papacy at the mercy of factions interested in their control; the Lombard king concerned with further encroachments into imperial territory and with dividing the Frankish kingdom; the circle of court and clerical functionaries competing for their own advancement and influence; the nobility, heirs of imperial commands in the country, seeking power from their own bases. The former imperial provinces had a common civic tradition and record of opposing the Lombards but had not yet been welded together under one acknowledged authority. Roman society itself was not homogeneous but was composed of separate strands each in origin distinct from the others, whose constitutional and social relationships were not resolved by the Frankish re-ordering of Italy. Although the papacy had acquired a wide diplomatic and administrative leadership in times of danger in addition to its religious primacy, it was also as a bishopric a local, Roman office; elected by the Roman clergy and citizens from among the Roman clergy, the pope was not fully representative of all elements in the whole range of his new dominions. His rule over these dominions was variously interpreted in the first generation of the new papal states; by the Franks as a vicariate for St. Peter; by Hadrian I as a residuary legateeship for lapsed Byzantine authority; by Leo III as a fully developed sovereignty in Roman law.

The emergence of family interest—an interest which had been dormant in the seventh century when Rome was dominated by refugees from the East—cut across the undefined sovereignty of the pope. The nobility that derived titles and authority independently of the papacy, from the Eastern Empire, was matched by the bureaucratic families that centred their activities on the Lateran. The father of Pope John VII as a high imperial functionary was domiciled in Rome; Gregory III had a Roman home which he converted into a monastery; Stephen II was succeded as pope by his brother Paul. Christopher had probably achieved his and the Lateran executive's dominance during the pontificate of Paul I, possibly to the exclusion of the pope himself; Paul's charitable record as an indefatigable visitor of prisons perhaps reflects the fate of Christopher's early rivals. Duke Toto's power was differently based; but he too had a city house, just as Christopher and Paul Afiarta received support from Campania. There was also the prospect of family advancement; Stephen III's brother John, who like his brother must have been a refugee from Sicily, was a Roman duke during his pontificate.

But while the nobility resented the papacy's insistence on resuming full legal claims and a strict Roman legal system of government, they remained conscious and proud of their distinction as Romans and of their particular place in the old imperial city. Indications are recorded of a revival of Roman patriotism prompted by the Lombard peril: a southerner's distaste at Aistulf's troops gorging themselves on looted beef as they ravaged the *campagna*; a flutter of pride, even from a hostile source, at Toto's overthrow of the mighty Lombard champion Racipert; Christopher's wish to be handed over to the equally harsh hands of his fellow-citizens rather than to the foreigners; dissent in the following century at the growing Lombard settlement in the city and at the dissipation of the relics of Rome's patrons. This pride was increased with the annexation by Charles of the Lombard kingdom and the revival of the imperial title–both unpremeditated acts, made with insufficient understanding of the territorial demands of an Italian kingdom. Charles himself had little personal interest in Rome; only twice did he wear the insignia of his patriciate and his Christian imperial vision was centred on his northern and eastern frontiers and his new Rome at Aix-la-Chapelle, but the city itself under Hadrian's successors was physically reshaped to a fresh grandeur, to the golden Rome of the middle ages. As the renaissance of learning reached Rome in the mid-ninth century it formed a new and intensive consciousness of republican and imperial history. However, the perpetuation of a separate Italian kingdom within the Empire kept alive the same geo-political problems, and the papacy continued to seek independence of a powerful neighbour while searching for internal balance.

Under Stephen III the papacy had been in weak hands; appointed by Christopher's influence, he had enjoyed little independence of action and while conventional praise was paid to his vigour, he had been deceived by Desiderius and Afiarta. Towards the end of his life the scales had fallen from his eyes; Desiderius had refused to consider the restoration of the cities owed to St. Peter once his immediate purposes in Rome had been served, and he thought Stephen's requests unjustifiable: had he not saved Stephen from domination by Christopher and from subjection to Christopher's ally Carloman? Before his death Stephen had remarked to Hadrian that in every instance of a promise on oath, Desiderius had proved a perjuror and liar.[1]

Hadrian himself presents another aspect of the Roman nobility: of authority and wealth gained in the Church's service and used to a better purpose. He was the son of Theodore, a member of a respected Roman family. His father died when he was young and Hadrian was brought up by his uncle Theodatus, a former consul and duke, and *primicerius* of the Roman Church. The family was intimately connected with the charitable organizations of the city; Theodatus repaired the *diaconia* of S. Maria *Antica* and also served as patron, *pater diaconiae* of S. Angelo *in Pescheria*. Hadrian as a young layman served in the church of St. Mark near his home in the Corso, where he distributed alms to the poor as far as his resources would permit–the practical administration of Rome's material needs was a prominent feature of his pontificate, in which he completed the work of Zachary. He attracted the attention of Pope Paul who enjoined him to become a cleric; he became a regional notary, again supervising material needs, and later subdeacon. But he had not neglected theological and scriptural studies. On the accession of Stephen III he was promoted to deacon, in which office he established a wide reputation as a preacher. A man of such ability was not content to accept the domination of Paul Afiarta; immediately on his election he ordered the recall of those city and clerical officials whom Paul had banished, pending full inquiry into recent events.[2]

Paul moved swiftly to reinforce his position. Desiderius sent an embassy to Hadrian's consecration but Hadrian rejected this overture, referring to Desiderius's continued faithlessness and repeating

[1] *LP*. I, 487.
[2] *LP*. I, 486, 514, n. 2; see W. de Gruneisen, *Sainte Marie Antique*, (1911).

papal demands for restitution of the cities of the exarchate. A legation was sent to Pavia to emphasize that the Pope desired not only peace but justice as well, and Paul Afiarta secured his attachment to the embassy. He assured Desiderius that he would bring Hadrian to Pavia and gain his support and acknowledgement of Carloman's children, but in his absence his position in Rome had been undermined. Hadrian had heard the rumours of his culpability for the death of Sergius and in his enquiry had received the evidence of Calventzulus and Leonatius; and Desiderius had now marched openly into the exarchate and, within two months of Hadrian's accession, had captured Faenza, Ferrara and Commachio and was hemming in Ravenna itself, plundering the countryside. A deputation from Ravenna of three tribunes, Peter, Vitalian and Julian, begged for papal intervention and Hadrian sent further letters to Pavia. Desiderius declined to negotiate, stating that as Hadrian would not come to talk with him as an equal he could not entertain the idea. Meanwhile the problem of Paul Afiarta remained; he was a danger in Lombard hands and a potential object of intrigue in the exarchate. The tribune Julian was sent back to Ravenna with instructions to Archbishop Leo for Paul's arrest if he entered the exarchate; he did and was detained at Rimini. By now the Roman enquiry had been completed and the Campanians' complicity with Paul established; but Hadrian did not presume to act as a civil authority in such a matter as murder and handed the culprits over to the prefect of the city to be tried according to the usual criminal process. They were publicly tried in the prison by the statue of the elephant at the foot of the capitol, and found guilty; the sentence was exile to Constantinople. A full report of the proceedings was sent to Archbishop Leo that he might proceed properly with Paul; but Leo without authorization handed Paul over to the highest civil authority in Ravenna, the *consularis*, for trial. The account of the Roman trial again publicly read out to him, was held to prove his guilt, and he was sentenced to death. Leo failed to inform Hadrian of this, who heard of it only through a third party; meanwhile he had written to the joint emperors, Constantine V and Leo IV, giving full details of Sergius's murder and asking that Paul should be held in exile in the imperial dominions. Instructions were delivered to Leo to send Paul to the East by way of Venice or any other available route, but Leo, a personal enemy of Paul, refused, asserting that Desiderius held as hostages the sons of duke Maurice of Venice and would surely kill them if harm befell Paul. Hadrian sent the *sacellarius* Gregory, first to interview Desiderius on his withdrawal from negotiations and then to Ravenna to bring Paul to Rome. Gregory immediately visited Ravenna and told Leo and the city officials of their strict instructions to keep Paul safe, adding that he would collect him for removal to Rome on his return from Pavia. But in Gregory's absence Leo ordered Paul's execution; he then belatedly asked Hadrian for approval which was refused as Paul had been denied opportunity for contrition.[3]

Faction and disaffection within Rome were now temporarily stilled, perhaps through Hadrian's studied respect for civic institutions and the Empire. But the external danger persisted – Desiderius had on the failure of subversion launched a full-scale attack against the Roman lands. The exarchate was invaded and a detachment of the Lombard army were sent to seize the towns connecting Rome with Ravenna – Sinigaglia, Jesi, Montefeltre, Urbino and Gubbio – which all fell. A Lombard force from Tuscany approached Blera, one of the northern defences of the duchy; the inhabitants of the town, coming out to harvest their crops, were taken in ambush, the leading men killed and vast plunder in cattle and prisoners seized. Twenty miles from Rome the castle of Otricoli was taken; Hadrian's protests were ignored. Abbot Probatus of Farfa with twenty of his senior monks was sent to plead with Desiderius, but without success. Desiderius did however send envoys to Rome, and to these Hadrian reiterated his willingness to meet the king at any place of his choice – Rome, Ravenna or Pavia – and his promise that the king would be at liberty to reoccupy the towns if the pope failed him: but the towns must be returned first. This and other suggestions achieved nothing, for Desiderius still clung to his plan for the anointing of Carloman's sons. Accompanied by the young Frankish princes he now moved against Rome itself, sending messengers to Hadrian demanding their coronation. Hadrian prepared the city for siege; the country folk were brought in, with contingents from Etruria, Campania, Perugia and Pentapolis, and the fortifications were made ready. The gates were bolted and some bricked up, the doors of St. Peter's locked and

<hr>

[3] *LP.* I, 487–91.

barricaded from within by carts, the ornaments and treasures brought into the city. As Desiderius reached Viterbo on the frontier of the duchy Hadrian sent three bishops, Eustratius of Albano, Andrew of Palestrina and Theodosius of Tivoli, with a solemn warning of excommunication if the king crossed the frontier. It was sufficient; Desiderius, basically a weak and vacillating man for all his bluster, withdrew.[4]

He had already informed King Charles that he had made full restitution to St. Peter, but now Frankish envoys arrived in Rome to find out if this were so. Hadrian informed them of recent events and returned them to Charles with a legate of his own to implore Charles to see to the fulfilment of his father's acts. The envoys went by way of Pavia, where once more Desiderius refused an audience, and so on to report to Charles. An offer by Charles of 14,000 *solidi* for the towns' return was rejected and the Franks decided on war. The army was mobilized and marched to occupy the passes, Charles himself with picked troops making for the Mont Cenis pass. Desiderius and the Lombard army had anticipated him and had fortified the passes with walls and earthworks; again he rejected diplomatic offers. His position was one of some strength and the Franks had little stomach for a direct assault; but a fortuitous panic seized the Lombard troops at night and they deserted their stations. The army was scattered: Desiderius escaped to Pavia and his son to Verona, the strongest of all the Lombard cities; the remainder of the army dispersed to their homes. Further south the unity of the kingdom had already collapsed; the leading men of the duchy of Spoleto spontaneously surrendered to the Roman Church. They swore fidelity to St. Peter and the pope and had their hair cut in the Roman fashion. On its return to the duchy, the Spoletan contingent from Desiderius's army joined the submission. Hadrian accepted their allegiance to himself and his successors and allowed them to elect their own duke, their leader Hildiprand. This example was followed in other parts of Italy; the inhabitants of Fermo, Osimo and Ancona, cities of the exarchate that had been under Lombard rule, also submitted.[5]

Charles had moved to besiege Pavia; blockading Desiderius there he detached forces to reduce the remaining Lombard cities, including Verona. Pavia resisted for six months and in 774, as Easter approached, Charles desired to celebrate the feast in Rome. Leaving Pavia still under siege, he moved with his whole court and a sizeable force through Tuscany to Rome, arriving in the city on Easter Saturday. As patrician of the Romans he was accorded the full protocol for the welcome of an exarch. Nearly thirty miles from the city Charles was greeted by Church officials; and a mile outside the military associations, the *scholae* with their banners, their patrons, the noble laity and the boys of the schools they maintained welcomed him by singing the acclamations that in Constantinople were granted to a newly-appointed patrician. When Charles observed the banners and the crosses of the regions he dismounted and entered the city on foot, making his way with his court to St. Peter's. There on the steps of the apostolic hall, Pope Hadrian waited with his clergy; Charles approached him, kissing each step out of reverence for the apostle, and at the top embraced the pope. It was the beginning of a firm friendship and trust which served to reinforce religious sentiment and political interest. They entered the basilica together as the choir sang 'Blessed is he who cometh in the name of the Lord'. Charles prayed before the body of St. Peter and then formally asked Hadrian's permission to enter the city. It was granted and together, with the two courts, they went up to the Lateran; there the pope, as was customary before Easter, performed the city's baptisms in the presence of the king. The Easter festival was kept with full splendour; Charles attended the papal Mass at S. Maria *Maggiore* and afterwards was entertained at a banquet in the Lateran: on Monday Hadrian said Mass at St. Peter's and the acclamations of Charles were again sung: on Tuesday the Mass was celebrated at St. Paul's.[6]

Charles had come to Rome primarily as a pilgrim out of reverence for St. Peter; he had made a personal friend of Pope Hadrian and had received visible and audible evidence of his status as patrician in the city. But what political discussions took place between the two courts is a matter of dispute. The later Roman theory, inserted into the *Life* of Pope Hadrian, was that Charles confirmed the donation of his father in as precise and definitive terms as those later held to have been used by Pepin, and that after the confirmation had been signed

[6] *LP*. I, 497–8. On Charles and Rome, see J. Deer, 'Die vorrechte des Kaisers in Rom, 772–800', (*Schweitzer Beiträge zur Allgemeinen Geschichte*, 15, 1957).

by Charles and the leading Franks it was deposited on the *confessio* of St. Peter. But at this time Charles may have not been fully decided on his future plans for Italy, and the sweeping concessions to Rome that this document contains were incompatible with the establishment of any stable Italian kingdom. The Roman Church still took literally the submission of Spoleto which was accordingly inserted, together with the possession of Benevento and of Venice and Istria. Charles's first concern may have been with the siege of Pavia to which he returned immediately after Easter; the town was reduced by famine and plague and was soon betrayed by an Italian, Peter, who was later rewarded with the bishopric of Verdun. Desiderius himself survived and was taken into exile in France, and Charles assumed the Lombard crown [7]

That only vague arrangements for the settlement of Italy had been made in Rome is indicated by the activities of Sergius's successor in Ravenna, Archbishop Leo. As *vicedominus* of Ravenna he had taken a lead in defying Pope Paul; scarcely had Charles returned to France from Pavia than he was again exercising civil authority throughout the exarchate. He sent a certain Theophylact throughout the provinces announcing that Charles had ceded Pentapolis to him and, expelling those of the Roman Church, he managed to establish his own agents in the towns of the province. There was some local protest at this for the inhabitants did not welcome the too-close administration of a traditionally harsh and corrupt see. Hadrian, calling attention to this in a letter to Charles, harped on the damage it did to both Church and Frankish prestige that explicit settlements should be so openly flouted. Hadrian compared Leo to the late Archbishop Sergius: 'All know that his thrice-beatitude [Stephen II] wielded authority there, in Ravenna and the exarchate, and even removed Archbishop Sergius when he strove in a spirit of pride to oppose him; our predecessor had taken measures to administer the exarchate and his agents had all received their commissions from Rome. He had sent magistrates from Rome, Philip, at that time a

---

[7] See L. Saltet, 'La lecture d'un texte et la critique contemporaire: II: les prétendues promesses de Qierzy (754) et de Rome (774) dans le Liber Pontificalis', (*Bulletin de littérature ecclésiastique*, 42, 1941), and E. Griffe, 'Aux Origines de l'Etat pontifical: Charlemagne et Hadrien I (772–775)', (*Bulletin de littérature ecclésiastique*, 55, 1954).

priest, and the duke Eustachius, to administer justice in Ravenna, for everything was being done there by force. If your most Christian Excellency requires fuller satisfaction over this, let him summon Bishop Philip and examine him on the truth of what we say.'[8] In October 775 Charles again visited Italy and Archbishop Leo hurried to interview him; to Charles Hadrian pointed out that the situation was now worsened and Leo's presumption even greater. Leo had returned from his audience 'in overweening pride and a tyrannical elation and as before shows not the slightest inclination to obey our instructions and will allow no one from Ravenna or Emilia to come here to receive our orders in various business. But the inhabitants of Pentapolis remain obedient to our rule and have come to us, just as in the time of our predecessor the lord Pope Stephen, to accept our orders concerning the individual cities of Emilia as well as Gavello. But of those whom we appointed to these places, some he has ejected, others detained in chains; he has spread propaganda throughout Imola and Bologna to the effect that your Excellency has not conceded these cities to us at all but that they were granted to the archbishop himself to remain under his jurisdiction. So he allows no-one from these cities to approach us but appoints his own agents without our authority and keeps our officers under restraint.'[9] A month later Leo was still denying papal officials access to the towns of Emilia; Dominicus, whom Hadrian had appointed count in Gavello, had been arrested by the archbishop's troops and was now held in custody in Ravenna. Leo, in his official acts, was styling himself 'exarch' but had as yet been unable to establish his power in Pentapolis; the cities there, from Rimini to Gubbio, remained loyal to Rome.[10]

Territorial disputes continued on all the frontiers of the new papal state as the papacy sought to gain effective possession of all to which it felt itself entitled. In 775 there was news of an alliance against pope and king between duke Hildiprand of Spoleto, duke Arichis of Benevento—whose duchy had not been absorbed with the rest of the Lombard kingdom into Charles's dominions—and duke Reginbald of Chiusi. Desiderius's son Adelchis had fled to the Greeks, had been appointed patrician and was threatening to join the dukes with Greek aid. Hadrian informed Charles that the following March they

[8] Cod. Carol., 49.   [9] Ibid., 53, 54.   [10] Ibid., 55.

planned 'to form their alliance and combine with the despised Greeks and Desiderius's son Adelchis, to launch an invasion against us on land and at sea, with the object of taking this our Roman city, sacking the Church of God and the treasury of your patron the blessed Peter; and, may God avert it, to carry us off as a prisoner and re-establish the Lombard kingdom.'[11] Duke Reginbald, who as a *gastald* of Desiderius had been prominent in his atrocities, seized some towns in Tuscany early in 776. There were also disconcerting signs of opposition to papal policy within the ranks of the Roman clergy; in 775 the chamberlain Anastasius had been sent as legate to Charles accompanied by a Lombard, Gaudefrid. The latter was detected in some plot against Charles which included the forgery of documents, and Anastasius may have been implicated as well for Charles arrested him too. In the same year the *sacellarius* Stephen was sent as envoy to Spoleto to make arrangements concerning hostages, and while there discovered the dukes' conspiracy on behalf of imperial or Lombard sentiment in Rome.[12]

But the conspiracy was not as co-ordinated as it appeared and mainly took the form of *razzias* like those of Reginbald. It was the papal and Lombard territory that principally suffered. 'We would bring to your honoured attention', Hadrian wrote to Charles in 776, 'the traffic we have discovered among our subjects who, sometimes even through the agency of our own Romans, are being sold to the unmentionable Saracens. Heaven forbid, we have not consented to this scandal, nor has it arisen through our wishes; but these indescribable Greeks are cruising constantly along the Lombard coasts, striking up friendship with the Lombards themselves, buying up their servants and from the Lombards taking possession of the peasants. We accordingly gave orders to duke Allo to prepare many ships and to capture the Greeks and burn their ships; but he objected to carrying out our orders, for we have neither ships nor seamen with which to take them. However, as God is our witness, we took upon ourself in our desire to end this scandal, this very considerable exertion, and managed to burn many of these Greek ships as they lay in our port of Civitavecchia and hold the Greeks themselves in prison for some time. But as we mentioned, when food shortage compelled them, many of the Lombards have sold their servants.'[13]

[11] *Ibid.*, 57, 58.   [12] *Ibid.*, 57.   [13] *Ibid.*, 59.

The bitterness caused by the new papal administration was not due solely to the wider aspects of Mediterranean politics involving the Empire, the Saracens, and the imperial towns and the Lombards of southern Italy. On a more local level resentment occurred as the papacy clung to the literal word of past agreements, perhaps made without full realization of the consequences. In May 778 Hadrian set the tone in a letter to Charles asking for a complete fulfilment of all promises made:

'As for all the rest, all in the regions of Tuscany, Spoleto, Benevento and Corsica, and in the Sabine patrimony, which had been granted to God's holy and apostolic Church and to the blessed apostle Peter by so many emperors, patricians and other God-fearing persons for mercy to their souls and pardon for their sins, and which over a long space of years have been removed and denied to us by the Lombards, all these ought to be restored to us in your time: for we have records in our sacred chancery of many such donations.'[14]

This was a revival of ancient claims to properties many of which must have been out of papal control for nearly eighty years since the Lombard expansion in the Sabine region during the early years of the century. Zachary had kept that claim alive at Terni but Hadrian's revival, based on old entries in the Lateran rent-books, involved the disruption of perhaps third-generation Lombard settlers; not merely inheritances but gifts in memory of the dead and for the soul's benefit to the local religious centre, the great abbey of Farfa, were jeopardized, outraging sentiment and pocket alike. Hadrian was continuing in the footsteps of Zachary in trying to establish a Roman occupied countryside, as his *domuscultae* show, and he was concerned also with the problem of feeding a growing city. Farfa had shown itself diligent in the reclamation of uncultivated land and the repair of disused irrigation channels. The effective tenure of these properties was a major aim of Hadrian's pontificate; at an early date he placed Sabine affairs under a separate minister, the *prior vestiarii*, who devoted himself to sorting out the claims and counter-claims.

Miccio's commission was comprehensive, to maintain order and ensure justice: 'Therefore Miccio and his successors shall have power to distrain on any person, either clerical or lay, of the Church's household or anyone's servant, at large or within the cities of our Roman

---

[14] *Ibid.*, 60 (p. 587).

republic, whether, as we have said, anyone's slave or a free man.'[15] This appointment, made on Hadrian's election in 772, had little effect at first; local opposition, led perhaps by the *gastald* Hilderic of Rieti–a man with strong family connections in the area who seems about this time to have been deprived of office–inhibited a direct transfer.[16] In May 778 bishops Philip and Andrew and duke Theodore were sent by Hadrian to repeat the claims, bearing with them the letter referring to the documents in the Lateran chancery. Renewed appeals to Charles resulted in 781 in the convening of a commission of inquiry whose members were Ittherius, abbot of St. Martin at Tours and Charles's secretary, the archchaplain Maginarius, the *sacellarius* Stephen and duke Theodore, at Foro Novo, the seat of the bishop of Sabina and the urban centre of the disputed area. There a hundred of the oldest inhabitants of the district were questioned on the extent of the papal patrimony and were asked 'what they knew and had seen formerly of St. Peter's Sabine patrimony'. The result was apparently favourable to the papal case, but once again possession was a more difficult matter. Ittherius and Maginarius moved south to settle disputes on the Beneventan frontier and Hadrian's legates found obstacles in their way, for 'various perverse, evil men put up excuses' for not complying with the judgement. The dispute was to continue for many years into the next century with increasing bitterness on both sides.[17]

Nor was the Sabine district of the new papal state the only one to experience these birth pains. The cities of the bay of Naples remained nominally to the Empire and independent of both the papacy and the Frankish crown. The duchy of Benevento under duke Arichis continued its opposition to Franks and pope and served as a shelter for Lombard refugees; from Sicily the Byzantine governor supported Desiderius's son Adelchis. There was now also the added danger of Saracen activity along the coast. In May 778 Hadrian sent warning to Charles of possible Saracen raids; he also gave an account of the

[15] *Chronicon Farfense Gregorii Catinensis*, ed. U. Balzani, (Fonti per la Storia d'Italia, 33, 34), 1903, p. 156: *Registrum Farfense*, ed. I. Giorgi and U. Balzani, 5 vols, 1914, vol. 11, p. 83.

[16] *Registrum Farfense*, II, pp. 77, 80, 82.

[17] Cod. Carol., 69; and O. Vehse, 'Die päpstliche Herrschaft in der Sabina bis zur Mitte des 12. Jahrhunderts', (*Quellen und Forschungen aus Italienschen Archiv und Bibliotheken*, 21, 1929–30).

(Photograph by Mr Charles Daniels

Plate 2. The papal *domusculta* of Capracorum (Sta Cornelia), founded on the family estate of Pope Hadrian I; recently excavated by members of the British School at Rome.

situation on his southern frontier. 'Your Excellency is unaware that our enemies and yours, these wicked Beneventans, are working on our cities in Campania, trying to persuade our people there to withdraw from our jurisdiction; they are in league with the inhabitants of the fortress of Gaieta and of Terracina and are binding themselves under oath to the governor of Sicily, who has taken up residence in Gaieta; they are trying to withdraw the Campanians from our jurisdiction and that of the blessed Peter and subject them to the patrician of Sicily. For as long as we have been aware of this we have again and again sent warning and exhortation by our bishops and those we trust, for we wish these Campanians not to be harmed or have any evil befall them.' Terracina was recovered for the papacy but within two years it had fallen to a combined Greek and Neapolitan attack. Duke Arichis and the patrician were advancing towards Rome, bringing Adelchis with them. The papal patrimonies in the area were lost in spite of Hadrian's attempt to guarantee them by treaty.[18]

The feeling in southern Italy towards the Frankish kingdom in Italy and the papal government was demonstrated in 781 by a disputed election in the great abbey of St. Vincent on the Volturno river. The abbot-elect Potho was accused of open disloyalty to Charles; a commission containing Frankish and Roman officials and clerics heard the accusations of one monk, Rodicausus: the abbot had refused to pray for Charles, saying that if it were not his duty to think for the monastery and for Beneventan territory, he would esteem Charles as highly as a dog, and that he valued those Franks in the district as so many vegetables. Rodicausus's evidence was discounted when the commission heard of his poor moral character, but a more serious charge against the abbot of mounting a guard on the bridge across the Volturno to prevent persons contacting Charles was less easily disposed of. Potho maintained that he was keeping guard against the king's enemies and, on papal advice, he was reinstated.[19]

The south remained a constant danger to Rome, providing an opportunity for imperial interference and a source of disunion and instability. In the following century when the Empire was driven from Sicily the papacy was to find great difficulty in forming a com-

[18] Cod. Carol., 61.   [19] Ibid., 66, 67.

241

mon front against the approaching Saracens out of the small, jealous states of the Neapolitan littoral, while the Beneventan duchy, advancing itself to a principality and inheriting Lombard royal claims, proved equally divisive. But these problems touched only the borders. In the heart of the Roman state, in the city and the country around, there was a new prosperity as Hadrian, secure in the friendship of Charles, managed to reimpose papal authority and policy on the administration. He relied largely on his own family, his nephews Paschal and duke Theodore, and on a small group of clerics whom he could trust, Bishop Philip, Miccio and the *sacellarius* Stephen. He was himself careful of the susceptibilities of the Roman nobility from whom he came and, as in the enquiry into Afiarta's associates, worked through the normal city machinery. In the purchase of the estate of the *primicerius* Mastalus to found a *domusculta*, there is also a hint of the sale of office to one of the dead man's heirs.

Time and resources were available for the rebuilding, endowment and decoration of churches, not merely of those in the city but also in the countryside; the aqueducts and city walls were also repaired. 'The walls and turrets', his biographer wrote, 'which were in ruins for the entire circuit and had collapsed almost to their foundations, he repaired and restored effectively; he spent large sums on this, on the wages of the builders, on their subsistence, on lime and other materials, to a total of 100 lb. of gold.' For twenty years, since Aistulf's siege, the Sabbatina aqueduct, from which water ran in large pipes to the atrium of St. Peter's and supplied baths for the pilgrims, had been damaged; this had also interfered with the mills on the Gianiculo which the aqueduct served. 'There seemed small chance of repairing it for a hundred of the arches, which were extremely high, had fallen to their foundations and lay derelict. But this most blessed and holy bishop gathered a crowd of people to restore and rebuild it themselves, and he showed such care and attention to the fabric of the aqueduct that he restored it from its foundations like new.'[20]

Personal physical energy with a practical ability to command distinguished Hadrian. He is to be found directing a fire-fighting operation: 'In the silence of the night the basilica of the monastery of Anastasius, martyr of Christ, together with the sacristy and the

[20] *LP.* I, 501, 503.

abbot's lodgings, was through the carelessness of the monks, burnt down and destroyed from its foundation to the very summit of the roof. When he heard of this the most merciful bishop came hurrying at dawn and found it still burning with only the arch of the martyr's shrine lying in the middle of the court. The fire had also damaged other sanctuaries and ministerial offices in the church and sacristy. Full of grief he made certain with his servants of extinguishing the fire and, immediately afterwards, through his strenuous efforts it was restored from a fire-swept ruin to a better state than before: church, sacristy, abbot's lodgings and all the other buildings.' When the Tiber overflowed and for three days the lower and more densely inhabited parts of the city were flooded, Hadrian organized a ferry service of punts along the Corso, carrying food to people who could not leave their houses.[21] Perhaps also he had an interest in practical engineering; his repairs to pipe-lines and aqueducts were more extensive than any during the previous two and a half centuries.

This physical resurgence of Rome was marked also by the foundation of new *domuscultae* of which Capracorum, near the ancient Veii about fifteen miles from Rome, was the chief. Hadrian inherited the Capracorum estate from his parents and at first held it for his own use. Later 'he added farms, farm-houses and properties, buying these at a fair valuation from various people. This *domusculta* of Capracorum with all its estates, farms, farm-buildings, vineyards, olive-groves, water-mills and all belonging to it, he founded under apostolic privilege and heavy bonds of anathema to remain for ever for the use of our brethren, the poor of Christ. The annual harvest of wheat and barley that grew on the *domusculta* was with diligence to be transported to the granaries of our holy Church and stored there separately. The wine and the various vegetables that grew in the fields and separate plots of the *domusculta* were similarly to be taken to the chief cellarer of our Holy Church and stored apart. The pigs fattened every year on the *domusculta*, one hundred, were to be killed and stored in the cellars.' All this was destined for the poor: 'Every day one hundred of our brethren, the poor of Christ, and more if more there were, should be assembled in the patriarchal Lateran palace and sat down in the portico next to the stairway leading up to the palace, where are the paintings of the poor; fifty loaves, each weighing two

[21] *LP.* I, 512, 513.

pounds, and two ten-gallon jars of wine, weighing sixty pounds, and cauldrons full of soup shall every day be distributed to the poor by one of our faithful cellarers; each pauper will receive a ration of bread and one measure of wine, that is two cupfuls, and a bowl of soup.' On the *domusculta* a church, lavishly decorated, was built and the bodies of the Popes Cornelius, Lucius, Felix and Innocent placed there; it was dedicated in a grand ceremony attended by the whole clergy and nobility.[22] Other *domuscultae* were established, two near Galeria on the Aurelia and Porto roads, ten and twelve miles to the north-west of the city, and another named Calvisianus fifteen miles to the south-west. Yet another to the north on the Flaminian road was made up of a series of legacies; the *primicerius* Mastalus bequeathed some of his property to the Roman Church for the poor, and Mastalus's other heirs agreed to give or sell to Hadrian the remainder of the property, so preserving it intact at a value of 200 mancuses. One heir, Gregory, ominously gave his share of the legacy in return for the office of *secundicerius*. To this was added an inheritance from one Paschal and an exchange was made with the heirs of Lucy, who had left property in the area, and with those of the *primicerius* John; other properties were added and, around the church of St. Leucius which was 'then derelict, with brambles around it, and snake-infested', the new *domusculta* was established.[23]

These settlements, showing the recovered peace of the countryside, were matched by restorations to the derelict churches of the *campagna*. To the north, near one of the *domuscultae* of Galeria, the cathedral of the cardinal-bishop of Silva Candida was repaired and enlarged with a baptistery to serve the newly-settled population, while on the Appian Way the basilica of St. Andrew at the thirteenth milestone was restored and also given a baptistery. Churches in other towns, Palestrina, Ferentinello and Perugia, were also put into repair, with others within the city. The increased stability and wealth of Rome is shown in the amount of decoration–bronzework and precious metal and dyed cloth-work–that he devoted to the city churches, making a significant impact on the appearance of the city.[24]

Hadrian's reign was externally a threatened one but for the first time under the papacy the city had a settled internal government; the initiative remained firmly in papal hands. Partly this was due to

[22] *LP*. I, 501–2, 506.   [23] *LP*. I, 502, 505, 509.   [24] *LP*. I, 508. 510–14.

Hadrian's recognition of the civic authorities and the nobility and to the use he made of members of his own family, especially his nephews. Respect was also paid to the shadowy claims of the Empire, as the arrangements made for Sergius's murderers indicate, and this may have served to mollify any remaining imperial sentiment in Rome; from 782 religious peace with the East and a temporary ending to the Iconoclast movement had been achieved. A scrupulous sense of justice marked Hadrian's capable administration; the creation of the *domuscultae* was carried through by fair negotiation and it is possible that after the first resistance he did not press the claims for the repossession of Sabine properties. He had perhaps a strong interest in legal affairs; he sent to Charles the collection of canons compiled in the sixth century by Dionysius Exiguus of which he must have had some personal knowledge. His insistence on the validity of claims based on Lateran records after so considerable a lapse of time reflects a close adherence to the letter of the law; of Archbishop Leo's activities in Emilia it was the lack of justice and fidelity that most aroused him. Counts were appointed in Pentapolis to report direct to the Pope, and Miccio's appointment to the Sabina was made expressly because Hadrian on his election found himself so overworked that justice, if dependent on him alone, might be delayed.

Above all, Hadrian's success rested on his friendship with Charles which dated from their first meeting in 774, and with members of the Frankish court including the English scholar Alcuin; the respect was mutual and deep throughout the twenty-three years of Hadrian's pontificate. To a certain extent this glossed over the weaknesses of the Roman state, the uncertain frontier relations, the lack of definition to papal sovereignty and the weakness of basic military power in Rome. There was no Roman fleet to protect a vulnerable coastline; although Hadrian received the gift of a horse from Charles, there is no indication that Rome was adequately self-sufficient to equip an army, and reliance was necessarily placed on aid from outside. But Hadrian had given Rome and the papacy a new stability and confidence, and when he died on Christmas Day 795 Charles 'wept as if he had lost a deeply-loved son or brother'. He ordered Alcuin to compose an epitaph in verse for the Pope's sepulchre which was engraved in marble and inlaid with gold and sent to Rome.[25]

[25] See L. Wallach, 'Alcuin's Epitaph of Hadrian', (*American Journal of*

His successor was elected and consecrated within two days, a haste that may have been the work of the Roman clergy who feared a *coup* by the nobility or Hadrian's family. Their choice was the priest of S. Susanna, Leo son of Azuppius; he was a man of no family, a bureaucrat by training who had worked in the vestarariate, presumably under Miccio, even as a priest. His position was delicate if he were not to be another Stephen III; although naturally of an authoritarian disposition he hastened to gain the support of Charles, going far beyond Hadrian in his overt acts. Charles had not yet been informed of Hadrian's death nor had his permission been sought–as that of emperors and exarchs had been–for the papal election, but Leo at once sent the keys of St. Peter's *confessio* and the standards of the city to the king. Also, in startling variance to his predecessor's views on the patriciate, he wrote asking that Charles might send one of his high ministers to receive an oath of loyalty from the Romans. He aimed to attach Rome more formally to Carolingian power; only once under Hadrian had Charles reluctantly appeared in the formal dress of a patrician, the long tunic and chlamys and the campagi, and Leo was also to persuade him to do this as an overt sign to the Romans of the power of the pope's protector. The adoption of Charles as the new Constantine was stressed by Leo in his programme of building, in which at least he showed himself a worthy successor to Hadrian and by which he emphasized the vast superiority of the papacy over existing Roman institutions. The *Triclinium Maior* of the Lateran, enlarged and magnificently decorated by Leo in the opening years of his pontificate, bore witness to the new symbolic pattern; Christ, pictured in the act of giving his commission to his disciples to teach all nations, was flanked on the one side by Constantine and Sylvester and on the other by Charles and Leo. Reminiscent of the appointment of imperial governors by the emperor, it was a representation of harmony and co-operation.[26]

Established safely, Leo appears to have insisted on the full sovereign rights of the papacy under Roman law with no such restraint and tact as Hadrian had shown. Many claims in the Sabine region were still outstanding, of which Leo may already have had

Philology, 72, 1951) and J. Ramackers, 'Die Werkstattheimat der Grabplatte Papst Hadrians I', (*Römische Quartalschrift*, 59, 1964).

[26] *LP*. II, 1, 3, 35, n. 14.

experience under Miccio; in 829 in a lawsuit held at the Lateran, Abbot Ingoald of Farfa claimed certain estates, for 'the lord popes Hadrian and Leo had by force invaded the property of the monastery itself . . . we repeatedly claimed in the time of Stephen, Paschal and Eugenius but never obtained judgement'. In the registry of Farfa's lands compiled later by the monk Gregory of Catino is included a list of those benefactors of the house whose donations had been claimed and taken by the papal authorities; they included ecclesiastics such as bishops Teuto and Alefrid of Rieti and local Lombard officials such as the *gastald* Hilderic. The tradition of the Sabine country attributed to Leo in the following centuries a widespread resumption of properties prosecuted under Roman law and to his agents a considerable rapacity in execution. The same story was told in the area north of Rome centred on the monasteries of Soratte.[27]

This discontent was not simply confined to properties on the fringes of the Roman duchy where there was still ample margin for legal dispute; it spread to the Roman nobility themselves against whom, and against the civic administration, Leo may have encroached in the Lateran's favour. Certainly many families, including that of Hadrian, had benefited under the last pontificate, and a threat to their estates would now find them sensitive. Within four years of his election rebellion broke out. On 25th April 799 Leo left the Lateran for S. Lorenzo *in Lucina* to conduct the major litanies and, as the papal procession passed the monastery of SS. Sylvester and Stephen, it was attacked by two of Pope Hadrian's nephews–Paschal and Campulus–who were joined by one Maurus, a native of Nepi, the home town of duke Toto. Leo was thrown from his horse and dragged into the monastery; an attempt to blind him and cut out his tongue failed–possibly it was not wholehearted–and that night he was smuggled to the monastery of S. Erasmo on the Coelian where he was kept under guard. The conspirators did not put forward an anti-pope; it was Leo's secular activities that they were determined to check. But Leo was rescued that night by the chamberlain Albinus who gained access to him and lowered him by a rope from the monastery wall; they at once fled to St. Peter's where they were

---

[27] *Registrum Farfense*, II, p. 221: see also L. M. Hartmann, 'Grundherrschaft und Bureaukratie im Kirchenstaate vom 8. bis zum 10. Jahrhundert', (*Vierteljahrschrift für Social-und-Wirtschaftsgeschichte*, 7, 1909).

greeted by some of the clergy. The conspirators did not dare to attack him there but contented themselves with sacking the city houses of both Albinus and the pope.[28]

Help for Leo came from Winichis, Charles's appointment as duke of Spoleto, who on hearing the news from Rome, arrived with a military force. He conducted Leo to Spoleto and sent word to Charles at Paderborn as he was preparing to march against the Saxons. Charles instructed Leo to be brought to him and sent the archbishop of Cologne and his own son, King Pepin, to welcome the pope. At Paderborn Leo was enthusiastically greeted by the Frankish army; a solemn Mass in the cathedral was followed by a banquet at which Charles entertained the pope.

Alcuin, Charles's scholarly companion from York, gave advice on the situation: the Saxon campaign was a matter of little importance compared to Rome. There the conspirators, strong in their sense of justice in opposing Leo, had made no further moves in self-defence; apart from some acts of violence against the recent papal acquisitions, their behaviour was peaceable. Formal charges were drawn up against Leo alleging, among other things, adultery and perjury–two stock charges against any cleric–and Charles's judgement was calmly awaited. In November Leo returned to Rome with a strong Frankish escort led by the archbishops of Cologne and Salzburg. He received an honourable welcome through the towns on his route and at the Milvian Bridge was greeted by the entire assembly of the Roman army in formal array. The procession went to St. Peter's where Leo said Mass; on the following day, in Leo's own *Triclinium Maior* in the Lateran, Paschal, Campulus and their associates presented themselves for trial before the Frankish counts and bishops. No detail of this trial has survived, an indication perhaps that the biographer of Pope Leo was not altogether correct in stating that the charges could not be maintained against him. The conspirators were found guilty but sentence was deferred to Charles himself.

Charles had told Leo that he would spend the Christmas of 800 in Rome, and left France in August. He travelled by way of Ravenna and Ancona and sent Pepin with a considerable force into southern Italy to reduce the duchy of Benevento. On 23rd November at

[28] *LP.* II, 4–6. See also W. Mohr, 'Karl der Grosse, Leo III und der römische Aufstand von 799' (*ALMA*, 1960).

Mentana, fourteen miles from Rome, he was greeted by Leo and the clergy, the militia and the people, with the formal ceremonial used for the reception of an exarch. There Charles and Leo dined and Leo informed the king of the situation in Rome. The following day Charles entered Rome, travelling indirectly northwards across the Milvian Bridge to arrive first at St. Peter's. There at the top of the steps Leo greeted him and they entered the basilica to pray.

On 23rd December Charles, wearing for only the second time the insignia of his patriciate, summoned an assembly of Franks and Romans to pass sentence on the rebels; he informed them that he had come to restore order to Rome, to punish the assault on the pope's person, and to judge between the pope and his accusers. Thereupon the Frankish bishops, primed perhaps by Alcuin, rose to declare that they might not sit in judgement on the highest bishop of all, whose office was rather to judge them; and Leo, following the general lines of the procedure used in the sixth century by Pelagius I when accused of complicity in Vigilius's death and also in legend by Popes Sixtus and Marcellinus, came forward and declared his lack of knowledge of the crimes imputed to him. This was accepted and a *Te Deum* was sung; then the plotters were brought forward for sentence. At Leo's plea the death penalty was commuted to exile in France; the deaths of such prominent men, of Hadrian's family, would have served only to increase Roman resentment. Throughout the proceedings Charles had emphasized that he regarded his protectorate over Rome as specifically a protectorate over the papacy; by rejecting the complaints of the rebels he stressed that the papacy upheld the legal government of the city in which he could not interfere on appeal from the citizens but only at the request of the pope. The same argument was contained in his diversion from the normal entry into Rome by crossing the river to arrive first at St. Peter's; the Carolingian recognition of St. Peter as the prime source of authority was undiminished. At the same time Charles and his advisers saw in the Roman troubles a parallel to another situation in which a German king, by moderation and a refusal to dictate policy to a sovereign Church, had yet been able to arrange a settlement.[29]

[29] See Adelson and Baker, 'The Oath of Purgation of Leo III', (*Traditio*, 8, 1952) and L. Wallach, 'The Genuine and the Forged Oath of Leo III',

Then the Christmas ceremonies began which Charles attended as he had promised. While in prayer before the *confessio* of St. Peter he was startled when Leo suddenly appeared to place a crown on his head, and he was acclaimed by pope and Romans as Emperor of the Romans. The historical and legendary parallels had long been drawn between the Christian emperors of the West and the new Christian dynasty of the Franks, and the territorial extent of Charles's dominions could only stand comparison with the old Empire. To Leo the imperial title was a fitting culmination to Charles's work on behalf of Church and papacy, a work which conformed to the ideal of the Christian Emperor hammered out more often in breach than observance. Furthermore the Empire itself might be deemed to be vacant; in Constantinople the Empress Irene had deposed and blinded her son Constantine VI and reigned without precedent as empress-regnant. But basically the coronation may be seen as the recognition rather than the conferment of a title, the recognition of services that could only stand comparison with those of Constantine the Great.[30]

Locally the imperial coronation–unexpected and unwelcome to Charles–left the domestic situation of Rome unaltered. Leo had been reinstated and with clear Frankish support had not moderated his views of government. The Italians recognized Charles as Emperor and as having the plenitude of imperial power, but Charles left to the papacy its own sovereignty. The Farfa tradition, from an area which suffered heavily as the papacy collected its dues, saw the papacy after 800 as usurping imperial and secular functions; a monk of St. Andrew on Monte Soratte a century later commented on Leo's policy after reinstatement that 'whatever was left to these

(*Traditio*, 11, 1955); L. Wallach, 'The Roman Synod of 800 and the alleged trial of Leo III', (*Harvard Theological Review*, 49, 1956).

[30] See E. Rota, 'La consacrazione imperiale di Carlo Magno', (*Studi per E. Besta*, 4, 1939); P. Schramm, 'Die Anerkennung Karls des Grossen als Kaiser', (*Historische Zeitschrift*, 172, 1951); E. Griffe, 'Aux origines de l'Etat pontifical: Le couronnement imperial de l'an 800 et Donatio Constantini', (*Bulletin de litterature ecclesiastique*, 59, 1958); W. Ohnsorge, 'Das Kaisertum der Eirene und die Kaiserkrönung Karls des Grossen', (*Saeculum*, 14, 1963); R. Folz, *Le couronnement impérial de Charlemagne*, 1964; F. L. Ganshof, *The Imperial Coronation of Charlemagne; Theories and Facts*, (1949).

monasteries [Farfa and Soratte] was swept away'.[31] As regards Farfa, the conflict was largely one of laws; the abbots of Farfa continued to insist on their right to have their tenures judged according to Lombardic law whereas Leo attempted to impose a Roman system on his dominions more favourable to a centralized state. He further tried to create his own power base by fortifying the Vatican region,[32] the traditional refuge of besieged popes, but this project was interrupted by his death and the materials collected were removed by the Roman citizens. Additions were made to the *domuscultae*, perhaps by confiscation and perhaps with the idea of using them as the basis of a militia loyal to the papacy which could be used to coerce the city.

Excuse for Leo can be found since he was undoubtedly hampered financially in his attempts to run a full administration and to make the city once more a worthy imperial capital. His building programme – of new churches, ceremonial halls, frescoes, mosaics and ornaments for the churches–was impressive. But already by 808 Frankish activity was clashing with what Leo regarded as his absolute sovereignty; in that year he wrote to Charles to complain of the *missus* Helmengaud's activities: 'These men [Helmengaud and his companions] are travelling around in the areas where the duke appointed by us is accustomed to levy the taxes of various kinds and remit them to us. They are making a heavy collection from the people there, so that the dukes themselves are entirely unable to make full remittance to us.' Lack of revenue was crippling his efforts to create a central government which reacted on the agents employed and increased dissatisfaction yet further.[33]

In 814, on the death of Charlemagne, the Romans revolted once more; Leo promptly and in accordance with the legal powers of a Roman sovereign, had the leaders executed for *lèse majesté*–a significant advance from Hadrian's method. Charles's son Louis, the new emperor, raised objections to this wider exercise of power in Rome and ordered his nephew King Bernard of Italy to investigate; Leo felt sufficiently uneasy about his action to send a legation headed by Bishop John of Silva Candida, the *nomenclator* Theodore and duke

---

[31] *De imperatoria potestate in Urbe Roma Libellus*, (ed. G. Zucchetti, Fonti per la Storia d'Italia, 1920), p. 196.
[32] *LP*. II, 123.
[33] *MGH. Epp.* V, p. 89.

Sergius to Louis with explanations. This satisfied the Franks, but as Leo himself entered his last illness the discontent continued: 'That season,' Louis' biographer recorded, 'as Pope Leo bore heavily on them the Romans attempted to destroy and take back for themselves the estates they call *domuscultae*, which had been newly established by the pope and which they claimed had been taken from them contrary to the law; nor did they expect any official.'[34] On the instructions of King Bernard, duke Winichis of Spoleto intervened but the *domuscultae*, evidence of papal domination, had been burnt. The biographer of Pope Hadrian had been at pains to demonstrate that the lands for *domuscultae* had been legally acquired, by fair purchase and exchange or by legacy, and that no hardship had been caused to private persons. Leo relied rather on sovereign powers – 'entered by force', as the abbot of Farfa complained of his acquisition of Sabine lands. The pope also had control of the judicial machinery which denied redress to the victims.

When Leo died in 816 many elements in the Western and Italian situation had altered. Charles had devolved the regional government of his dominions on his sons as sub-kings, the eldest of whom, Pepin, became king of Italy, transmitting the kingdom to his son Bernard on his death in 813. Charles was survived by only one son, Louis, whom he had associated with himself in the imperial titles but who, as king of Aquitaine, had shown little military or executive capacity and was to demonstrate a lack of that force of character necessary to assert the unity of the empire over the sub-kingdoms. His first concern was to institute an administrative and moral reform of the Empire, correcting the weaknesses of Charles's old age. Rome and Italy at first held little interest for him. Leo's successor, Stephen, had been educated in the Lateran under Hadrian and promoted to the subdiaconate under Leo; he was moreover of the Roman nobility, of a family that produced three popes in the course of the ninth century, and was a man of less authoritarian temper than Leo. His short pontificate of nineteen months was marked by a visit to the court of Louis at Rheims; not only was Louis reassured about Roman conditions but, in this first succession to the imperial title, the religious and Roman aspects were once again emphasized. The visit was successful; Stephen was triumphantly received and crowned Louis in

[34] Astronomus, *Vita Hludowici Imperatoris*, c. 25 (*MGH. SS.* II, 607).

the cathedral of Rheims, securing from him a confirmation of the privileges and independence of the papal states. This pact, ratified by Stephen's successor Paschal, shows Louis' lack of interest in Italian affairs and his satisfaction with his father's arrangements. The territorial possessions of the papacy, and its rights of full jurisdiction, were acknowledged; Louis was to guarantee the freedom of papal elections, the return of fugitives from Roman justice and respect for the papacy throughout the Empire. Stephen, concerned with healing the rifts in Roman society, brought back from exile the rebels against Leo and restored their estates to them; but his premature death in 817 prevented the completion of his work of stabilization.[35]

Within a year of Stephen's death Italian affairs had forced themselves upon Louis' attention and led to a new relationship with the papal monarchy. In 817 Louis undertook a partition of his Empire among his three sons—the elder, Lothair, received no kingdom but was associated with his father in the imperial title. In the following year his nephew King Bernard of Italy fell under suspicion of disloyalty; he did not owe his royal title to Louis but to Charles and having succeeded his father had become heir also to Lombard hopes of independence. He was summoned to France, arrested, summarily tried and blinded; an act into which Louis had probably been bullied and which he ever after repented. Lothair was thereupon given the vacant kingdom and came to Rome for his coronation as co-emperor.

The new pope to succeed Stephen IV was Paschal who had risen through the ranks of the Roman clergy from the subdiaconate to the priesthood, and had then been appointed by Leo abbot of St. Stephen's monastery near St. Peter's. This unusual *cursus* was the result of an interest in monastic reform matching the movement in France of the same period, directed by Louis' adviser and friend, Benedict of Aniane. As abbot, Paschal's activities were marked by a devotion to the care of foreign pilgrims in Rome, and as pope he was distinguished by his care and concern for the preservation of the relics of the saints, exhumed from the suburban cemeteries and brought into the city churches. The prosperity brought to Rome by these relics, by pilgrims come to venerate them and churchmen to buy them, is seen in a new outburst of building and decoration in the

[35] *LP.* II, 49–50.

city and—a symptom of the dangers that were overtaking the Mediterranean world—in the ransoming of prisoners taken by the Arabs and sold overseas in Spain and Africa. The pilgrims living in their communities in Rome preserved national characteristics not always popular with the Romans; it was in Paschal's pontificate that the English colony of the Borgo, near St. Peter's, which followed its native custom of building in wood, lost its houses in a disastrous fire, the first of many to sweep the crowded quarter around the basilica. Paschal, roused at midnight, hurried barefoot to the scene and supervised the fire-fighting operations himself; ever solicitous of pilgrims, he granted the Saxon community estates and money for rebuilding, with woods for a supply of timber.[36]

But practical charity was not the sole feature of Paschal's pontificate; selected by Leo for the reform of the Roman monasteries he too was imbued with Leo's authoritarian ideals. Towards the end of his life a clash occurred with Abbot Ingoald of Farfa in a lawsuit concerning some of the abbey's holdings in the Sabine Hills which were claimed by the papacy. In the presence of Lothair the papal claims, in accordance with Roman law, were upheld while Ingoald, himself a Frank, entered a vigorous protest against this extension of Roman law to a long-settled Lombard area and against the harsh arbitrary methods of the papal agents.[37] His protest was shared by the Roman nobility who, under the more settled conditions of the Empire, were taking their attitude and desire for greater security of tenure from the Lombard and Frankish society around them, while within the city they were excluded from the profits of government. The Lateran did not moderate its position; two prominent Romans, the *primicerius* Theodore and his son-in-law the *nomenclator* Leo, were arrested for *lèse-majesté* and either summarily executed or murdered by papal servants. Paschal wrote at once to Louis in explanation of their arrest and to purge himself of their murder, but the nobility also appealed to him as their emperor and invited his intervention in the internal affairs of Rome.[38]

Louis was now forced to take note of Italian and Roman affairs, and in November 824 Lothair was commissioned to hold an inquiry into the City's internal state. Paschal died before Lothair's appoint-

[36] *LP.* II, 52–63. [37] *Registrum Farfense*, III, 137.
[38] Einhart, *Annales*, a. 824.

ment and the Roman nobility gained the greater part of their case by the election of Eugenius, the archpriest and titular of S. Sabina on the Aventine, the aristocratic region of the city. Although Roman born, his father's name was Boemund, a name that may reflect Lombard antecedents. At the time of his election he was elderly and in uncertain health and was dependent on his two advisers, Quirinus the governor of the Lateran, and the *nomenclator* Theophylact. Lothair's inquiry, of which Eugenius was co-chairman, was a heavy indictment of papal government under Leo and Paschal; in a constitution promulgated after its completion Lothair gave the city a precise form of government, defining its relationship to the Empire and the Empire's responsibility for good order. The papal officials were ordered to Louis' presence to be examined on their fitness for office, while the Romans themselves were permitted to register themselves as bound by either Roman or Lombard law, at their choice, gaining security of tenure and freedom from arbitrary government. A final court of appeal was established of two *missi*, one appointed by the Emperor, the other by the pope; and certain regulations, such as a prohibition on the long-established practice of plundering the Lateran on a pope's death, were made to preserve internal order. It was a victory for the nobility who for the remainder of the century had their place in the government; but it introduced direct imperial and royal authority into Rome.[39]

[39] *Constitutio Romana*, a. 824, in MGH. LL. Capit. 1.See also O. Bertolini, 'Osservazioni sulla "Constitutio romana" e sul "Sacramentum cleri et populi" dell' 824', (*Festschrift di Stefano*, 1956).

9

ROME AND
THE CAROLINGIAN EMPIRE

The pontificate of Eugenius II laid Roman society fully open to the conditions of the Carolingian Empire: the politics of the sub-kingdoms which introduced into the city for the first time in three centuries an international nobility; the relations of local governments to imperial unity; the growth of external attacks against which the vast extent of territory could provide no co-ordinated response.The nobility called in the imperial power of the Franks to check the misrule of Paschal I; in 824, unlike 799, the imperial authorities accepted their responsibility for Rome and the Romans and not for the papacy only. The nobility was secure within the city, a security assured by the person of Eugenius – his biographer, reflecting the viewpoint of the nobility, described his pontificate as a period of great peace and prosperity for the Romans. But this debt to imperial authority could not be extended to imply a subservience to the empire or to Italy; Roman sentiment and ecclesiastical principle were united on that. Radoin, supported by the Frankish Abbot Ingoald, reminded Eugenius of his ultimate dependence on the emperor's goodwill; this suggestion was hotly contended by the clerics of the Lateran service but they were in brutal fact unable to disprove it.

The problems facing Rome in the ninth century display in microcosm the symptoms of the decline of Carolingian power through the external threat of invasion and the internal localization of authority. Louis had established his son and co-emperor Lothair as king of Italy but in 833 Louis was forced to retire from active government when his sons, distrustful of a new partition he planned, combined in arms against him. The part played by the papacy as a supranational force was unhappy; Pope Gregory IV who had succeeded Eugenius in 827 after the month-long pontificate of Valentine and was the candidate of the nobility, hastened north over the Alps to make peace between the factions; but he was caught up in Lothair's train and brought merely as a witness to the Field of Lies. To the Frankish bishops, supporters of Louis and imperial unity, he appeared as Lothair's tame bishop; he had no opportunity for arbitration and was accused by the episcopate of the empire of succumbing to Lothair's bribes and was threatened with deposition by a meeting of Frankish bishops. On his return to Rome he abandoned international affairs and until his death in 844 concerned himself with domestic matters.

These included some repairs–for example, to the Aqua Traiana, the main aqueduct bringing water from Lake Bracciano to the city– and the construction of a papal summer villa at Dragone, between the city and Ostia. But his principal undertaking was the refortification of Ostia at the mouth of the Tiber in response to the imminent threat of Saracen raids along the seaboard. The Romans had no experience of naval matters, while a shortage of timber forced Gregory to rely on defensive measures alone. After centuries of neglect the defences of Ostia were placed on a sound footing, for river mouths were the traditional targets of seaborne raiders. The walls were heightened and 'he strengthened its entire perimeter with gates, portcullises and man-traps and with great skill he manufactured catapults for throwing stones from above to drive back any approaching enemy': a ditch was placed around the restored wall. The new defence-work was solemnly consecrated and named after himself Gregoriopolis, the first time a pope's name was commemorated in this way.[1]

The Arab power in North Africa had been growing steadily during the previous twenty years. In 827 Euphemius, the Byzantine governor of Sicily, had rebelled and called in Arab mercenaries; these had remained, overrunning the island in the course of the next few years. Paschal had spent heavily on ransoms for captives–the young Elias, for example, later one of the greatest of the Sicilian-Greek saints, was ransomed from captivity only to be captured again two years later in 835 and sold in North Africa.[2] From their base on Sicily, and profiting by the disorders of the south Italian states, the

---

[1] *LP.* II, 81–2.

[2] *AASS. Aug.* III, 479–89; see G. Da Costa-Louillet, 'Saints de Sicile et de l'Italie meridionale aux VIIIᵉ, IXᵉ et Xᵉ siècles', (*Byzantion*, 29, 1959).

Arabs entered the mainland, occupying Brindisi in 838. They defeated the Venetians the following year off Taranto, and ravaged the Adriatic. From Messina, which fell to them in 843, they reached into the Tyrrhenian Sea; already in 813 and 827 raids had been directed against Civitavecchia. In 848 the island of Ponza was taken, followed by Miseno, the former naval base commanding the Bay of Naples.[3]

These raids were compounded by the internal divisions of the Lombard and former imperial states of southern Italy which were engaged in destructive fratricidal rivalry. The principality of Benevento, which had been the scene of savage bloodfeuds, was disintegrating as a powerful bloc and was no longer able to represent separatist Lombard ambitions. In 839 Prince Sicard was murdered, and in the course of a civil war his treasurer Radelchis seized power in Benevento itself while Sicard's brother Sikenolf established himself in Salerno with the support of the Campanian *gastalds* of Conza, Capua and Acerenza. Further subdivisions followed, especially among the gastaldates of the upper Liris valley; Sikenolf's principal supporter, Landolf of Capua, divided his possessions among his sons on his death in 842, creating three small lordships at Capua, Teano and Sora.[4] Between these, and Benevento and the imperial cities of Gaeta, Amalfi and Naples, rivalry sprang up as each attempted to expand its own territories and to avoid domination by any of the great powers. For southern Italy was disputed territory: the two Empires had equal claims to domination and equal rights to intervention in face of the Arab threat. The establishment of a defensive system against the Arabs and of a coalition to protect central Italy was to be the major military and diplomatic preoccupation of the ninth century.[5]

[3] For the Arab invasion of Sicily see A. A. Vasiliev, *Byzance et les Arabs*, pt. I, 1934.

[4] See N. Cilento, *Italia meridionale longobarda*, 1966, 'Le origini della signoria capuana nella Longobardia minore', (*Istituto Storico Italiano per il Medio Evo, Studi Storici*, 69–70, 1966), and 'Le condizioni della vita nella contea longobarda di Capua nella seconda metà del IX secolo', (*Rivista Storica Italiana*, 63, 1951).

[5] G. Galasso, 'Le città Campane nell' alto medio evo', (*Archivio Storico per la provincia Napoletana*, n.s. 38, 1959; 39, 1960). M. Leccese, *Le origini del ducato di Gaeta e le sue relazioni con Roma e con Napoli*, (1942).

During the pontificate of Gregory IV the possibility of an effective and unified leadership in Italy appeared to be good. In 840 the Emperor Louis died, having regained much of his authority through the quarrels of his sons, and confining Lothair once more to his Italian kingdom. On his father's death Lothair again became effective Emperor and gave his Italian kingdom to his son, Louis II–Italy had passed once again to a king of the second generation whose interests were forcibly confined to the peninsula itself. In 843, by the partition of Verdun, Louis was confirmed in the rule of Italy, and granted not the old *Regnum Italicum* of Charlemagne–effectively limited to the north and the Lombardic plain–but 'the whole Italian kingdom with the city of Rome itself, which is venerated with a special status by all the Churches through the presence there of the apostles Peter and Paul and which, through the former invincible might of the Roman name, used to be called the mistress of the whole world'. The consequences of the known ambitions of Lothair and Louis to create a monolithic Italian state–the establishment of Rome's status as that of an Italian capital and of the pope as the Italian king's bishop, for so Gregory had appeared to the Frankish episcopate–were now apparent to the Romans. The revival of the Roman Empire, the delayed arrival in Rome of the Carolingian rebirth of learning, and the religious and civil pretensions of the New Rome, were awakening the Roman people to a consciousness of their particularity and great past. They were not prepared to be exploited or dismissed by the Frankish powers.

Roman resentment came to a head when Gregory IV died in 844, the year after Louis' appointment as king of Italy. His successor was the archpriest Sergius, a candidate of the nobility, a member of the same family that had already produced Stephen IV and later in the century produced Hadrian II. The election was disputed; the deacon

M. Berza, 'Un' autonomia periferica bizantina: Amalfi, sec. VI–IX', (*Atti del V Congresso Internazionale di Studi Bizantini*, 1939) and 'Amalfi preducale', (*Ephemeris Daco–Romana*, 8, 1938). N. Cilento, 'I Saraceni nell' Italia meridionale nei secoli IX e X', (*Archivio Storico per la provincia Napoletana*, n.s. 38, 1959). On the two empires, see O. Bertolini, 'Longobardi e bizantini nell' Italia meridionale', (*Atti del 3° Congresso internazionale di Studi sull' Alto Medio Evo*, 1959); P. Lamma, 'Il problema dei due imperi e dell' Italia meridionale', (*ibid.,*); W. Ohnsorge, 'L'idea d'impero nel secolo nono e l'Italia meridionale', (*ibid.*).

John gathered a crowd of rough country folk and attempted to seize the Lateran by force. It was a short-lived attempt: 'Swiftly the princes of the Quirites gathered with a large mounted force' to expel the intruder and Sergius's consecration, which was marked by an unusual fall of snow, quickly followed.[6] The incident recalled two features of Roman life; their adoption of Frankish military methods – and specifically of mounted troops – and the deliberate archaism of the *Quirites*, harking back to the heroic days of their city. But in current politics it was not sufficient; the consecration, made without the prior confirmation of Lothair and Louis, directly contravened imperial policy. The Emperor ordered his son to reassert visible authority over Rome, and Louis left Pavia with a large army and many Frankish bishops to assume royal and imperial rights over the city. His troops *en route* gave expression to their feelings by plundering and committing atrocities in Bologna, a city belonging to the papal states. Italian and Roman alarm increased at the accounts of their disorderly march, accomplished in severe weather, but the king's arrival outside the city was met with the usual protocol, the assembly of the city militia and the Greek acclamations accorded to the Emperor. The meeting of king and pope outside St. Peter's was cordial, to the initial relief of both, but the Frankish army made its temper known. Sergius ordered the great bronze doors of the basilica to be closed and turned to the king: 'If you are come to this church with sincere mind and goodwill towards the republic and the whole world, then at my invitation enter; but if not then neither by me nor by my leave will these doors be opened.' Louis assured the pope of his good intentions and together with their counsellors they entered St. Peter's to pray at the apostle's tomb.[7]

But the Frankish army encamped outside the city was restless; by papal command the gates of the city were shut and barred to the troops, who began to plunder the suburbs and the countryside so that the Romans compared them to a plague that had settled on them. News came of a second army approaching Rome, that of Sikenolf of Salerno who was coming to lay his claim before Louis to the whole principality of Benevento; his approach was equally disorderly and he plundered Monte Cassino on his march to bribe Louis with 100,000 *solidi* from the proceeds. The prospect of a

[6] *LP*. II, 87.   [7] *LP*. II, 87–8.

combination of the armies was a threat to Rome's liberties; within the city, disputes over the validity of Sergius's election continued, and the antipathy of the Frankish episcopate to the papacy was renewed when Sergius queried the claims of Louis' counsellor Drogo of Metz to metropolitan status. Sergius finally won recognition from Louis and a second time blessed him and conferred on him the insignia of the Italian kingdom. But this merely aroused in Louis a desire for total sovereignty within Italy; he demanded from the pope and the assembled Roman nobility an oath of allegiance to him personally as king of Italy. This Sergius refused for both himself and the nobility; Rome, he declared, was subject to no Italian kingdom but to the Empire alone and he expressed his willingness to swear fidelity to the Empire. Louis grudgingly acquiesced and the oaths of pope and nobility to Lothair were registered, but the danger was renewed with the arrival of Sikenolf. Rome seemed to be surrounded by armed camps, but Sergius with consummate diplomacy persuaded Louis to recognize Sikenolf at least as prince of Salerno and to withdraw both armies from the city. Sikenolf acknowledged Louis as king and Louis, partially satisfied, withdrew to the north.[8]

The relief of the Romans was great. Sergius, hailed as the author of their salvation and the restorer of peace, had by taking his stand on the highest concept of Empire preserved Rome's independence. He had been the nobility's candidate, from among their own number, and they had suppressed his rival; he in turn had preserved their status and freedom from the danger of becoming a vassal of the Italian king. The remainder of his pontificate, until his death three years later, demonstrated the hold that the nobility had acquired over the papacy and its offices, clerical and lay. Sergius was not himself physically a strong man and towards the end of his life control was taken by his brother Benedict, whom he had appointed bishop of Albano. Sergius's biographer has little good to say of Benedict, 'an uncouth and ungainly man, lustful and given over to boorish habits', and who went further to secure his personal position; by bribes to Louis he gained from the Emperor Lothair the 'lordship and rule over Rome'– most probably the office of imperial *missus* established by the constitution of 824 as the overseer of the Lateran administration which he could hold in the imperial interest. The

8 *LP.* II, 88–91.

papacy, as the Roman bishopric, was being localized: the symptom of the loss of central Carolingian authority, the devolution of imperial appointments to local interests, was being worked out in Rome also. This too affected the increase in Roman pride and particularism.[9]

The resentment of the Romans was increased by the tragic events of the year of Sergius's death. The justification for Carolingian power in Italy had in papal eyes been the protection of St. Peter's city from its enemies; this was the origin of the patriciate and the empire. On 10th August 846 a message was received from count Adalbert of Corsica which warned that a concentration of Arab ships – estimated at seventy-three and carrying 500 horses, indicating a more protracted foray than usual – was gathering off the mouth of the Tiber. Little attention was paid; the newly fortified Gregoriopolis was considered adequate and Benedict of Albano was not apparently a man of great energy or efficiency. On 23rd August the Arabs landed; Gregoriopolis fell at once and the unfortified Porto was abandoned by its inhabitants. Pope Sergius was dying; the only troops that could be mobilized sufficiently quickly were those of the *scholae*, the foreign communities of the city and, 'at this disaster the courage of the Romans waned and eroded'. The *scholae* marched at once to the coast, too late to save the towns and arriving only to defeat a few Arabs who had scattered for plunder. On the 24th the *scholae* remained at Porto, protected by the river from the main body of the enemy; the following day the main Roman army marched down to join them. The enemy was too numerous and the Romans fell back towards the city; on their retreat they were overtaken by the Arabs and put to rout. Defeated, they reached Rome and manned the defences.

On 26th August the Arab forces arrived before the city. The walls could withstand the assaults of a marauding expedition, but the shrine and basilica of St. Peter's with its attendant monasteries and *diaconiae* and the Saxon quarter of the Borgo lay undefended beyond the river and outside the walls. On these the pirates fell, looting the basilica of all its accumulated treasures, removing even the great high altar and the silver covering the *confessio* of St. Peter, and the great bronze doors. They then spread over the countryside north of

[9] *LP.* II, 97–8.

the river, devastating the *domusculta* of Galeria and the adjacent basilica of St. Rufina; one party crossed the Tiber and sacked the unprotected church of St. Paul. Rescue came at last from duke Guy of Spoleto who led down an army of Lombards from the hills. He attacked the Arabs in their main encampment on the Vatican hill and drove them from the city after fierce fighting in the Borgo. They were pursued across the open country to Civitavecchia, while some fled south down the Appia to Fondi and their base at Miseno. The Arab fleet itself cleared Ostia but ran into severe storms and suffered losses on the coast; bodies washed ashore provided rich profit to the Italians from the booty still in their clothes.[10]

For Rome it had been a nightmare experience and served to increase resentment of the pretensions of the kingdom of Italy. Later legend was to credit Louis with having been throughout the sack encamped on Monte Mario, venturing down with his troops who had formerly shown themselves so brave in terrorizing the district only to suffer defeat in the Field of Nero and retire helpless to watch the horror.[11] He was in fact too far to the north to have intervened before the sack was over, but to the Romans it was apparent that the claims of the king of Italy were not matched by a corresponding ability or inclination to defend his would-be capital. It was apparent also that the only local power that could act effectively was the duchy of Spoleto which had long had a watching brief over Rome on the Franks' behalf; nor was the part played by the foreign communities forgotten. But the creation of absolute security for the Italian littoral was to be the unaided work of the Italians themselves under the leadership of the new pope.

Sergius had died during the sack; his successor, elected after the pirates' repulse, was Leo, a monk of St. Martin's by St. Peter's who had been appointed subdeacon by Gregory IV and priest of the *Quattuor Coronati* by Sergius. In the first years of his pontificate he prepared his campaign; the shock of the sack temporarily secured the support of the maritime cities of the south and, with a foretaste of the indulgences later granted to crusaders, spiritual benefits were promised to all who fought. Early in 849 news came of a second Arab

[10] *LP*. II, 99–101.
[11] See Ph. Lauer, 'La poème de la destruction de Rome et les origines de la cité Leonine', (*MAH*, 19, 1899).

concentration off Sardinia; the combined fleets of Amalfi, Gaeta and Naples assembled at Ostia under the command of Caesarius, son of duke Sergius of Naples, and there Pope Leo visited them to bless and communicate the troops. The Arab fleet appeared and battle was joined off-shore, the Neapolitan galleys leading the attack. The battle was interrupted by a storm which separated the combatants; the allied fleet made its way back to harbour but the Arabs, unable to ride out the storm, were dispersed and large numbers of ships were flung ashore. The scattered remnants were easily picked up by the allies when the storm had blown itself out; many prisoners were taken and sent to work in chain-gangs on the new defences of Rome.[12]

Before the naval campaign Leo had already undertaken the reconstruction of Rome's defences. In October 846 the Emperor Lothair had summoned an assembly to deliberate 'on the building of a new Rome' and had called for a special tax from the entire Empire to finance it. The prime task lay in the provision of defence for the unprotected group of buildings on the Vatican hill, dominated by St. Peter's. Leo III had begun the construction of a fortress there but at his death the materials collected had been removed by the Romans. Leo IV was no civil autocrat to be feared, and for the building of the new wall to protect the Vatican the entire resources of the duchy were called upon. Labour forces were provided by contingents from every estate, from the *domuscultae*, and from the monastic properties and towns of the duchy; to each work-party, called *militiae*, was assigned the construction of a section of the wall and inscriptions recording the work of each placed there. Two of these have survived, mentioning the contingents of the Saltasina estate and the Capracorum *domusculta* under its *corrector* Agatho. The completed work took four years; it stretched in a narrow horse-shoe from the Mausoleum of Hadrian (long since fortified) inland from the river around the St. Peter complex, and back again to the river bank by the Borgo. The walls, of *tufa* and tile, forty feet high, were strengthened by forty-four towers and interrupted by only three gates. The work was completed in 852 and on 27th July of that year a solemn ceremony of dedication was performed. A procession of the entire clergy, barefoot, accompanied by the militia and nobility, made a circuit of the walls, blessing them and the gates; it

[12] *LP.* II, 118–19; Leo IV, *Ep.* 28, (*MGH. Epp.* V, p. 601).

was followed by a distribution of money, food and clothing to the people.[13]

The Leonine city was the first extension of Rome beyond the circuit of the Aurelian Walls and the first definite additions to the shape of the city made by a pope, yet it represented only a part of the papacy's work. The coasts were again fortified; Porto, by now almost deserted, was rebuilt with walls and settled by refugees from Corsica who were granted farms in the adjacent countryside as colonists under papal and imperial patronage in return for military service. Chains were prepared to block the river itself. Civitavecchia, the second great port of Rome which had already suffered attack twice in the century, was also refounded; the remaining inhabitants were moved by Leo to a new site about twelve miles away which was built, fortified and dedicated under the name of Leopolis. Inland on the northern boundary of the duchy, Orte and Ameria were also re-fortified. The work of Rome's defence was completed later in the century when Pope John VIII built a wall round the basilica of St. Paul and its surrounding monasteries, calling the complex Johanno-polis; lying on the plain to the south of the river the new fortress served, as it had in the Gothic Wars, to defend the southern flank of the river approach.[14]

King Louis of Italy was commissioned at Lothair's assembly of 846 to raise an army and secure the defence of the Italian peninsula. The Arab bases in Italy were consolidating themselves. At Fondi in Lazio an almost permanent base had been established within raiding distance of the great Campanian towns, and in the south an Arab emirate centred on Bari had won possession of Taranto as well.[15] The principalities and states of the south were unable to achieve any alliance or unity to resist Arab aggression; the count of Capua, on Sikenolf's death, had renounced allegiance to Salerno and was at war with Naples; the gastaldates of the Liris valley were unable to co-operate to block the invasion route provided by the river. To Louis,

[13] *LP.* II, 123–5 and p. 137, n. 47: see also A. Prandi, 'Un' iscrizione frammentaria di Leone IV recentemente scoperta', (*ASR*, 74, 1951).

[14] *LP.* II, 117, 126–7: see also Ph. Lauer, 'Lacité de Cencelli', (*MAH*, 20, 1900).

[15] G. Musca, 'L'Emirato di Bari, 847–871', (*Università degli Studi di Bari, Istituto di Storia medievale e moderna, Saggi,* 4) 1964; *MGH. LL.* II, *Capitularia* II, p. 65.

searching for a firm command before embarking no the long campaign needed to oust the Arabs, it seemed essential to break up the
blocs that were forming in Italy and to unite them under his crown
and sole leadership. The principality of Benevento was already
strained by civil war and in 847 Louis moved south against the Arabs
to instigate the division of the principality into two–Benevento and
Salerno–but this failed to give him any solid support for his campaign. In 850 he was associated with his father in the imperial title
and the following year, to win Lombard sympathies, he married a
prominent Lombard heiress, Engelberga. In 852 Louis received
appeals for protection from the abbeys of Monte Cassino and St.
Vincent on the Volturno. The adventures that befell the body of St.
Magnus, the patron of Trani who had been moved to Fondi for
sake-keeping, provide a striking illustration of the conditions of
Campania and Lazio at this time. Fondi was sacked in 846 and 'one
of the leading persons of Campania, no intellectual but a tribune by
office, called Plato' took the body for safety to Veroli. On arrival, the
nearby town of Anagni was under siege by an Arab raiding party
that had come across the peninsula from Calabria; its commander
Musa turned on Veroli, stabling the horses in the church of St.
Andrew. St. Magnus's body was not found, buried beneath the pavement of the church–indeed, its miraculous powers killed the animals
and forced the raiders to ask for its removal to Anagni. The sufferings
of the Italians were correspondingly great: twenty years later when
the monk Bernard was travelling to the Holy Land he saw in the
Arab-held port of Taranto, six ships with 9,000 Christian captives
ready to sail to the slave-markets of Tripoli. But Louis still could not
obtain sufficient support to end this menace. His next campaign in
the south was supported by Benevento and Spoleto, but not by
Capua or Salerno.[16]

The support of the papal states and the Romans could not be
relied upon in creating an effective Italian kingdom, and Louis was
compelled to encourage movements that weakened the papal government. In December 850 a new archbishop, John, was elected in

[16] C. Odegaard, 'The Empress Engelberga', (*Speculum*, 26, 1951);
Translatio S. Magni Ep. Tranensis, *AASS. Aug.* III, 708; F. Avril and J – R.
Gaborit, 'L'Itinerarium Bernardi Monachi et les pélérinages d'Italie
pendant l'Haut Moyen Age', (*MAH*, 79, 1967).

Ravenna. He was a member of one of the city's leading families and was at the head of the antipapal faction of Emilia that looked to the archbishop for protection from Rome. Aided by his brother duke Gregory who ruled Emilia as a bandit, John began to shake free of Roman rule; his suffragan bishops were denied contact with Rome and hindered in their *ad limina* visits; a systematic despoiling of papal supporters, mainly the clergy and lesser nobility of the adjacent towns, was begun by the two brothers, and papal tenants in Emilia were dispossessed. Duke Gregory was joined by two of Louis' envoys in an attack on a papal agent, Regimbald, whom they killed; John himself hounded another papal officer, the *vestararius* Hilary. Leo's death and the disorders of Benedict III's accession gave John an opportunity to extend his power; he kept a bodyguard of fifty horsemen and obliged his bishops to supply him with three or more horsemen each; tributes of up to 200 *mancuses* were levied on the suffragans and distributed to his followers; diocesan and monastic lands, some under papal protection, were forcibly added to the archiepiscopal fisc and suffragans' tenants compelled to cultivate the archbishop's lands. The administration of justice was taken directly into his own hands.[17]

In Rome also there was discord. A prominent Roman, the *magister militum* Daniel, fled to Louis in about 854 with accusations that his colleague Gratian, the military governor of the Lateran palace, had plotted the restoration of Byzantine power in Italy. Certainly the Roman dislike of an active monarchy established too close to the city made the prospect of a more distant sovereign attractive; and sympathy for the East remained strong. Louis came to Rome for an inquiry and Daniel's charges proved baseless; he was handed over for trial under Roman law, found guilty but pardoned at Gratian's intercession.[18]

A more serious dislocation of Roman society occurred during Leo's pontificate. The pope had undertaken to reform both the spiritual and clerical sides of Roman life and consequently reissued the synodal admonition, but in so doing he had run into opposition from one of the most powerful clerical dynasties of Rome. The

---

[17] G. Buzzi, 'Ricerche per la Storia di Ravenna e di Roma dall' 850 al 1118', (*ASR*, 38, 1915).

[18] *LP*. II, 134.

Carolingian renaissance of learning had come late to Rome and was in the mid-ninth century confined to a small group of clerics who were closely identified with the nobility and their politics; their ideas found expression in an awareness of the historical and geographical extent of the old Empire and an archaic attempt to revive its ancient powers and forms. The use of old terms, the senate and the consulship, and a consciousness of the Latin myths of Rome's origins, became increasingly apparent; a few years later one scholar of this school, the deacon John Immonides, attempted in his *Life* of Gregory the Great to rescue that pope from the near-monopoly that the Anglo-Saxons exercised over his cult and, for the delectation of his patron Bishop Gaudericus of Velletri, traced the history of the bishop's diocesan town back to the arrival of Aeneas. But under Leo IV the leader of the clerical group was Bishop Arsenius of Orte who had been appointed one of the two resident *missi* in Rome in about 848 and had taken the opportunity to enrich himself–a Breton appellant to Rome was so struck by his authoritative air in synod that he styled him archbishop. His family–symptomatic of the changes brought about by Frankish domination–was an international one; a nephew was the later archbishop of Vienne and martyrologist, Ado. Another nephew was an even more celebrated scholar, Anastasius, who while still a young man had been appointed priest of S. Marcello by Pope Leo in 847-8. But his ambition and neglect of his spiritual duties aroused Leo's anger and within a few months of his appointment he was compelled to flee from Rome.[19]

Anastasius fled to Louis' territory; Leo's demands for his extradition were unsuccessful and he settled in Chiusi just beyond the papal frontier. He was several times excommunicated by Leo in synods in which his serious shortcomings were proclaimed. In November 853 he was solemnly deprived of his priestly orders; Leo emphasized the sentence by having a fresco representing the anathemas of Christ and the Virgin on the culprit set up in St. Peter's. To the pope he was a potentially dangerous focus of imperialist tendencies for already the antiquarian group of Romans was urging Louis to a new conception of imperial authority and to 'seek out again the ancient dominion of the Emperors'. The firm reunification of Italy and the establishment

[19] (Excerpta e) *Vita S. Conwoinis* (*MGH. SS.* XV, 455-9); Mansi, **14**, 1018.

of Rome as an actual and visible capital were the prime steps towards this end. It was a lay conception, untouched by ecclesiastical influence. Arsenius and Anastasius, despite their religious orders, were primarily politicians competing for power with other members of the nobility and lent support to the imperial concept to further their own ambitions. To Leo this attitude spelt the end of an independent papacy, as it had to Sergius II. Although a party favourable to him which might one day hold power in Rome was useful to Louis in his attempts to unite Italy, he owed too much to Frankish and Carolingian attitudes to adopt the ancient idea. Twenty years later he was to write to the Emperor Basil I in the East in justification of his imperial title using specifically Frankish terms: 'we have taken this name and dignity from the Romans among whom this highest of styles and appellations first arose'; it was conferred by 'imposition and unction at the hands of the highest bishop and by the judgement of the Church' for 'the defence and glorification of the mother of all God's churches'. That remained the lasting principle of the Christian Carolingian empire; but in the mid-ninth century the defection of Anastasius was a useful temporary advantage to Louis.[20]

Leo IV continued his programme of reform of the clerical life in the papal states. At the synod of 853 which deposed Anastasius he sought to withdraw the clergy from too close an involvement in secular life. Except to avoid injustice, and then only with episcopal assent, priests were not to act as witnesses or recognizors in secular business, nor could they act as advocates. The politician-bishops were reminded of their prime duties: a bishop could not be absent from his diocese without canonical consent for more than three weeks, 'for the absence of the bishop is a great calamity for the people'; he was to visit with diligence the outlying parishes of his see and not confine his activities to his diocesan town; he might not dispose of the immovable properties of the parish; following Frankish influence, he was to establish a cloister near his cathedral for his clergy. The educational system needed revision: 'It has been brought to our notice that some places have neither teachers nor provision for pious study in letters. Therefore in every cathedral and in the subordinate parishes and elsewhere as need may dictate full care and diligence must be taken to establish masters and teachers who shall

[20] *MGH. Epp.* V, 386–94.

conscientiously instruct in letters and the liberal arts, for in these above all are manifest and made clear the divine commands.'[21]

Other priests were deprived for unworthiness, but the attempt to widen the basis of education and provide a trustworthy and disciplined clergy failed. The Roman clergy–drawn from a narrow and specifically Roman background–were too sensitive to the political complexities of the city to provide an independent agency for the papacy. The papacy could attach no trustworthy Greek scholars to the legations to Constantinople in 861, 869 and 879: those clerics who did serve were themselves open to the prevailing opportunities for temporal advancement that the Empire provided. Successive legates, Radoald of Porto at the court of Lothair in 860, Radoald and Zachary of Anagni at Constantinople in 863, succumbed to bribes and were excommunicated. The ambitions of Formosus of Porto when legate to the Bulgarian mission proved the first stage in his tumultuous career. The Roman nobility flirted only temporarily with an imperialist policy; the antiquarian view put forward by Roman scholars of Rome's prerogative and status became the possession, not of the Carolingian dynasty nor of the papacy, but of the clergy's associates and relatives among the aristocracy.

In July 855 Leo IV died, a man widely respected for his sanctity, his reforms and his leadership. Louis wished now to force Anastasius's election canonically but a party of the nobility forestalled him by choosing Benedict, the priest of St. Cecilia. In accordance with the constitution of 824, confirmation was necessary and both parties wished to remain within the letter of the law. Bishop Nicholas of Anagni and the *magister militum* Mercurius were sent as envoys to Lothair and Louis to obtain their consent but were intercepted on their journey by Arsenius who persuaded them to support his nephew. Louis refused to accept Benedict and sent envoys of his own led by the marquis Adalbert of Tuscany to enforce his will on Rome. These reached Orte where they were joined by Bishop Arsenius and Anastasius; shortly afterwards Bishop Nicholas and Mercurius with other military leaders, the *magistri militum* Gregory and Christopher, slipped out of Rome to join them, followed by two prominent churchmen, Bishops Agatho of Todi and Radoald of Porto. The imperial envoys and their followers approached Rome; Benedict's

[21] Mansi, 14, 1009.

spokesmen, Gratianus and the secretary Theodore, were detained in custody and two more of his followers, the *secundicerius* Hadrian and duke Gregory, were also arrested. Arsenius's advance stage-management of public opinion secured a welcome that could be construed as enthusiastic and Anastasius in some semblance of triumph entered Rome after seven years' exile.

One home, however, he ruined what support he had in the city by the violence of his revenge on his opponents. He went first to St. Peter's where he supervised the destruction of Pope Leo's fresco commemorating his excommunication; this, involving the destruction of images of Christ and the Virgin, aroused the anger of the Romans. The Frankish *missi* tried to apply pressure on the bishops of Albano and Ostia to perform Anastasius's consecration, and Anastasius ordered one of his partisans, Bishop Romanus of Bagnorea, to eject Benedict from the Lateran and hand him over to the custody of two priests, John and Hadrian, who had been deprived of their orders by Leo. But the Romans, led by a majority of the clergy, were now fully roused; the spectre of domination by the civil power seemed almost to have materialized and the attack on the memory of the saintly Leo and the doubtful records of Anastasius and his partisans produced a wave of support for Benedict. The clergy, meeting in Leo's former church, the *Quattuor Coronati*, instituted a three-day fast for divine intervention, and the Frankish *missi* yielded, appreciating that Louis could not sustain an unwelcome candidate in Rome against constant hostility. Benedict was again brought out, mounted on Leo's own horse and led once more through the streets to the Lateran. It was a compromise–Anastasius was not proceeded against but given the abbacy of S. Maria in Trastevere in compensation.[22]

The two year pontificate of Benedict III passed quietly since neither party dared to press the compromise arrived at. St. Peter's basilica was restored to its former splendour and gifts for the purpose were received from as far away as the Emperor Michael in Constantinople. This compromise was maintained on Benedict's death in 858 when Louis again looked for a favourable candidate, Anastasius now being discredited. One was found, the deacon Nicholas, acceptable both to the Emperor and to the Romans. Louis, who was present in Rome for the election, saw that his choice was a good one; he was sumptuously

[22] *LP.* II, 141–3.

entertained by the pope on the *domusculta* of S. Leucio and held frank discussions with him in which Nicholas declared his policy of intervening in temporal affairs only under exceptional circumstances. The need for unity was strong.In Italy the principality of Salerno was still engaged in a civil war in which duke Guy of Spoleto meddled profitably, and the Arab power based on Bari remained unchallenged. In Europe the descendants of Charlemagne, ruling the successor kingdoms of the Empire, were in a state of permanent enmity as they strove for personal advantage. But the memory and form of unity was still strong, as it had been in the time of Gregory I, and its accomplishment not beyond the bounds of possibility. However, the visible aspect of unity was now the possession of the Church, since its international and hierarchical character cut across the shifting boundaries of kingdoms that were dragging down the Christian Empire.

Imperialism of a kind was represented in the ethos of the False Decretals, that body of documents appearing in Northern France in the mid-century and gaining wide currency, which emphasized the structure of the church culminating naturally at Rome– it was the episcopate that preserved the concept of unity. The imperialist aspect of the Church was expanding; the Greek brothers Cyril and Methodius were active in the conversion of the Slavs beyond the Danube, a mission conducted under Roman auspices that was to bring new Christian states into being. Obedience to the Christian law was the hall-mark of the pontificate of Nicholas. To Boris of Bulgaria he laid down the details of every aspect of the Christian life; he attempted to control the private morals of the Western kings; he induced into the Greek Church a sense of Rome's authority. The personality of Nicholas stands out in the mid-ninth century, wielding an authority on behalf of the papacy that contrasts with the factious local base of power in Rome.[23]

In this work he was to marshal the intellects of the Roman Church in defence of its overriding primacy, especially in its relations with Archbishop Hincmar of Rheims and the patriarch Photius of Con-

---

[23] F. Dvornik, *Les Slavs, Byzance et Rome au IX siècle*, (1926), and *Le Schisme de Photius: Histoire et Légende*, (1950); J. Dujzev, 'Die Responsa Nicolai I Papae ad Consulta Bulgarorum', (*Festschrift zur Feier des 200 iahr. Bestandes des Haus-, Hof-, und Staatsarchiv, Wien*, 1949, vol. I).

stantinople. Chief among his aides was Anastasius who, secular ambition now unattainable, had embarked on a career of scholarship in the papal service that was impressive in scope and range. As papal librarian and secretary to Nicholas he drafted the letters to patriarchs and kings that hammered home Nicholas's conception of the Roman Church as the fount of all authority; in his programme of translations of Greek spiritual writings he made the Western world aware of the full extent of Christianity; in his historical writings and editions of the sufferings of Pope Martin at Greek hands in the seventh century he made Europe aware of the papacy's central position in its history. The adoption of the principles of the pseudo-Isidorean decretals by Rome were matched by other collections made to correspond with Italian and Roman circumstances. One such collection, which drew heavily on Pope Gelasius's writings and on the Symmachian forgeries, was possibly the work of Anastasius himself and dealt with a wide variety of disciplinary matters, including the validity of episcopal translation–later to become a burning question–and, an interesting comment on Anastasius's own career, the problems of deprivation of orders.[24]

Nicholas's authoritarian temper revealed itself in his relations with Ravenna. During the pontificate of Benedict Archbishop John of Ravenna had increased his local power, but Nicholas soon received from the suffragans of Ravenna and from 'the senators of Ravenna and its uncounted population' appeals for protection from their archbishop. Letters and legates that were sent to John without effect were followed by a summons to Rome. At a synod in Rome early in 861 John was excommunicated by the pope and at once fled to Pavia

[24] G. Lapotre, *De Anastasio Bibliothecario Sedis Apostolicae*, (1885); E. Perels, *Papst Nikolaus I und Anastasius Bibliothekarius*, (1920); J. Haller, *Nikolaus I und Pseudo-Isidor*, (1936); C. Laehr, 'Die Briefe und Prologe des Bibliothekarius Anastasius', (*Neue Archiv für Deutsche Geschichts-kunde*, 47, 1928); Yves M-J. Congar, 'S. Nicolas Ier: ses positions ecclésio-logiques', (*Rivista di Storia della Chiesa in Italia*, 21, 1967); S. Lindemans, 'Auxilius et le manuscrit Vallicellan tome XVIII', (*Revue d'histoire ecclesiastique*, 57, 1962); J. Pozzi, 'Le MS. Tomus XVIII de la Vallicellana et le libelle De episcoporum transmigratione et quod non temere iudicentur regulae quadraginta quattuor', (*Apollinaris*, 31, 1958); P. Devos, 'Anastase le Bibliothecaire: Sa contribution à la correspondence pontificale: la date de sa mort', (*Byzantion*, 32, 1962).

to ask for help from Louis. Louis offered him the company of two imperial *missi* to Rome, but Nicholas refused to accept them and John's enemies in Ravenna invited the pope there. Louis, anxious to avoid a rupture with the papacy, withdrew his support from John, and Nicholas in Ravenna was able to reinstate the papal officials and arrange the return of property confiscated by John and his brother duke Gregory. When John was finally received in Rome with two *missi* as guarantors of his personal safety, he was compelled at a synod in December 861 to renounce all territorial ambitions. He swore to make a visit *ad limina* every two years, to allow no episcopal elections in Emilia save those canonically managed, and to raise only the canonical tribute from his suffragans. He was to restore all stolen property and above all to exercise no civil jurisdiction in private cases. The right of appeal to the resident papal *missus* in Ravenna and to the papal *vestararius* was always to remain open.[25]

It was a moral and legal victory for Nicholas, the papacy and for Rome, but it threatened Louis' hold over Italy and the prospects of a successful war against the Arabs. In 860 his position had become precarious through the opposition of two great feudatories of central Italy, Lambert the son of duke Guy of Spoleto and count Ildebert of Camerino. These fled, Ildebert to the sultan of Bari and Lambert to Adelchis of Benevento. Their flight gave Louis an opportunity to assert his control over central Italy and to prepare for his great campaign. Pentapolis was occupied by his troops and the payment of tribute to the papal authorities forbidden; instead public land was distributed to Franks to outweigh the influence of the papalist party. Two years later there came another occasion to establish his power over Rome. When Louis' brother Lothair, King of Lorraine, repudiated his wife and married and crowned his mistress Waldrade, a synod of bishops at Metz had, under pressure from the king, and giving voice to national aspirations among the episcopate, condoned the act; the papal legate, Bishop Radoald of Porto, had succumbed to bribes and also given his assent. Nicholas promptly excommunicated the king, and Archbishop John's partisans in Emilia prevailed on Louis to support his brother and march on Rome. As the Frankish army approached, Nicholas organized fasts and processions for

[25] H. Fuhrmann, 'Papst Nikolaus I und die Absetzung des Erzbischofs Johann von Ravenna', (*Zeitschrift für Savigny–Stiftung*, 75, 1958).

divine intervention. One of these was attacked and broken up in the street by Louis' supporters in the city; the crosses and relics, including a part of the True Cross, were thrown to the ground and the pope himself was barely able to escape by river to the Leonine City. He remained there for two days until, with the promise of a safe-conduct, he went to interview Louis. In the Emperor's camp the archbishops overwhelmed him with reproaches and accused him, in Louis' presence, of trying to make himself emperor and of wishing to dominate the whole world–the expressions of resentment felt by a national episcopate in conflict with a supranational authority. Nicholas's excommunication of the bishops was rejected and they in turn anathematized him. The document condemning the pope was carried by armed men into St. Peter's and thrown before the *confessio*; one of the sacristans who tried to prevent the outrage was killed, and for several days Louis' troops ravaged the city. But Nicholas stood firm, reiterating his condemnations; Louis, who would have profited only from a quick surrender, withdrew from Rome, realizing that he had neither the moral right nor the physical power to hold it. The archbishops and Bishop Radoald, deprived of their orders, were confined in monasteries within the city, and when Lothair came to Italy later in the year to beg his brother's aid, he was refused, for Louis could not afford a continued rupture with Rome.[26]

Louis' pretensions in Rome had suffered a third defeat, with more damaging results for he was forced to recognize the principle of Roman exclusiveness in papal elections, whereby the weight of influence remained with the nobility. But his grand design for the reduction of all Italy was nearing fruition. Alliances had been made with the Eastern Empire, with Venice and with the Slav tribes of Dalmatia for naval co-operation, and in 866 he decreed a general mobilization throughout northern Italy, in eleven recruiting districts, with orders to assemble in March of that year at Lucera in Apulia, giving detailed instructions about service, equipment and discipline. This was to be the final test of his policy, but the distrust of the separatist Lombards of the south still hampered him. His advance through Molise and Samnium was bitterly contested by the local

---

[26] *LP.* II, 160: Hincmar, *Annales*, a. 864 (*MGH. SS.* I, 405ff); *De Imperatoria Potestate in Urbe Roma Libellus*, (ed. G. Zucchetti, Fonti per la Storia d'Italia, 1920), pp. 203–4.

gastalds, he received little support from Spoleto or Camerino, and it was with difficulty that the siege of Bari was established. Despite naval aid, the city resisted until February 872, when it capitulated. The sultan was made prisoner and Louis, his forces attenuated and the rest of his dominions demanding attention, withdrew. At Benevento that year the final blow to his ambitions in south Italy was delivered when Louis was seized at the palace by the Beneventans under prince Adelchis. His army, which had been dispersed in billets around the countryside, withdrew to Pavia without a leader. Adelchis could not detain so eminent a prisoner and therefore released him after extorting a promise not to exercise sovereignty over southern Italy. Louis' claim over a united Italy was demonstrably in ruins.[27]

Louis turned to the only potential allies now left to him: the Romans. Nicholas had died in 867; his domestic reign had been peaceable and prosperous. In Europe he had seen the Empire vanish in all but name, Louis' authority being confined to Italy, and his style one of prestige only. Nicholas had given the papacy an authoritative place in what remained of the European consciousness of unity, although by so doing he aroused the distrust of the Frankish church. On his death a Frankish chronicler remarked 'Since the blessed Gregory to the present day there has been no such prelate in Rome— to him alone can he be compared. He dominated kings and tyrants as though the Lord of the whole world had granted them and authority to him.' His successor, Hadrian, lacked his personality, but was placed in the papal chair by the nobility to whom he belonged. A priest of St. Mark and a member of the family of Sergius II and Stephen IV, his father Talarus had also been a bishop. The disorders of his election were a reaction against Nicholas's firmness, led by the indomitable bishop Arsenius. The Lateran was sacked and the *magister militum* Sergius absconded with the papal treasury; then duke Lambert of Spoleto intervened with a riotous mob of Franks and Lombards. His intervention was unofficial for Louis' representatives had already accepted Hadrian's election and confirmation had been received from the Emperor. It was a *razzia* looking for plunder and the opportunity to annexe border lands; churches were sacked, properties confiscated and presented to Lambert's supporters,

[27] F. Seneca, 'L'avventura di Louis II nell' Italia meridionale', (*Annali della Scuola Friulana*, 1951).

Germans or Franks resident in the city. In Emilia Archbishop John once again began to dispossess papal tenants and to disrupt administrative communications with Rome.[28]

Lambert at length withdrew and Hadrian, a milder man than Nicholas, began his policy of conciliating the Roman factions. Nicholas, he declared, had by his lack of compromise accentuated the troubles of the age; the Roman church, although its authority had been vindicated, was embroiled in ecclesiastical disputes in the East, in Italy and throughout France. Hadrian was more accommodating and exiles were recalled: the two leading Roman scholars, Bishop Gaudericus of Velletri and the deacon John Immonides, who had been banished by Louis, and Bishop Stephen of Nepi returned to Rome; the deposed archbishops and Bishop Zachary of Anagni, deprived by Nicholas, were reinstated. He was unable to heal the breaches in Roman politics, however. The adherents and admirers of Nicholas accused him of undoing the great pope's work, or wishing to nullify his acts and condemn his memory. Hadrian was compelled publicly to acknowledge his approval of the policy of his predecessor, to ratify his acts, and to complete the buildings works he had begun. This merely aroused the suspicion of Nicholas's opponents, led by Bishop Arsenius and his family.[29]

Roman politics were dominated by personal and family matters as individuals strove for influence to determine the policy that could lead to a local superiority or to the perpetuation of Nicholas's design for the papacy. Nicholas's supporters, led by Formosus of Porto, forced Hadrian round to their party; the reaction from Arsenius's family, when it came, was violent. Arsenius had a son, Eleutherius, who wishing to reinforce his family's position, proposed a marriage alliance between himself and a daughter of Hadrian–the pope had been married before ordination and had voluntarily separated from his wife. Such a marriage brought great advantages and wealth. A few years before one George had married a niece of Benedict III and had risen from obscurity to wealth in the process. But Hadrian's daughter was engaged to another and refused Eleutherius who thereupon abducted her and her mother from the Lateran. Making his escape, he wounded the pope; fearing pursuit he raped the girl and murdered both her and her mother. It wrecked his family's

[28] *LP*. II, 176–7.   [29] *LP*. II, 175.

ambitions. Arsenius fled with his treasure to Louis to gain his and the Empress Engelberga's support, but Eleutherius was surrendered to imperial envoys and condemned to death. Arsenius, his influence gone and travelling neglected in Louis' train, shortly afterwards died 'conversing with the devil'. Anastasius was arraigned before a church tribunal but declared his innocence of the whole affair; he was bound under heavy penalty to remain in Rome and to take no further part in affairs. This sentence he swore to observe and continued to act as papal secretary.[30]

At Pentecost in 872 Louis came to Rome after his release from Benevento, to an honourable welcome from pope, clergy and citizens. His prestige was weakened and he was in a mood to conciliate rather than to dominate the city. His hopes of creating an Italian kingdom were gone. To the Romans, clergy and nobility alike, this was advantageous; the recent activities of Rome's powerful neighbours, the dukes of Tuscany and Spoleto especially, demanded the services of a champion. The Romans now cast Louis to play the same role as the Frankish kingdom had in the previous century, with Spoleto taking the place of the Lombard kingdom – by that measure had the scale of power diminished. His reception in Rome was therefore enthusiastic, each party outdoing the other in flattery. As the triumphant captor of Bari he was 'crowned with the imperial laurel on the Capitol by the lord Pope Hadrian, the Roman people and the senate'. The pope released him from the vow extorted by Adelchis and the nobility, with their dreams of Rome's imperial status and the ancient partnership of senate and emperor, joined Louis in condemning Adelchis 'as an usurper and enemy to the republic', and in declaring war against him. It was an empty gesture; Louis withdrew to the north, leaving his wife Engelberga to conduct the vendetta against Benevento in her own name and in accordance with the family rivalries that dominated Italian politics. In any case the chief actors on the Italian stage shortly died, Hadrian in December 872, and Louis three years later.[31]

[30] Hincmar, *Annales*, a. 868.

[31] S. Pivano, 'La "Declaratio Senatus" dell' anno 872 contro il principe Adelchi di Benevento', (*Rivista di Storia del Diritto Italiano*, 23, 1950); on the re-emergent senate, see A. Paravicini, *Il Senato Romano*, (1901); A. Solmi, *Il senato Romano, 757–1143*, 1944.

Louis died without sons, after six direct successions in the Carolingian line from Charles Martel; the inheritance of both the Empire and the Italian kingdom lay vacant. Of the Carolingian line there remained Louis' two uncles, Charles, King of France and Louis, King of Germany, who had two sons, Charles the Fat and Carloman. Italian sympathy, led by Engelberga and the marquis Berengar of Friuli, himself a grandson of Louis the Pious, favoured the German branch, but the papacy had recently had more contact with Charles the Bald. His realm—longer settled, and more highly civilized—was militarily weaker, since it was open to the attacks of the Northmen and had suffered a diminution of the central power as defence became localized. Charles himself was almost a symbol of the Empire's loss of unity; the youngest son of Louis I by his Bavarian second wife, his father's attempts to create a kingdom for him from his half-brothers' shares had led to Louis' deposition. The French and German parts of the Empire were growing apart linguistically and politically; the Empire to which Charles succeeded in 875 differed greatly from that of his father and grandfather. The emperor was an equal of his kingly colleagues and spent his life contending with them; his style was a personal distinction only, while the openness of the accession after a series of hereditary transmissions gave the papacy and senate a sense of satisfaction which accorded with both the original creation of the Empire and antiquarian sentiment.

The pope who selected him was John VIII, the previous archdeacon of the city, who had been reigning for three years. He was a man of wide vision and statesmanship approaching that of Nicholas but his character was marred by an intransigence and intemperance that embroiled him unnecessarily in disputes within Rome and abroad. Determined to be master in all circumstances he sent an embassy, headed by Bishop Formosus of Porto, inviting Charles to Rome for imperial coronation. The news aroused resentment in Germany and Italy where a *diet* at Pavia had already invited Carloman to be king of Italy. But Charles accepted with alacrity and his journey through Italy in the autumn of 875 was unimpeded; on Christmas Day 875 he was crowned Emperor in St. Peter's having, a German chronicler noted bitterly, 'like Jugurtha, corrupted the senate and the whole Roman people with money'. But his authority was weak north of the Alps; in the south it was non-existent and with the Norman menace increasing no resources could be spared to revive it. His one ally was the papacy and this he planned to strengthen, as a counterweight to the Italian princes and a bulwark against the Arabs. He did not revoke his vestigial imperial powers, but the senate had been associated in his elevation and the traditional confirmation of the papal states was granted, with extensions that gave John authority over Campania and the county of Capua. Having therefore on paper created a strong and trustworthy power in central Italy he withdrew, first to Pavia to receive the Italian crown, and thence to France.

But John, whose purpose was to dominate Europe as firmly as Nicholas had done, found within Rome the same opposition to the French candidature that was common throughout Italy.[32] The Italian princes Adalbert of Tuscany and Guy of Spoleto, whom Charles had weakly confirmed in his protectorate over Rome, led the opposition to the French house. Each had interests in Rome; Adalbert had been commissioned by Louis II to secure Anastasius's election on the death of Leo IV, and Guy's brother Lambert had found a large body of German residents in the city to support his raid following the death of Nicholas. These German sympathizers formed a family network of Lateran and city officials, led by the formidable Bishop Formosus of Porto. Their position had already been threatened by John who had taken the opportunity of Charles's presence in the city to dismiss one of his ministers inherited from the previous reign, the *nomenclator* Gregory, replacing him with his own nephew Leo. Violent clashes between the two families followed. The leader of the opposition to John, Formosus, was a man who had already come under suspicion for his ambition; with a reputation for personal holiness he had been appointed Bishop of Porto by Nicholas in 864 and sent as legate to the Bulgarian mission in 866, but he was suspected of intriguing to gain the archiepiscopate of the newly-established Church and recalled within a year. He had contested John's election—although he later accepted the embassy to Charles of 875—and he had also maintained in Rome the tradition of Nicholas's vision for the papacy.[33] But the

[32] See G. Lapotre, *L'Europe et le Saint Siège a l'époque carolingienne: le pape Jean VIII*, (1895).

[33] See J. Duhr, 'Humble vestige d'un grand éspoir deçu. Episode de la vie de Formose', (*RSR*, 42, 1954).

wider policies before the Roman Church were overwhelmed in the struggles of family factions for power within the city.

The fighting between the factions increased in the early months of 876, and before Easter Formosus and his supporters were compelled to flee the city. They comprised a powerful group of Lateran officials but the threat of a summons to a synod to answer charges of corruption, ambition and immorality was one that could not be ignored. Their leaders, under Formosus, were the recently dismissed *nomenclator* Gregory, himself the son of a *nomenclator*, Theophylact; Gregory's brother the *secundicerius* Stephen who had a reputation as a plunderer of churches; the *magister militum* Sergius who had married a niece of Nicholas and having spent her money, deserted her for a concubine; and Gregory's daughter Constantina. Also belonging to the party was the man who had led the fighting against John's family, George surnamed 'of the Aventine'. He had risen from obscurity by marrying a niece of Pope Benedict III, but had been living openly with Constantina as man and wife. This group, threatened with various charges, fled through the St. Pancras gate on the night before Easter, using forged keys and taking with them as much of the papal treasury as they could.[34]

The consequences of this 'flight of the Tarquins' were for Italy and Rome the most divisive of the many defections from the city. They fled to duke Guy at Spoleto who refused John's demands for their return; from Spoleto they were able to build up a Formosan party in Pavia and the other pro-German towns of the Lombard north, and in Ravenna found a welcome supporter in Archbishop John. Papal legates, including John's nephew Bishop Leo, were arrested when they sought the extradition of the Formosans from Pavia. Archbishop John welcomed the defectors into Ravenna and a Formosan leader, Maurinus, raided Emilia, confiscated the holdings of papal tenants, and seized the *vestararius* who represented the papal government there, removing from him the keys of Ravenna and presenting them to the archbishop. From September to December 876 Spoletan troops raided Roman territory and Guy sent, in the emperor's name, demands for homage and hostages from the city. Pope John indignantly refused; the demand, he announced, had aroused the anger

[34] See P. Devos, 'La mystérieuse episode finale de la Vita Gregorii de Jean Diacre: La fuite de Formose', (*AB*, 82, 1964).

of the Roman assembly for 'nowhere is it to be read that under any sky had the sons of Romans been given as hostages'.

In Rome the enemies of Formosus and Gregory were triumphant. Their leaders were those whom John had sent to summon the rebels to answer charges in synod–Bishop Zachary of Anagni, the papal librarian, Bishop Gaudericus of Velletri and the *primicerius* Christopher, perhaps the father of the later Pope Leo VI. The two bishops belonged to the group of Roman scholars, erudite in the terms of the day, who were continuing the literary and historical tradition of Anastasius. It was one of this group, the deacon John Immonides, who in a literary pleasantry gave expression to their triumph. He had already lambasted the reputation of Bishop Formosus in a supplement to his *Life* of Gregory I which he had composed at John's request; his second effort was more popular, more ribald and more savage in its account of Roman personalities. The setting was the preparation for a supper-party; the literary device–traditionally ascribed to St. Cyprian to instruct the unlettered in the Scriptures–was that Biblical personages each took an appropriate part in laying the table. Deacon John complacently described his audience's reaction; Bishop Gaudericus rolling helpless with laughter on his couch, the more austere Zachary gazing with admiration at his skill. A local butt for humour was the subdeacon Crescentius, prior of the *Schola Cantorum*, an old man with a stammer and dyspepsia; the difficulties he encountered with these two afflictions in controlling small boys and in singing before the pope are, with perhaps not over-much subtlety, subject for John's attentions.[35]

Literary crowing was not sufficient. With Rome and Italy permanently split, it was vital that John should gain greater control of the papal government, weakened by the loss of many personnel. In March 877 he convoked a synod at Ravenna, the centre of opposition to him, to review and reorganize his temporal power. An attack was launched against the 'tyrant dukes' who were trying to make appointive offices hereditary, exploiting the administration of justice and denying the Church its proper revenues. Leases of church properties to private persons had become uncontrolled; further

[35] A. Lapotre, 'Le Souper de Jean Diacre', (*MAH*, 21, 1901): see also G. Arnaldi, 'Giovanni Immonide e la cultura Romana al tempo di Giovanni VIII', (*BISI*, 68, 1956).

alienations and the granting of church offices, abbacies and convents, were prohibited. There was a review of all taxation, of harbourage and riverage dues, and of the organization of the Roman mint. The traditional structure of the papal patrimonies was strengthened. The great Sabine patrimony, which had grown considerably during the previous century, was divided into two and these lands were to remain under direct papal administration, with no benefices granted from them.[36]

John had every need of money to counteract the Arab situation which had deteriorated since the withdrawal of Louis II. From their now permanent encampment on the Garigliano river they dominated Campania and raided into Lazio, the Sabine Hills and southern Tuscany. One of the gravest charges against the 'Tarquins' was that in their flight they had left the gate open and, with wandering bands of Arab marauders in the area, had placed the city at real risk. The Campanian dynasts and cities were at permanent loggerheads. Naples was under the domination of a dynasty which held both the duchy and the bishopric, but disputes within the family produced no assured hope of unanimous co-operation. The last of the brothers of the house of Capua, Landolf, had formed an alliance with Salerno, Naples, Gaeta and Amalfi to regain Capua for himself; for this he was also using mercenaries. John made several offers to form a united front; the papal patrimonies of Traetto and Fondi were offered to count Pandulf of Capua but this antagonized the senior magistrate of Gaeta, the *hypatos* Docibilis, who threatened to form an alliance with the Arabs. In 877 John went to Naples to try to end Campanian intrigue; he had some success with the prince of Salerno but duke Sergius of Naples refused co-operation and was excommunicated. In June 877 the pope summoned a conference of all interested parties to be held at Traetto. The papal city of Terracina was granted to Gaeta as a naval base but the conference ultimately failed since the jealous states would not combine.[37]

In the North the German Carolingians were preparing for war. Charles the Bald made only one more visit to Italy, in the autumn of 877, and the pope went to meet him at Vercelli but in October the

[36] Mansi, 17, 336.

[37] F. E. Engreen, 'Pope John the Eighth and the Arabs', (*Speculum*, 20, 1945).

Emperor died, by poison it was rumoured. The German Carloman, who was in North Italy with an army, easily secured recognition as king of Italy and John's whole political position collapsed. He was in urgent need of a protector and played, with some desperation and duplicity, for time. There were three choices before him. Charles had left a son, the incapable Louis the Stammerer and a cousin, duke Boso of Provence; in the East the general Basil had seized the throne and was vigorously prosecuting the war in the central Mediterranean. His admiral Basil Nazar was on the point of driving the Arabs from Sicily, permitting Elias after forty-five years exile in the East to return to his home in Palermo. Finally, there was the dominant Germany party in Italy. The decision was taken out of John's hands. Plague compelled Carloman to withdraw to Bavaria, but meanwhile his Italian supporters acted. John wrote in flattering terms to duke Lambert of Spoleto, acclaiming him as the Church's protector but prohibiting him or Adalbert from entering Rome. Early in 878, however, the combined Spoletan and Tuscan armies appeared before Rome, bringing with them the Formosan exiles. John , in the Leonine City, was cut off from Rome, which was soon surrendered by the magnates who swore allegiance to Carloman. Although John was shut up in the Vatican for a month under strict duress, he refused to consider a German candidate for the Empire; the Spoletan troops, as usual, looted within the city. But Lambert could not keep his army in Rome for long and, after reinstating the exiles, withdrew. John, emerging from the Vatican, proclaimed a state of mourning; no pilgrims were admitted, the treasures were removed from St. Peter's and the altars covered with sackcloth. To the Emperor Basil he wrote a lament on Rome's plight: 'She sits in sorrow, or rather in ruin, this mistress of the nations, the queen of cities, the mother of churches, the consolation of the sorrowful, the refuge of the endangered.' Rome's influence appeared to have vanished.

With the reinstated Formosans disputing his control of the city, John could not remain in Rome. In April he fled by sea to France and was taken by duke Boso to Troyes, where he crowned Louis the Stammerer as Emperor. But questioned on intervention in Italy Louis showed his incapacity; John thereupon turned to the more vigorous, unscrupulous Boso, promising him a royal title in Provence, hopes of the imperial crown, and naming him as his adoptive son. In the spring of 878 Boso accompanied the pope back to Italy but they were unable to win over the bishops and counts of Lombardy to Louis' cause. John was able once more to take up residence in Rome for Lambert stood in awe of Boso, and was able to continue the search for a champion who would unite Italy against the Arabs and yet not overbear on Rome herself. His last years were spent in feverish and wide-ranging diplomacy, negotiating in France, in Germany and in the East. At last some fruit was borne; the brothers of the German branch proposed in consideration of Carloman's illness to place their second brother Charles the Fat on the imperial throne. John reluctantly agreed and in 879 Charles was crowned King of Italy at Pavia; early in 881 he came to Rome for his imperial coronation.

Thenceforth he did nothing for Rome and John, who had fulfilled his part by denouncing his former champion Boso as an usurper, was left without allies. Within Rome the Formosans gave him no peace and Spoletan raids into Roman territory were carried on by Guy III who succeeded his brother Lambert as duke. John continued to plead with Charles, but the loss of papal properties and the mutilation of papal tenants and murders of the country-people, could not induce the Emperor to intervene. John's agony of helplessness, acute for so masterful a soul, continued until he died, ten days before Christmas 882. Rumour had it that he was murdered by his servants who fractured his head after poison had been found too slow in working. His pontificate marked the last attempt to revive a united Empire against common enemies, the last initiative of the papacy to dictate to rival princes. He had failed in the tangle of local feuds and ambitions and through the defects of his own hasty, devious temperament. Under Spoletan influence his enemies were supreme in Rome and Ravenna, and the papacy's independence was at an end.

10

ROME AND THE DYNASTS

The interruption of the direct succession to the Empire on the death of Louis II and the throwing open of the supreme honour to rival branches of the Carolingian family introduced a new dominant feature into the European politics of the late ninth century. The Empire had recreated in Europe an international nobility; families whose power was locally based also retained, through their winding genealogies, royal or semi-royal claims to higher status. Duke Boso of Provence exemplified this, for his sister had married Charles the Bald and he himself, having reputedly poisoned his first wife, married Irmengard, the sole child and heiress of Louis II. He had inherited his father-in-law's Italian interests and his ruthlessness marked him out as a potential king of Italy to Pope John, who granted him the royal style for Provence. The major potentate of northern Italy was the marquis Berengar of Friuli, who was through his mother a grandson of Louis I; his father Everard was a Frank who had settled in Italy under Lothair and was made by him marquis of Friuli. Berengar married Bertilla, heiress of a Lombard family of Parma who was also the niece of the Empress Engelberga. Marquis Adalbert of Tuscany had succeeded his father Boniface, another of Lothair's appointments, and had married a sister of duke Lambert of Spoleto with whose house he remained closely allied. The house of Spoleto shows similar origins and growth. A count Lambert was in Italy by 834 and his son Guy, marrying a niece of Louis I's second wife Judith, became duke of Spoleto in 842; dying in 866 he was succeeded by his elder son Lambert until 879, then briefly by Lambert's son Guy II, and then by Lambert's brother Guy III. The family took advantage of the disordered state of Italy to increase its territories, intervening in the struggles of the Campanian towns and counties; Sora, Arpino, Atina and Vicalbo were all annexed to the duchy, as well as papal territory in the Sabine region, the duchy of Rome and Emilia. Guy III married Ageltrude, sister of prince Radelchis of Benevento, and as champions of the German party within Italy he and Lambert built up a network of influence throughout the country.[1]

Nor was this dilution of royal and imperial claims confined to the Western Empire. In Constantinople the new imperial Macedonian dynasty was faced with a long regency from 912 on behalf of the six-year-old Constantine Porphyrogennitus. Successive noble families, the Argyri and the Phocae, directed the government until, in 919, the *arriviste* admiral Romanus Lecapenus was crowned emperor-regent and married his large family into the imperial dynasty and into those of his rivals. More resources were brought to the service of the emerging dynasts by the capture of ecclesiastical posts in the East, in the cities of southern Italy such as Naples, and in northern Europe. The scale of effective power throughout Europe had dwindled; the reign of Louis II and the diplomacy of John VIII had firmly tied the imperial crown to Italian and Roman interests, but had emasculated the office – it was a time of great opportunities for the lesser dynasts.[2]

The Roman scene reflected the larger. There the senate, the digni-fied name granted to an oligarchy of nobles, had the preponderant influence, but the term covered shifting factions and struggles for ascendancy. The basis of power was the resources of the Roman Church, its dignities, lands and revenues. In spite of John VIII's decrees, more papal property was falling into the hands of the nobility as benefice-holders or administrators, and this made avail-able to them military power and riches.[3] The richest prizes were open only to churchmen, as titulars of the city churches or the diaconal regions, or of the suburbicarian sees. Politics were embittered since the disavowal of a pope's policy involved also a disavowal of his acts, his appointments and his ordinations. A new set of appointments or the return of dispossessed clerics served to put offices in constant dispute, and so revolution, through the questioning of personal worthiness and of the validity of orders, brought a new, deeper divi-sion into Roman politics.

[1] For a summary of post-Carolingian Italy see G. Parazzoli, *Dis-soluzione dell' impero carolingio e regno feudale in Italia*, (1960).

[2] S. Runciman, *The Emperor Romanus Lecapenus and his reign*, (1929).

[3] See for senatorial acquisition of papal lands, P. Partner, 'Notes on the lands of the Roman Church in the early Middle Ages', (*Papers of the British School at Rome*, 21, 1966). See also G. Falco, 'L'amministrazione papale nella Campagna e nella Marittima', (*ASR*, 38, 1915).

This bitterness was amply demonstrated during the pontificates of the two successors to John, both in themselves nonentities. Marinus, elected in December 882, had served as a papal legate in Constantinople where he had become a bitter enemy of the patriarch Photius. His election was an innovation for he was already bishop of Cervetri and although there had been during the ninth century a movement towards the relaxation of the rule, the canons of the Church traditionally forbade translation: a bishop remained wedded to his see until death. The two years of Marinus's pontificate showed some amelioration of the papacy's situation–Charles the Fat had grown alarmed at the rapid rise of the house of Spoleto and was looking for an ally. In 883 Marinus and Charles met at the abbey of Nonantola near Bologna to plan concerted action, and the marquis Berengar was commissioned to invade Spoletan territory. But Guy, already in touch with the Byzantines and with his eye on southern Italy, hired Arab mercenaries from Campania and defeated the Friulian army. In accordance with his German sympathies, Marinus had recalled and reinstated Formosus and George of the Aventine, but his death in 884 was the occasion for another revolution. The new pope, Hadrian III, inherited John's anti-German sympathies and was elected only amid considerable disorder. He had George of the Aventine, the leading civil member of the Formosan party, arrested and blinded, along with others of John's enemies. Maria, the wife of a *superista* who had murdered a colleague in the gardens by St. Peter's, was arrested, bound, and dragged naked through the streets, and the imperial *missus* in the city was also detained. The aristocracy closed its ranks against the pope who set off to seek help from the Emperor. The enmity of the Romans, especially of Maria's husband, and of Ravenna pursued him; his death in September 885 near Nonantola was perhaps procured by the Formosans. His body was rifled by the monks of the abbey, and in Rome the nobility and people once more plundered the Lateran. Charles made efforts to obtain the election of a friendly successor but the Romans put forward a noble, Stephen, priest of the *Quattuor Coronati*, whose election was approved by the imperial *missus* and throughout the duchy; he received the homage of all classes and groups within the city.

Late in 887 Charles the Fat abdicated in favour of his brother's bastard son Arnulf, and died in January 888. On his death, Arnulf

288

retained possession of Germany; Louis, son of Boso, held Provence, and Odo, the count of Paris, relying on personal prestige gained in the defence of Paris against the Northmen, took the title of king of France. Only in Italy was there a vacuum of power. It was soon filled by Guy of Spoleto who had no rival after his defeat of Berengar, and was acclaimed king at Pavia in 889 with the especial support of the bishops, having 'deserved well of Italy'. Stephen V saw in this the worst dangers of the reign of Louis II revived – a king dominant in Italy and an end to Rome's independence. The city and the papal government were bankrupt, a severe famine threatened after a bad harvest, and the plundered Lateran could not supply food from outside. In Ravenna the successor to Archbishop John, Romanus, had used his good offices with Charles the Fat to secure his recognition of Stephen. His price had been a formal acknowledgement of his see's independence of Rome, and he was able at last to unite the clergy and people of Emilia under him. The papal search for a counterpoise to the Italian king continued. Messages were sent to the Emperor Leo the Wise, son of Basil, asking that the Byzantine fleet take responsibility for the protection of the Campanian coast from the Arabs, and appeals for aid against the Lombards, couched in terms similar to those of the previous century, were made to Swentibold, Arnulf's son who was king in Moravia. But external help was not available: in Eastern Europe the Hungarian menace was building up, and Rome was unable to resist Spoletan pressure. Guy had been temporarily distracted by the opportunities of obtaining recognition as king in France where a relative, Archbishop Folco of Rheims, was working on his behalf. His absence enabled Berengar to assume for a short time the style of king of Italy, but on his return Guy reasserted his position and in February 891 constrained Stephen to crown him and his wife as Emperor and Empress in St. Peter's. In the autumn of that year Stephen died, leaving behind a reputation for peace-making, charity and holiness.

He was succeeded by the man who, before his election, during his pontificate and after his death, was a perpetual centre of faction and controversy and had given his name to the party that divided Italy – Formosus of Porto. As one of Nicholas's principal legates, he had served in Constantinople and had aimed at the archbishopric of the newly-established Bulgarian Church, but Nicholas forced him to decline the office. John VIII had distrusted him and they had fallen out over the succession to Louis II: Formosus was excommunicated and deprived of his orders. In exile he had skilfully built up a party throughout Italy of those opposed to papal policy and favourable to the German cause–the dissidents of Emilia, members of the Roman nobility, and the house of Spoleto. In 883 Marinus restored him to his full honours and now, after a career that had left bitterness and division wherever it had touched, he became pope in his own turn. He had a reputation for personal sanctity and his election, his apologists maintained, was popular, even enthusiastic: 'The princes, the regiments and the commanders, the crowd and the foreign communities, from the highest to the lowest, chose him, acclaimed him, praised and reverenced him; and the bishops, with the officials of the Lateran, enthroned him.'[4]

There was, however, some violence during his election, for a deacon Sergius, the leader of Spoleto's partisans in the city, put himself forward as a rival and from the start of Formosus' pontificate conflicting influences weakened his policies. Although in the past he had been friendly to the house of Spoleto which had championed him in exile, as pope he wished to rid Rome of a dangerous neighbour. His own instincts now inclined him towards Guy's defeated rival Berengar, but the Roman magnates, more imperialist in tendency, urged him to call in Arnulf, and Formosus, torn between the two, played a double game. Spoleto was assured of his friendship, and in 892 at Ravenna the pope crowned Guy's son Lambert as co-emperor. It was an unwilling alliance but Guy had a strong party within the city, led by Sergius and two nobles, Constantine and Stephen, which could not be ignored. Formosus tried to neutralize Sergius as a rival by consecrating him bishop of Cere, and so jeopardizing his chances of gaining the papacy. Guy's campaign against Berengar was successful. The marquis fled to Arnulf; to him also came messages from Formosus, begging for the liberation of Italy from those evil Christians who menaced both the Holy See and the Italian kingdom. Swentibold was sent into Italy by his father, but Adalbert of Tuscany stood firm in his alliance with Guy, and the Germans withdrew.

[4] See G. Domenici, 'Il Papa Formoso', (*Civiltà Cattolica*, an. 75, vols. I and II, 1924).

In December 894 the death of Guy gave new hope for a successful intervention, and Arnulf himself led an army into Italy. Resistance was led by the indomitable Ageltrude, Guy's widow, on behalf of her son, but Arnulf took Pavia and Milan and Adalbert yielded himself as his vassal. Ageltrude withdrew through Tuscany, offering strong local resistance which cost Arnulf severe casualties, to Rome where her supporters 'were preponderant within the senate'. By October 895 Arnulf had reached Rome and camped by the St. Pancras gate. Ageltrude had prepared a vigorous defence. She supervised the watch on the walls herself and arrested Formosus, appointing in his place an anti-pope, Boniface. For a moment Arnulf hesitated, but German contempt for the Romans, degenerate since their imperial days, counselled a surprise attack. Resistance was severe; it broke only in late February and even then the Spoletans and their supporters were able to escape from the city. Arnulf formally entered the city across the Milvian Bridge, the imperial entry, and was welcomed by senate and *scholae*; the liberated Formosus crowned him Emperor on the steps of St. Peter's. The Romans, summoned to the basilica, took an oath of loyalty to the new Emperor: 'I swear, by these, all God's mysteries and saving my honour, the law I live by and my fidelity to the lord Pope Formosus that I am and will remain all my days faithful to the Emperor Arnulf, and will never associate myself with any man in disloyalty to him; that I will never show to Lambert or to Ageltrude his mother, any help to obtain secular power; nor will I betray this city of Rome to Lambert or to his mother Ageltrude or their men, for any consideration or argument.' Ageltrude's Roman supporters, Constantine and Stephen, were arrested and exiled to Germany; one of Arnulf's vassals, Faroald, was installed as his representative in Rome. But Arnulf's triumph was brief. Suffering a stroke, he withdrew to Germany and his chief Italian ally Berengar, deciding that it was useless to continue the struggle against Spoleto, agreed with Lambert on a delimitation of spheres of influence within Italy. On 4th April 896 the aged Formosus died. Italy was once more self-contained.[5]

---

[5] See G. Arnaldi, 'Papa Formoso e gli imperatori della Casa di Spoleto', (*Annuario della Facoltà di Letteratura e filosofia dell' Università di Napoli,* I, 1951).

Formosus's policy had proved an anachronism. Roman society was already looking inward upon itself and Formosus's attempts to relate it to a wider, European horizon, such as he had known as Nicholas's legate, resulted only in the temporary and destructive irruption of external forces that had not the strength to sustain a permanent power and government. His failure likewise meant the local reaction in Rome which had become a feature of Roman life, leading to further discord and bitterness. On Formosus's death Ageltrude's anti-pope Boniface VI made a brief reappearance, probably elevated by popular tumult and anti-German feeling, but within a fortnight he had succumbed to gout and his place was taken by the bishop of Anagni, a relative of Bishop Zachary, under Spoletan influence, who became Stephen VI.

Stephen's vengeance–directed by Spoleto–turned on the memory, reputation and remains of Formosus and on his followers. In February or March 897 a synod was assembled in the presence of the Emperor Lambert and his mother. The tomb of Formosus was broken open and his corpse, dressed in full pontificals, was placed in a chair as defendant before the synod; a deacon stood by as his advocate. The grisly scene was fully played out. Pope Stephen shrieked his accusations at the corpse–of usurping as Bishop of Porto the papal throne, of his enmity against John VIII, of his amibition and of his re-entry into Rome while the ban still ran against him. The wretched deacon offered no defence for his principal and Formosus was condemned. Three fingers of his right hand, the hand of benediction, were cut off, his vestments stripped from him, and his corpse thrown into the river. All his acts and ordinations were annulled, consequently securing the position of Stephen himself since his consecration to Anagni was made void. Although the trial took the form of a synod, it was a political action, reflecting the localization of the struggle for power and the enmities and policies it bred. The papal government had sunk so far since the days of Nicholas that Formosus could be accused of meddling in foreign affairs to the damage of the Roman state. Under the house of Spoleto Rome was to be another local Italian power, easily controlled, and in Stephen they had a puppet. 'To whom shall I liken you, Stephen, more cruel than the most cruel?' wrote a supporter of Formosus, 'Surely not to Nero or to Diocletian or to the other tyrants? Nowhere can we read that they did such things to a corpse already so many days old.'[6]

Stephen himself survived his synod by six months; in reaction against its horror the Romans, led by those clerics who had lost orders, offices and influence by the annulling of Formosus's acts, rose against him. Formosus's qualities were remembered: his vigour as papal legate in defence of Catholicism, his work of repairing and decorating the Roman churches. Stephen was seized, stripped in his turn of his pontifical vestments, and thrown into prison. A few days later he was strangled. A certain Romanus was chosen in his place and ruled for four months. He was succeeded by Theodore who lived only twenty days, but in that time assembled a synod of local bishops to rehabilitate Formosus and to restore those involved in his degradation. Formosus' body had been found, washed ashore at a bend in the river. Redressed in its vestments, it was given honourable burial in St. Peter's. Theodore's death, early in 898, was followed by a double election. Ageltrude's partisan, the deacon Sergius whom Formosus had forcibly consecrated to Cere, which he later renounced, and who had participated in the synod of the corpse, made a reappearance, but the Formosans put forward John, son of a Lombard of Tivoli, whom they enthroned as John IX. For six years he and his successors, managing to exclude Sergius, attempted to reach a more moderate and pacifying policy and to hold out against the localizing tendencies that threatened to enclose Rome. A synod in St. Peter's examined the conduct of those who had taken part in the synod of the corpse and the status of many whose ordinations were now of uncertain validity—John himself had been ordained priest by Formosus. Formosus's accusers begged for absolution since they had been acting under fear and compulsion and, in accordance with his moderation, John absolved and reinstated them. The prime offenders were excluded, the anti-pope Sergius, the priests Benedict and Marinus, and the deacons Leo, Paschal and John. They had taken refuge in Tuscan territory and were preparing armed invasion.

More important was a *rapprochement* with Lambert whom John encouraged in his desire to rule in peace, and to whom he gave wholehearted co-operation. In the synod of St. Peter's it was declared

[6] Liutprand of Cremona, *Antapodosis*, I, 30: Auxilius, *In defensionem Sacrae Ordinationis papae Formosi*, (in E. Dummler, *Auxilius und Vulgaris*, 1866).

that future papal elections must be held under the supervision of imperial representatives, to prevent the bloodshed of recent events. Lambert's position was strengthened by John's declaration that Arnulf's coronation had been forced upon Formosus; Arnulf was dying in Germany and Berengar alone could not challenge Spoleto. Later in the same year John went further in his acknowledgement of imperial supremacy. A second synod at Ravenna declared the emperor to be sovereign of all, to whom all Romans had the right of appeal–the hindrance of this right was a major crime. The property of the Roman Church was stabilized as from the coronation of Guy, all subsequent alienations being revoked, and the protection of the secular power was invoked for the maintenance of order during papal interregna.[7]

Such a compact giving, on paper, the greatest powers over Rome enjoyed by any emperor was sorely needed, for the condition of Rome and the countryside was distressful. In the tumults and the successive sackings the Lateran palace was burnt and greatly weakened; during the pontificate of Stephen VI it collapsed and could not be fully repaired. In the countryside, Pope John complained, the magnates were living by banditry, terrorizing or murdering the *contadini*; the roads were too unsafe to transport the beams he had acquired for the repair of the Lateran. Above all the Arabs, from their great camp on the Garigliano, were plundering Campania, Lazio and Tuscany. The Neapolitans deliberately destroyed the great Lucullanum monastery outside the walls, in case it should serve as cover for an attack on the city itself. In 840 St. Benedict's monastery at Subiaco was sacked by an Arab band: rebuilt a few years later, it was again destroyed. Farfa–the richest of the central Italian monasteries, in the Sabine Hills–which had thrived on the patronage of emperors, Lombard kings and dukes of Spoleto for nearly two centuries, was besieged in 890. The abbot Peter summoned the abbey's vassals from its extensive holdings and endured the siege for seven years in the fortress-like foundation while its estates were ravaged. Then, realizing the impossibility of survival, he sent the abbey's treasures to Rome, Rieti and Spoleto for safe-keeping and abandoned the monastery. The Arabs spared it, using it merely as an

[7] Mansi, 18, 233; J. Duhr, 'Le Concile de Ravenne, 898: Le rehabilitation du pape Formose', (*RSR*, 22, 1932).

encampment, but Italian stragglers from the disorders, finding it empty, continued the looting and burnt it; it was not rebuilt for thirty years. Smaller bands of Arabs held strongpoints in the hills, at Ciciliano and Saracinesco, dominating the entire county of Narni and threatening the roads from Spoleto and Rieti into Rome. North of Rome the basilica of Silva-Candida, the seat of a cardinal-bishop and the site of a *domusculta*, was also plundered. 'For thirty years the Saracens ruled in the Roman countryside and the land was made a desert,' wrote the monk Benedict of the monastery of St. Andrew on Monte Soratte.[8] Lambert–young, energetic and sincere in his desire for good government–held out to Italy a hope that the country had not seen for nearly half a century, and although he had been forced into the alliance, John was working hard to make it a success, even at the expense of many traditional Roman prejudices. The full realization of how far authority imperial and religous, had departed from Rome was expressed in the contemporary *Versus Romae*–only in the East was any success being achieved against the common enemy of Christianity. In Italy opposition to the alliance was not dead. Sergius had joined the marquis of Tuscany who presented himself as a candidate for the crown of Italy in the summer of 898. He marched on Pavia, but was intercepted and defeated by Lambert.

Italian hopes were dashed when Lambert was killed while hunting in north Italy. Once more the opportunity was seized by Berengar, who hastened from his capital at Verona and established himself as king in Pavia, from where he naturally looked towards Rome and the imperial crown. He was supported by Adalbert of Tuscany and Guy's widow Ageltrude, and the death of Arnulf in 899 secured his position further. But his misfortunes continued. At this favourable moment there burst upon Italy the terrible onslaught of the Magyar tribes, mounted archers from the Hungarian plains, who overwhelmed Berengar's army on the Brenta in September 899, destroying his hopes and prestige. His enemies in Italy rallied and invited Louis, the son of Boso of Provence, to be their king. He came amid great acclaim but before he reached Rome the second architect of the brief revival of Italian concord–'the mirror of the Church, the most shining jewel

[8] Benedict of St. Andrew, *Chronicon*, (ed. G. Zucchetti). *Destructio Monasterii Farfensis*, in Gregory of Catino, *Chronicon Farfensis*, (ed. U. Balzani, 1903).

of goodness'–John IX, had died. For a brief moment he and Lambert had seemed to remove the papacy from the round of local politics, and at Ravenna to have initiated a reform of Church and civil life. The synod there, attended by one hundred and twenty bishops, was the largest audience the papacy was to have for nearly a century.

The posthumous career of Formosus was not yet over. John's successor was Benedict IV who followed in Formosus' footsteps by crowning the last member of the French Carolingians, the lords of Provence, to counterbalance to Berengar's power, but the alliance took little effect. The anti-Formosans under Sergius had a powerful influence in the major Italian cities and the French were chary of Italian adventures. Benedict was rapidly succeeded by Leo V and Christopher, neither of whom made much impact on either Rome or the Church. Christopher lasted one month before the anti-Formosans gained control of the city. Sergius had found a new ally, a Frankish adventurer named Alberic who in 898 had murdered the young son of Lambert and seized Spoleto for himself. With his help and through the 'machinations of certain Romans' Sergius returned to power. Once more the full fury of persecution was directed against the memory and the partisans of Formosus; he and his acts were condemned and a bishop was deposed for speaking unguardedly of Formosus as a priest. Sergius dated his pontificate from 897 when he had first sought power and charges of desertion to the Saracens were issued against the dissident clergy. The savagery of the reign of Stephen IV was renewed.[9]

It was however only a temporary reaction. The disorders had increased the power of the oligarchy of nobles, collectively the senate, who since the days of John VIII had looked more frequently for support to Spoleto–it had been through their invitation that Alberic was brought to Rome. The acts of Louis of Provence during his brief visit to Rome for his coronation show him surrounded by a bloc of the nobility–the magistrates of Rome, consuls and dukes–who under weak popes disposed of the papal administration and estates. As the nobility extended its influence it captured the well-endowed secular

[9] P. Fedele, 'Ricerche per la storia di Roma e del papato nel secolo X: I: Sergio III', (*ASR*, 33, 1910).

and clerical posts and, since the standards of the monks were in decline as the lands of the monasteries were wasted by the Saracens or Hungarians, the papacy had no independent source of official personnel.

Within this oligarchy, in the years following the death of John IX, one family rose to pre-eminence, controlling much of the patronage of office and managing Rome's shrunken connections with the outside world. The founder of the family's power, Theophylact, may have been connected with the *nomenclator* Gregory who was dismissed by John VIII. Theophylact rose steadily in the official *cursus* of honours: in 901 he was recorded as *iudex*, a simple official; in 904 he was *vestararius*, head of the papal treasury, possibly with outside functions as well, and shortly afterwards *magister militum*, commander of the army. Other titles were *gloriosissimus dux*, and in 915 'senator of the Romans', the singular emphasizing his pre-eminence over the other nobles of the city. His wife the *vestararissa* Theodora was a vigorous woman but, unlike the other remarkable women of this family, charitable, pious and faithful to her husband. 'The scent of your piety spreads everywhere; everywhere you diffuse the sweet smell of Christ, as your sacred piety delights the world. We have heard from many the tale of your holy life and conduct and we rejoice with a spiritual joy that God has placed you as a lamp to be an example to the men of this age. Further in you we embrace what we should especially observe in mankind, a holy marriage, a chaste bed, hospitality, alms, a watchfulness over the guardians of the saints, a divine eloquence, a care that preserves us.' Theophylact was 'lord of one city but that city comprised the whole world'. Their home was in the aristocratic quarter of Rome, the Via Lata where the family of Hadrian I had lived; there they restored and beautified the church of S. Maria *in Via Lata*.[10]

The society over which they presided was an enclosed one. European unity was destroyed in the ruin of the Carolingian Empire, the papacy was no longer a universal office, and the flow of pilgrims from the north had slackened through fear of the Saracens in southern France and Italy. But the consciousness of Roman

[10] G. Falco, 'La prima dinastia di Roma medievale', (*Albori d'Europa, pagine di storia medievale*, 1947).

particularity was at its height; Eugenius Vulgaris's eulogy of Theophylact and Theodora echoes the words of Sidonius Apollinaris in the fifth century in acknowledging the universality of Rome. Through the ninth century the Romans had fought for their independence of a local power and for their special status within the Empire; in the absence of an Empire the Roman past was preserved there alone. When the Saxon dynasty revived the Empire in the mid-tenth century, they received from Rome a more vigorous consciousness of its ancient antecedents, a consciousness that Charlemagne's Empire, built up away from Rome, had never possessed.[11]

This appreciation fed the reaction to Sergius's violent partisan policies which were seen as detracting from Rome's nobility; the tradition of Formosus continued as that of an earnest and statesmanlike pope who had worked for the good of religion and the Christian world. A vigorous pamphlet warfare grew up in defence of his memory and of the memory of Rome as the visible, active centre of the world. Auxilius, a southern Frank living in Naples, wrote primarily in defence of the orders conferred by Formosus or his followers which Sergius was declaring to be invalid – he had himself been ordained by Formosus and the matter was of immediate concern. Eugenius Vulgaris was perhaps a native of the Sabine region, an area which from the eighth century had shown a marked distrust of successive Roman governments. Above all the anonymous author of the *Invectiva in Urbem Romam*, writing probably between 914 and 928, shows a love of Rome as the unique city – her crimes are acknowledged but her imperial and Christian associations are emphasized almost to excuse them. One thing only betrays and prostitutes her, the imprisonment of the papacy by the senate who are incapable of rising above local interests and allowing the city and the Church to resume their proper place. The author pictures the anger of Christ: 'Where, O Rome, is your great nobility and your ancient, unconquered strength? For if the cabal of your princes carries off the apostolic see, then the valour of your nobles and the wisdom of your leaders will slumber in waste. . . . O Rome, backslider and apostate, in madness and frenzy you rave . . . turn to the Lord and you will be

[11] G. Arnaldi, 'Appunti sulla crisi dell' autorità pontificia in età postCarolingia', (*Studi Romani*, 9, 1961); G. Falco, 'Particolarismo e universalismo nella Roma del secolo X', (*Studi Romani*, II, 1954).

saved ... we beg for peace, we seek concord and for you, O Rome, who are the head of us all, for you we beg healing.'[12]

Sergius's rancour against the memory of Formosus was transitory, and his authority was soon limited by the nobility led by the Theophylacts. An approach from the pope to Berengar offering him the imperial crown was countered by the Romans and their allies – Alberic of Spoleto, Adalbert of Tuscany and Archbishop John of Ravenna. The alignment itself shows that Rome was claiming no imperial role but was to be regarded as a power on the level of Spoleto, Tuscany and Emilia, and this equality removed much of the tension in Italian politics. Personal relationships were established with the other Italian states; Alberic of Spoleto was to marry Marozia, the daughter of Theophylact and Theodora, and Archbishop John who was a friend of Theodora acted as intermediary to establish peace with Berengar. The domination of Theophylact's party provided continuity and order following the death in 911 of Sergius III. He was succeeded by Anastasius III and Lando, both shadowy figures. The first reigned for two years and the latter for six months; on his death, the Theophylacts summoned to the papal throne their friend and colleague, John of Ravenna.[13]

The reputation of the Theophylact dynasty and of its women, Theodora and her daughter Marozia especially, has been largely coloured by later Italian and imperialist sentiment, expressed most vividly by Bishop Liutprand of Cremona later in the century. That Rome, the *urbs ecclesiae*, should be dominated not by clerics but by a lay family in which the women took an equal initiative with the men; that the city and the papacy should have seemingly abdicated their special positions in relation to the world and be content to remain the local power base for a minor dynasty – these conditions were insupportable to those formed in the tradition of Formosus and

[12] The principal polemical writings are: Auxilius, *In defensionem sacrae ordinationis papae Formosi*; Auxilius, *De Ordinationibus a Formoso factis*; Auxilius, *Tractatus qui infensor et defensor dicitur*; Auxilius, *Libellus in defensionem Stephani episcopi*. Eugenius Vulgaris, *De causa formosiana libellus*; Eugenius Vulgaris, *Libellus super causa et negotio Formosi papae*. Anon., *Invectiva in Urbem Romam*, (*PL.* 129, 823ff); see also O. Pop, *La defence du pape Formose*, (1933).

[13] See P. Fedele, *Ricerche* (*cit.*); III, 'Le lettere dell' arcivescovo Giovanni di Ravenna,' (*ASR*, 34, 1911); IV, 'L'elezione di Giovanni X', (*ibid.*).

Nicholas. Eugenius, Auxilius and the author of the *Invectiva* all loved Rome and abhorred those who had thus diminished her status; and Liutprand–writing after the event and uncertain of chronology and facts–as a servant of the revived Roman Empire in the West seeking to justify it in the East, could only explain this sinister domination by citing moral degradation. So archbishop John of Ravenna, who as a deacon had been on a mission to Rome, was credited with having been the lover of Theodora; Marozia in her turn was accused of having been, as a young girl, the mistress of Sergius III by whom she had a son, the future John XI. The chronology of the latter is hardly possible and the likelihood of the former small; even Sergius's contemporary Eugenius welcomed the work of the pope and of the senator in restoring the physical aspect of Rome after its disorders. The Lateran basilica was at last rebuilt, with greater splendour. Pope Sergius added the dedication to St. John to the old patronage of the Saviour and the basilica now replaced St. Peter's as the normal burial place for the popes. The papal palace was also restored and redecorated; magnificent mosaics and frescoes and adulatory inscriptions made it once more a palace worthy of the leading functionary of Europe. 'Now let golden Rome rejoice, for the broken leaves now rise again; the republic, so evilly fallen, now glowingly revives and blossoms like a showery spring.'[14]

The partnership–rather than the domination that Liutprand saw– between senator and pope came to its full development during the pontificate of John X. He had previously been elected to the bishopric of Bologna but this, perhaps on Theodora's advice, he had declined in order to wait for a vacancy at Ravenna. This came within a year of Sergius's occupation of Rome and the ascendancy of Theophylact, and perhaps from 905 until 914 he had ruled Ravenna in the anti-Formosan interest. The burning questions of the Formosan controversy, the validity of episcopal translations and hence of subsequent ordinations which had hurt so many pockets, careers and positions, were now dead, leaving only the more general but less urgent argument about the status of Rome and the papacy. John had been able to retain excellent relations both with King Berengar and with Alberic of Spoleto, and while reviled by many for his ambition, he

[14] L. Duchesne, 'Serge III et Jean XI', (*MAH*, 33, 1913); G. Arnaldi, 'Liutprando e l'idea di Roma nell' alto medio evo', (*ASR*, 79, 1956).

showed in the fourteen years of his pontificate that he was a capable man with vision of his own and a wide experience, by no means a mere puppet.[15]

The most pressing problem facing Rome was still that of the Arabs, whose thirty-year domination of the countryside from their base on the Garigliano was as yet unbroken. From the inception of his pontificate John sought to revive the work of John VIII in forming an alliance of the Italian states and cities to put a final end to the menace. The reign of Basil I in the East had seen significant advances made for the reconquest of southern Italy by the Byzantines. The themes of Longobardia, approximating to the modern Apulia, and of Calabria had been formed and, while gains in Sicily itself were largely lost under Basil's son Leo, the refugees, including many monks and hermits, had given Calabria a firmly Greek culture and loyalty. This Eastern contact with the West was extended to the south Italian towns, and a nominal Byzantine suzerainty was claimed over Salerno, Benevento and Capua as well as Naples and Amalfi– Byzantine patriciates were conferred in 909 on Landulf of Capua and Guaimar of Salerno, both of whom visited Constantinople for investiture. In 914 a new commander for Longobardia, Nicholas Picingli, was sent out with a powerful fleet and with the titles of patrician for the rulers of Naples and Amalfi.

Pope John had also been making preparations; the Beneventans and Capuans had been approached and John was already sure of the adherence of Spoleto and Camerino under Alberic. But the beginnings of the land campaign appear to have been spontaneous. The *gastald* Aciprand of Rieti, with a force of Lombards and Sabines, surrounded and routed Arab marauders at nearby Trebula and, at about the same time, the inhabitants of Nepi and Sutri successfully encountered another band near Baccano to the north of Rome. These two successes encouraged John and Alberic to concentrate their forces and to pursue the survivors who had retreated to the camp on the Garigliano; the Arabs who had been occupying the territories of Narni, Orte and Eciculi had also fled, clearing central Italy of their presence. As the Spoletan and Roman armies marched south they gathered allies, contingents from Benevento, Naples and Amalfi. The town of Gaeta, naturally strong and with a harbour, presented a

[15] See T. Venni, 'Giovanni X', (*ASR*, 49, 1936).

major problem since the loyalty of its two *hypatoi*, John and Docibilis, was uncertain. In 903 they had already ruined the possibility of
a Capuan and Neapolitan victory over the Arabs by switching sides.
The princes insisted on Gaetan adherence, but Gaeta's price was the
donation of the Roman Church's possessions in Fondi and Traetto.
In camp on the Garigliano the document was drawn up, witnessed by
Picingli and the southern princes and on the Roman side signed by
the leading nobles including Theophylact and Hadrian, the father of
Stephen VI.[16]

The Arab camp was now blockaded from the land by the combined
Italian armies, but the decisive factor was the presence of the Byzantine fleet which denied the Arabs any chance of reinforcement or
of escape by sea. For two months they resisted, their numbers
swelled by refugees from the north, and then in desperation attempted
to break out. The allies, with Alberic and Pope John himself fighting
in the front-rank, decisively defeated them; the few who escaped were
rounded up and destroyed.[17] Both John and Alberic returned to
Rome as Italian national heroes, and the alliance between Rome
and Spoleto was further strengthened. Marquis of Spoleto, Alberic
had now become a Roman personage as well; following the battle of
the Garigliano he married the leading Roman heiress, Theophylact's
daughter Marozia, and was rewarded by John with Roman properties,
and also perhaps with the style of a Roman consul. The political
balance within Rome revealed by the signatures to the donation of
Caeta, which the city magnates, senators and dukes, had signed
before the curial administrators, was now strengthened by the
removal of possible Spoletan hostility against Rome.

King Berengar of Italy had been approached by John for support
during the preparatory stages for the campaign, but had not been
able to supply a contingent. In December 915 he came to Rome and
was granted the usual imperial honours in the Field of Nero; the two
effective powers in Rome were represented by the two young men who

[16] See O. Vehse, 'Das Bündnis gegen die Sarazenen vom Jahr 915',
(*Quellen und Forschungen aus Italienischen Archiv und Bibliotheken*, 19,
1927). G. Arnaldi, 'Le fasi preparative della battaglia del Garigliano del
915', (*Annuario della Facoltà di letteratura e filosofia dell' Università di
Napoli*, 4, 1954).

[17] P. Fedele, 'La battaglia del Garigliano dell' anno 915, ed i monumenti
che la ricordano', (*ASR*, 22, 1899).

led his horse, Pope John's brother Peter and the son of Theophylact. Berengar received imperial coronation, and at St. Peter's before a large crowd, took the oath granting protection to the Church, afterwards praying at the apostle's shrine, but his visit was brief and he exercised no authority in the city. This balance of power continued in Rome and in Italy for some years until it was shattered in 924 when the Tuscan and Lombard magnates rebelled against Berengar and invited Rudolf of Burgundy, from beyond the Alps, to become king. In despair Berengar called in Magyar mercenaries who a second time entered Italy, sacked Pavia and ravaged across the peninsula; in the same year Berengar was murdered in Verona. Events are uncertain in Rome, but Alberic perhaps tried to seize the patriciate of the Romans by summoning the Hungarians to his aid, and was lynched by the outraged Romans. For John it was the undoing of his work, since Theophylact also died at about the same time. The harmony of Italy was destroyed, the Empire vacant and the nobility of Rome once more at daggers drawn. He tried to fill the vacuum by appointments of his own; in 924 his brother Peter succeeded to many of Theophylact's offices and also to the vacant marquisate of Spoleto in the place of Alberic. But Peter was unpopular with the Romans and withdrew to Orte, on the borders of the papal states, where he established himself in a strong fortress and raided the Roman *campagna*, perhaps in conjunction with the Hungarians.

For four years the confusion continued until the family of Theophylact, in the person of the widowed Marozia, reasserted itself. In 927 she turned to the remaining great feudatory of central Italy, the marquis Guy of Tuscany, married him and in the following year carried out a *coup d'état* to regain possession of Rome. The marquis Peter was arrested and executed before the eyes of his brother the pope; then John himself was thrown into prison where in June 928 he was suffocated. For four years Marozia was dominant in Rome, fighting for her supremacy and that of her family, raising it to equality with the semi-royal dynasties of Europe. Her new husband Guy was the half-brother of Hugh of Provence and grandson of Louis II's brother King Lothair; Lothair's daughter, by the mistress condemned by Nicholas I, had married first of all count Boso of Provence, and then the marquis Adalbert of Tuscany, bearing Hugh by the first marriage and Guy, Lambert and Irmengard by the second. This clan intrigued for their advancement; Irmengard's influence in Italy as widow of the marquis of Ivrea was sufficient to induce the magnates to desert Rudolf of Burgundy as king in favour of Hugh of Provence, and her energy was matched by Marozia. By Alberic, Marozia had four sons and a daughter. The eldest, John, she made pope in 931; the second, Alberic, succeeded his father, after Peter's death, as marquis of Spoleto, although perhaps too young for personal rule; a third son, Sergius, was appointed bishop of Nepi. Through these her hold on power was maintained for she herself was the directing factor. The popes she appointed to succeed John X, Leo VI and Stephen VII, and her own son John XI, were nonentities. A visitor to Rome during her ascendancy, the chronicler of Rheims Flodoard, gave his impression of John, 'empty of power, caring only for splendour, having only ceremonial duties'. Marozia took her father's titles as *senatrix* and patrician, claiming a formal power within the city.

But as a woman she was in a precarious position since she could rule only by this subversion of lay or clerical offices, and when within three years Guy died she urgently needed a new protector. It was to her husband's half-brother Hugh of Provence and King of Italy that she turned. The young Liutprand, later bishop of Cremona, had been a page at his court and was an enthusiastic admirer of his qualities, but he had already shown a ruthlessness and lack of scruple in his career. The opportunity of acquiring power in Rome brought out his chilling qualities; canon law forbidding the marriage of a brother to his widowed sister-in-law, he declared that his mother's three children by Adalbert of Tuscany were supposititious, so annulling both Marozia's relationship to him and the claims of Guy's brother Lambert to Tuscany. Lambert challenged Hugh in defence of his legitimacy but was captured, imprisoned and blinded. Hugh's half-brother on his father's side, Boso, was installed as marquis of Tuscany and Hugh came to Rome for his marriage.

The marriage was celebrated with splendour in the Castel S. Angelo, the mausoleum of the Emperor Hadrian; on the north bank of the river it was the strongest building in Rome, strengthened by the Leonine Walls which at that point reach the river bank, and commanding the major bridge across the river. To the Romans the locale was ominous. The Vatican region had a long tradition of use as a refuge from Rome and latterly of attempted domination of the city, and Hugh had come with a considerable force of Burgundians to annexe Rome to his dominions.[18] To no one was this more dangerous than to the younger Alberic, Marozia's son. Hugh had already revealed his true quality by removing Lambert and absorbing Tuscany into his family, and Alberic as marquis of Spoleto and heir of the Theophylact family presented a double obstacle. The Romans felt humiliated by this subjection, after a long independence, to a foreigner as the gift of a woman. The occasion for their protest was reputedly a personal quarrel between Hugh and Alberic when the latter acted as the king's page at the festivities. Bishop Liutprand, like Alberic's contemporaries, regarded Alberic's appeal to the Romans as a nationalistic and patriotic move: 'Rome's dignity has now been reduced to such emptiness that it appears rather as an empire of prostitutes. . . . What is viler, more disgraceful than that these former slaves of the Romans, these Burgundians, should now rule the Romans?' The militia, responding to Alberic's appeal, assembled by its districts to storm the castle. Marozia was arrested and imprisoned, but Hugh was allowed to escape and make his way to his army.

The revolution of 932 completed the independence of Rome as a city-state. For twenty years, as the monk Benedict noted, no king, of Italy or from beyond the Alps, visited Rome to infringe its liberties. The twenty years of Alberic's rule were appreciated by the Romans and their near neighbours; his reputation was high, and his popularity, despite his sternness, great: 'fair of face, like his father . . . but to be feared, and his hold was heavy on the Romans'. But Rome lost by this exclusion, since pilgrims, scholars, bishops, and kings did not now come to the city nor see her as the active head of Christendom. This, to the later supporters of the revived Ottonian Empire, represented his and his family's great betrayal of Rome's natural destiny. Alberic's effective strokes of policy reflect this shrinking of horizons: the marriage of his cousin Theodora to duke John III of Naples to cement an alliance reveals Rome as just one of the Italian towns concerned with its own immediate environment.

[18] On Castel S. Angelo, see C. Cecchelli, 'Documenti per la storia antica e medioevale di Castel S. Angelo', (*ASR*, 74, 1951).

The revolution of 932 had a double aspect. It was a Roman affair. reflecting Rome's interest in itself alone, and it was a family revolution; power had changed hands within the family of Theophylact, not all of whose members were happy to see Alberic's personal aggrandisement at their expense. This found expression in a plot against him, led by two bishops and his own sisters, which he easily suppressed.[19]

The basis of his rule was the gathering of all offices into his own hands, leaving the pope his brother liturgical functions only. He ruled as '*princeps* and senator of all the Romans' and was acknowledged as *princeps* by the protocol-minded Constantine VII. It is possible, but not likely, that he used the term *patricius* on his coins. A Frankish abbot addressed him as '*vestararius*, first senator and also sole commander of the Romans'. Like Augustus, whose first name Octavian he gave to his son, his pre-eminence was a paramountcy over his peers of the city by an absorption of all individual powers and offices in his own person, including the offices of Lateran or civil service which reflected the aspirations of the Roman nobility with whom he ruled. But while the nobility were associated with him their dependence was made plainly visible. The administration of Rome was conducted from his family palace in the Via Lata, near the church of the Apostles, where he kept a court-like household headed by a *camerlengo* who was used as an agent on official business, and it was at his palace that judgements, attended and witnessed by the nobility, were issued. These, with their titles, *primicerius*, *secundicerius*, *arcarius* and *sacellarius*, continued to transact business under Alberic, classed together as his *curiales*. Pope Marinus II, one of the successors of John XI, 'dared touch no business except at the command of the *princeps* Alberic'.[20]

The major problems before him were the maintenance of Rome's independence of foreign powers–made easier by his possession of Spoleto–and the control of the nobility who had enriched themselves at the papacy's expense from the land of the *campagna* and who, like the marquis Peter, were capable and willing to build castles from

[19] See G. Arnaldi, 'Profilo di Alberico di Roma', (*Atti dell' Accademia di Scienze di Napoli*, 68, 1957).

[20] For Alberic's titles see F. Labruzzi, 'Di una moneta di Alberico principe e senatore dei Romani', (*ASR*, 35, 1912).

which to defy the central government. But Rome was still a city and the centre of political life. Alberic's insistence on the forms of Byzantine administration and court hierarchy was a real weapon to secure the allegiance of the nobility. This checked the growth of any real feudal devolution of government such as the rest of Europe was experiencing. Although some of the instincts of northern Europe were making themselves felt, the forms remained strictly those of a bureaucracy. When in 946 Bishop Leo of Velletri gave permission to Demetrius to build a castle, this permission was signed and witnessed by a representative of the city government, the *secundicerius*. The Sabine district, which for a century and a half had been hotly disputed by the papacy and Spoleto, was now definitely transferred to the Roman duchy, but its administration was kept under the close scrutiny of Alberic's court. As in the papal patrimonies, an official called the rector was appointed. The first known of these, Ingebald, was a Frank who was connected through his wife with the Roman aristocracy. His title in 939, 'duke and rector of the Sabine territory', gives both his personal rank in Rome and his official post–the use of both duke and count as titles was derived from contemporary usage elsewhere rather than from a sense of personal inherent authority. Alberic also employed the services of the episcopate, both at his Roman court and in rural administration; for example, the dioceses of Foronovo and Mentana were united to facilitate the administration of the Sabina.

The defence of Rome from external enemies also demanded Alberic's attention, for Hugh of Provence did not abandon his claims when he was forced from Rome. Two attempts, in 933 and 936, by Hugh to regain possession of the city failed, and these caused Alberic to place a greater reliance on the *scholae* of the militia, which had helped him to obtain power. The death, probably in 936, of Marozia, still under restraint, for the time being brought to an end Hugh's hopes of regaining Rome, and he formed a compact with Alberic who married his daughter Alda. But this came only after negotiations for a grander match had failed. In the East, the Emperor Romanus Lecapenus was placed in rather similar circumstances to Alberic. He was acting as regent for the Macedonian heir Constantine VII and was attempting to reinforce his family's position in the state. Three of his sons were crowned as associate emperors, and his daughters were

307

married to prominent Byzantine officials. In 930 he sought to make his youngest son Theophylact, then thirteen, patriarch of Constantinople. Two years' delay was necessary, but in 932 ambassadors from the East arrived to seek papal approval to counter the indignation of the Greek hierarchy. To Alberic, who had just assumed power, this seemed an excellent opportunity to strengthen his position; his brother the pope gave the necessary permission and four Italian bishops were sent to Constantinople for Theophylact's enthronement. Alberic then made further offers, that he marry a daughter of Romanus and that one of Romanus's emperor-sons should come to Rome to marry his sister. Romanus hesitated; he was engaged in a final campaign against the Arabs of the central Mediterranean and King Hugh, with his Provençal and Lombard possessions, was a useful ally.

The Byzantine alliance was useful to Hugh. The pact of 936 by which Alberic married Alda, who was at least of Carolingian descent, had been negotiated by the Abbot Odo of Cluny after Hugh had realized that his two abortive marches against Rome had merely devastated the countryside and reduced still further his chances of obtaining popular acceptance in the city. He had not abandoned hope of gaining an ascendancy in central and southern Italy and an alliance with the Eastern Empire was the principal means to do so. In 935 the alliance was formed and the Greek governor of the south was able with help from the north to drive the Lombards from Apulia and the other Byzantine provinces they had occupied. In 941 a combined Byzantine naval and Provençal land attack destroyed the last major Arab base on Christian territory, at Frejus. The alliance was further cemented by marriage; an illegitimate daughter of Hugh was sent to the East to marry Romanus's grandson Romanus, son of the hereditary Emperor Constantine. This marriage, in 944, took place just one year before the final fall of the house of Lecapenus.

Abbot Odo of Cluny ,who negotiated the peace between Hugh and Alberic in 936, had been invited that year to Rome by Alberic to undertake a reform of the monastic life of the duchy. This had sunk to a low level, largely in consequence of the ravages of the Saracens in the previous three-quarters of a century that had destroyed the estates supporting the city monasteries, as well as the fabric of the rural ones. Furthermore, the nobility had seized on the well-endowed clerical posts of the city, thereby depriving an independent papacy of a source of personnel. The fate of Farfa in Alberic's early years illustrates the conditions brought about in the countryside by the disorders and lack of firm government. The abbey had been rebuilt from its ruins by Abbot Roffred, but in 936 he was murdered by two of his monks, Campo and Hildebrand. Through Hugh's influence Campo became abbot but after a year of riotous living quarreled with Hildebrand, who fled and established himself as anti-abbot on the monastery's outlying properties. Both men lived as laymen, with wives, troops and palatial establishments, a grotesque example of the secularization that had overcome the Church, and of the pattern of civil strife, war and partition that marked the Italian lordships. The monks followed their abbots' example, living on the estates with their families, and meeting in the abbey only for communal celebrations; many of the treasures of the abbey had been stolen and the gold of the sacristy ornaments melted down. Other houses had also fallen in penury, their lands annexed by powerful neighbours.[21]

Odo was appointed by Alberic as archimandrite of Rome, with authority to reform all houses in the district. Visitations were made to the monasteries of Soratte, to Farfa and to Monte Cassino, and the stricter rule of Cluny introduced. At Farfa there was resistance and Alberic sent the Roman militia to force Odo's choice of a new abbot on the community. In Tuscany the monasteries of St. Elia and Soratte were reformed; to St. Andrew on Soratte Alberic gave his family's estate of Nazzano, associating his relations with him in the gift. Within the city the smaller houses were reformed and rebuilt and others were founded–St. Paul, then in ruins, St. Laurence and St. Agnes and St. Erasmo on the Coelian. One of his own palaces on the Aventine was converted into a monastery, S. Maria *in Aventino*, while Alberic's sisters may have been responsible for the foundation of St. Stephen and St. Cyriacus, near S. Maria *in Via Lata* and the main Theophylact residence.

Alberic's purpose was both religious and political: from his grandparents he may have received a piety that had missed his mother's generation. The re-endowment of monasteries was a direct encouragement to the recovery of agriculture in the battered *campagna* and the

---

[21] *Chronicon Farfense*, (ed. U. Balzani, 1903).

monasteries could, as in the instance of Subiaco, be given a wide civil jurisdiction over their regions and so buttress the Roman government. The extent of lands granted to the monasteries, which Alberic persuaded the magnates to imitate, also served to break up the growth of formidable territorial blocs in the hands of the counts of the countryside which threatened the stability of the administration. Furthermore a rich, disciplined monasticism would serve as a useful counterweight to clerical dissatisfaction with their loss of control over the government and the quiescence of the papacy. Alberic's brother John XI died in 936 and was succeeded by a monk, Leo VII, a pious and withdrawn man. He was followed by Stephen VIII in 939 and Marinus II in 942; neither intervened in politics nor took any initiative in monastic reform, nor was either of them implicated in the plot, instigated by Hugh, against Alberic. The leaders were two cardinal-bishops, Benedict and Marius who hoped to regain clerical patronage over the administration, but the plot failed, for an associate, a sister of Alberic, revealed it to her brother and the ringleaders' punishment was swift.

But the most important factor in Alberic's monastic reform was that it revealed him clearly as a ruler in the Christian tradition. Since the elevation of Pepin in the eighth century an essential aspect of the ruler was the care and protection of the Church, not merely of its properties and personnel, but of its spiritual and intellectual life as well. From kings and emperors who fell short of this ideal, Rome and the Roman Church had already suffered sufficiently. Alberic's own father had achieved what no Carolingian ruler in Italy had—the suppression of the Arab menace on the Garigliano in 915. The *princeps* was of necessity obliged to complete this work with the moral defence of Christianity. From the death of Berengar I in 923 until the coronation of Otto I in 962 there was a vacancy in the Empire of the West. Alberic, who styled himself as ruler by the grace of the Lord and had such close contacts with the Byzantine world, may have seen himself as custodian of the imperial and Roman concept of Christian rulership that had been inherent in Pepin's patriciate and Charlemagne's imperial title—a concept that could only validly be realized by denying all initiative to the clergy.[22]

[22] G. Antonelli, 'L'opera di Odone di Cluny in Italia', (*Benedictina*, 4, 1950); A. Rota, 'La riforma monastica del "princeps" Alberico II nello

Alberic's determination to keep Rome free of northern kings was amply demonstrated in 941 and 951. In 941 Hugh was again able to employ direct methods to resume his Roman claims. He appeared in arms before the city and for a whole summer and winter tried to force his way in by threats, bribes and promises, but the Romans stood firm behind Alberic in resisting this attempt by a foreign monarch to impose himself on the city. After devastating the countryside Hugh was forced to withdraw. It was his last effort to win Rome and the imperial crown; his leading Italian rival, his relative Berengar of Ivrea, had for some years directed an opposition party to Hugh, enjoying the support of Otto of Saxony, King of Germany. In 945 Berengar re-entered Italy from Germany and rapidly gained the support of all Lombardy, and especially of the bishops. Hugh made peace with Alberic, withdrawing his claims to Rome and recognizing Alberic as ruler of the city. He could not however hold his position in the north. His son Lothair was recognized as king by the Lombards, who were thus able, as so often before, to play off two rival kings against each other, and so preserve their own independence. Hugh withdrew to Provence and died two years later; Lothair retained a shadowy claim to Italy until his death in 950. Berengar assumed the style of king and associated his son Adalbert with him.

But Berengar did not secure undisputed sovereignty at the head of a national party. His persecution of Lothair's widow, the recurrent fears of the north Italians for their liberty, his encroachments on property of the Roman Church and Alberic's suspicions that he was ambitious for an imperial crown, created a party united against him. In 951 his former protector Otto was invited to Italy at the instance of Pope Agapetus and in the following year, under pretext of a pilgrimage to Rome, Otto came south. He and his father, King Henry the Fowler, had for the previous thirty years been reconstructing a strong state out of the German duchies, a state which looked eastward in defence of Europe from the Magyars and to the occupation and conversion of the Slav lands of Eastern Europe, welding political and religious expansion together. But Otto too looked for an imperial crown in recognition of his predominance and

Stato Romano ed il suo significato per il potere indipendente del "princeps" ', (*ASR*, 79, 1956); B. Hamilton, 'Monastic Revival in 10th century Rome', (*Studia Monastica*, 4, 1962).

as a sure confirmation of his German power; and the imperial name was indissolubly linked to Rome. Alberic welcomed Otto's intervention in Italy to weaken the danger from Berengar II, but he could not permit a northern monarch in Rome. His success in Italy was immediate. Berengar, appreciating that resistance was useless, submitted to Otto as vassal king of Italy and received the Lombard crown at a German diet in Augsburg, while Otto's brother Henry of Bavaria was given an Italian lordship created from the union of Verona and Aquileia. Ambassadors, ostensibly to Pope Agapetus, came to Rome but Alberic refused permission for Otto to enter the city. Otto obediently returned to Germany.

It was a remarkable demonstration of Alberic's assured position and mastery in Rome that the most powerful king in the West should be refused entry, but his ascendancy was a purely personal one. Otto had approached the pope and Rome's invitation to him had also been made in the name of Pope Agapetus, a Roman whose ten-year pontificate showed some stirrings of papal initiative. Alberic recognized this, aware also that in northern eyes his lordship meant nothing in comparison with the mystique of St. Peter's heirs, who alone represented Rome. In 954, after a principate of twenty-two years, he fell ill, still comparatively young, and took measures for the continuance of both his family's pre-eminence and the independence of Rome. With a revived imperial aspiration in the north, union between the papacy and the temporal rule in Rome was required. Before his death he summoned the magnates of Rome to St. Peter's for them to swear that on Agapetus's death his own son Octavian should be elected to the papal throne.

Alberic's death marked the end of a period of comparative peace and dignity in Roman life. His moderation in temporal affairs had suited well the pride of the Romans who had supported him against foreign intrusion, yet beneath his mastery there remained the threat of internecine family strife that could tear apart a weak or masterless Rome. He had made the surviving vestiges of the imperial power a domestic Roman matter, but while he could exclude the persons of northern kings, he could not check their covetous eyes nor their resentment of his monopoly of the source of prestige and authority. The foreign nations which also fought for the Church had some rights in the papacy which Alberic's exclusiveness in local Roman and

family interests was denying to them. His son Octavian who succeeded him as *princeps*, and then two years later became pope as
John XII on Agapetus's death, showed the dependence of Alberic's
system on his own person. Sixteen at his father's death, eighteen
when he became pope, Octavian threw himself into a full enjoyment
of his inherited position; high living within the Lateran was matched
by ambitions beyond the duchy of Rome, towards a resumption of
papal rule over Campania and Emilia. His lack of discipline and
respect for the ceremonies of the Church, his ordinations of boon
companions in the Lateran stables, alienated the Romans; his
aggressions outside the boundaries set by his father led to conflict and
threatened defeat at Berengar's hands. Rome's isolation from the
northern world was broken down, and in despair at Berengar's
advance an appeal was made in 960 to the Saxon king. Otto responded, entered Pavia in 961 and early in 962 marched for Rome.
Before the walls of the city his ambassadors negotiated conditions of
entry. Otto promised to the papacy full restitution and protection
of its property, to respect Roman jurisdiction, and to protect and
exalt the Roman Church. But his entry into the city in February was
not welcome. He received imperial coronation, but instructed his
swordbearer, as he prayed in St. Peter's, to hold a naked sword above
his head, 'for I know my predecessors have suffered from Roman
faith; it is only wise to safeguard against enmity with prudence'.

Otto's coronation marked the beginning of a new era in Rome's
history and its relationship with external powers, for he commanded
an authority that was not hesitant to make itself felt and an earnest-
ness that would not allow local obstacles to hinder its aims. In the
north the ruthless war against German separatism and against the
Magyar and Slav states of central Europe had produced a masterful-
ness that Rome had not experienced—a boy of the instability of Pope
John could not command the respect of a man who had dominated
his own national Church. John's clumsy intrigues against Rome's
new lord earned his deposition and the election of a pope of Otto's
choice. While the domination of the Theophylacts had won the
enmity of those who followed in the tradition of Formosus and
Nicholas in seeing Rome as the visible centre and lawgiver of
Christian Europe, the principate and pontificate of John had earned
for the Romans themselves the greatest contempt in the Western

world. Otto's suspicions were not unique. Liutprand of Cremona mentioned that the phrase 'you Roman' was an insult in the west, and recalled Ennodius's plea to a Roman lady to prove that despite the factions of the city there was some good in Rome.

What Rome and the Roman families, who were checked but not stifled by the Ottonian power, contributed to the new Empire was the vivid consciousness of Rome's imperial heritage. Alberic's government had been Byzantine in form and in sympathy in a century that, as Bishop Liutprand found, saw the Eastern Empire still conscious of its ancient Roman title to rule. The nobility of Rome, drawn from imperial office-holders, had never fully acknowledged the papal title to govern through the donation to Sylvester and its recognition by the Carolingians. The literary and political groups of the ninth century had, like their predecessors of the sixth, reverted to an emphasis on the republican past, the foundation of the 'Romulean city', the curule chair that John Immonides offered to a bishop, the equation of the Scipios and the Anicii as the epitome of nobility. But this nobility also, as its counterpart in the fifth and sixth century, sought to exercise a patronage over the church offices, keeping alive, alone in Western Europe, the traditions of urban political life.

But that Rome had survived through four and a half centuries was the work of the papacy. Inevitably it is around the papacy and the Roman clergy that the history of that time must revolve, for it was the papacy and the transmission of St. Peter that was the sustaining principle. Only in St. Peter and his heirs could the new nations of the West recognize an authority above theirs. To rulers St. Peter supplied the guarantee of legitimate authority; to ecclesiastics, that spiritual, literary and administrative tradition upon which the Church's structure had been built; to pilgrims, immediate contact with the relics and legends that constituted the new, Christian history. The great imperial monuments decayed as the physical margin of survival narrowed, and were replaced by the smaller, intimate chapels of the saints, glittering with mosaic, gold and enamels. The imperial monolith had vanished, replaced by local powers and lesser states; new arts and new polities alike looked to papal Rome for patronage. All Rome's rulers, from Theodoric and Justinian to the younger Alberic and Otto, were conscious that Rome remained a capital, unique in the world, in descent from Romulus and Peter:

no passive influence or inert and antiquarian reminder of the ancient world, a phantom preserving the shape without substance, but a power which had in the eighth, and would again in the eleventh, reach out and refashion the world.

GENERAL BIBLIOGRAPHY

M. Armellini, C. Cecchelli: *Le chiese di Roma*, 1942.

E. R. Barker, *Rome of the Pilgrims and Martyrs*, 1913.

O. Bertolini, *Roma di fronte a Bisanzio e ai Longobardi*, (Istituto di Studi Romani, Storia di Roma, 9, 1941).

P. Brezzi, *Roma e l'impero medioevale*, (id. 10, 1947).

F. Castagnoli, C. Cecchelli, C. Giovanni, M. Zocca, *Topografia e Urbanistica di Roma*, (id. 22, 1958).

C. Cecchelli, *Vita di Roma nel medio evo*, 1951.

L. Duchesne, *L'Eglise au VIe siècle*, 1925.

—*Les premiers temps de l'Etat pontifical*, (2nd ed. 1904), English trans. A. H. Mathew, *The beginnings of the temporal sovereignty of the Popes, 754–1073*, 1903.

G. Falco, *The Holy Roman Republic*, (trans. K. V. Kent) 1964.

F. Gregorovius, *History of Rome in the Middle Ages*, (English trans. by A. Hamilton), 1894.

H. Grisar, *Geschichte Roms und der Päpste im Mittelalter, I: Rom beim Ausgang der antiken Welt*, 1902.

L. Halphen, *Les origines du pouvoir temporal de la Papauté*, 1922.

L. M. Hartmann, *Geschichte Italiens im Mittelalter*, 1923.

— *Untersuchungen zur Geschichte der byzantinischen Verwaltung in Italien* (540–750), 1889.

T. Hodgkin, *Italy and her Invaders*, (8 vols.), 1880.

E. K. Mann, *The Lives of the Popes in the Early Middle Ages*, (18 vols), 1902.

G. Matthiae, *Le chiese di Roma dal IV al X secolo*, 1962.

— *Mosaici medioevali delle Chiese di Roma*, (2 vols,) 1967.

E. H. Schneider, *Rom und Romgedanke im Mittelalter: die geistliche Grundlagen der Renaissance*, 1926.

W. Ullman, *The Growth of Papal Government in the Middle Ages*, 1955.

INDEX

317

Gregory II, Pope, 94, 112, 122, 137, 139, 166–8, 195–6, 199–200, 206, 212

Gregory III, Pope, 112, 136, 200–2, 206, 229

Gregory IV, Pope, 185, 192, 194, 256–7, 259

Gregory, bishop of Tours, 87, 175–6

Gregory, exarch of Africa, 149–50, 153, 156

Guide books, 117–18

Guy I, duke of Spoleto, 263, 272

Guy II, duke of Spoleto, 280–1

Guy III, duke of Spoleto, 285–6, 288–91

Hadrian I, Pope, 112–13, 122, 138, 185, 191, 194–5, 198, 227–240, 242–7, 252

Hadrian II, Pope, 112, 259, 276–8

Hadrian III, Pope, 288

Heraclius, Emperor, 142, 145–9, 157

Hildiprand, duke of Spoleto, 234, 237

Hilduin, abbot of Soissons, 184, 187, 189–90

Honorius I, Pope, 94, 103, 105, 139, 141, 147–8, 196

Hormisdas, Pope, 30, 43–5, 47–8, 59, 65

Hugh, king of Provence, 303–5, 307–11

Hungarians, in Italy, 295, 303

Iconoclasm, 166–8, 172, 200, 206, 219, 245

Ingoald, abbot of Farfa, 185, 247, 254, 256

Isaac, exarch of Italy, 145–8

Johannopolis, 265

John I, Pope, 47–8

John II, Pope, 64

John III, Pope, 83

John IV, Pope, 103, 123

John V, Pope, 131, 134, 139, 156, 168

John VI, Pope, 163

John VII, Pope, 94, 170, 197, 229

John VIII, Pope, 265, 279–88, 290, 296, 301

John IX, Pope, 293–6

John X, Pope, 299–303

John XI, Pope, 300, 304, 308

John XII, Pope, 312–13

John, archbishop of Ravenna, 266–267, 273–4, 277, 281

John Immonides, deacon, 91–2, 95, 111, 114, 268, 277, 282, 314

John, bishop of Porto, 119, 160

John Platyn, exarch of Italy, 159–60

John Rizocopus, exarch of Italy, 163

Justin I, Emperor, 44–5, 47

Justin II, Emperor, 82, 84, 90

Justinian I, Emperor, 30, 44–5, 47, 49–51, 54–7, 64, 68–9, 74, 76, 78, 80–2, 118, 142

Justinian II, Emperor, 110, 119, 122, 160–1, 163, 168, 211

Lambert, duke of Spoleto, 274, 276–7, 284–5

Lambert of Spoleto, Emperor, 290–295

Lando, Pope, 299

Laurentian Schism, 41–2

Law, canon, 43–4, 245, 272–3
  lombardic, 251, 255
  Roman, 203–4, 229, 239, 247, 251, 254–5, 267

Lawrence, antipope, 40–2

Lawrence, St., 137, 174–5

Learning, in Rome; see Education

Lehun, priest of Soissons, 187–90

Leo I, Pope, 171

Leo II, Pope, 123, 134

Leo III, Pope, 162, 185, 192, 198, 229, 246–52, 254, 264

Leo IV, Pope, 120, 232, 263–4, 267–271

Leo V, Pope, 296

Leo VI, Pope, 304